Fundamentals of Information Technology

WILEY SERIES IN COMPUTING

Consulting Editor
Professor D. W. Barron
Department of Computer Studies, University of Southampton, UK

BEZIER · Numerical Control—Mathematics and Applications
DAVIES and BARBER · Communication Networks for Computers
BROWN · Macro Processors and Techniques for Portable Software
PAGAN · A Practical Guide to Algol 68
BIRD · Programs and Machines
OLLE · The Codasyl Approach to Data Base Management
DAVIES, BARBER, PRICE, and SOLOMONIDES · Computer Networks and their Protocols
KRONSJO · Algorithms: Their Complexity and Efficiency
RUS · Data Structures and Operating Systems
BROWN · Writing Interactive Compilers and Interpreters
HUTT · The Design of a Relational Data Base Management System
O'DONOVAN · GPSS—Simulation Made Simple
LONGBOTTOM · Computer System Reliability
AUMIAUX · The Use of Microprocessors
ATKINSON · Pascal Programming
KUPKA and WILSING · Conversational Languages
SCHMIDT · GPSS–Fortran
PUZMAN/PORIZEK · Communication Control in Computer Networks
SPANIOL · Computer Arithmetic
BARRON · Pascal–The Language and its Implementation
HUNTER · The Design and Construction of Compilers
MAYOH · Problem Solving with ADA
AUMIAUX · Microprocessor Systems
CHEONG and HIRSCHEIM · Local Area Networks
BARRON and BISHOP · Advanced Programming–A Practical Course
DAVIES and PRICE · Security in Computer Networks
KRONSJÖ · Computational Complexity of Sequential and Parallel Algorithms
SHIRAI and TSUJII · Artificial Intelligence—Concepts, Techniques and Applications
AMMERAAL: C For Programmers
KRONSJÖ: Algorithms: Their Complexity and Efficiency. 2nd ed.

Fundamentals of Information Technology

Edited by

G G Wilkinson

and

A R Winterflood

JOHN WILEY AND SONS

Chichester · New York · Brisbane · Toronto · Singapore

Library of Congress Cataloging-in-Publication Data:

Fundamentals of information technology.
(Wiley series in computing)
Bibliography: p.
1. Electronic digital computers. 2. Computer
software. I. Wilkinson, G. G. II. Winterflood, A. R.
(Anthony R.) III. Series.
QA76.5.F855 1987 004 86–19018

ISBN 0 471 91003 1

British Library Cataloguing in Publication Data:

Fundamentals of information technology.—
(Wiley series in computing)
1. Electronic digital computers
I. Wilkinson, G. G. II. Winterflood, A. R.
004 QA76.5

ISBN 0 471 91003 1

Typeset by Activity Ltd, Salisbury, Wilts, England
Printed and bound in Great Britain

Contributors

David Cornwell **Michael Denham**
Andrew O'Keeffe **Janet Sinclair**
Anthony Winterflood

School of Computing,
Kingston Polytechnic, Surrey, UK

Graeme Wilkinson

Department of Computer Science
University College London

Contents List

Acknowledgements

Cover photograph reproduced by kind permission of The Trustees of the Goodwood Collection, Chichester.
Figure 2.6 reproduced by permission of P. Wright, Cray Research (UK) Ltd.
Figure 2.11 reproduced by permission of INMOS.
Figure 12.4 reproduced by permission of PA Consulting Services Ltd.
Figure 14.6 reproduced by permission of G. Peacegood.

Editors' Preface

In September 1983 Kingston Polytechnic, like many other higher education establishments in the UK, launched a new one-year MSc degree course in Information Technology (IT). Many of these courses, including the one at Kingston, are 'conversion courses' aimed at re-training graduates from other disciplines in the new field of information technology. These courses have been made possible by special government funding to academic departments in universities and polytechnics and through student sponsorship by the Science and Engineering Research Council. Right from the very beginning places on the Kingston course were in heavy demand—this demand continues today and shows no sign of diminishing. There is no shortage of graduates wishing to re-train and no lack of opportunities in industry for those trained in the grey arts of software engineering, knowledge-based systems, and data communications (to name but a few of the topics covered in this book).

At a very early stage, the course team became aware of the unprecedented problems involved in training graduates to Master's level in IT within the space of one year given that some had come from arts or humanities backgrounds. Many of our first graduate students had little formal education in 'technical' subjects beyond O-level (and this continues to be the situation today). This placed new demands on the ingenuity and educational skills of the lecturing team. It soon became apparent that there was a need for a textbook to present the discipline of IT in a unified way to the intelligent graduate without specialist knowledge of computing or mathematics. In 1985 we formally decided to produce such a book ourselves and this text is the product of that decision.

The book is intended primarily as an introductory text for students on the IT postgraduate conversion courses in the UK, though it should be suitable for anyone with O-level mathematics, an inquiring mind, and a desire to understand the hardware and software techniques which are at the heart of the new technological revolution. It should therefore be of value not only to the post-graduate student of IT but also to undergraduates and BEC/TEC students in science, technology and business-related studies. We also believe it will be of value to the many managers, engineers and skilled technicians in industry and commerce today who find themselves increasingly both working with new information technology and faced with (frequently expensive) decision-taking in relation to new innovations in information handling. Also it should be useful to the many programmers and systems analysts who need to update their awareness of a field in which the half-life for knowledge is now reckoned to be less than three years.

The thrust of this book lies primarily but not completely in software techniques. This reflects the dominant theme of the Kingston course, which is itself a reflection of the current realization that software expertise is central to the exploitation of new technology to the full. Our aim has therefore been to survey the capabilities of modern computing machines and trends in their development and to use this as a basis for exploring the important and exciting developments in the software field—particularly in regard to formal methods in software design, information management systems, intelligent knowledge-based systems, and human–machine interfaces.

Finally we would like to thank everyone who has helped in the production of this text, particularly Ian Shelley and Gaynor Redvers-Mutton at John Wiley. We are also indebted to Dr. Martin McCaig who, as the first leader of the Kingston course, was instrumental in helping us at the planning stage. We must also express our gratitude to the many Kingston students who in their perseverance on the IT course helped us, often unwittingly, to refine our ideas and to adapt this material to the rather special needs of the 'conversion graduate'.

Introduction

What is Information Technology?

'Information Technology' is a term which has become extremely fashionable in the last few years. It has little relation to eithe information theory—concerned with the information content of signals—or to information science—concerned mainly with the management of libraries. Information technology is an all-embracing term which is applied collectively to the modern techniques associated with advanced computing systems and data communications.

Its origins lie in the 'microchip revolution' of the 1970s which caused the price of computers to plummet in the 1980s. This led to the realization that renewed economic prosperity would not come only from building and selling the physical machines that process data. It would come primarily from imagining and creating the intellectual tools that could exploit these inanimate machines and give meaning to the data. The exploitation of inanimate objects is 'technology'; data with meaning is 'information'.

We are clearly witnessing a revolution which is at its most visible in the number of homes and businesses which now possess a computing machine or appliance of some sort which contains a microchip, in the rapid growth of computer education and training programmes, and in the inception of advanced research and development programmes intended to push the capabilities and functions of computers even further. 1982 was officially designated 'information technology year' in the UK and the 'IT82' symbol appeared in surprising places—even on postage stamps.

In academic circles new areas of research activity have been opening up, principally concerned with making computers and information systems more powerful, more user-friendly, and more capable of intelligent behaviour. Although these new topics have been grouped under the information-technology umbrella, there are no rigid definitions or demarcations of which subjects constitute IT and which do not. Arguments on this matter are somewhat futile and largely irrelevant. What is perhaps more important is precisely how we have interpreted and used the term in this book. To a large extent we have taken our lead from the Alvey Programme for Advanced

Information Technology—a UK Government initiative begun in 1982 to develop more advanced computing systems. The core components of the Alvey Programme represent the nationally perceived thrust areas for future technological development in the computer field. These are the areas which we have chosen to concentrate on and the major parts of the book reflect this decision.

How Did it All Begin?

Around 1982 a number of governments started taking IT very seriously and formulated national plans for education, research and development. The catalyst for this activity seems to have been the report produced in October 1981 by the Japanese Information Processing Development Centre (JIPDEC) advocating an advanced programme to develop fifth-generation machines. This resulted in the formation of the Institute for New Generation Computer Technology (ICOT) in Tokyo with the support of all the major Japanese electronics companies and the Japanese Ministry of International Trade and Industry (MITI). The fifth-generation computer systems (FGCS) project began in 1982 and is planned to run for 10 years (see Moto-Oka and Store 1984 for more details). In addition an eight-year Very High Speed Computing Systems Project was set up to create machines for special numerically intensive scientific and engineering applications.

These developments clearly caused considerable interest around the world, for Japan had already known great success in building up its electronics industry and in applying automation and computer technology in industry (far more effectively than, for example, the UK). There was also a worldwide feeling that however ambitious the FGCS project might seem, the strength of its inspiration could enable it to succeed. This had for instance been the case of the US Apollo Project of the 1960s, aimed at placing a man on the moon within the decade, with which the FGCS project is often compared.

In March 1982 the British Government set up the Alvey Committee to report back on the scope for originating a similar advanced IT research programme in the UK. The report noted that the Japanese had identified an overlap between those areas of society where the application of IT could be most beneficial in terms of increases in efficiency and productivity and those in which it had not so far been successfully applied. The Alvey Report noted that the Japanese had identified:

> ... the clear necessity to overcome the limitations inherent in existing technology, as well as the need to improve understanding of how successfully to apply the technology. Apart from making the technology more widely and cheaply available ... the Fifth Generation Project is aimed particularly at improving the ease with which the technology can

be used, and at the use of I.T. for knowledge processing as opposed to data processing and computation.

(Alvey Committee 1982)

Clearly the aims of the Japanese Programme are by no means insignificant. The Alvey Committee went on to recommend the implementation of an advanced IT programme in the UK similar to the FGCS project. Within two years the EEC launched a scheme called ESPRIT along the same lines with the aim of improving the application of computer technology in European industry (see EEC 1984). Many of the recent projects sponsored by the US Defense Advanced Research Projects Agency (DARPA) have similar objectives.

The Alvey Programme and the New IT Growth Areas

As a result of the Alvey Committee's investigation a Directorate was set up by the UK Department of Trade and Industry to foster collaborative research between industry and academia with a £350 million budget over five years. The research projects under this advanced IT initiative have been grouped under four main headings covering the principal 'enabling' technologies which are seen as essential to progress in information handling. These are:

- software engineering;
- intelligent knowledge-based systems (IKBS);
- man–machine interfaces (MMI);
- very large-scale integration (VLSI) and computer-aided design (CAD).

These topics represent the *new information technology* and they will almost certainly become the major growth areas for computer-system development in the next decade or so. They define our view of IT. With the exception of VLSI we have tried to give a thorough introduction to each of these main topics in this book. The rationale behind the development of each of these areas is abundantly clear.

Software engineering (the application of formal mathematical techniques and rigorous engineering methods to software development) is crucial if future information systems are to be reliable and effective. At present it is woefully apparent that the majority of software systems developed commercially are poorly specified, poorly designed, poorly documented, difficult to use, inadequately tested, unmaintainable and not easily portable from one machine to another. Also software development projects frequently go over-budget and involve major rewrites to extensive sets of programs simply because of inadequate specification of requirements at the outset. As software systems become increasingly complex and represent substantial financial and human investment it is clear that stricter, more formal approaches to specification, design, and implementation are required rather than the *ad hoc* methods currently employed by many practitioners in the commercial world. One of the overriding objectives of software engineering is thus to make the production of reliable software more cost-effective in industry and commerce. The purpose of Part 2 of this book is to introduce the engineering approaches so required and to point to the important developments now taking place.

The development of *intelligent knowledge-based systems* is another key growth area. The bulk of computing systems in commercial use at the present time are data-processing systems which simply store, manipulate and re-create records of information (e.g. accounting systems, database and information-retrieval systems, word-processing systems, inventory control systems). Such systems as they now stand are basically 'unintelligent'. They can only apply their algorithms in a straightforward and inflexible manner. Yet it is beginning to be widely recognized that systems should be developed to incorporate 'knowledge' to help them solve complex logical problems. Such systems could have wide application in, for example, decision-making, design, planning and diagnosis (see Hayes-Roth *et al.* (1983) for more examples). Although 'artificial intelligence' (AI) research has been proceeding for some years, its commercial exploitation has until recently been negligible, despite considerable potential. Work is now going ahead on developing appropriate theoretical approaches and software tools for constructing and exploiting intelligent systems within the FGCS, Alvey and ESPRIT programmes. Part 4 of this book is devoted to the fundamentals of AI which underpin these new developments.

Research in *man–machine interfaces* is also important for future computing. At present communication with computers is primarily carried out by means of a typewriter-like keyboard. Communication is slow and dialogue is limited. Machines often only understand a very narrow set of commands which must be given in a very precise syntax—for the uninitiated access is impossible. The aim of MMI development is to enable humans to communicate with computers via speech, natural language, visual images, icons and even by touch. Apart from easing the job of professional programmers, such developments would enable unskilled operators to work with the machines, thus facilitating increased use of the technology. In Part 5 we consider some of the principles behind the development of human interfaces to advanced computers.

The fourth development area identified by Alvey is in *very large-scale integration*—i.e. fabrication technologies for extremely compact integrated circuit chips containing up to several million components. We have not devoted a major part of this book to this topic directly. Instead we have included a major part (Part 1) on the trends in computer hardware and the

Table 1 Alvey large-scale demonstrator projects

1. *Design to product*
Purpose: to demonstrate the automation of the total manufacturing production process incorporating IKBS techniques, advanced MMI approaches, and VLSI technology for high-speed processing and large database implementation.

2. *DHSS demonstrator*
Purpose: to evaluate the role of advanced IT in the application and interpretation of complex rule-based policies in an organization such as the UK Department of Health and Social Security. This will include topics such as automatic determination of benefits to be paid to claimants. The project will draw heavily on IKBS and MMI techniques.

3. *Speech-input word processor*
Purpose: to construct a word-processing system for office use capable of adaptively recognizing a vocabulary of 5000 words from a variety of speakers. This will demand considerable computer-processing power and will draw heavily on algorithms developed within MMI research for the understanding of natural languages.

4. *Mobile information systems*
Purpose: to design highly intelligent computer terminals for vehicles enabling communication with public and private databases. This could lead to the development of in-car information systems for route-guidance and the creation of mobile electronic offices.

(*Source:* Alvey Directorate (1984))

necessity for VLSI technology in advanced high-speed computer systems to support the processing demanded by sophisticated MMI and IKBS programs.

Apart from sponsoring a large number of individual research and development projects on these topics, the Alvey Directorate has established four large-scale demonstrator projects to bring together many of these enabling technologies and to demonstrate what could be achieved by future computer systems. These projects are listed in Table 1.

Whatever degree of success is achieved by the demonstrator projects, it is now clear that there will be many exciting developments in IT in the next few years which will lead to sophisticated, highly intelligent, friendly, compact, very fast, and readily accessible computer systems. Such systems are likely to revolutionize homes, offices and manufacturing plants (and indirectly to have a profound impact on society which politicians will skillfully have to deal with). In this book we try to give a flavour of the capabilities and complexities of those future computing systems. We begin with an examination of basic computer architecture and how this is changing in the light of the new technological requirements.

PART 1

COMPUTER SYSTEMS

Fundamentals of Information Technology
Edited by G. G. Wilkinson and A. R. Winterflood

Chapter 1

Computer Systems Organization

1.1 HISTORICAL DEVELOPMENT OF COMPUTING MACHINES

Despite interest in numerical computation since the earliest civilizations of the East, the first serious attempts to design a general-purpose computing machine did not occur until the first half of the nineteenth century when Charles Babbage designed his famous 'analytical engine'. Babbage and his co-worker Ada Lovelace identified the key components which are now regarded as the basis of any computer:

- an input system (to permit numbers to be fed to a calculating engine);
- a store or memory (to hold numbers used in calculations);
- an 'arithmetic mill' (to carry out calculations);
- a control unit (to direct the computational operations);
- an output system (to enable the results to be presented to the user).

Remarkably, perhaps, little progress was made in the practical construction of a general-purpose digital computer until a century later at around the time of the second world war (although some mechanical adding machines and special-purpose analogue machines were developed before this). The most significant early developments took place between 1943 and 1948, when the modern computer was effectively created out of the enormous research effort that accompanied the war. Arguably the first electronic computer was Colossus 1, developed at Bletchley Park in England, where teams of mathematicians had been assembled to work on deciphering German military codes. Colossus consisted of 2000 thermionic valves and was therefore extremely large and difficult to keep running. Within three years a second machine, the ENIAC (electronic numerical integrator and calculator), was developed in the University of Pennsylvania—this one was based on 18 000 valves and weighed 30 tons! Although such machines were intrinsically highly unreliable they were capable of high-speed numerical computation at rates of hundreds to several thousands of additions per second.

In 1945, alongside the development of these massive computing engines, John Von Neumann at Princeton introduced the concept of the stored-program machine and thereby laid the foundations for the design of most modern computers. Indeed Von Neumann's design may be regarded as the basis of the conventional computer. His design for an 'electronic discrete variable automatic computer' (EDVAC) was revolutionary in that it contemplated the use of a programmed sequence of mathematical instructions besides the possibility that such a *program* could even modify its own instructions. The EDVAC design also incorporated a large two-level store for instructions and data exactly as we find with most present-day computers. Von Neumann's EDVAC can be regarded as the classic example of the first generation of modern general-purpose electronic computer.

Most computer scientists now classify post-war computer designs into five amorphous generations, beginning with the Von Neumann stored-program machine. (No fifth-generation machine currently exists but we shall consider some possible designs and capabilities in Chapter 2).

The main advances in computing machines since 1948 have come about through the increasing miniaturization and cheapness of computing elements and storage devices for data together with changes in general approaches to control and computation management (e.g. use of concurrency through which several computational tasks may be tackled at the same time on one or more than one processing engine)—see Table 1.1.

Perhaps the most significant driving force behind the rapid growth in computer capabilities has been the advance in integrated circuit technology. Numerical computation is primarily based on binary number representation, so that simple switching devices can be used to store and process data (on = 1, off = 0). Simple *logic gates* which perform Boolean logic operations between binary digits (e.g. logical AND, OR, NOT, NAND, etc.) now form the basic building blocks of all digital systems. The basic discovery in 1948 that miniature switches in the form of transistors could be fabricated from semiconductor material such as silicon or germanium caused the first major revolution in computer hardware. The subsequent invention of the integrated circuit (chip) in 1959 comprising several logic gates built into one piece of semiconductor brought a further dramatic change in computer miniaturization. Since then chip complexity and component miniaturization have gone through several quantitative leaps (see Table 1.2) and chip complexity now appears to be doubling approximately every 1.5 to 2 years—see Figure 1.1.

The development of large-scale integration (LSI) in the late 1960s and early 1970s with thousands of components per chip led to the appearance of the first *microprocessor* in 1971 developed at Intel Corporation in the United States. The microprocessor essentially consists of a basic computing engine on a small piece of semiconductor—a remarkable feat. The advent of such devices has enabled computer designers to contemplate the use of large numbers of multiple processing engines working together to tackle extremely complex computational problems. The use of parallel computation is one of the

Table 1.1 Generations of Modern Digital Computer

Generation	Approximate dates	Main features
1	1945–55	Based on thermionic valves, stored-program machine, single processing unit, basis of generations 1–3.
2	1955–64	Based on transistors (invented in 1948), use of machine-independent programming languages, delegation of input/output to subsidiary processing units, provision of systems software.
3	1965–80?	Based on semiconductor integrated circuits, improved memory-management techniques to handle very large programs, introduction of concurrent programming.
4	1980–present day	Use of large-scale integration, highly parallel processing units, supercomputers, sophisticated programming support tools, novel control approaches (e.g. data flow), sophisticated personal workstations, artificial intelligence machines.
5	1990s?	Very large-scale integration, preliminary conceptual designs appeared early 1980s. Main features include 'knowledge processing' capability and sophisticated man–machine interaction (e.g. via speech).

Table 1.2 Quantitative leaps in chip complexity (After Burger *et al.* 1984)

		Components per chip
Small-scale integration	(SSI)	2–64
Medium-scale integration	(MSI)	64–2 000
Large-scale integration	(LSI)	2 000–64 000
Very large-scale integration	(VLSI)	64 000–2 000 000
Ultra large-scale integration	(ULSI)	2 000 000–64 000 000

dominant themes of present-day computer organization, as we shall see shortly.

Readers who wish to trace the history of computer development in more depth are referred to Hayes (1978). Further information on integrated circuit technology can be found in Burger *et al.* (1984), and Mead and Conway (1980).

1.1.1 Sequential Computers

We can regard a single Von Neumann machine as a 'single-instruction-stream–single-data-stream' (SISD) computer (see Figure 1.2). This is the

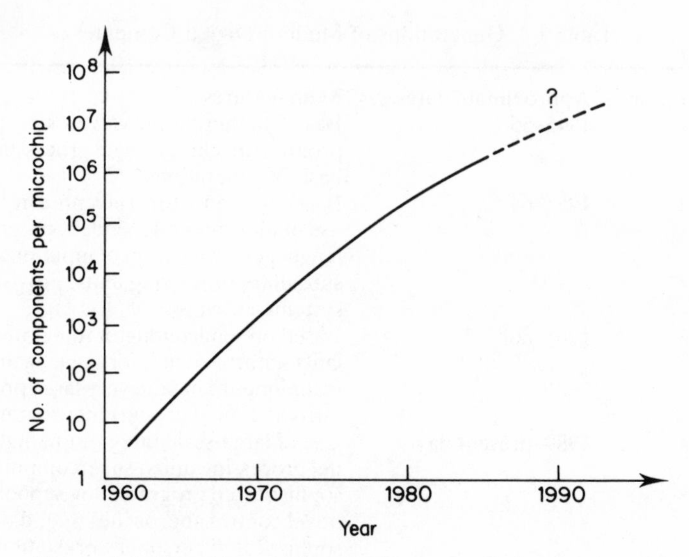

Figure 1.1 Trend in complexity of integrated circuit microchips

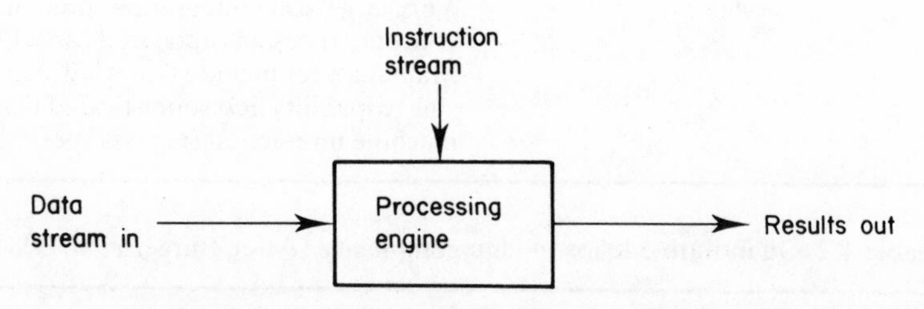

Figure 1.2 The basis of the Von Neumann computer

simplest architecture for a general-purpose computer. Such a machine accepts a stream of data items (numbers which are to be input to the processing engine) and manipulates them according to a set of pre-defined instructions which are applied in a sequence. It can therefore only perform numerical calculation based on a specified **sequential** algorithm. Before commencing execution of any numerical procedures the Von Neumann machine requires both data and algorithmic instructions to be loaded into a memory. The instructions (selected one at a time by a program control unit) pick data items from specified storage locations in memory and compute results which are returned to the same or other locations in the memory. To complete the process the machine requires an output device to communicate the results to the human operator.

Although most computers operate in this way it is perhaps not difficult to appreciate that if a particular computing problem possesses considerable inherent parallelism (if for example the same set of algorithmic instructions must be applied to multiple sets of input values), then a single Von Neumann machine operating in a sequential fashion is not very efficient. There are now many computational problems in advanced scientific applications where such parallelism is apparent and where the overall complexity of the problem and the number of data items is so enormous that computational efficiency is at a premium. Such problems are not well-served by a single Von Neumann machine and alternative architectures are preferable, as we shall see later. (Numerical weather forecasting is a good example of such a problem: complex atmospheric fluid dynamics calculations must be carried out over a numerical model of the globe using thousands of data items acquired from worldwide weather reports and satellite observations.)

1.2 IMPLEMENTATION OF THE CONVENTIONAL MACHINE

Figure 1.3 shows the *architecture* of a conventional stored-program machine at the macroscopic level—i.e. the main functional units are shown simply as black boxes (the microscopic system architecture—individual components, logic circuits, data pathways etc. which go to make up these functional units—is not shown). Figure 1.3 also indicates typical parameters which can be used to characterize such a system. These parameters represent the rates at which information can be transferred within the system, the rate at which computations can be carried out and the storage capacities of the memory units. The figures indicate a wide range of system performance reflecting the enormous spectrum of computer systems currently on the market.

The heart of any stored-program machine is the central processing unit (CPU) which carries out the basic numerical or logical operations on data which is supplied to it (the CPU is equivalent to Babbage's 'arithmetic mill'). Usually the CPU comprises two main functional units: the arithmetic and logic unit (ALU) and the program control unit. The CPU is linked directly to the main memory unit which holds the sequence of algorithmic instructions of the stored program together with items of data (and coded representations of numbers and characters) which are being processed in the numerical or logical computations.

The performance of the CPU is usually specified in terms of the number of program instructions which can be executed in a given period of time (assuming that a constant stream of data and instructions is available). Most computer programs include instructions for the following types of operation:

- integer arithmetic;
- floating-point (real) number arithmetic;
- transfers to/from main memory;
- branching to new points in the program;
- logical operations (e.g. character comparisons).

Performance measurement must therefore be carried out using a representative program—one which contains a set of algorithmic instructions which are typical

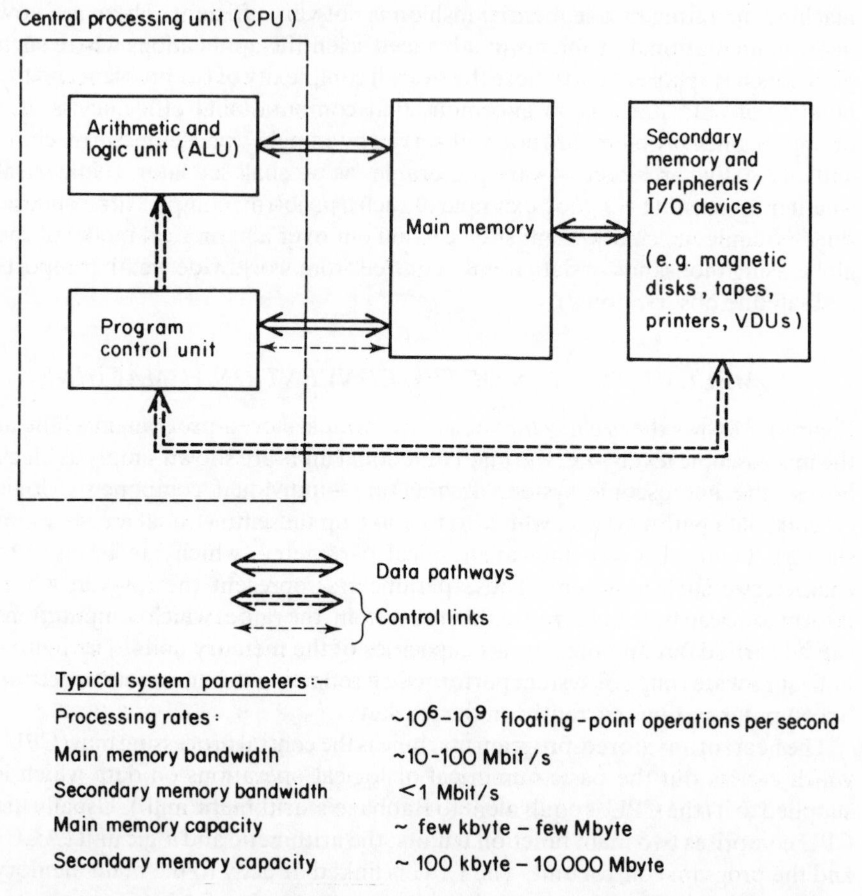

Figure 1.3 Macroscopic architecture of a typical modern stored program machine

of the use to which the machine is being put. Often the performance is quoted in terms of the average program instruction execution time $\bar{T}$, defined by:

$$\bar{T} = \sum_{i=1}^{n} T_i p_i,$$

where T_i is the execution time for an instruction type i, and p_i is the probability of that instruction type occurring in a typical program. This performance measurement can be alternatively quoted as the number of instructions executed per second. Most high-performance processors now achieve rates of the order of millions of instructions per second, giving rise to the so-called 'MIP rate' (1 MIP = 1 million instructions per second). For scientific or engineering applications in which the bulk of the computing involves floating-point numbers the performance is affectionately quoted in terms of a 'megaflop rate'—1 megaflop = 1 million floating-point operations per second.*

The main memory which stores program instructions consists of storage locations for groups of binary digits (memory words). Usually main memory is fabricated from semiconductor integrated circuits, although in the early days it consisted of tiny electromagnets (magnetic cores) hence it is still often referred to as 'core memory'. The memory is linked to the CPU by a data bus (parallel set of wires) to permit the transfer of whole words simultaneously.

During the execution of a stored program successive instructions should ideally be transferred to the CPU at high speed. The CPU must therefore be capable of accessing main memory and the data transfer rate between memory and the CPU (the main memory bandwidth) should ideally match the rate at which instructions are being executed by the CPU. This necessitates fast storage element technology for the semiconductor memory.

Although the CPU and main memory make up the heart of any stored-program machine, they may only form a very small part of the total physical system.

Any computing machine clearly requires appropriate devices for information input and output. Data and programs can be input from a considerable variety of modern computer peripherals, including visual display units (VDUs), magnetic tape readers, magnetic disk units, and optical character or bar-code readers. Magnetic tapes and disks can also be used as long-term mass storage for the results of computations. Visual display units, teletype writers, printers, and graphic display terminals can be used to present output in the form of text, diagram, or image. It is likely that quality voice synthesizers and recognizers will become commonplace for direct speech output within the next decade or so.

Since most peripheral devices and mass-storage units involve electromechanical operations which are slow compared to the purely electronic operations of the CPU and main memory, the secondary-memory bandwidth (i.e. transfer rate between peripherals and main memory) is substantially lower than the main-memory bandwidth. This has implications for system efficiency which will be discussed in Section 1.3.2.

*Floating-point numbers are represented by two binary numbers: a *mantissa* (m) and an *exponent* (e) with an assumed *radix* (r):

$$n = m \times r^e$$

e.g. $r = 10$, $m = 12\,345$, and $e = 4$, then represents
$n = 0.12345 \times 10^4 \quad (= 1234.5)$

The benefit of handling floating-point numbers in this way is that the mantissa and exponent can be individually treated as integers.

1.2.1 The Internal Architecture of a Processor

The internal architecture of a CPU or processor can be specified in terms of its main functioning components and the data pathways between them in the same way that we described macroscopic system architecture.

The most vital part of a processor is the circuitry which performs the basic micro-operations on binary numbers. These operations can be arithmetic (e.g. subtract, add) or logical (e.g. AND, OR, COMPLEMENT); hence the use of the term 'arithmetic and logic unit' for this part of the processor. Besides the ALU and the control unit the processor contains a set of registers (fast-access storage locations) for binary data words (instructions, data, or addresses). Some registers are general purpose—for example they can be used to store the intermediate results of micro-operations. Others are used only for special purposes such as storing binary data values arriving from or being sent to main memory via a bus connection. Figure 1.4 illustrates a basic processor architecture.

The memory address register (MAR) and the memory buffer register (MBR—sometimes called by alternative names, e.g. memory data register) are used for processor–main memory communication through the data and address buses which link directly to external buses connected to the main memory unit. The MAR is used to store the number of the main memory storage location (i.e. the address) which the CPU needs to access. A data word can be either read from that main-memory storage location into the MBR or written back to it from the MBR (see Figure 1.5). Generally speaking the width k of the address bus (i.e. the no. of wires it contains) is related to the capacity of the memory unit by the following relationship:

$$m = 2^k \qquad (m = \text{capacity (words)})$$

since the maximum number of addresses which can be specified by a k-bit binary number is 2^k.

1.2.2 Stored-program Execution

Normally a stored program will consist of a sequence of machine instructions loaded into successive storage locations in main memory. To execute such a program the individual instructions must be read sequentially by the processor. The normal sequence of events for program execution is as follows:

1. The program counter register (PC) is loaded with the address of the first program instruction in main memory.
2. The contents of the PC are transferred to the MAR. The instruction can then be read into the MBR.
3. The PC is incremented by 1 to point to the *next* instruction of the program. The contents of the MBR (i.e. the instruction which has just

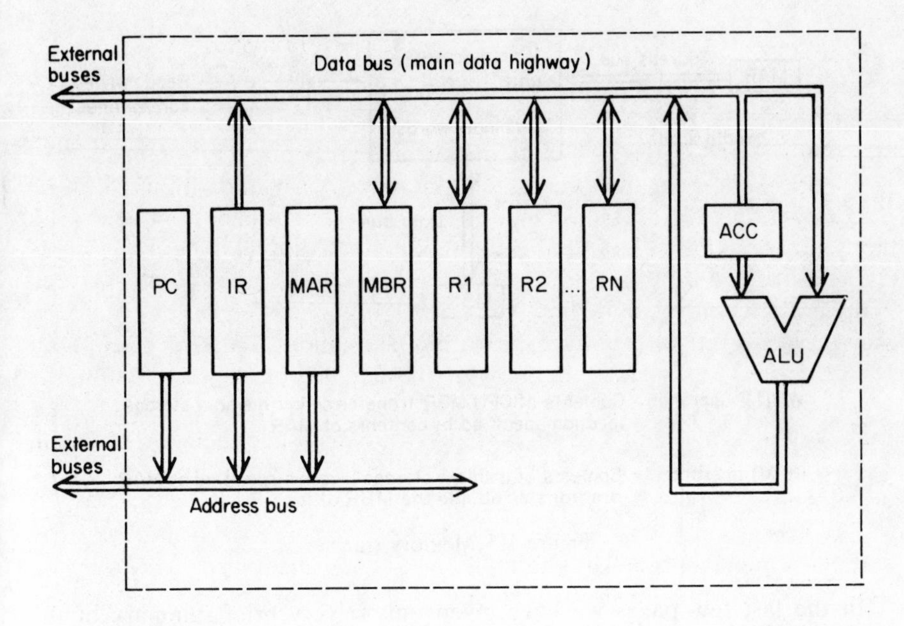

R1, R2, ... RN General-purpose registers
PC, IR, MAR, MBR, ACC Special-purpose registers

PC = program counter
IR = instruction register
MAR = memory address register
MBR = memory buffer register
ACC = accumulator register
ALU = arithemetic and logic unit

Figure 1.4 Simplified internal processor architecture

been read) are also copied into the special-purpose instruction register (IR) where it is decoded into the appropriate computational micro-operations. (Note that one program instruction may be decoded into a sequence of several ALU micro-operations.)

4. The instruction will be executed (this may involve accessing main memory again to bring in data values—hence the need for the PC and IR to free the MAR and MBR for use during the execution step).
5. The procedure is repeated from step 2 as many times as are necessary to complete the program.

Notice that steps 1, 2 and 3 are concerned with *fetching* the program instruction from main memory and that step 4 is concerned with *executing* it. This gives rise to the concept of the *fetch–execute cycle* for processor operation. (The CPU may go through other kinds of cycle—for example if an instruction sequence is interrupted by some external event—but we shall not consider this here.)

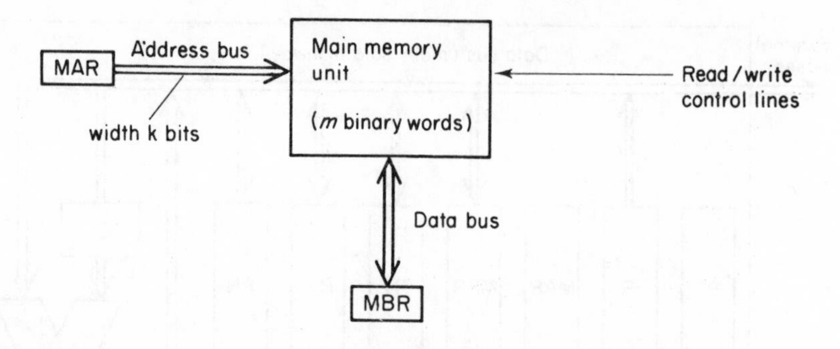
MAR
Address bus
width k bits
Main memory unit
(m binary words)
Read / write control lines
Data bus
MBR
WRITE operation : Contents of CPU MBR transferred into memory storage location specified by contents of MAR
READ operation : Contents of memory storage location specified by MAR are transferred into the MBR of the CPU

Figure 1.5 Memory transfer

In the last few pages we have given only a very brief summary of the operation of a typical processor to set the scene for discussion of efficiency, system management, and advanced architectures. Readers who want to delve more deeply into processor design, processor instruction sets, machine cycles, etc. are advised to consult the numerous excellent texts which cover these topics e.g. Downton (1984), Willis and Kerridge (1983), and Mano (1982). Readers with a strong interest in design of digital logic circuits to construct registers, binary storage elements, arithmetic and logic units, etc. should consult texts such as Stonham (1984), Fletcher (1984) and Shiva (1985).

1.2.3 Memory Devices for a Stored Program Machine

The main memory of a stored program machine must be a *random access memory* (RAM) which can permit memory locations to be read in a totally random sequence. Although program instructions normally occupy contiguous areas of main memory, during program execution the CPU may need to access data values stored some distance from the sequence of instructions it is dealing with. It would then be highly inefficient to have to read sequentially through a large part of main memory to find the data items required; hence the need for randomly accessible storage locations. There are two types of semiconductor RAM: static and dynamic (see Figure 1.6). Most computers also possess read only memories (ROM) which are also random access devices but their contents cannot be changed. They are mainly used to store the values of vital system parameters, control programs or initialization programs (bootstraps).

There is also considerable variety of secondary memory systems for modern stored-program machines. These include of course magnetic tapes and disks mentioned earlier. Tapes can be accessed serially only by unwinding and reading successive data words along the tracks. They are, however, fairly cheap and are ideal for mass *off-line* data storage—i.e. for archiving digital information.

Disks provide several advantages compared to tapes—principally random access and higher data transfer speeds. However, disks can be much more expensive than magnetic tapes. The physical configuration of a magnetic disk unit is shown in Figure 1.7. Some disk systems (e.g. Winchester disks) consist of sealed units containing the drive unit, the read/write heads and the hard disk as well; some consist of drive units which may take removable disk packs. Removable disks come in several varieties, ranging from single-surface flexible disks to rigid disks with up to 20 or so separate storage surfaces. Data capacities range from ~250 kbyte up to ~500 Mbytes (1 byte = 8 bits). Large disks are therefore capable of storing the equivalent of several hundred million characters.

There has also been much interest in the last 10 years in developing semiconductor mass memories. Two kinds are now in existence: magnetic bubble memories and charge coupled devices (CCDs)—see Figure 1.6. These devices are able to store data at very high densities (up to 1 million bits per chip for bubble devices) and are non-mechanical. However, they can only be accessed serially, which is a major disadvantage. Nevertheless it is likely that there will be considerable investment in the development of high-density non-mechanical storage devices for future generations of computer system. This is simply because reliance on bulky mechanical devices like disks is fundamentally undesirable from the point of view of designing highly compact and very fast computing machines.

We have not discussed in this section how information in secondary storage may be managed—this is a major topic in its own right. Most users of large-scale computer systems, particularly in a commercial environment, now use machines to maintain substantial on-line databases. Indeed, it is apparent that many machines are no longer used primarily as 'computational engines' as Babbage and Von Neumann envisaged, but more importantly as systems providing rapid access to information—i.e. *information management and retrieval systems*. Such systems will be considered in more depth in Part 3.

1.3 SYSTEMS SOFTWARE

So far we have presented the computer simply as a processing engine for executing sequences of instructions. The software written by individual users to perform specific calculations, information retrieval and manipulation etc. constitutes *applications software*. It may consist of one-off programs written by

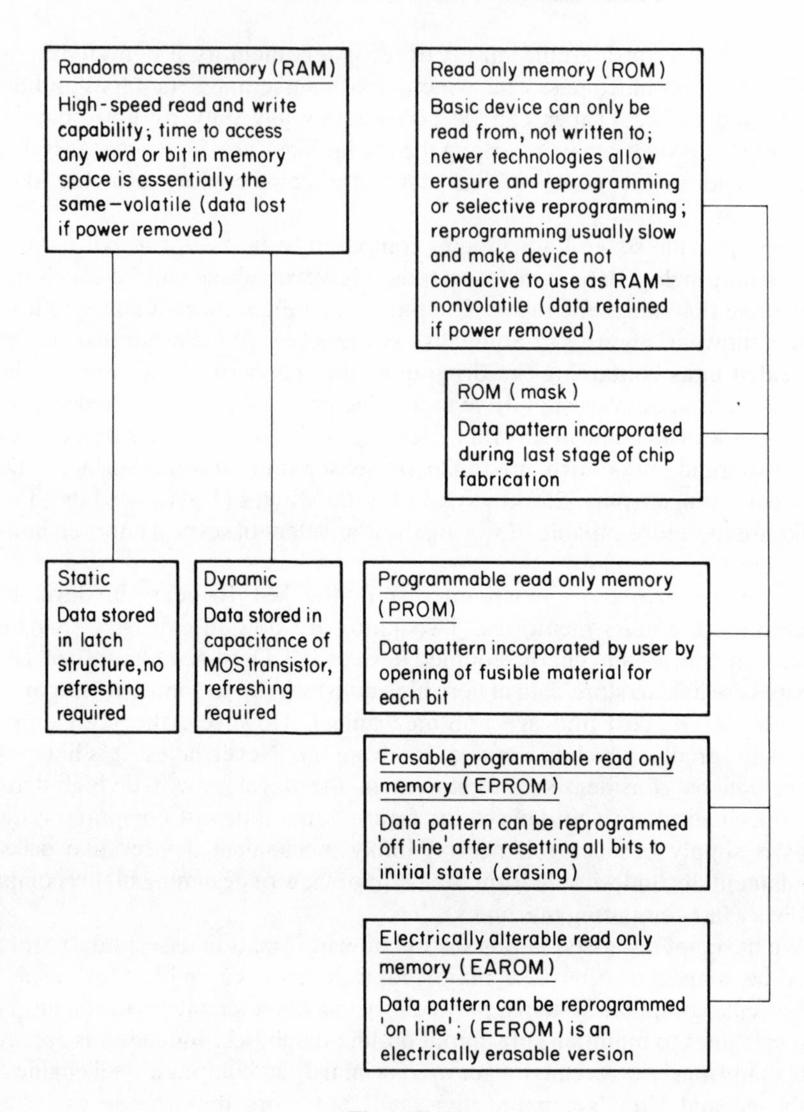

Figure 1.6

the user or alternatively of packages written by commercial software houses and bought by the user to accomplish specific tasks (e.g. accounting). However, computers also require *systems software* which is concerned with making them efficient in operation and easy to work with. Systems software exists to supervise the operation of the machine and to facilitate easy access to the various hardware resources.

Systems software can be broken down into several categories:

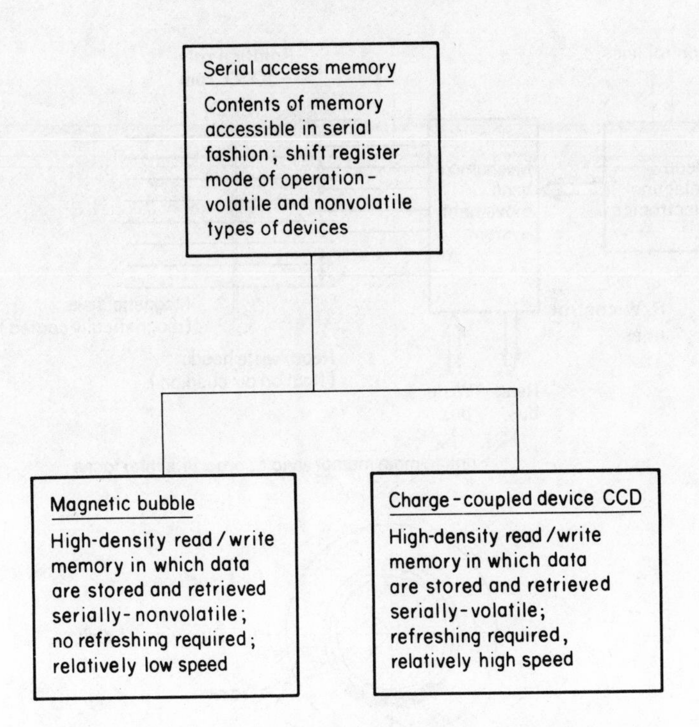

Figure 1.6 (Continued)
Major semiconductor memory categories (after Krutz 1980)

1. *The operating system:* programs which supervise the operation of the entire system including controlling the execution of all other software and diagnosing faults.
2. *Language processors:* programs which translate applications software written in *high-level languages* (e.g. Pascal, COBOL, LISP) into the *low-level* binary machine instructions which the processor executes. There are three main types: compilers, assemblers, and interpreters.
3. *Library and utility programs:* software to help the applications programmer. It consists of standard commonly used software routines which the user may invoke (e.g. for copying files of data).

In the rest of this chapter we shall examine some of the features of category 1 (the operating system) as this is directly concerned with system management and efficiency. The discussion will be restricted to a consideration of the main functions of the operating system. Category 2 (computer-language translation) is treated separately under the software-engineering part (Chapter 4). Library and utility programs have no special attributes which make them worthy of further consideration.

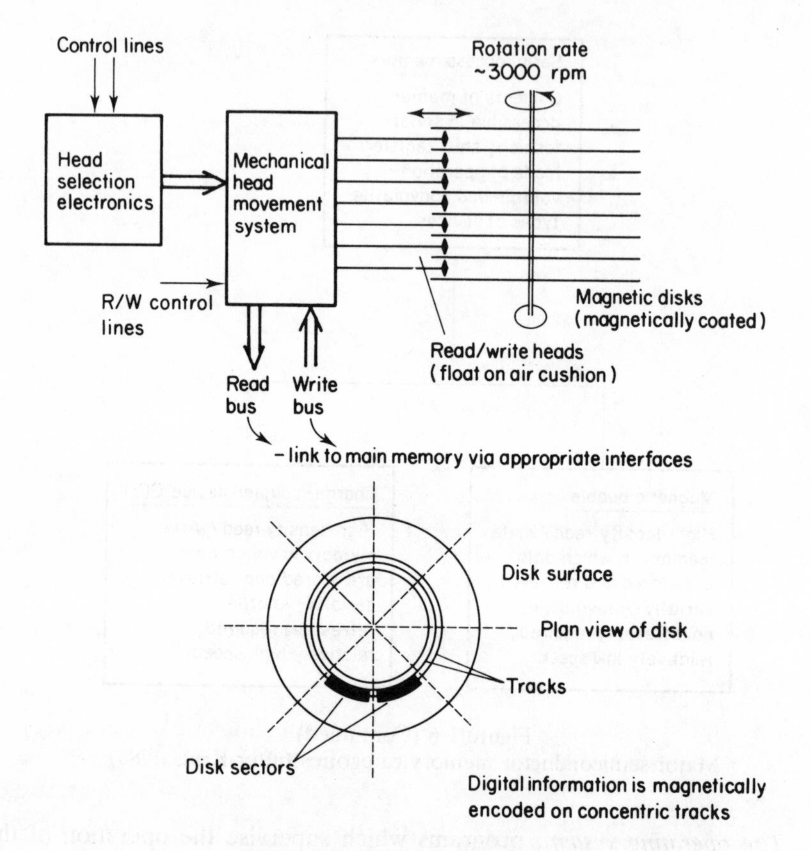

Figure 1.7 Magnetic disk systems

1.3.1 Functions of the Operating System

A typical modern stored-program computing system can be modelled analytically as a set of one or more *servers* executing a queue of *processes* (Figure 1.8). A server is effectively a CPU in action; a process can be regarded as a program in execution. Modern systems which possess more than one CPU effectively have multiple servers. Also most systems in use today need to support multiple users each of which may request service for sequences of several processes (jobs). Such systems therefore normally have a queue of waiting processes which may become lengthy during some parts of the day when several users wish to perform computation at the same time.

The operating system for a multi-user stored-program machine has five main functions. These are:

1. *Process management:* to schedule and select processes for the individual process servers (CPUs) and to facilitate inter-process communication.

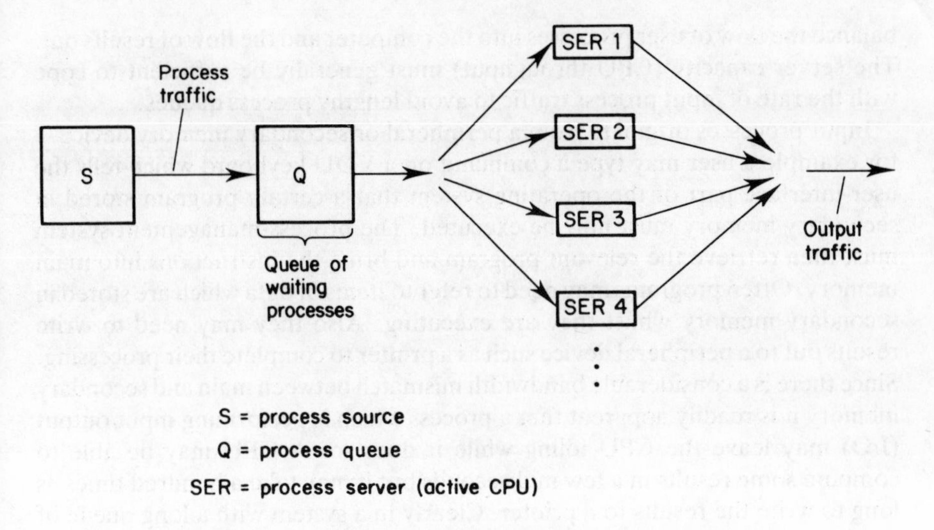

Figure 1.8 Analytical model of job-processing system

2. *Main-memory management:* to allocate regions of main memory to individual user- or system-defined processes.
3. *Secondary-memory management:* to supervise the use of secondary memory space, including allocating space to individual users, keeping track of locations of files of data and programs, and controlling access.
4. *Management of input/output:* to control the reading or writing of data and program instructions to/from main memory out of/into peripheral devices and secondary memory.
5. *Provision of a user interface:* to facilitate user–machine communication via an appropriate command language, systems utility programs, text handling software, etc.

The operating system itself consists principally of a set of software procedures together with a variety of system tables which keep track of vital system parameters (e.g. status of processes, job priorities, queue orderings, file locations in memory, etc.). System tables and the operating-system software routines normally reside in main memory when the system is running; the tables are effectively maintained and updated by the software routines. All five management tasks outlined above are essential to the efficient operation of a multi-user stored-program machine. Tasks 3 and 4 will not be considered here as they are less central to computer organization. But the interested reader is referred to other operating-system texts.

1.3.2 Efficiency, Multiprogramming and Process Management

In the system environment which we have outlined above it is important to balance the flow of user processes into the computer and the flow of results out. The server capacity (CPU throughput) must generally be sufficient to cope with the rate of input process traffic to avoid lengthy process queues.

Input processes originate from a peripheral or secondary memory device—for example a user may type a command on a VDU keyboard which tells the user-interface part of the operating system that a certain program stored in secondary memory must now be executed. The process-management system must then retrieve the relevant program and bring the instructions into main memory. Often programs may need to refer to items of data which are stored in secondary memory whilst they are executing. Also they may need to write results out to a peripheral device such as a printer to complete their processing. Since there is a considerable bandwidth mismatch between main and secondary memory it is readily apparent that a process which is performing input/output (I/O) may leave the CPU idling while it does so. A CPU may be able to compute some results in a few milliseconds but it may take a hundred times as long to write the results to a printer. Clearly in a system with a long queue of processes awaiting execution this is a very inefficient mode of operation, and one of the main aims of process management is to overcome this particular problem which fundamentally arises from hardware constraints.

We can illustrate its solution by reference to a very simple process structure (Figure 1.9). The function of this model process is to repeatedly read a collection of data items (a record) from secondary memory, to carry out some processing on it, and then to write it back to secondary memory. For such a process we can define a quantity known as the CPU utilization efficiency:

$$\text{CPU utilization efficiency (\%)} = \frac{\text{Useful computing time (CPU time)} \times 100}{\text{total time used}}$$

We can envisage two extreme situations exemplified by the following cases:

(a) Suppose: input takes 50 ms,
processing takes 1 ms,
output takes 49 ms
⇒ CPU utilization efficiency = 1%.

(b) Suppose: input takes 1 ms,
processing takes 98 ms,
output takes 1 ms
⇒ CPU utilization efficiency = 98%.

A process which behaves as in case (a) is called an *I/O-limited process*. This is by far the most common type of user-defined process. It has a very low efficiency and leaves the processor idling for 99% of the time—this is totally unacceptable in a multi-user process-queue environment.

A process which behaves as in case (b) is called a *CPU-limited process*. This makes good use of the processor.

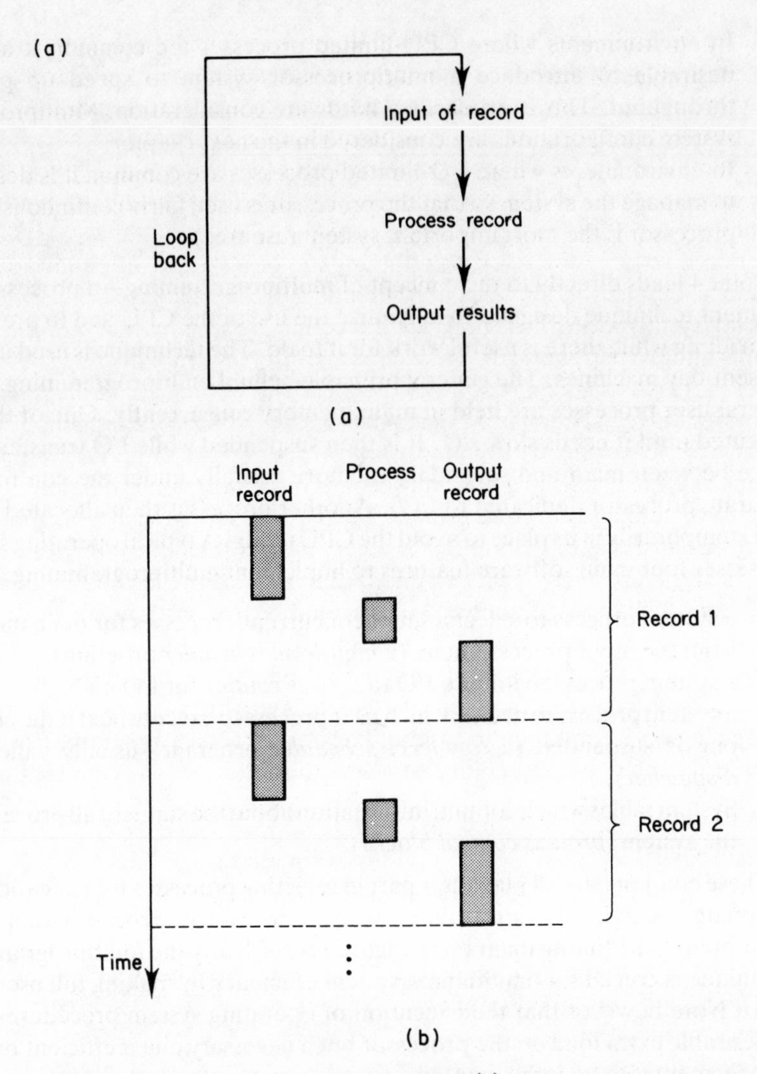

Figure 1.9 A simple process structure: (a) process structure; (b) timing diagram

Four points arise from this which are important for process management:

1. Most processes in normal computing environments are I/O-limited due to the relatively slow transfer of data between main memory and peripherals compared to instruction execution times. (Most programs read data from secondary memory.)
2. Some special-purpose numerical applications are CPU-limited (e.g. computing atmospheric behaviour).

3. In environments where CPU-limited processes are common it may be desirable to introduce a multiprocessor system to speed up process throughput. This is primarily a hardware consideration. Multiprocessor system configurations are considered in the next chapter.
4. In environments where I/O-limited processes are common it is desirable to manage the system so that the processor is used fairly continuously (the processor is the most important system resource).

Point 4 leads directly to the concept of **multiprogramming**—a process-management technique designed to maximize the use of the CPU and to prevent it from idling while there is useful work for it to do. The technique is used in most present-day machines. The general principle behind multiprogramming is that several user processes are held in main memory **concurrently**. One of them is executed until it needs slow I/O. It is then suspended while I/O transfers take place between main and secondary memory (usually under the control of a separate processor dedicated to I/O). Another process is then allocated to the CPU temporarily in its place to avoid the CPU idling. A typical operating system possesses four main software features to implement multiprogramming:

1. a system process to select a set of concurrent processes for main memory from the input process queue (a *high-level scheduler* program);
2. a system process to initiate I/O (a *service routine* for I/O);
3. a system process to decide which user process to execute next if the current one is suspended (a *low-level scheduler* program—usually called the *dispatcher*);
4. System tables which contain information about the status of all processes in the system (*process control blocks*).

These components all play their part in selecting processes for execution and swapping them if I/O constraints make it necessary. Process swapping is illustrated in the timing diagram in Figure 1.10. Clearly the multiprogramming technique is crucial for maintaining system efficiency by making full use of the CPU. Note however that the execution of operating system procedures is an undesirable extra load on the processor but a necessary one if efficient process management is to be implemented.

1.3.3 Concurrency and Process Communication

In a single-processor multiprogrammed computer several processes are resident in main memory at the same time. This is a situation of concurrency, that is several processes are in the stage of being executed at the same time. Note that the CPU can only actually handle the instructions from *one* process at a time. This is therefore an example of *apparent* concurrency. In a computer with multiple processors it is possible to have several processes executing simultaneously—this constitutes *true* concurrency.

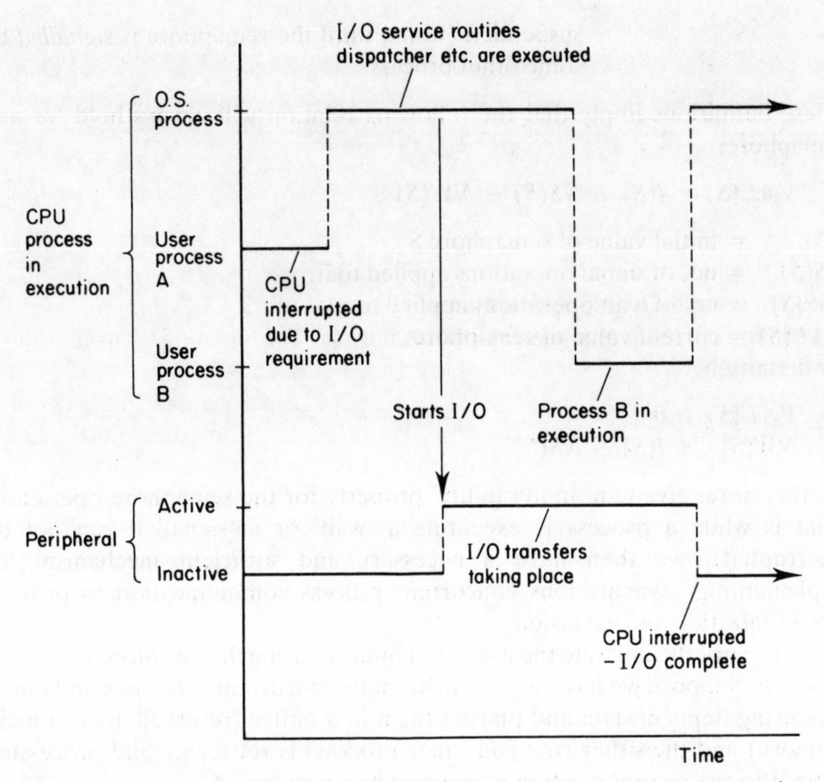

Figure 1.10 Timing diagram of process swapping in a multiprogramming environment

Both true and apparent concurrency imply a need for process communication—primarily for synchronization and/or exclusion. For example:

Situation (a): Process 1 must not pass some point in its processing until results are available from Process 2. This requires process synchronization.
Situation (b): Processes 1 and 2 need to access the same piece of utility program. They can not both gain access to the same area of memory at the same time (otherwise data corruption could occur). This requires process exclusion.

Process synchronization and exclusion are usually implemented within an operating system using a special data object—the **semaphore**. Semaphores are non-negative integer variables maintained within the operating-system tables. Apart from initialization to a set value, they can only be operated on by two procedures:

signal (semaphore) increases value of semaphore by 1.
wait (semaphore) decreases value of semaphore by 1 but *only if* result is to be non-negative. When it acts on a zero-valued semaphore the process requesting the operation is

suspended (waits) until the semaphore is *signalled* by some other process.

These definitions imply that the following relation will always hold for any semaphore:

$$VAL(S) = I(S) + NS(S) - NW(S)$$

$I(S)$ = initial value of semaphore S;
$NS(S)$ = no. of signal operations applied to it;
$NW(S)$ = no. of wait operations applied to it;
$VAL(S)$ = current value of semaphore.
By definition,

$$VAL(S) \geqslant 0$$
$$NW(S) \leqslant I(S) + NS(S)$$

Furthermore, given an 'indivisibility' property for the semaphore operations (that is while a process is executing a 'wait' or a 'signal' it can not be interrupted), we then have a necessary and sufficient mechanism for implementing asynchronous concurrent process communication to provide synchronization and exclusion.

We can briefly illustrate the use of semaphores using the *producer–consumer problem*. Suppose we have two asynchronous concurrent processes and one is producing items of data and placing them in a buffer (reserved area of main memory) and the other (the consumer process) is retrieving and processing them. Process communication is required because:

- the consumer process must wait if no data is available for it;
- the buffer area can not be accessed by both processes simultaneously (need for exclusion):
- the buffer area will be bounded and so the producer can not keep adding to it indefinitely unless space is being cleared by the consumer.

A solution to this process-communication problem using semaphores is shown in Figure 1.11.

1.3.4 Virtual Memory: The One-level Store

When a user program is to be executed it is brought from secondary memory into main memory where, in a multiprogramming environment, it joins a number of other concurrent processes. This simple model assumes that there is room in main memory for this program. It is not uncommon, however, to find programs which either exceed the total storage capacity of main memory or at least exceed that part of it which can reasonably be devoted to one concurrent user process. With the advent of high-bandwidth storage peripherals a solution

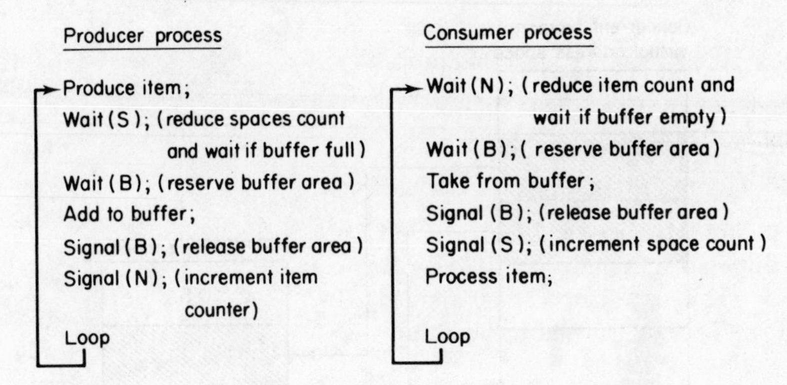

Producer process
Produce item;
Wait (S); (reduce spaces count and wait if buffer full)
Wait (B); (reserve buffer area)
Add to buffer;
Signal (B); (release buffer area)
Signal (N); (increment item counter)
Loop
Consumer process
Wait (N); (reduce item count and wait if buffer empty)
Wait (B); (reserve buffer area)
Take from buffer;
Signal (B); (release buffer area)
Signal (S); (increment space count)
Process item;
Loop

Figure 1.11 Semaphore solution to the producer–consumer problem

Three semaphores are required:
S—counter for spaces remaining in buffer
B—buffer access control semaphore (to ensure exclusion)
N—produced item counter
Initialization values are:
$S = M$, $B = 1$, $N = 0$, where
M = maximum no. of items that can be stored in the buffer

was found to this problem: namely to use part of secondary storage as an extension of main memory—hence the concept of the one-level store. A memory management technique was developed to exploit the one-level store concept—this is **virtual memory** (VM).

The implementation of VM in third-generation operating systems was an important step forward as it freed programmers from restrictions on program length. VM is now implemented on most current computers. Its introduction is sometimes regarded as a distinguishing characteristic of third-generation stored-program machines.

VM is usually implemented by dividing main memory space into a number of equal-sized sections called *page frames*. The total volume of a user program (its *virtual address space* which includes both instructions and space for data) is then effectively divided into a number of chunks called *pages* of the same size as the page frames. When a program is executed only a few pages of it are brought into main memory (where they fit within the page frames); the remainder stay out in secondary memory (see Figure 1.12). This technique is feasible because more often than not a particular program instruction will refer either to variables or other instructions stored within the same page or within neighbouring pages—the so-called *principle of locality of reference*. Execution can usually therefore proceed uninterrupted through many instructions within

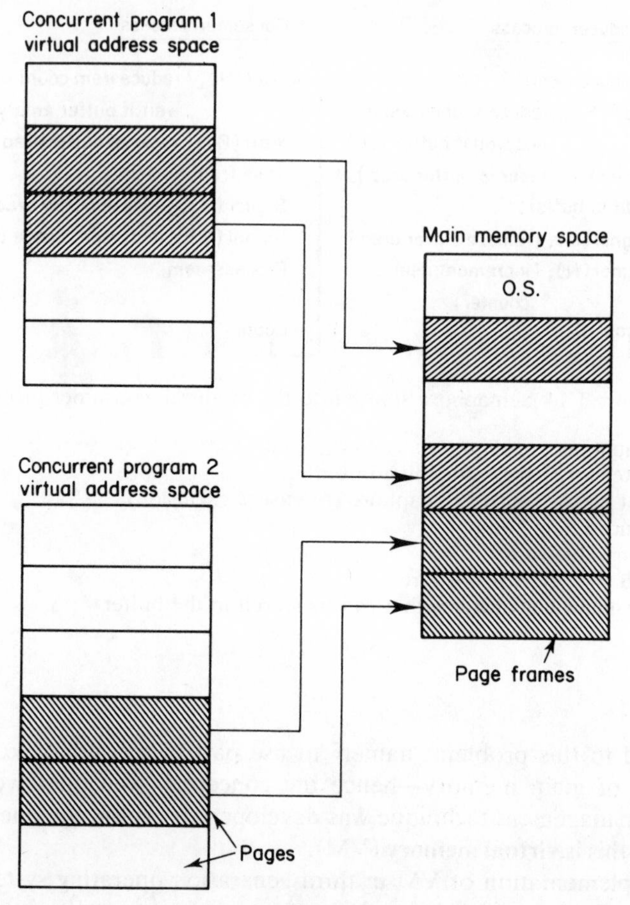

Figure 1.12 Two concurrent programs sharing main memory under VM
Unallocated pages remain in secondary memory

the currently available pages before reference must be made to instructions or variables which exist out in secondary memory. When this point is reached, however, a *page fault* occurs—that is a required page is not resident in main memory but must be brought in to replace an existing one. This necessitates I/O and the current process must be temporarily suspended and another concurrent process executed instead for a while.

It is important to realize here that virtual memory has an effect on system efficiency. In general the more processes in main memory the more chance there is of finding one which is not waiting for I/O and so CPU utilization efficiency should increase. However, as the number of concurrent processes increases the number of page frames allowed per process must decrease, thereby

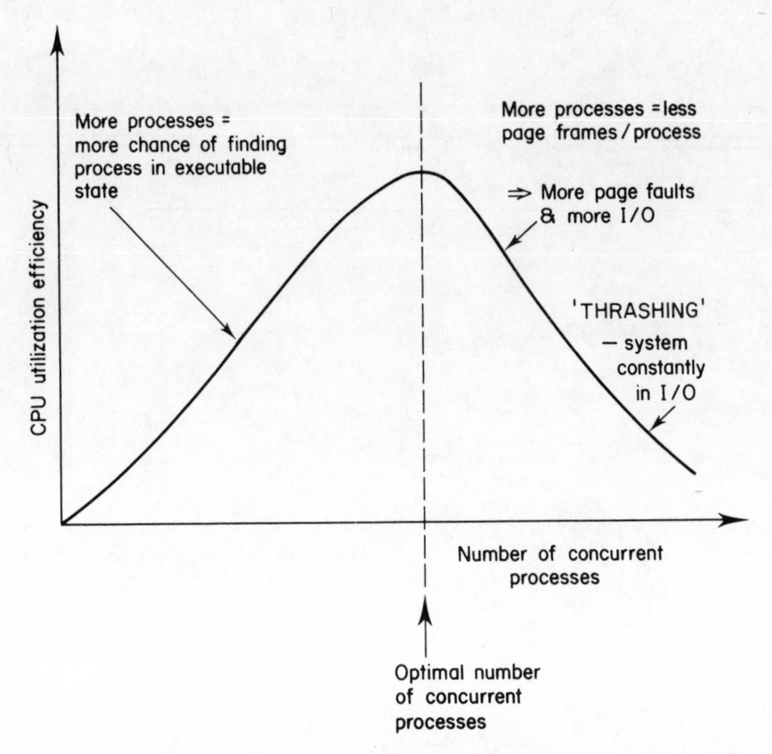

Figure 1.13 Effect of VM on CPU efficiency

increasing the frequency of page faults and the need for I/O (see Figure 1.13). Ideally operating-system software should monitor the system performance and optimize the number of concurrent processes sharing main memory.

We do not discuss the details of VM implementation here as there are many possible schemes which are to a large extent hardware dependent. However, readers interested in VM implementation and related topics covered briefly in the last few sections are referred to the more recent operating system texts, e.g. Deitel (1984) and Peterson and Silberschatz (1985). Comer (1984) interestingly provides a practical guide to construction of a complete prototype operating system.

This chapter has laid the foundations for an exploration of the more exotic and powerful computer architectures now being contemplated and designed around the world. In the next chapter we shall examine some of the limitations of the sequential stored-program machine and look at more advanced system architectures including the hypothetical fifth-generation machine. In Chapter 3 for completeness we shall discuss data communications and computer-system networking—an increasingly important aspect of modern computing.

Fundamentals of Information Technology
Edited by G. G. Wilkinson and A. R. Winterflood

Chapter 2

Advanced Computer Systems

2.1 LIMITATIONS OF THE SEQUENTIAL MACHINE

In the last chapter we identified the main components of a stored-program machine and explored how it could be efficiently managed by system software. In this chapter we need to go further, in particular to see how the capabilities of modern computing machines can be dramatically increased. In the last chapter we also briefly introduced the notion of parallelism in computer architecture and established that some modern machines use several processors to handle quite separate tasks, e.g. numerical computation, input–output control. Not only can parallelism lead to significant speed improvements but also novel control approaches quite different to the stored-program concept may lead to important new breakthroughs in machine processing capability.

If we consider a stored-program machine with a single CPU (we shall call this a uniprocessor) we can readily recognize two fundamental limitations: firstly inability to take advantage of any inherent parallelism in computational algorithms and secondly inability to keep going if the CPU fails in some way. The use of more than one processor could potentially overcome both problems. Not all computational algorithms possess inherent parallelism, though many do. Even with only a few program instructions it is possible to see when parallelism does and does not apply. For example, in the following short program extract there is no inherent parallelism:

```
z: = 1;
a: = 2;
b: = a + 1;
c: = b + 1;
```

The third instruction can not be executed before or at the same time as the second. Likewise the fourth can not be executed before or at the same time as the third because the value of *b* is required from the previous step. However, in the following example, which effectively creates the same results, parallelism is readily apparent:

```
z: = 1;
a: = z + 1;
```

b: = z + 2;
c: = z + 3;

Once the first instruction has been executed to assign a value to z, then the remaining instructions can be carried out in parallel—on different processors if several are available. In the following example not only is parallelism inherent to the program structure but also there is an equivalence in the function (increment by 1) of the individual instructions:

a: = a + 1;
b: = b + 1;
c: = c + 1;

Already we have identified two different forms of parallelism—control parallelism and functional parallelism which may exist in any computing problem. Such parallelisms can not be used by a uniprocessor in any way. A uniprocessor can only execute one instruction at a time.

Apart from parallelism within sequences of instructions there may be parallelism at a higher level; for example, the parallelism of several concurrent computing tasks or programs submitted to the same machine at the same time. On a uniprocessor these would have to be scheduled for sequential execution—they would be apparently concurrent, not truly concurrent. Clearly a uniprocessor stored-program sequential machine is far from ideal for achieving rapid computation in absolute terms or for a given cost. In this chapter we shall first consider ways of configuring a multiprocessor to exploit parallelism. We shall then question the concept of a stored sequence of program instructions. This may not be the best mechanism for achieving maximum computational throughput, even within current technological constraints.

2.2 PARALLEL-PROCESSOR SYSTEMS

A uniprocessor stored-program machine can be described architecturally as a single-instruction-stream–single-data-stream (SISD) computer (see Figure 1.2). As we have seen, apparent concurrency can be achieved with this architecture by multi**programming**—i.e. separate processes time-share the processor (see Figure 2.1). Although this improves program throughput by keeping the processor occupied while slow I/O takes place it does not facilitate parallel *computation*. This can be achieved only by using parallel processors, i.e. multi**processing** systems.

The term 'multiprocessing' can encompass a variety of different architectural configurations and scales of computer system. In the discussion which follows the term will be restricted to complete systems in which several processors share the same memory and peripherals. These are called tightly-coupled

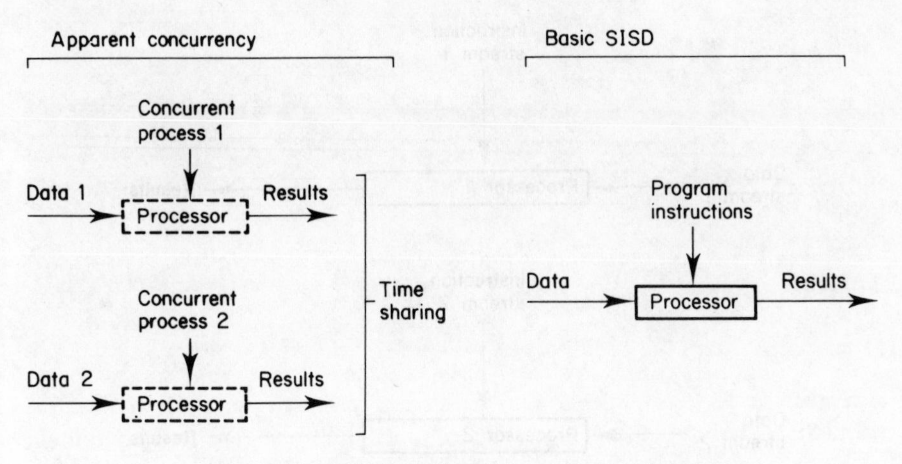

Figure 2.1 Multiprogramming on a uniprocessor

systems. By comparison, some systems which are also referred to as multiprocessors actually consist of quite separate machines linked only by a communication network. These are usually called *loosely-coupled* or *distributed* systems. These will not be considered further until Chapter 3 although it is worth noting that with modern high-speed data communications systems (e.g. based on Cambridge Ring or Ethernet technology) it is now possible to imagine a network of scattered computers behaving like a single machine.

The most obvious extension to the SISD architecture is to move from a uniprocessor to a multiprocessor system in which several processors each execute their own instruction streams with their own data streams (Figure 2.2). This architecture would be called multiple-instruction-stream–multiple-data-stream (MIMD). One might imagine that N processors could achieve a factor of N increase in computation speed compared to a uniprocessor. This would only be true when the N processors could work independently. Generally there are contentions over access to shared memory and there are overheads associated with communication between the various concurrent processes (which may now be truly concurrent). Also the software structure may not support degree-N parallelism. The MIMD architecture is the most general we can conceive while still restricting ourselves to the stored-program (instruction-stream) concept. There is much interest in the use of MIMD systems for high-speed computation, but memory contention resolution and strategies for optimal allocation of tasks to processors are still the subject of continuing research.

A simpler parallel architecture from a practical point of view is the single-instruction-stream–multiple-data-stream (SIMD) architecture (Figure 2.3). With this configuration several processors are arranged in an array and given identical instruction streams, which they execute synchronously, though

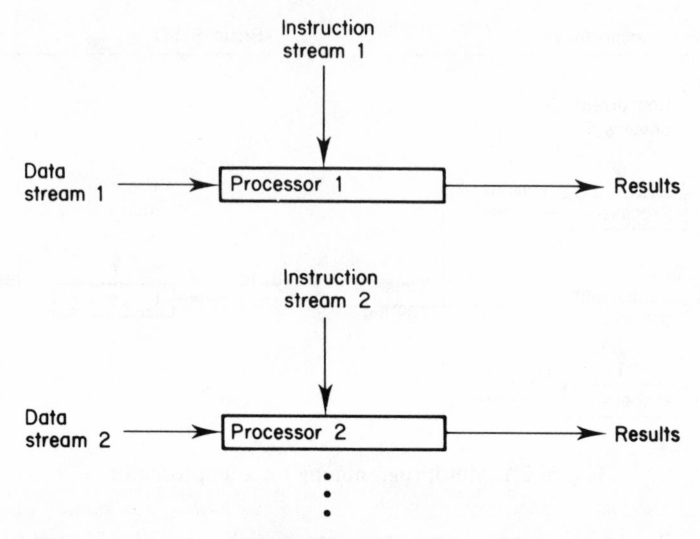

Figure 2.2 The multiple-instruction-stream–multiple-data-stream (MIMD) architecture

using different items of data. These machines are often called **array processors** and can be physically configured as linear or square arrays. These machines are ideal for algorithms in which there is a high degree of functional equivalence between successive algorithmic instructions (see the third example in Section 2.1) and where a large number of variables must be subjected to identical numerical operations. A typical example of a commercial SIMD machine is the ICL distributed array processor (DAP)—see Figure 2.4. This machine has been used for a number of numerically intensive computational problems, e.g. image processing, galactic evolution simulation, oil-field simulation. Like many commercial parallel machines it has its own high-level programming language (DAP-FORTRAN) in which variable names can refer to whole sets of data items such as complete vectors or arrays. Also its language includes many instructions with a simple syntax for carrying out quite complex procedures, e.g. finding the maximum value in a large array of numbers. Some features of this language and the use of such machines for image processing are briefly discussed in Chapter 14. More information on the DAP can be found in Flanders *et al.* (1977) and Gostick (1979).

The third approach to architectural parallelism is the **pipeline** technique which, depending on the circumstances, may be regarded as being an SISD or MISD architecture (in fact it is difficult to classify and does not conform well to the standard instruction-stream–data-stream model). In a pipelined system a set of processors can act together to progressively transform items of data (Figure 2.5). This is analogous to assembly-line manufacturing or packing.

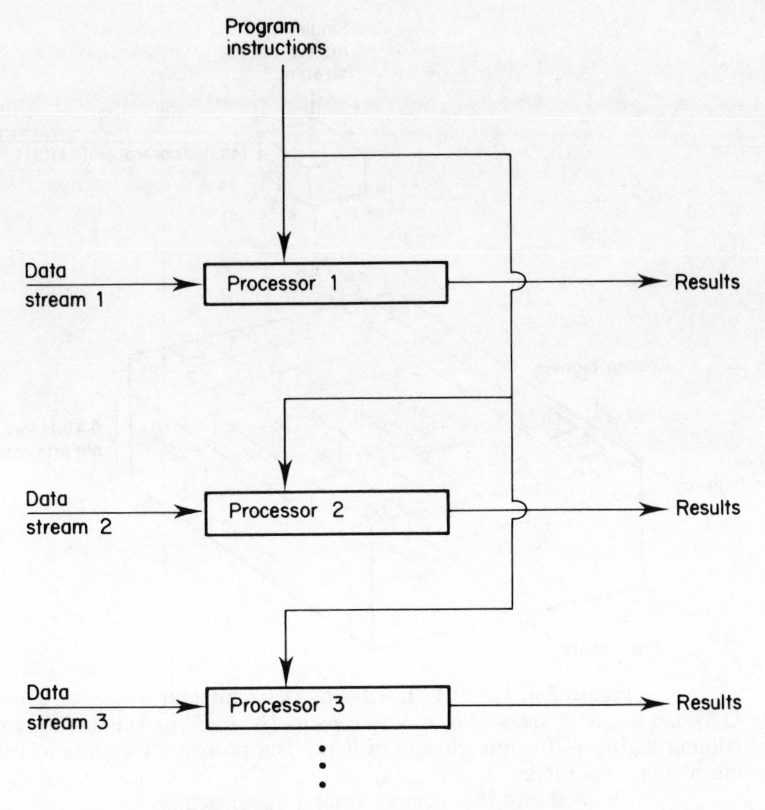

Figure 2.3 The single-instruction-stream–multiple-data-stream (SIMD) architecture

Take for example a large bottling plant which is preparing bottles of wine for a supermarket chain. At successive work-stations bottles are filled with the requisite amount of wine, have corks inserted, and finally labels stuck on. The three operations (filling, corking and labelling) can be carried out independently and in parallel, though obviously on different sets of bottles. Returning to the computer we can see that a set of data items (e.g. a vector) which must be processed identically could be handled by a similar assembly-line technique—this is the rationale for the pipelined architecture. A typical example of a commercial pipelined machine is the CRAY-1—a modern 'supercomputer' (see photograph, Figure 2.6). The CRAY-1 contains a set of vector registers which can store up to 64 floating-point numbers—these are operands which are sent to pipelined functional units ('arithmetic assembly lines'). It is not possible to examine the architecture of the CRAY in detail here but readers interested in this machine (and other recent pipelined machines) should consult Hockney and Jesshope (1981).

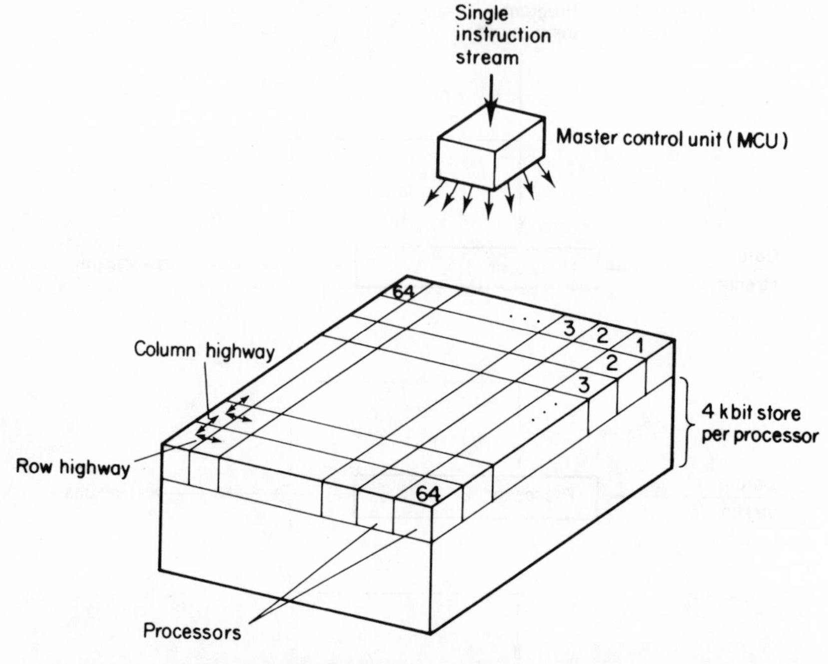

Figure 2.4 The ICL–DAP (SIMD Architecture)
The DAP has a square array of $N \times N$ processors ($N = 32$ or 64) linked by row and column highways for interchange of data. The processors simultaneously execute a single instruction broadcast from the MCU. Initial data values are loaded into the memory from a host machine

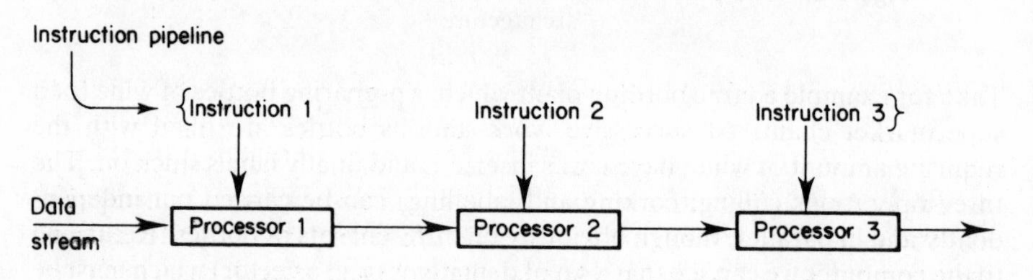

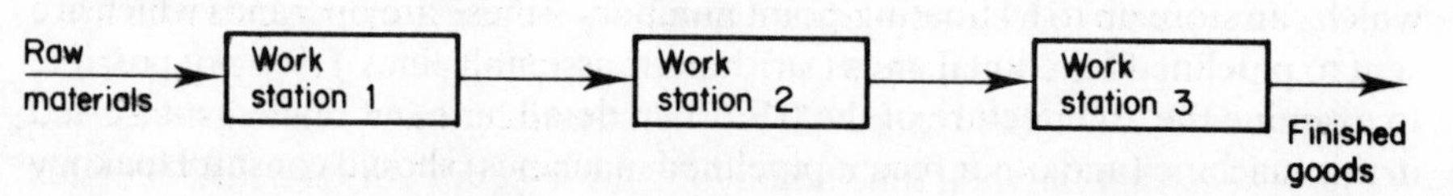

Figure 2.5 Parallelism by pipelining

2.3 COMPARING COMPUTATION TIMES FOR PARALLEL ARCHITECTURES

The computer architectures introduced in the previous section perform very differently on simple numerical problems. We can gain some insight into their relative capabilities by comparing the time each takes to execute a model problem. A suitable one for this purpose has been identified by Hockney and Jesshope (1981). It is the addition of two floating-point vectors $\boldsymbol{x}$ and $\boldsymbol{y}$ (with say components x_i and y_i, $i = 1, 2, 3$) to obtain a sum vector z. The addition of any pair of components x_i and y_i involves four sub-operations:

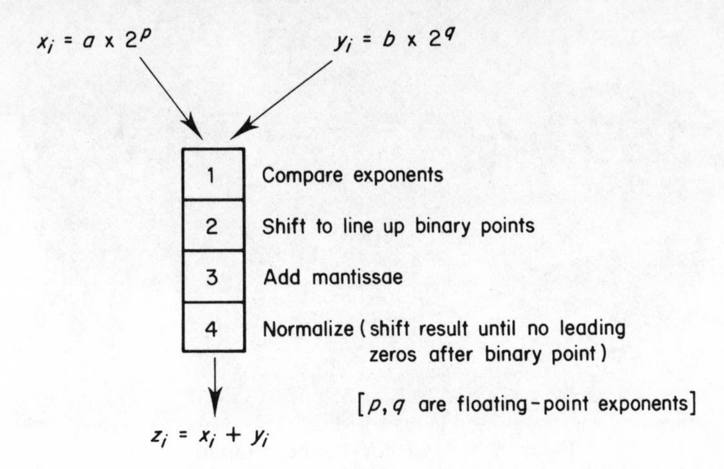

$x_i = a \times 2^p$
$y_i = b \times 2^q$
1 Compare exponents
2 Shift to line up binary points
3 Add mantissae
4 Normalize (shift result until no leading zeros after binary point)
[p, q are floating-point exponents]
$z_i = x_i + y_i$

The precise nature of these four sub-operations is immaterial for our purposes. Indeed it can be assumed for simplicity that each involves precisely one fetch–execute cycle in a processor. Note that from the way the problem has been defined this set of four operations must be carried out on *three* pairs of vector components. Figure 2.7 shows how the uniprocessor, pipelined parallel processor, and array-processor architectures each cope with this problem.

Notice that the array-processor architecture is the most efficient for this particular problem where exploitation of the inherent degree-3 parallelism in the problem establishes a considerable speed advantage compared with the uniprocessor. The pipeline architecture is also very efficient, though there is clearly a vector start-up period during which its efficiency is reduced. This is a natural consequence of the fact that an assembly line is not fully operational until the first components have reached the end.

2.4 PERFORMANCE TRENDS FOR PARALLEL MACHINES

We have seen that the total time taken for a given computational task depends very much on the machine architecture on which it is being executed besides

Figure 2.6 A CRAY-1 supercomputer
Reproduced with permission from P. Wright, CRAY Research (UK) Ltd

being dependent on the exact nature of the problem itself. Different tasks with different types of inherent parallelism are suitable for different classes of architecture. In general computer users may only have one machine available to them and rarely have total freedom to select a specific architecture for a given problem. Usually a computer user who desires high-speed computing is interested in average performance figures for a system as a whole covering a diversity of applications programs. Typical or representative performance figures are therefore essential for selecting a commercial machine.

As mentioned in Chapter 1, machine performance can be measured using programs containing a realistic mix of instruction types (benchmark programs). Execution speed can then be quantitatively specified in terms of a MIP rate or megaflop rate. The limitation on execution speed comes primarily from the finite switching speed of semiconductor devices, main-memory access times, and signal-propagation delays through interconnecting buses etc. Although these physical limitations are constantly being reduced by improved device technology it is certain that parallel processing will continue to play a major role in setting high-performance capabilities. In some cases the need to

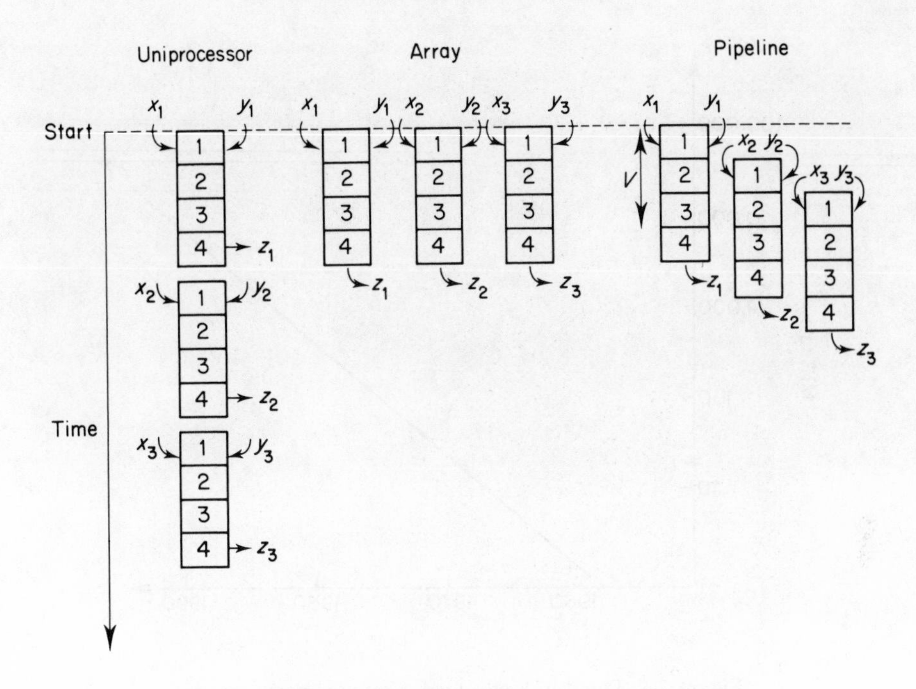

Computation-time comparison:

4 cycles/result   4 cycles for 3 results   1 cycle/result after V^*

($^*V$ = vector start-up time = 3 cycles in this case)

Figure 2.7 Comparison of computation times for floating-point vector addition on different machine architectures (adapted from Hockney and Jesshope 1981)

minimize signal propagation delays has led to very compact system configurations. The CRAY-1, for example, consists of an open cylinder of height 2 m (6.5 ft) with very densely packed components and short wire lengths to minimize signal delays (Figure 2.6). The whole machine is cooled by a liquid refrigerant to prevent heat build-up in the dense electronics.

The general trend in machine performances over the last few decades is illustrated in Figure 2.8. Certainly the highest-performance uniprocessors at present are limited to cycle times down to about 10 nanoseconds* at best. The maximum achievable instruction rate for current uniprocessors is of the order of 30 MIPs. Performance figures shown on Figure 2.8 in excess of this are primarily due to the use of parallelism.

It is important to note that it is rare to be able to achieve a theoretical maximum computing rate for a given machine in practical applications. For

*1 nanosecond (ns) = 10^{-9} s.

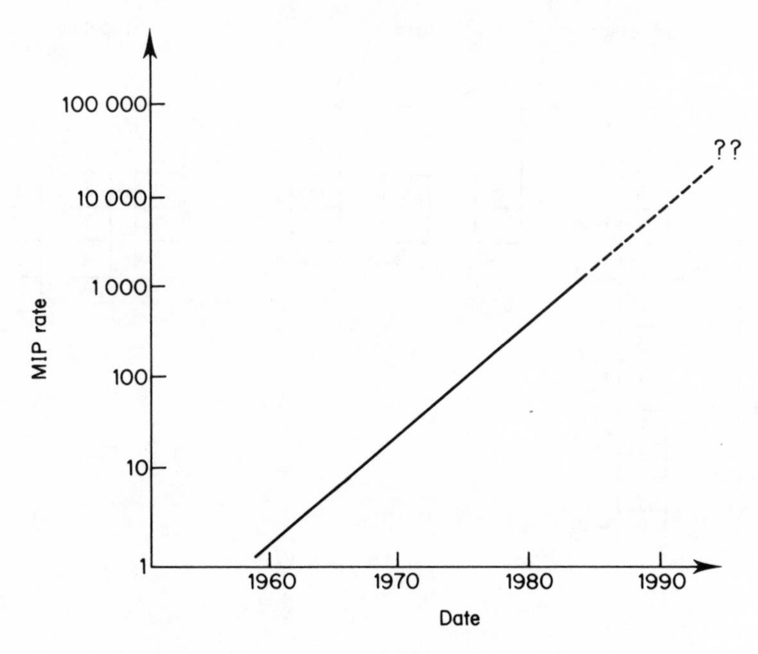

Figure 2.8 Trend in high-speed computer performance

example, performance rates in the 'gigaflop' (1000 megaflops) range are sometimes quoted for highly parallel array-processing machines (e.g. the DAP which could have up to 4096 processors working simultaneously). However, it is very unlikely that the parallelism of such machines would ever be fully exploited in general computational problems. The effect of this on performance can be illustrated with a little algebra.

Suppose we have a program consisting of a total of N instructions which must be executed on a computer on which a processor takes time t to execute one instruction. If this program must be executed entirely in serial mode, then the total time taken is:

$$T = Nt$$

Suppose, however, that the machine has N parallel processors available and that each instruction could be executed in parallel. In this case the total execution time would only be t. In general the program will contain pN instructions which can be executed in parallel and $(1 - p)N$ which can not. The total execution time in this case is given by the more general formula:

$$T' = \underbrace{(1 - p)Nt}_{\text{serial execution}} + \underbrace{t}_{\text{parallel execution}}.$$

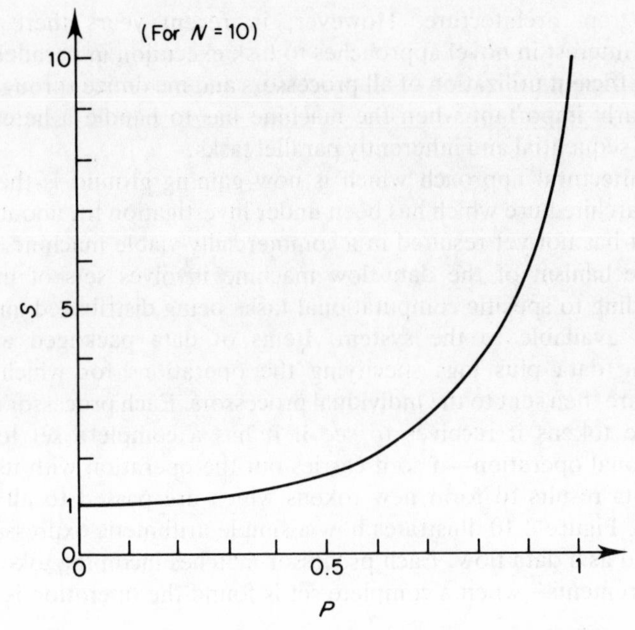

Figure 2.9 Relationship between speed-up factor and proportion of instructions which can be executed in parallel

The net speed-up factor S for a program on this machine is thus given by:

$$S = \frac{T}{T'} = \frac{N}{(1-p)N + 1}$$

This relationship is illustrated in Figure 2.9. Interestingly a speed-up factor of only 2 is achieved by a program with 60% parallelism on an $N = 10$ machine. Clearly performance is seriously reduced by any requirement to do serial processing on a parallel machine. Overall we can therefore say that good machine performance requires not only highly parallel architectural configurations but also high-speed capability for individual processors within the total system to minimize serial computation times.

2.5 NOVEL APPROACHES TO CONTROL: THE DATA-FLOW CONCEPT

So far we have restricted our architectural discussion to conventional approaches based on parallel processors working with stored sequences of instructions which may be applied to multiple data items which are held in arrays or passing through pipelines. We can regard this centralized 'control flow' approach to task execution as characteristic of the Von Neumann stored-program architecture. However, in recent years there has been increasing interest in novel approaches to task execution in parallel machines to ensure efficient utilization of all processors and maximize throughput. This is particularly important when the machine has to handle a heterogeneous mixture of sequential and inherently parallel tasks.

An architectural approach which is now gaining ground is the so-called data-flow architecture which has been under investigation for about a decade, although it has not yet resulted in a commercially viable machine. The basic control mechanism of the data-flow machine involves sets of instructions corresponding to specific computational tasks being distributed amongst the processors available to the system. Items of data packaged as 'tokens' (comprising data plus tags specifying the operations for which they are required) are then sent to the individual processors. Each processor checks the tags of the tokens it receives to see if it has a complete set for a given computational operation—if so it carries out the operation with its data and packages its results to form new tokens which are passed to all the other processors. Figure 2.10 illustrates how a simple arithmetic expression can be represented as a data flow. Each processor matches incoming tokens with its data requirements—when a complete set is found the operation is executed.

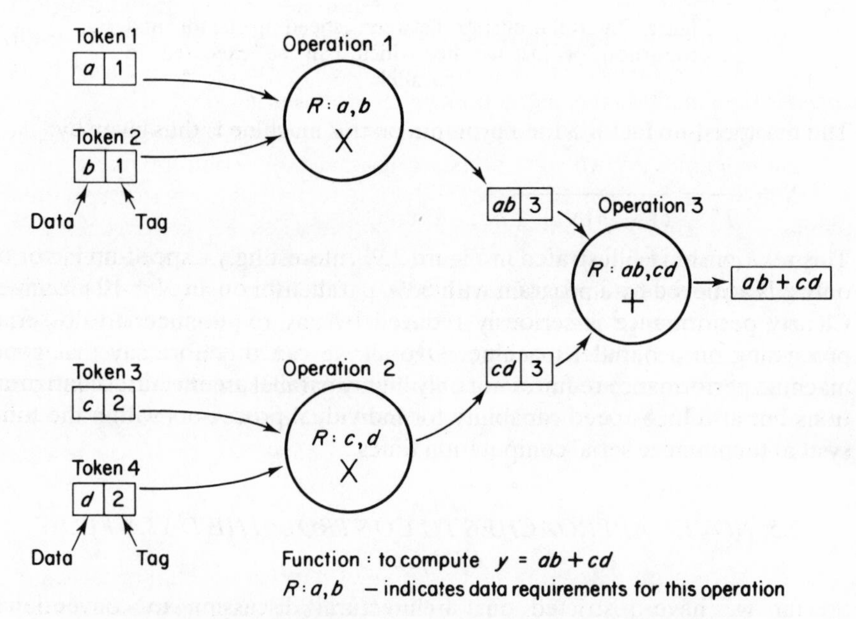

Figure 2.10 Data-flow diagram of arithmetic computation
In a data-flow machine operations 1–3 can be performed by different processors. Square boxes indicate tokens, i.e. data plus tags. Note that data-flow diagrams are also used to specify software designs, although the graphical conventions are somewhat different—see part 2

Implementation of this kind of computational approach requires an extensive bus network linking all the processors together so that tokens can be rapidly exchanged.

In principle the data-flow architecture is extremely flexible and provides a suitable solution for general heterogeneous computing problems—it simply handles them as a set of inter-related tasks which individually 'fire' as soon as data becomes available. In practice, however, there are several problems associated with such machines. These are:

- processing bottlebecks;
- necessity for extensive processor communication network (costly);
- need for novel programming languages (based on graphical representation of the data-flow).

So far these problems have precluded the introduction of commercial data-flow machines (although some prototypes are now in existence). The whole approach is, however, undergoing extensive research and is being looked at as a candidate architecture for fifth-generation machines. Further information can be obtained from Lerner (1984), *Computer* (1982) and Treleaven and Lima (1984).

A possible alternative to the data-flow approach is the demand-driven control mechanism in which a processor executes an instruction when its result is required. If the instruction requires some data to perform its operation a request is then made to the instruction which produces it.

Yet another possible control mechanism is the 'pattern-driven' mechanism for 'logic machines'. With such a system the machine would invoke certain operations when data conditions have been detected which match specified patterns. This kind of approach may be appropriate for systems used in knowledge-processing applications where logical inferences are made on the basis of data inputs matching specified rules.

At present there is much interest in developing machines with novel architectural and control features. Several projects are being carried out to exploit alternatives to the Von Neumann control-flow principle. These include the Japanese fifth-generation project and the 'Flagship' project run by the Alvey programme in the UK.

2.6 THE TRANSPUTER

So far we have been discussing the benefits of various novel approaches to computer organization. However, developments in processor technology are likely to be equally important in the future. It is certain that future high-performance computing machines will take advantage of whatever new developments take place in individual processor technology. One noteworthy development is the *transputer*, which can be regarded as a computer on a chip.

The transputer (a VLSI device comprising 200 000 logic gates) is a comparatively recent development distinguishable from a microprocessor in that processing power, some working memory and extensive communications capability are all provided within one integrated circuit. The inclusion of memory on the same chip as the processor removes the need for too many memory-address lines. Pins are therefore freed for establishing direct I/O links to external devices, including other transputers.

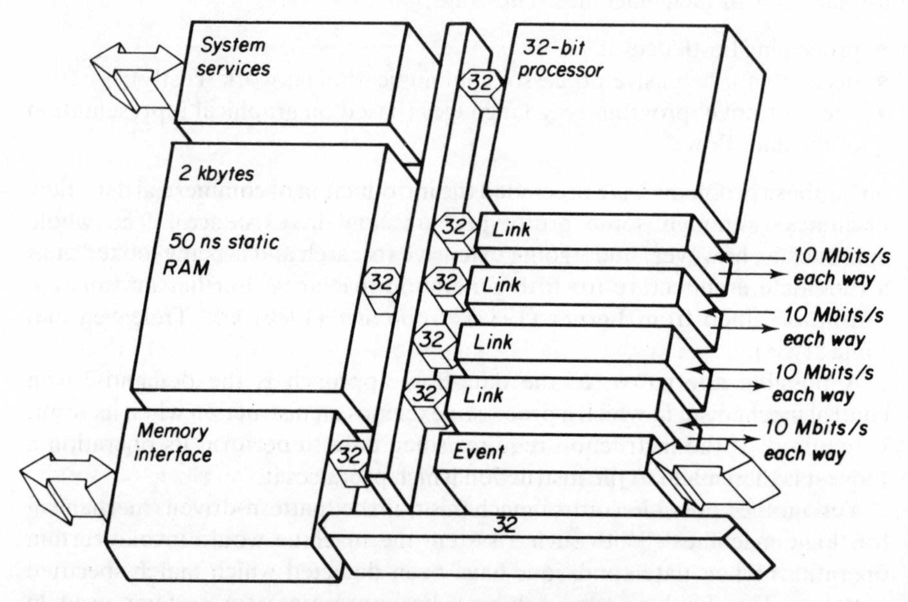

Figure 2.11 The INMOS T-414 transputer
32-bit processor, 10-MIP processing power, fabricated on 84-pin CMOS chip (With permission from INMOS)

The IMS T414 transputer (Figure 2.11) developed by the UK Inmos Company is capable of performance rated at 10 MIPs. It also has an integral 2 kbyte memory and four 10 Mbit/s links which can be used to create transputer networks to handle concurrent processing tasks. Inmos also originated work on a new concurrent programming language, Occam, specially tailored to the transputer. Occam enables the user to specify a set of concurrent intercommunicating processes which can be executed on a given transputer system.

Devices like it are likely to become very important in the future for constructing massively parallel computing machines. The transputer's main strengths lie in its compact size, high performance rates, and fast network links. It will be most useful as a building block for large processor networks—some experiments are already under way to use it in image-processing and machine-vision applications. Further information about the transputer concept can be found in Barron (1978).

2.7 THE OPTICAL COMPUTER

It is usually taken for granted that electronic techniques provide the basis for all computing at the present time. To a very large extent this is unquestionably true—all computers are currently built from integrated circuitry and computations are effectively performed by electronic switches in the form of transistors (a VLSI device, for example, can be considered to be a network of hundreds of thousands of transistors etched into wafers of semiconductor). Electrical signals are therefore at the heart of all modern computation. However, even though there are trends towards the use of massive parallelism and towards the development of more compact and faster electronic devices, it is generally recognized that a major leap forward in processing speed (of several orders of magnitude) is unlikely to come about from advances in electronics. Certainly advances are being made all the time but the capabilities of electronic devices are approaching the point where they are limited by the fundamental laws of physics. A significant leap forward in computer power now requires a radically new approach to signal-processing technology.

One such approach is the use of light beams rather than electric currents. Researchers at Heriot-Watt University have recently constructed simple optical analogues of transistor devices (so-called transphasors) using optically bistable crystals which can change rapidly between states of transmitting and not transmitting incident laser beams, depending on the intensity of the incident light. This leads directly to the possibility of constructing 'optical computers'. Basic logic functions (fundamental to current computers) can be achieved using optically bistable crystals (see Figure 2.12). Recent research has indicated that switching times of as little as 10^{-12} s are possible for such devices (roughly 1000 times faster than current technology). Since the laser beams carrying 'signals' would also propagate at or close to the speed of light (depending on the medium) and that parallelism should be fairly easy to achieve in optical systems, it is possible that optical computers will be able to achieve performance rates of the order of 10^6 MIPs or even more. Although the technology is still a long way from the point at which optical computers can be realized, some significant early progress has been made in building simple 'optical circuits'. For further details see Abraham *et al.* (1983).

2.8 THE FIFTH-GENERATION MACHINE

No discussion of advanced computer architectures would be complete without some examination of the fifth-generation machines.

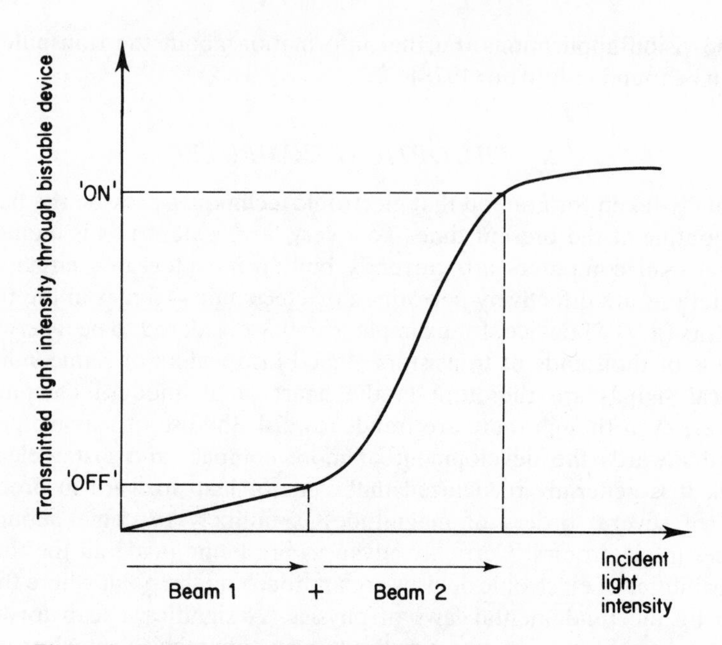

Figure 2.12 Optical bistability and implementation of AND logic function (adapted from Abraham *et al.* 1983)
The graph shows that the intensity of light passing through a bistable crystal is dramatically affected by the intensity of the incident light. Such a crystal could be used as an AND logic gate: the device only switches 'ON' (high transmission) when *both* beams are applied

Despite the lack of a tangible machine, there are some fairly detailed models of the functions these machines are intended to carry out and of the architectures on which they will be based.

Fundamentally, fifth-generation machines are envisaged to be knowledge-processing machines handling not only algorithmic programs but also human knowledge encoded in logical constructs which facilitate complex problem-solving. Clearly there is much activity at present on the development of knowledge-based software (part 4 is devoted to this) besides intelligent man–machine interfaces (part 5) which are expected to form a key part of future generation systems. But the JIPDEC, Alvey, and ESPRIT research and development programmes referred to in the introduction all include major projects on advanced architecture development as well—a necessary requirement if the complex software algorithms envisaged are to be executable in a finite and realistic period of time.

The basic configuration of a fifth-generation machine is shown in Figure 2.13. It is intended that such machines will provide access via natural language

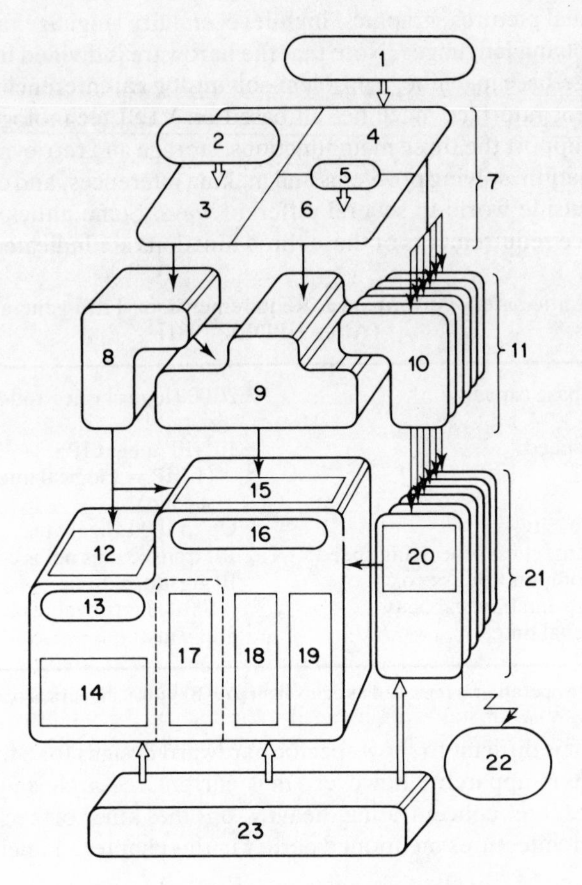

Figure 2.13 Proposed structure for fifth-generation machines (After Moto-Oka and Kitsuregawa 1985)
(1) access using natural language, speech and graphics etc.; (2) high-level enquiry language; (3) knowledge-base management system; (4) intelligent interface system; (5) kernel language; (6) problem-solving and inference system; (7) external interface with the basic software system; (8) knowledge-base management system; (9) problem-solving and inference system; (10) intelligent interface system; (11) basic software system; (12) knowledge-base machine; (13) relational algebra; (14) relational database mechanism; (15) problem-solving and inference machines; (16) predicate calculus type language; (17) abstract data type support mechanism; (18) data flow parallel implementation mechanism (data-flow processing mechanism); (19) innovative von Neumann mechanism; (20) intelligent interface machine; (21) hardware system; (22) distributed function network system; (23) VLSI architecture

speech, visual pictures, graphics, high-level enquiry languages and logic-based problem-solving languages. Note that the hardware is divided into three parts: a knowledge-base machine, a problem-solving logical-inferencing machine and an intelligent interface machine, all based on VLSI technology. These three machines support the three main functions: storage and retrieval of knowledge and information, solving problems and making inferences, and communication with the outside world in several different ways. Some anticipated machine-performance requirements of these three functions are indicated in Table 2.1.

Table 2.1 Anticipated Performance Requirements of Fifth-generation Hardware. (After JIPDEC 1981)

Knowledge-base capacity:	20 000 logical rules and 100 gigabytes of data
Inferencing speed:	10^2–10^3 megaLIPS (1 LIP = 1 logical inference per second)*
Database capacity:	Up to 1000 Gigabytes
Database transaction processing speed:	10^4 transactions per second
Numerical computation speed:	10 gigaflops
Picture/image database capacity:	~100 000 retrievable pictures
Picture retrieval time:	< 100 ms.

*One inference operation is regarded as equivalent to ~100–1000 numerical operations.

At present it is difficult to show specific hardward designs for a fifth-generation machine. It is apparent, however, that current research and development programmes are concentrating heavily on the kind of technologies and advanced architectures mentioned earlier in this chapter, namely:

- VLSI technology (e.g. transputer-like devices);
- Massive parallelism;
- Data-flow architecture;
- Data-driven, demand-driven or pattern-driven control.

It is unlikely that optical computer technology will form part of fifth-generation machines, owing to its primitive state at present. Nevertheless, it is perhaps predictable that optical technology and even 'biological chip technology' (based on layers of organic molecules acting as switches) will form the basis of sixth and subsequent generations, but this is still many years away. For further information on fifth-generation systems see JIPDEC (1981), Simons (1983), or Moto-Oka and Kitsuregawa (1985).

Fundamentals of Information Technology
Edited by G. G. Wilkinson and A. R. Winterflood

Chapter 3
Computer Networks

3.1 INTRODUCTION: THE NEED FOR COMPUTER NETWORKS

In the last chapter we saw that the power of a single computer system can be significantly improved by the use of parallel processing within the same physical machine. In a similar way, the power of a single computer installation can be substantially enhanced by linking it to other machines by means of a data communications network. Such a network may simply consist at one end of the spectrum of a few machines linked together in the same room (e.g. an office automation system). At the other end of the spectrum it might consist of an intercontinental network of computers belonging to a multinational company which communicate via sub-ocean cables and satellites. The two most important benefits of computer networking are:

1. it facilitates faster more effective transfer of information, e.g. by 'electronic mail';
2. it permits the distribution of computing tasks around the network in the interests of economy and efficiency.

For example, a large company with factories in several parts of the UK may have a requirement that each factory site should have available to it a huge database of product and customer information. It would be uneconomic and impractical to provide each site with a large duplicated database system. It is thus far more efficient for the company to maintain one central database system to which smaller machines on diverse sites have access. An analogous situation occurs in scientific computing: many scientific researchers in universities require the use of supercomputers such as the CRAY machines, the DAP and others. These machines are expensive and it would not be feasible to equip every university research laboratory with a machine of this power for 'number crunching'—it is far better to provide a network allowing access to centrally placed machines. In Britain, for example, the universities' network allows users to access supercomputers at regional computer centres in London and Manchester.

Computer networking is becoming an increasingly important part of computer systems development. Most of the coordinated information technology programmes taking place around the world now give computer communications a very high priority. The extension of parallel processing within one machine to the quasi-parallel processing of multiple computer installations operating on a global scale is also a development of the single CPU Von Neumann machine, but on a different scale. (It is interesting to note that some observers have pointed out that the total number of interconnections in the various worldwide telecommunication and computer communication networks now exceeds that of the cerebral cortex of man. But so far the system has not demonstrated any tendency towards intelligent or conscious behaviour!)

3.2 INFORMATION NETWORKS IN COMMERCE

At a conceptual level we can view computer networks as mechanisms for improving the information flow both horizontally and vertically within a company structure—they therefore create 'information networks'.

There are many examples of companies that operate as a group of independent outlets. Each outlet may at some point have equipped itself with its own computing facilities to carry out basic functions such as stock control or accounting. In many cases the result of localized processing is transmitted by traditional means to a head office which carries out further consolidation of information. Horizontal integration then consists of organizing some form of advanced communications network to automate the links between the outlets and head office.

In other cases an enterprise might have computerized seemingly independent activities such as sales, stock control, purchasing, accounting, reporting and management. The company's products could, for instance, carry a code which, once fed to the information system at the point of sale, would not only provide the till with the pricing information necessary for establishing the customer's invoice, but would also contain a product description which would enable the inventory to be updated and new stock to be ordered automatically. Price, cost and description could even be passed directly to the accounting function, and up-to-the-minute reports could then be generated for management analysis.

Thus vertical integration aims at suppressing intermediary traditional transmission stages (and delays) and integrating different types of information subfunctions into a single complete, end-to-end, activity-monitoring function.

There are of course many cases (e.g. a group of independently run subsidiary companies) where one can imagine complex patterns composed of a combination of vertical and horizontal integration, all designed to build up a single corporate information function. Although the technology is progressing fast, this integration is still in its infancy and remains faced with the gigantic problem of linking very different types of complex equipment over possibly wide distances and getting them to exchange data without loss of meaning.

3.3 LOOSELY-COUPLED AND TIGHTLY-COUPLED SYSTEMS

Any computer system consisting of multiple processors which are linked not only to their own sets of peripherals but also to each other is capable of distributed processing. However, it is important to distinguish between those systems which are essentially only single multiprocessing computers and those which are true computer networks. Although the distinction is sometimes difficult to make (e.g. what is a network of transputers?) we can conceive of two kinds of systems illustrated in Figure 3.1—these are the tightly-coupled and the loosely-coupled systems respectively.

In Chapter 2 we noted certain technical constraints on tightly-coupled systems (e.g. prevention of memory contention).

With loosely-coupled systems there are other equally important considerations. For example, the formats for the exchange of data between the two systems must be rigorously defined—this must include definitions of everything from data-message structure down to electrical signal voltages and even plug-pin connections. Also there may be a requirement to ensure privacy and security of any data exhanged between the two systems. Such considerations are an important aspect of computer networking. Indeed, for communications to be at all possible between different parties it is essential that 'protocols' are defined specifying the procedures to follow for encoding, protecting and physically transmitting items of data. Such protocols must be accepted, published, and adopted by equipment manufacturers (e.g. the infamous RS232 standard terminal interface).

3.4 TRANSMISSION MEDIA AND NETWORK SCALES

Data can be transferred between computers using a variety of different media. Data transmission rates vary enormously over media from, say, 100 bits per second to ~100 megabits per second. The types of media used for data communication depend to some extent on the scale of the network under consideration. Networks which are designed to support local distributed processing within one company site (a local area network or LAN) usually rely on twisted-wire pairs or coaxial cables which are specially laid between the various machines and peripherals on the network. Those networks which involve computers at widely dispersed locations (wide area networks or WANs) normally require access to some external public telecommunications agency where data may be transferred along a variety of media including telephone cables originally designed to carry analogue signals, integrated digital networks carrying pulse-code modulated digital signals at megabit/s

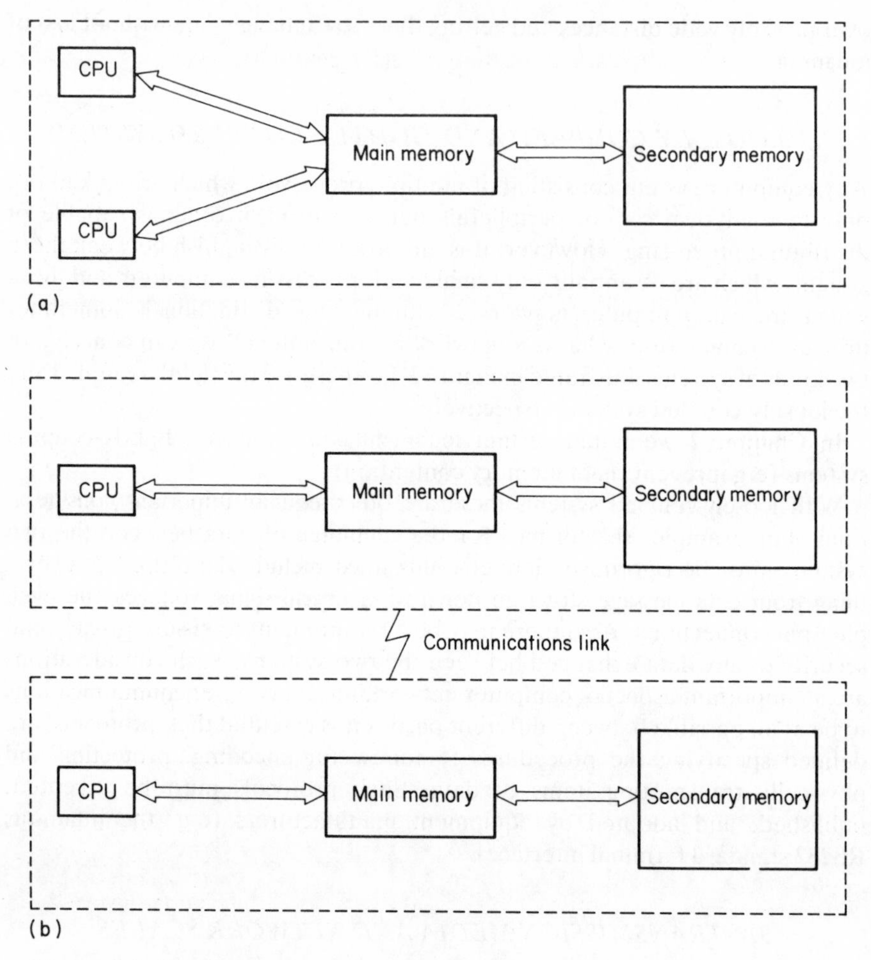

Figure 3.1 (a) Tightly-coupled multiprocessor system; (b) Loosely-coupled multiprocessor system

rates (e.g. British Telecom's IDN network and System X exchanges), and optical fibre links carrying data encoded as light pulses at similarly high data rates. International networks also make use of undersea cables and radio transmissions relayed via satellites in geostationary orbit over the equator.

3.5 DATA ORGANIZATION IN NETWORKS

Data can be organized in a variety of different ways on modern networks. Characters still form the major part of the data held on computer systems and transmitted across networks. Not surprisingly most of the coding and transmission techniques used in data communications are character oriented. At this level successful communication requires the following:

- Defining the set of all symbols it will be possible to use in a transmission, e.g. the International Alphabet no. 5 (IA5)—see NCC 1982.
- Defining the basic signal values to be used in transmission and the number and sequence of such values that will represent each character. The most common definition uses two signal levels assigned values 0 and 1 with sequences of seven such binary digits forming a character as defined in IA5. (Other representations exist, however, such as the 6-bit EBCDIC code or schemes based on four signal levels rather than two.)
- Defining error-detection mechanisms (such as parity checking using an 8th bit in IA5—see section on error checking below.)

At a higher level characters may be grouped in variable-length messages or fixed-length 'packets'. Packet switching is now very much a favoured way of transmitting data between individual computers (nodes) on a network. Packets usually contain several thousand bits of useful data besides a smaller number of bits (typically 32) to indicate their origin and destination addresses. They also contain some bits which act as error checking information. A typical packet structure is illustrated in Figure 3.2.

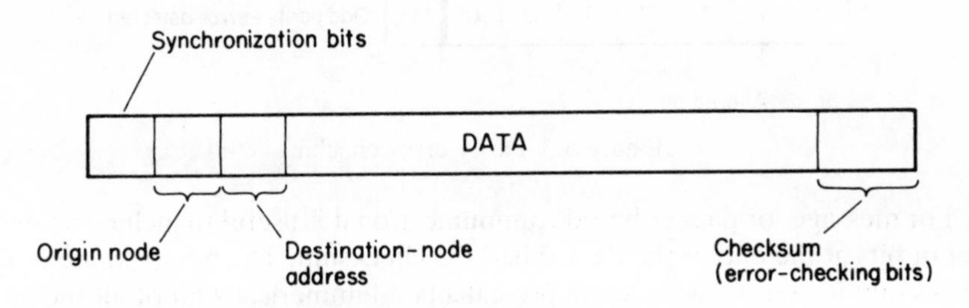

Figure 3.2 Typical 'packet' structure
Typical packet length ~2000–4000 bits
Within one network the packet structure must be pre-defined: all packets will be of identical format and length.
Synchronization bits indicate the start of the packet.

3.6 ERROR-CHECKING METHODS

Error checking is essential in data communication networks. Whenever data is to be transmitted over long distances via electronic circuitry, cables, radio links, etc., there is always a possibility of data corruption due to electronic noise or signal interference.

Error checking can be achieved by the inclusion of redundant information in the data message. Where character messages are being transmitted, an additional 'parity bit' may be added to the set of bits which define the character in our standard alphabet. This parity bit is set to 1 or 0 to make the total number of 1s in the binary-coded character either even or odd depending on which convention is adopted. With an even parity convention every character which is received must have an even number of binary 1s. If a character is received which does not possess the correct parity, then clearly a transmission error has occurred and we know that one of the bits in the character has flipped from 1 to 0 or vice versa (see Figure 3.3).

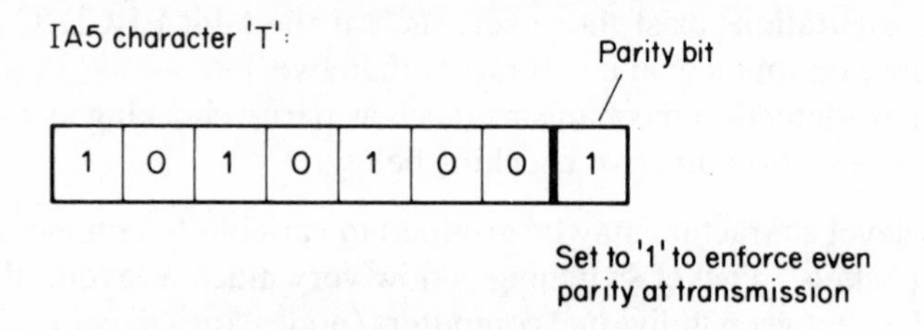

If after transmission through a network one of the bits is corrupted there will be a parity violation:

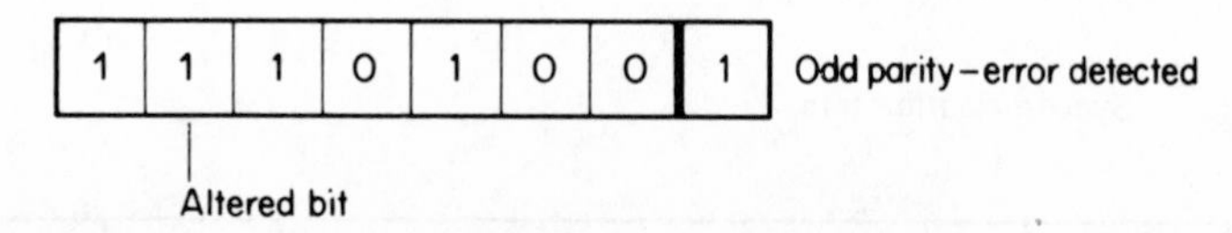

Figure 3.3 Parity-error checking

For message- or packet-based communication it is useful to include an extra set of bits at the end of the data called the checksum. The binary value of the checksum is used to store some pre-calculated numerical sum of all the 1s in the data message. At reception the addition operation is repeated and compared to the value in the received checksum. If the two do not tally, then there has been a transmission error. It may then be appropriate for the receiving computer to request that the original message or packet be repeated. Note that the transmission error could have corrupted either the actual data bits or the checksum. The inclusion of the checksum does not indicate where in the message or packet the problem has arisen, only that an error has occurred.

3.7 TERMINAL NETWORKS

So far we have glossed over an important network distinction: that between character-based terminal networks (i.e. networks of peripherals linked to a central computer) and message- or packet-based computer networks (i.e.

networks of several computers (nodes) communicating by the exchange of messages or packets). It is appropriate to consider each of these in turn.

Let us start with the case of a single terminal directly connected to a computer. Within the computer and within the terminal the eight bits that constitute a character (in the case of IA5) are transmitted in parallel over eight wires. Even if the computer and the terminal are only separated by a few yards, the distance is sufficient to make parallel communication between them using a data bus economically unviable. The data must then be serialized (transformed into a single bit stream) as shown in Figure 3.4.

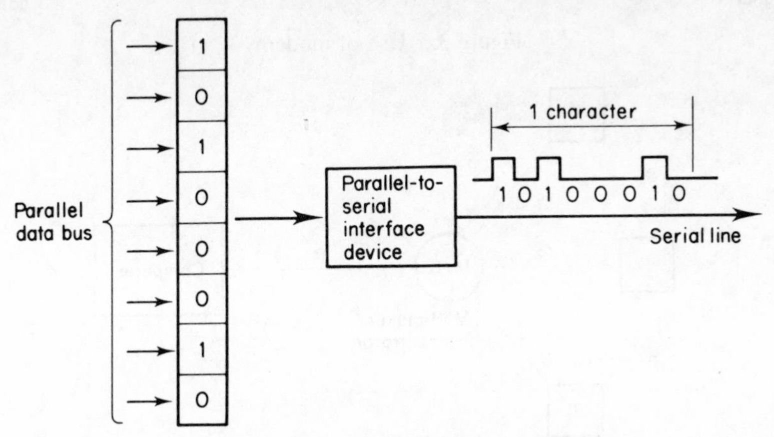

Figure 3.4 Parallel-to-serial data conversion

Standard 'universal asynchronous receiver transmitter' (UART) chips are manufactured for conversion between parallel and serial character representation for networking microprocessors. Normally these place special bits around serial characters to delimit their start and end points.

If the communication is to use a public telephone network (which was initially designed to carry voice) the bit patterns which the computer or terminal produce as variations of amplitude must be transformed into variations of frequency. The *modem* (modulator–demodulator) is the piece of equipment that carries out this task (see Figure 3.5).

In constructing a practical terminal network, we must also bear in mind that:

- user interaction with a terminal is intermittent rather than continuous;
- an active user's typing speed is far lower than the processing speed of the computer;
- a cost is attached to the installation and usage of the link between terminal and computer.

It is clear that sensible management of resources requires that communications from several terminals to the computer should be interleaved to enable

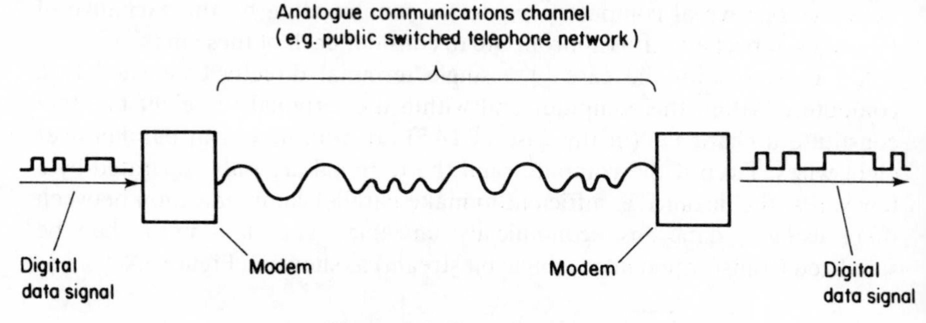

Figure 3.5 Use of modems

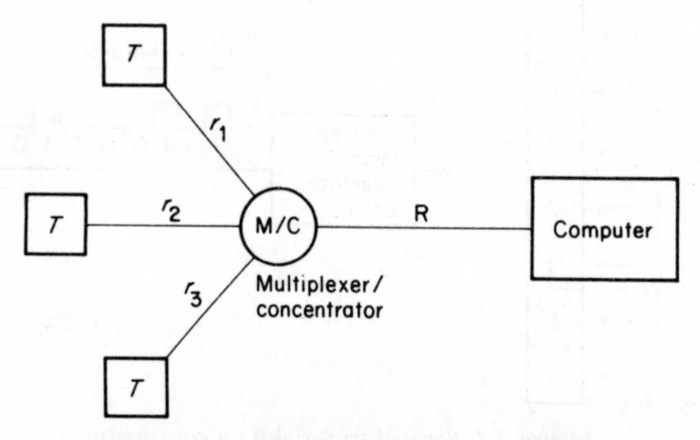

Figure 3.6 Use of multiplexers and concentrators
R = transmission speed of link into computer (no. of characters transmitted per second)
r_1, r_2, r_3 = transmission speeds of terminal lines to multiplexer/concentrator
If $r_1+r_2+r_3 \leq R$ then a *multiplexer* (switch) can be used
If $r_1+r_2+r_3 > R$ a *concentrator* must be used as there will be times when there is too much data to send—a concentrator can store data and spread the onward transmission over a longer period (providing the time averaged sum of r_1, r_2, and r_3 does not exceed R).

better use of each line. This task is carried out by *multiplexers* and *concentrators* (see Figure 3.6).

3.8 COMPUTER-NETWORK TOPOLOGIES

The integration of computing functions mentioned in the introduction would typically require that one or more users (or computers) be able to communicate with any one of a number of computers. A terminal network such as the one described in the previous section implicitly provides a fixed link between each

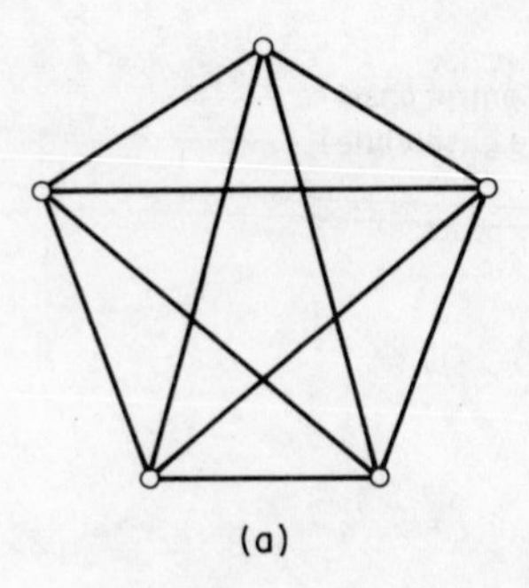

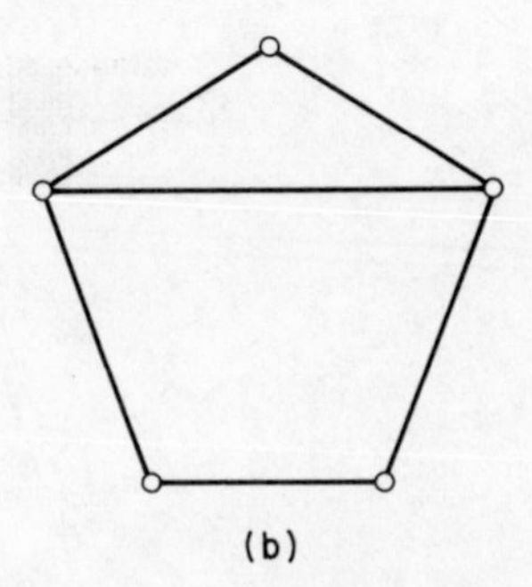

Figure 3.7 (a) Fully connected and (b) partially connected networks In partially connected networks data can still be passed between any two nodes provided that it is routed via others

terminal and a computer. Simply extending this service to provide direct access to a number of computers would require a network that was fully connected, i.e. where each terminal was directly linked to each computer (see Figure 3.7). This type of network gets unmanageable as soon as there are more than a very small number of nodes. It is also extremely inflexible as regards adding new nodes to the network.

Any practical way of allowing several machines to communicate therefore requires (a) a network that is not fully interconnected, and (b) a way of selecting one particular interlocutor amongst the different machines on the network.

The first problem (which is that of choosing a network topology) has seen three major classes of solution:

1. *Broadcasting:* This type of network uses a special *central agent* (typically a satellite) to which all nodes are linked. Communication takes place by the user sending a message to the central agent, which then broadcasts it to all stations on the network, including the originator of the message and its intended recipient (see Figures 3.8 and 3.9).
2. *Star-shaped networks:* Usually these have a hierarchy of several levels (such as a telephone network); in this case the user sends a message to a 'superior' node, which then passes it on to another node on a similar path. This procedure is repeated until the message reaches its destination (Figure 3.10).
3. *Ring structures:* In this case the nodes are arranged in a closed sequence so that each is connected to only two neighbours. A message can thus be put on the ring by an originator and passed from station to station until its recipient takes it off the ring (Figure 3.11).

A typical example of a ring network is the *Cambridge ring* local area network system. This uses mini-packets which are circulated around the network. Any

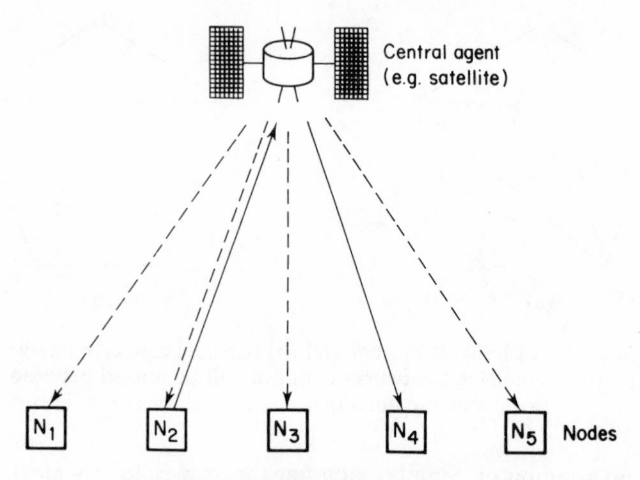

Figure 3.8 Satellite broadcast network

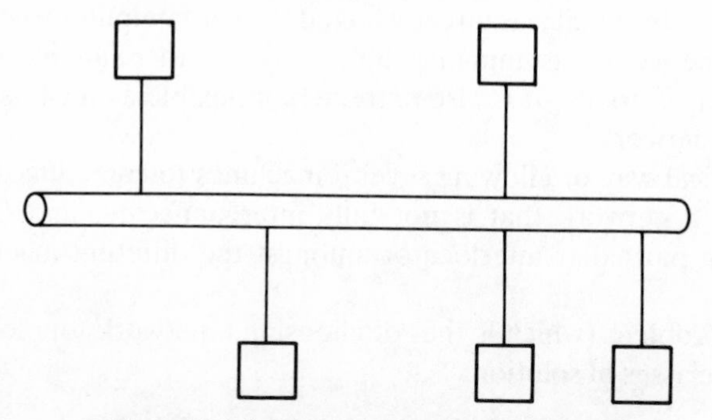

Figure 3.9 Multipoint linear bus network
This is a broadcast network with a cable acting as 'central agent'. A practical example of this is the commercial ETHERNET system first developed by Xerox—see Hutchison (1983), for example.

node wishing to send data must wait for an empty packet to come by. It then fills it with data and adds an appropriate destination address. Each node of the circuit inspects the destination fields of passing packets to decide whether or not the data is intended for itself. Packets are not emptied until they have done a complete circuit back to the originator. The originator verifies that the packet has remained unchanged during its circuit as a means of error checking (see Cole (1981) or Hutchison (1983), for example, for more details).

The second practical problem (routing) is of varying importance for each of the three topologies described above:

- Broadcast systems do not have routing decisions to make, but they have the difficult task of ensuring that simultaneous transmission attempts by two or

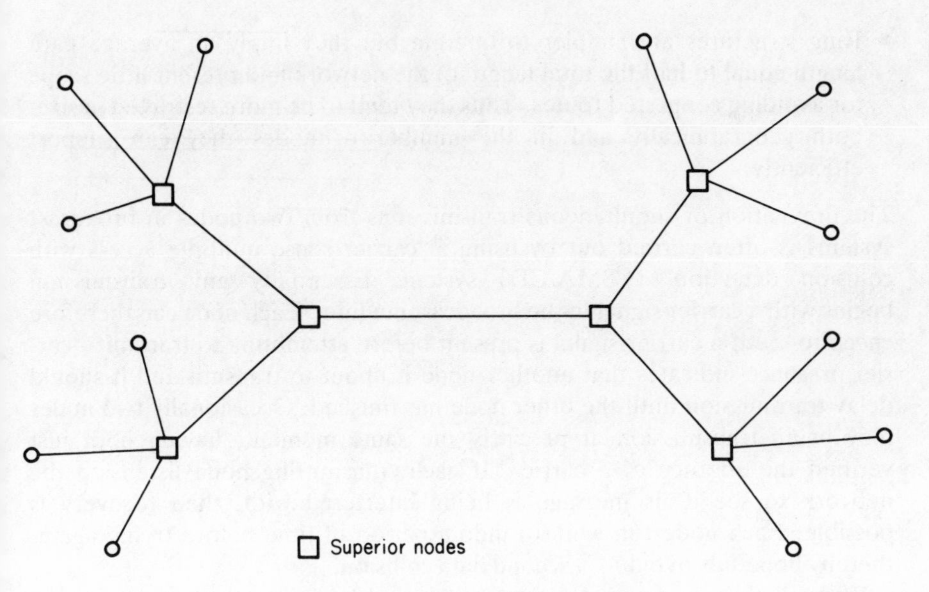

Figure 3.10 Star network topology

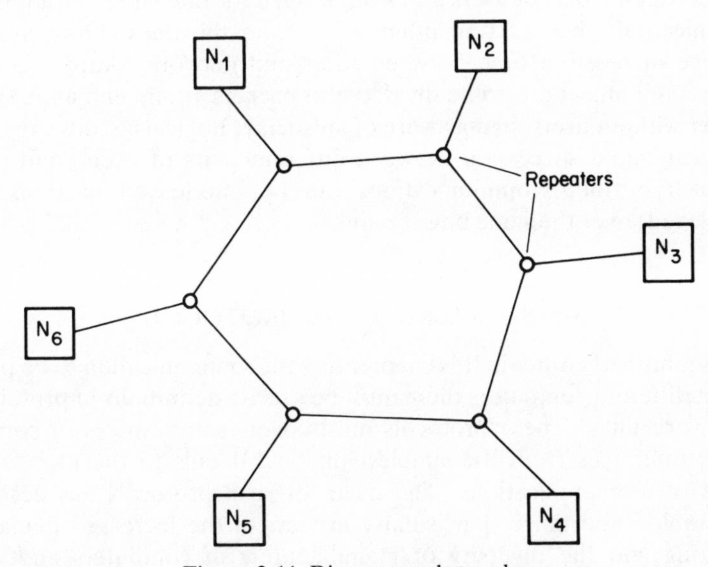

Figure 3.11 Ring network topology

more users do not result in a garbled broadcast. They also have to guard against eavesdropping by listeners which are not part of the network.

- Hierarchical networks do not have these problems, but due to the relative centralization of their structure they must try to provide a number of alternative routes to cope with node breakdown and path congestion.

- Ring structures are simpler to operate but they imply an average path length equal to half the total length of the network and present little scope for avoiding congested routes. Thus they tend to be more restricted in size, both geographically and in the number of nodes they can support efficiently.

The prevention of simultaneous transmissions from two nodes in broadcast systems is often carried out by using a 'carrier sense multiple access with collision detection' (CSMA/CD) system. Essentially any transmission begins with a carrier signal in the broadcast medium. Each node can therefore check to see if a carrier signal is present before attempting to transmit—carrier presence indicates that another node is about to transmit and it should delay transmission until the other node has finished. Occasionally two nodes may begin transmission at precisely the same moment, having both just verified the absence of a carrier. If each transmitting node listens to the network to see if its message is being interfered with, then recovery is possible. Each node can wait a random period of time before trying again, thereby hopefully avoiding a second data collision.

With all three network topologies it would be impractical to establish a circuit between a pair of users and keep it open for the whole duration of the communication, thus barring other users from the lines. Once again the difference in reaction time between users and network-control equipment enables communications to be divided into packets at one end and rebuilt at the other without users' being aware of any delay. Logical circuits can then be switched in rapid succession between different pairs of users, and packets from each of their communications can be interleaved in transmission (multiplexed) over the same physical links.

3.9 STANDARDS AND PROTOCOLS

It was established earlier in this chapter that for communication to be possible between different computers there must be precise definitions of protocols for the network links. These protocols must cover many aspects of computer/network interfaces from the simplest physical details to the most abstract features of user applications. The need for such protocols has become of considerable importance, particularly in view of the increased demand for networking and the diversity of manufacturers of computers and related equipment. The International Standards Organization has established committees to define appropriate protocols for all levels of data communications. Their work is based on a 'seven-layer reference model' for the interconnection of 'open' systems. This model views the communication process as a hierarchy of related layers, each of which requires its own standards and protocols (see Table 3.1).

Table 3.1 The ISO Seven-layer Reference Model for Open Systems Interconnection

Layer	Main features, standards required etc.
7. Application layer	Definitions of services for programs, file transfers, job transfers, distributed databases.
6. Presentation layer	Specification of syntaxes for structured data etc., message services.
5. Session layer	Definitions of connected session services and dialogue coordination, management of network resources.
4. Transport layer	Control of data transport from process to process.
3. Network layer	Definition of packet format, protocols for LANs to provide network services, routing, node-to-node communication.
2. Data-link layer	Protocols for link connection, character transmissions, error checking.
1. Physical layer	Definitions of signal qualities, interface connectors, pin assignments etc.

To conclude this chapter it is worth making the observation that although many computer networks are now well established both on local and intercontinental levels, it is still the case that real flexibility to link any two machines in the world together is unlikely to be achieved until all the ISO protocols have been established and adopted by equipment manufacturers. At present, although dozens of protocols have been defined for different aspects of the seven-layer hierarchy, it will be many years before a complete specification is ever published.

For further information on networks see Davies *et al.* (1979), Tanenbaum (1981) or Cheong and Hirschheim (1983).

PART 2

SOFTWARE ENGINEERING

Fundamentals of Information Technology
Edited by G. G. Wilkinson and A. R. Winterflood

Chapter 4

The Programming Environment

4.1 INTRODUCTION TO SOFTWARE ENGINEERING

Some twenty years after the first computer programs executed successfully, it was realized that although computers had considerable processing power, the abilities of humans to write complex yet reliable programs for them were limited. This realization led to the emergence of the still ill-defined discipline of *software engineering*. The term expresses the idea that until the design and construction of programs is based as securely on mathematical, scientific, and engineering principles as is the design and construction of other engineered artefacts we shall never realize the full potential of the computer. More seriously, we shall be tempted to entrust to badly-constructed and ill-understood programs tasks whose correct performance is vital (like controlling nuclear plants, for instance). Since a programming language is the medium in which a program is ultimately defined we may expect the quality of that language, and of the environment in which it is used, to make a significant contribution to program quality.

4.2 LANGUAGES AND MACHINES

If we were to make a representative selection of the programs run by a large general-purpose computer installation, in a university, say, and were to ask their authors to describe them in terms of their own subject disciplines, it would quickly become obvious that the professional languages of historians, mathematicians, psychologists and geologists, for example, are very different. We shall call these languages domain languages. If we were then to get the computer to print out the programs, and their data, in the form in which it stores and manipulates them, we should see another, common, language which would not bear the remotest resemblance to the domain languages. This language, which is called machine language or machine code, consists of sequences made up of precisely two symbols, conventionally represented as the binary digits 1 and 0.

This reflects the fact that the computer hardware can execute only programs which are sequences of precisely two electrical states and only upon data represented in exactly the same way. A programmer is therefore faced with a translation problem. The representation of the algorithm and input data in the domain language must be converted into the corresponding representation in machine code and the output data generated by the machine's execution of the algorithm must be translated back into the domain-language representation.

In the earliest days of computing the translation had to be done by the human programmer, who therefore needed a detailed knowledge of the machine code of the particular computer to be used. The syntax and semantics of a machine code are determined directly by the hardware of the machine. A machine-code program consists of a sequence of instructions each of which is a sequence of binary digits, or 'bits'.

Each data item in a machine code program is, physically, a sequence of bits stored in a memory location identified by its *address*. A memory location is the most basic instance of what is called a data object, a receptacle for data values. The semantics of data objects are determined by the machine operations they can be subjected to as well as by the values, i.e. the particular bit sequences, which they contain. This property of objects is captured in the concept of a data type; a concept which turns out to be fundamental in computing. A data type can be defined as a class of data objects with specifications for a set of attributes which they possess, for a set of values which they can contain and for a set of operations which can be performed upon them.

Some data types are built into the machine hardware in the sense that it implements their values and operations directly. A typical machine might offer integer, real, bit-string and possibly character or character string as built-in (or intrinsic) data types. The machine language will then include a special code (called the op-code) for each of the operations defined on these types. For type integer, for example, it might have op-codes for add, subtract, multiply, divide, test for zero and compare. The hardware interprets a bit sequence as, say, an integer if an integer operation is applied to it but it will interpret the same bit sequence in an entirely different way if a character operation is applied to it.

If a machine-code program fails to execute correctly the programmer has the problem of locating the error, or errors, in the machine code and/or the loading process. Errors are inevitable, not least because one sequence of 16 or 32 binary digit values looks very much like another to human eyes. Consequently, simple transliteration errors such as writing a 1 for a 0 or vice versa or omitting a digit are very easy to make and very difficult to find. Even if these errors are avoided, the readability of machine code is so poor that looking for an error in the logical structure of the program is a major investigative process. The appearance of the code simply does not reflect any of the logical structure it implements, nor any of the properties of the conceptual data types which are being modelled.

4.3 ABSTRACTION AND VIRTUAL MACHINES

Early programmers soon developed, out of sheer necessity, notations which made their programs easier to construct. Various graphical methods were devised to give a picture of the logical structure of a program or data object. Squares, circles, diamonds and other geometrical shapes were used to symbolize particular types of operations. Details of the operations could be written inside the shapes using abbreviations of English words and mathematical or other domain notations. The sequences in which operations were performed could be shown by lines or arrows connecting the shapes. These were the precursors of the flow charts, data-flow diagrams and design-structure diagrams discussed in Chapter 5. Of course, these graphical notations could not replace machine-code programs. They were aids to the design of a program which, at the end of the day, still had to be written out in binary machine code.

Textual notations, however, are a different matter. Instead of writing machine-code instructions as sequences of bits during the development of the program, it was much quicker and easier to represent each op-code by an English word, or abbreviation of it, which named the operation it stood for. Thus different bit sequences could be replaced by the much more mnemonic ADD, SUB, MULT, etc. The use of bit sequences for the addresses of main-memory locations containing data values could similarly be avoided by giving each location a name, or 'symbolic' address, which reflected its conceptual data type. Names like LENGTH, AVERAGE, PRICE, etc. convey information which a binary address cannot. This practice obviously made the development of programs much quicker and safer, since the program text itself reflects conceptual relationships and makes errors at that level easier to avoid. Once this text had been written the programmer could sit down with a table of mnemonic op-codes and their bit-sequence equivalents and translate the first into the second for each instruction. Similarly a memory map of the symbolic addresses was used to replace them in instructions by the actual addresses. Since this is a purely mechanical exercise relatively easily specifiable by an algorithm, programs called *assemblers* were soon developed to translate sequences of symbolic op-codes and addresses into machine-code programs.

These developments had enormous significance. The assembly-language programmer does not need to know the bit-sequence codes nor to specify actual hardware addresses. The existence of the assembler creates a new and different machine. The real machine is concealed below a layer of software which offers a **virtual machine** to the programmer. The virtual machine is easier to program than the real machine is: it can be programmed as if the hardware could cope directly with mnemonics and symbolic addresses. Assembly language offers an abstraction away from details of the real, hardware, machine which are not usually of interest of the programmer. Since this virtual machine is created by a program, other virtual machines could be created by writing other programs, a task made more feasible by the virtual machine we have just created.

The ultimate virtual machine would require only details which are meaningful in the domain context of the programs it executes. Any hope of constructing such a machine requires the identification of the kinds of abstraction required.

Symbolic addresses of memory locations offer **data abstraction**. The programmer can think of the location addressed as *LENGTH* as a mathematical variable whose value is the length in metres of the object being modelled in the program. The assembler provides **operational abstraction**: the programmer need no longer be concerned with how to place instructions and data values in memory.

The need for a third type of abstraction was soon perceived and provided for. In some machines the intrinsic data type integer did not include the operations of multiplication and division, so the programmer had to write a sequence of instructions to implement them in software. Since these operations occur very frequently in commercial and scientific applications it was convenient to provide them as single instructions built into the virtual machine. The assembler could then replace the single mnemonics MULT or DIV with the appropriate sequences of machine-code instructions. An even more useful facility of a virtual machine is one which allows a programmer to define and use his or her own abstract operations, and assemblers eventually provided a mechanism for this. The *subroutine* mechanism causes the relevant sequence of intrinsic instructions to be stored in main memory, starting at a location named by the programmer. When the name is later encountered as the operand of a 'branch to subroutine' (bsr) instruction, control is transferred to the named location and the sequence executed. At the end of the sequence control is transferred back to the instruction immediately following the bsr instruction. It became normal practice for computer installations to accumulate libraries of subroutines for programmers to use as required.

This facility removes the need for the programmer to provide specific details of how particular operations are performed and constitutes **procedural abstraction**. It can also be said to provide **control abstraction** since the details of how control is effectively transferred are hidden, or in computing jargon, 'transparent to the programmer'.

4.4 HIGH-LEVEL LANGUAGES

The obvious advantages of assembly language over machine code stimulated the development of languages which offered higher levels of built-in abstraction and better mechanisms for programmers to define their own abstractions. The late 1950s saw the appearance of a number of such languages, three of which, modified somewhat over the years, are still in wide use today. Two of them, FORTRAN and COBOL, are almost certainly responsible for more currently used software than all other programming languages put together. The third, LISP, adopted by the artificial intelligence (AI) community soon after its birth, is now actually increasing its user base as commercial exploitation of AI increases. The fourth major language of the period, ALGOL60, although in the opinion of many a huge advance on

FORTRAN, was never so widely used (for reasons mostly irrelevant to its qualities as a programming language) but exerted great influence on later developments in programming languages.

The two domains in which improvements in programmer productivity were of major interest at the time were science and engineering calculations and commercial and financial record-keeping and accounting. FORTRAN (language for FORmula TRANslation) was developed specifically to cater for the former, and COBOL (COmmon Business Oriented Language) to cater for the latter. The designers of FORTRAN were convinced that the difficulty, and hence the cost, of program development could only be reduced if the programmers could use a language very similar to their domain language; in this case conventional algebraic and decimal arithmetic notation. COBOL was designed with similar reference to the domain language of its targeted user group.

There are basically three ways of implementing a programming language. The first is hardware implementation; construction of a real machine whose machine code is the language. This has never been an economic proposition for high-level languages (except LISP, which is a special case) but it would be rash to say, in view of the rate of innovation in hardware design and production, that it never will be.

Faced with using a real machine with the conventional kind of machine code discussed in Section 4.2, there are two alternatives. The high-level code can either be translated into a machine-code representation which is then executed by the real machine hardware or a virtual machine can be constructed to execute the high-level code directly. Both methods require a sizable amount of enabling software to be constructed: a translator, called a compiler, for the first and an executor, called an interpreter, for the second.

To the programmer there is no difference, in principle, between the two methods, but there is an important difference in practice since a compiled (i.e. machine-code) version of a program actually executes many times faster than the high-level language version running on an interpreter. The compiler has already decoded the statements as far as machine-code instructions, which themselves are decoded very rapidly by the machine hardware. The interpreter has to decode each statement at run time every time it meets it, which makes interpretation very much less efficient (see Figure 4.1).

The first compiler to achieve wide use was that produced by the FORTRAN project team. Efficient execution was (and still is) a major requirement for its application domain, so an interpreter was never considered. The language was designed to be compiled into efficient machine code with extensive code optimization being performed by the compiler. The FORTRAN program in Figure 4.2 shows a main program (lines 1 to 9) and a subprogram (lines 11 to 28). The line numbers are not part of the program text but the numbers 100, 200, 300 are program statement labels. Comment lines begin

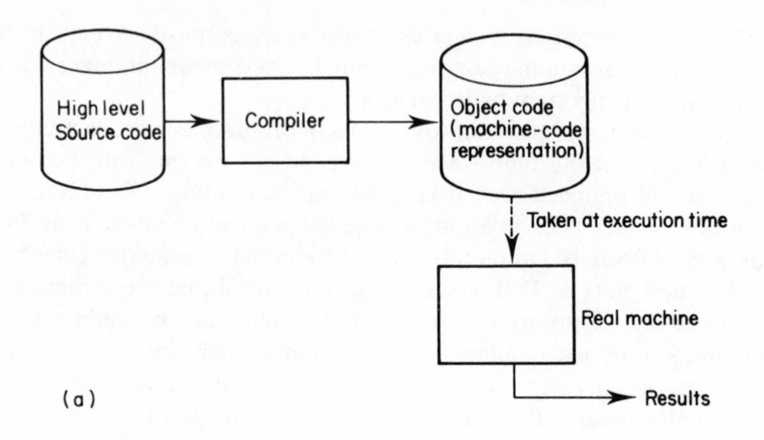

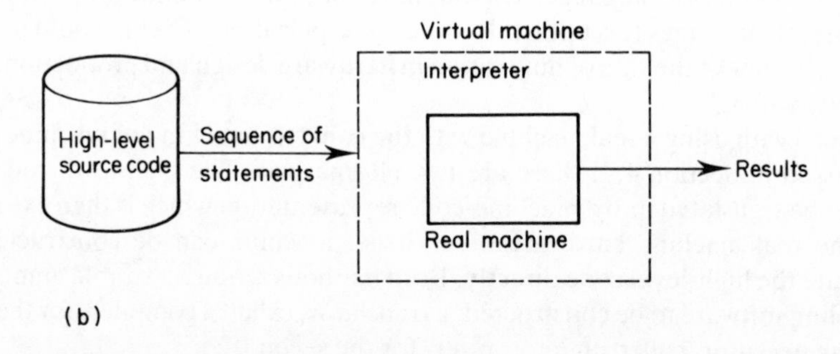

Figure 4.1 Translation of high-level source code by (a) compiler and (b) interpreter

with a 'C'. Corresponding roughly to the directives and instructions of assembly languages FORTRAN has declarations and (executable) statements. Declarations specify the names (symbolic addresses) and types of variables (memory locations) and must precede the statements within a program or subroutine. See lines 3, 4, 12 and 13 of the example program. The built-in data types are *INTEGER, REAL, DOUBLE PRECISION* and *COMPLEX*, all decimal numerical types, and *LOGICAL*, whose values are the Boolean truch values represented in FORTRAN by the constants *.TRUE.* and *.FALSE.*.

FORTRAN also provides one data-structuring facility, called an array. The declaration *DIMENSION M*(6) declares six objects of type *INTEGER* whose names are *M*(1), *M*(2), *M*(3), *M*(4), *M*(5), *M*(6).

Numerical computation is defined in FORTRAN by *expressions*, which consist of a combination of constants, variables and operators: for example,

```
 1          PROGRAM BUBBLE
 2  C
 3          INTEGER LENGTH
 4          DIMENSION M(50)
 5  C
 6          CALL INPUT(M,50,LENGTH)
 7          CALL SORT(M,50,LENGTH)
 8          CALL OUTPUT(M,50,LENGTH)
 9          END
10  C
11          SUBROUTINE SORT(ARR,I,ICOUNT)
12          INTEGER ARR(I)
13          LOGICAL FLAG
14          LIMIT=ICOUNT-1
15          DO 100 J=1,LIMIT
16             FLAG=.FALSE.
17             K=ICOUNT-J
18             DO 200 L=1,K
19                      IF(ARR(L).GE.ARR(L+1)) GOTO 200
20                      ITEMP=ARR(L)
21                      ARR(L)=ARR(L+1)
22                      ARR(L+1)=ITEMP
23                      FLAG=.TRUE.
24  200        CONTINUE
25             IF (.NOT.FLAG) GOTO 300
26  100     CONTINUE
27  300     RETURN
28          END
29  C       needs:
30  C       SUBROUTINE INPUT(ARR,I,ICOUNT)
31  C       reads number of integers to be sorted into ICOUNT
32  C       reads integers into ARR(I)
33  C       SUBROUTINE OUTPUT(ARR,I,ICOUNT)
34  C       outputs the first ICOUNT integers in ARR(I)
```

Figure 4.2 A FORTRAN program which sorts integers

$$I = J - K + I + 2$$
$$A(I) = A(I - 2) * 10 + 432.7 * Y/Z$$

(See for example line 14 of Figure 4.2).

The expression is a major advance over assembly-language provision since it removes the necessity for the programmer to specify the locations in which constants and the intermediate results of a computation are to be stored.

The two major control statements of FORTRAN are the *IF* and *GOTO* statements. Unconditional branching is performed by a statement of the form

GO TO ⟨label⟩

which transfers control to the statement bearing the specified label.

The most generally useful of several *IF* statements is the logical *IF*, which has the syntax:

IF ⟨logical expression⟩ ⟨statement⟩

and the meaning 'if and only if the logical expression evaluates to *.TRUE.* then execute the statement'. Line 19 of the example program shows the combination of *IF* and *GOTO* statements to achieve conditional branching.

The *DO* loop construct is illustrated by the example

DO 200 L = 1, K
⟨sequence of statements⟩
200 CONTINUE

of lines 18–24 of Figure 4.2. The sequence of statements (the *loop body*) is executed *K* times with the 'index variable' *L* taking the value *i* for the *i*th traversal of the loop, providing that control has not been transferred out of the loop by the *IF* ... *GOTO* ... statement on line 19.

Procedural abstraction is supported by a subroutine declaration which has a first line of the form:

⟨subprogram kind⟩ ⟨name⟩ (⟨list of formal parameters⟩)

where ⟨subprogram kind⟩ is either *SUBPROGRAM* or *FUNCTION*. At least one of the executable statements should be *RETURN*, which terminates execution of the subprogram.

A subprogram is invoked by a *CALL* statement which has the form

CALL ⟨name⟩ (⟨list of actual parameters⟩).

Execution of the *CALL* statement causes the formal parameters of the subroutine to be 'bound' to the positionally corresponding actual parameters of the call and the statements of the subprogram to be executed with these bindings. The binding, or *parameter-passing*, mechanism used is *call-by-reference*, in which every occurrence of a formal parameter is replaced at execution time by the address of the actual parameter it is bound to so that the actual parameters are accessed ('referenced') directly. Thus all operations on *ARR* in subroutine *SORT* in the example are actually performed on the array *M* when *SORT* is called on line 7.

A function subprogram is called by placing its name followed by an appropriate formal parameter list anywhere where an expression could occur and is used to produce a value determined by the last assignment to the name of the function within the body of the function. Supposing we have:

```
FUNCTION SQR(X)
SQR = X*X
RETURN
END
```

Then

```
Y=3
Z=Y+SQR(Y)
```

places the value 12 in *Z*. A number of commonly used functions are pre-defined in all FORTRAN implementations.

A subroutine or function is a fully independent subprogram which can be included in any program whose main program or subprograms require its services. Communication between the subprogram and the calling unit is via the parameter-passing mechanism. All the variables and labels used within a subprogram are said to be *local* to it; they are not visible to the calling unit or other subprograms. Conversely, a subprogram cannot see the variables and labels of the main program and other subprograms.

The *scope* of a binding of a name to a memory location is defined as the region of the program text within which the binding is maintained. Thus the scope of a (sub)program variable is its own (sub)program. The scope of a subprogram name is the entire program, it is said to be *global* to the main program and all subprograms except its own.

FORTRAN very quickly became the standard programming language for all applications except those in the area specifically catered for by COBOL. The majority of applications in its early days were in the domain it was designed for, so it became automatic for any manufacturer who wanted to sell machines to provide a FORTRAN implementation. This wide use led to the generation of very extensive libraries of subroutines for doing standard mathematical, statistical, scientific and engineering calculations which in turn made it even more useful. The final component in FORTRAN's recipe for continuing success was its universality. In principle, at least, a FORTRAN program written to run on one model of computer will run on any model with a FORTRAN compiler.

4.5 STRUCTURED PROGRAMMING

FORTRAN is still one of the world's most widely used programming languages. In domains requiring extensive numerical computations it is for many practitioners still the language of choice. Nevertheless, as far back as the late 1960s a number of computer scientists, in the course of developing a group of techniques for designing computer programs which became known collectively as *structured programming*, came to the conclusion that FORTRAN and languages like it were fundamentally unsatisfactory for writing structurally complex programs.

Structured programming constituted part of the response to the *software crisis*: the realization by industry that the then prevalent techniques of software production were hopelessly inadequate for applications of the size and complexity made possible by the storage capacities and processing power of third-generation hardware.

Structured programming involves the use of abstraction to decompose a complex programming task into smaller, simpler and hence more manageable subtasks. The subtasks can be decomposed in turn and the process continued until the tasks are simple enough to be expressed directly as statements in a programming language. The resulting program can then be viewed as a hierarchy of abstractions of both data and control. At the top level the program models operations and objects of a real-world domain. At the next level each higher-level operation is represented in more detail by a group of simpler operations which combine together to perform the higher-level one. The data objects which the higher-level operations are performed upon are similarly decomposed into components appropriate to the lower-level operations.

This applies to every level in the hierarchy below the top one, including the program code at the bottom which is thus structured by the whole of the design hierarchy which gave rise to it.

Because of this structuring the code can be written, and read, in small units whose relationships to other units are defined by the different levels of abstraction. This makes it easier to understand and therefore easier to write, test, debug (remove errors) and verify. Any modifications required can be made without reference to the details of the rest of the program providing that the relationships with other units are preserved.

These principles apply within the program code itself. The structuring methods which are used at the higher levels of the design hierarchy should also be applied at the program-code level to combine the basic (or *atomic* in the sense of indivisible) operations such as assignment and the basic data objects such as variables into larger units of operations and data. Much work was devoted to investigating structuring methods and its results have greatly influenced both programming techniques and the design of new programming languages. This work is well documented, notably in Dahl *et al.* (1972).

Its conclusion is that programmers should discipline themselves to use a severely restricted number (three) of logically simple structuring methods for both operations and data which would produce understandable and verifiable programs. The methods should be applicable at any level of abstraction and support top-down (decomposition to a lower level) or bottom-up (composition to a higher level) program design.

The simplest is composition. In terms of operations a number of statements are composed to form a single compound statement. The control structure imposed by composition is sequence; the component statements are executed one after the other in the order in which they appear in the program text. FORTRAN does not support this structuring method below the level of a complete program or subprogram.

The second structuring method is selection from one of a finite number of alternatives. As a control structure this is implemented directly in FORTRAN only for the simplest case of selection of a single statement in the logical *IF* statement.

The third method of structuring operations is iteration, or repetition, in which a statement is executed repeatedly zero or a finite number of times. FORTRAN implements this structure directly in the *DO* loop, only for the case in which the number of repetitions is defined before entry to the structure.

The three methods of structuring operations, the basic control structures, have been proved to be sufficient to construct any program which has a single entry point and a single exit point, however large and complex the program is. Since each of the three control structures has only one entry point and one exit point, the *GOTO* statement becomes entirely superfluous except insofar as it is needed to implement the basic control structures in languages, like FORTRAN, which do not implement them directly as atomic statements. Dijkstra (1968) condemned the use of the *GOTO* statement as harmful to the construction of understandable and reliable programs because it allows enormously complicated control structures to be implemented in which control can jump backwards and forwards from one end of the text to the other, out of *DO* loops before they complete and into and out of loops implemented using *IF ... GOTO*.

In a structured program control flows through the program purely sequentially in the sense that once a top-level instance of one of the basic control structures has been exited it can never be returned to. Within a given composition only those structures which are nested inside an explicit repetition structure can be executed more than once. Thus the static structure of the program text is a better representation of the dynamic structure of the computations it represents (see Figure 4.3).

A subprogram facility allows a composition to be used at different stages of execution by making it an atomic operation represented in the program text by a single statement. This enforces the abstraction represented by the composition by removing the text of its implementation from the program text. The details of how the operation is performed can be ignored, just as the implementation details of the built-in operations can be ignored. The user can be forced to ignore the implementation details by separate compilation of the subprogram declaration as is done for functions like *SQR* in the FORTRAN subprogram library.

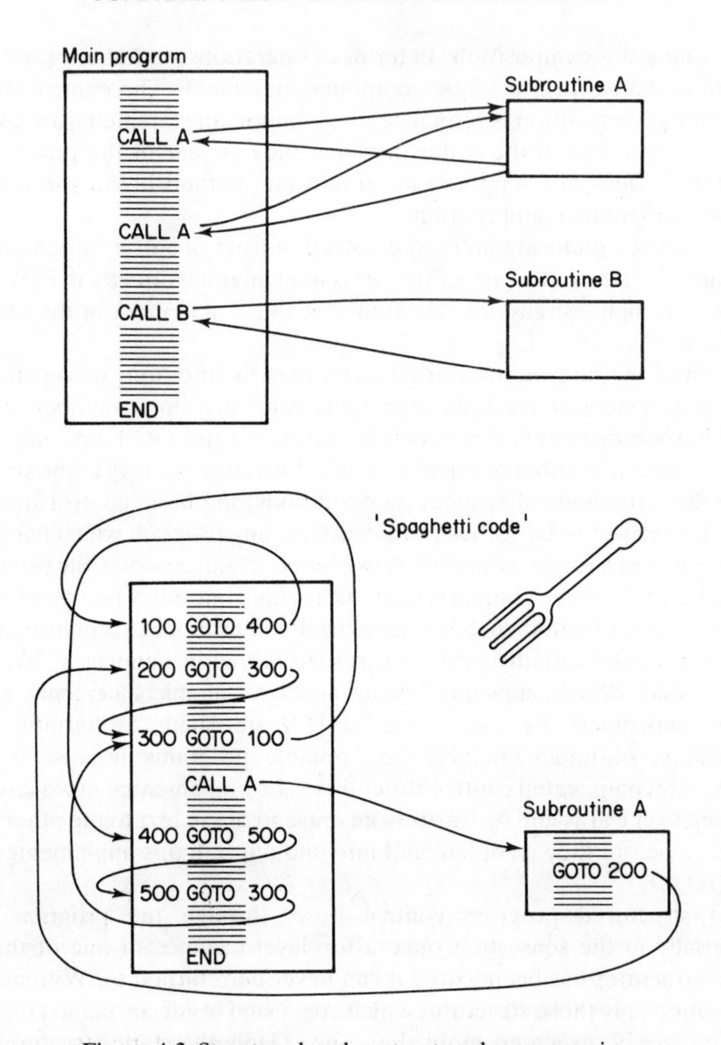

Figure 4.3 Structured and unstructured programming

FORTRAN has no comparable facility for implementing data abstractions. The data equivalent of the subprogram is the data type and FORTRAN has no data-type definition facility which allows a data structure to be declared and its name used to declare new objects of the type in the way that intrinsic type names like *INTEGER* and *LOGICAL* can be used.

The first enduring language to explicitly incorporate concepts of structured programming, including definition of new data types, was Pascal, which was originally designed as a vehicle for teaching the principles of programming (Wirth 1971a).

program ⟨name⟩ (⟨program parameters⟩);
⟨block⟩.

(a) Program structure.

const
        ⟨constant definitions⟩
type
        ⟨type definitions⟩
var
        ⟨variable declarations⟩
⟨procedure and function declarations⟩
begin
        ⟨sequence of statements⟩
end

(b) Block structure.

procedure ⟨name⟩ (⟨formal parameters⟩);
⟨block⟩;
function ⟨name⟩ (⟨formal parameters⟩):⟨result type⟩;
⟨block⟩;

(c) Subprogram structures.

Figure 4.4 Pascal program and subprogram structures

The structure of a Pascal program is shown in Figure 4.4 and a Pascal version of the FORTRAN sorting program discussed above is shown in Figure 4.5. The words in bold type, called reserved words, are single symbols which may only be used as specified in the language definition. The program parameters are the names of files which the program uses to read data from and write data to.

Constant definitions allow names to be bound to literal values of built-in types as shown in line 3.

The general form of a type definition is

⟨name⟩ = ⟨type denoter⟩;

where a type denoter may be the name of an existing type or a specification of a new type.

Pascal is strongly typed, which means that every data item in a program belongs to a particular type and that, in general, a variable may only be assigned (:=) a value of a compatible type computed from an expression which contains only data items and operators defined for that type. A data object (symbolic constant or variable) is bound to a type when it is declared and

```
 1  program bubble (input,output);
 2  const
 3          max = 10;
 4  type
 5          intarray = array [1...max] of integer;
 6  var
 7          i,length          : integer;
 8          number            : intarray;
 9  procedure sort(count: integer; var arr: intarray);
10  var
11          temp,limit,i      :integer;
12          flag              :boolean;
13  begin
14          if count>1 then
15                begin
16                   limit:=count-1;
17                   repeat
18                        flag:=true;
19                        for i:=1 to limit do
20                              if arr[i]<=arr[i+1] then
21                              begin
22                                 temp:=arr[i];
23                                 arr[i]:=arr[i+1];
24                                 arr[i+1]:=temp;
25                                 flag:=false
26                              end;
27                        limit:=limit-1
28                   until flag or (limit = 0)
29                end;
30  end;
31  begin
32          read(input,length);
33          for i:=1 to length do
34                 read(input,number[i]);
35          sort(length,number);
36          for i:=1 to length do write(output, number[i]:2)
37  end.
```

Figure 4.5 A simple Pascal program

data objects must be explicitly declared before use so that the compiler can check that the type rules are not violated by inappropriate and presumably erroneous operations upon data objects.

The general form of a variable declaration is

⟨list of names⟩ : ⟨type denoter⟩;.

Examples are shown in the **var** parts of the program and procedure of Figure 4.5.

The four built-in types are *integer*, *real*, *boolean* (like FORTRAN's *LOGICAL*) and *char* (which takes single characters as values). *Char*, *boolean* and *integer* are called *ordinal types* since their values form an ordered sequence.

Two kinds of new simple type can be defined by the programmer. Enumerated types are so called because the values defined for the type are listed explicitly as literal constants: for example,

day = (sun, mon, tue, wed, thur, fri, sat);
colour = (red, orange, yellow, green, blue);

The operations defined for variables of enumerated types include assignment and the relational operations.

Subrange types have a subrange of the values of an existing ordinal type and inherit its operations: for example,

workday = mon..fri; monthnumber = 1..12;.

Pascal provides five structuring methods for the construction of new composite types from previously defined types.

File types implement the structured programming concept of iteration and are defined using type denoters of the form

file of ⟨component type⟩

where ⟨component type⟩ can be any type except another file type. The files *input* and *output* used in the program of Figure 4.5 are predefined files of char.

Array types are defined type denoters of the form

array [⟨index type⟩] of ⟨component type⟩

where ⟨index type⟩ can denote any ordinal type. A subrange of integer is used on line 5 of Figure 4.5. ⟨component type⟩ can be any type including another array type.

The structuring devices of composition and discriminated union (selection of alternatives) are provided by record types.

A set type is provided and implements the mathematical set structure and set operations (discussed in Chapter 7) for sets whose elements are all of the same ordinal type.

Pointer types provide the most powerful of Pascal's data-structuring facilities. A variable of a pointer type contains as value the address of a second, anonymous, variable which it is therefore said to *reference* or *point to*. Since the variable pointed to can be a record with one or more fields of the same or different pointer type, it is possible to build structures with complex forms such as networks. Pointed-to variables can be created at run time so that the structures can vary dynamically in size and form.

In terms of control structures, the single most significant advantage of Pascal over FORTRAN is the provision of the compound statement which has the form

begin
⟨sequence of statements⟩
end.

and can be used wherever a simple statement could be. The selection structure is implemented by

if ⟨condition⟩ **then** ⟨statement⟩,
if ⟨condition⟩ **then** ⟨statement1⟩ **else** ⟨statement2⟩

and by the *case* statement, which allows the selection of one of any number of statements according to the value of an ordinal selector variable.

Repetition is implemented by three control structures:

while ⟨condition⟩ **do** ⟨statement⟩
repeat ⟨sequence of statements⟩ **until** ⟨condition⟩

and a **for** statement, analogous to FORTRAN's *DO*, which is illustrated in procedure *sort* in Figure 4.5.

The provision of the compound statement allows any number of statements to be placed under the control of any of the control structures.

Subprogram declarations in Pascal have the same structure as a program, as shown in figure 4.4, and can thus include other (*nested*) subprogram declarations to any depth. The block is the major method of controlling name bindings in Pascal, the scope of a name being the block it is declared in or in which it is a formal parameter. A name binding is effective throughout its scope, including inner blocks nested in that scope, unless it is redeclared (or used as a formal parameter) within an inner block. The old binding is then hidden by the new one for the duration of its (the new one's) scope.

The value of using subprograms to implement abstractions has been discussed in connection with assembly language and FORTRAN. Block structuring allows a greater degree of enforcement of an essential property of an abstraction, that of hiding lower-level information from program units which do not require it. Entities should be declared in the block within which they are needed or, if needed in more than one block, in the block which most closely encloses all the blocks which need them.

Pascal makes some advance on the parameter-passing mechanism of FORTRAN in providing *call-by-value* as well as call-by-reference, and in checking that actual parameters are of the same type as corresponding formal parameters.

Procedure *sort* in the program of Figure 4.5 has a call-by-reference parameter *arr* and a call-by-value parameter *count*. When the procedure is called (line 35 in Figure 4.5) the name of the formal value parameter is bound to an unallocated memory location, which is then initialized with the value of the actual parameter (and deallocated when execution of the subprogram terminates). This allows variables to be used to pass values into subprograms with no danger of those values being inadvertently altered by the subprogram and also allows expressions of the appropriate type to be used as actual parameters.

The name of a subprogram is visible inside its own block. In a function the name is assigned the value to be returned, as in FORTRAN, but the use of the name in an expression constitutes a call of the function within its own body. This is allowed in Pascal (but not in FORTRAN) and is called **recursion**. Each call creates a completely new set of formal parameters and local variables which causes existing data objects with the same names to be hidden. Procedures can call themselves recursively in exactly the same way.

Pascal has been very successful in achieving its design objectives. It is widely used in computing education and its small size and efficient implementations have encouraged its use as a general-purpose language on small systems. It has exerted a powerful influence on the design of more recent languages, many of which are basically Pascal extended with constructs for the definition of abstract data types (discussed in Chapter 7) and with facilities for concurrent programming. Its most important descendant is Ada, which is discussed briefly in Chapter 5.

4.6 THE 'MACHO' APPROACH TO PROGRAMMING

A particularly interesting programming language is C, which was first used to write most of the UNIX operating system for minicomputers. Since then it has become the foremost systems-programming language.

C is a descendant of a language called BCPL (Richards and Whitby-Strevens 1980) which originated in the late 1960s. This remarkable and elegant language incorporates a comprehensive set of control structures but has only one built-in data type, the bit-sequence. It has operators appropriate to numeric and character types but consistent use of them is entirely the programmer's responsibility. Its major data-structuring facility is the pointer, which allows it to implement the complicated data structures typical of systems software. It also implements recursion, necessary in a language originally designed for compiler writing. C's designers took BCPL as a starting point and added the data-structuring facilities expected in a post-Pascal language (Kernighan and Ritchie 1978). C follows BCPL in relegating I/O and other facilities for higher-level data type operations such as character-string handling to function libraries which (unlike those of FORTRAN and Pascal) are easily user-extendable.

This approach, of a small, efficient and flexible core with ready access to such additional facilities as may be useful for a particular application area encourages use of the language both for high-level general-purpose applications programming and for systems programming. As UNIX gains almost universal distribution it carries C with it and its use as a general-purpose language appears to be increasing rapidly.

Converts from Pascal and its predecessors find its syntax rather cryptic at first (it is possible, but not necessary, to achieve extreme conciseness in expression in C). They also tend to be disconcerted by the C compiler's very permissive attitude to type checking and taciturn intolerance of syntax errors.

In many ways C and Pascal represent two very different attitudes to programming. The C attitude, like the UNIX attitude, is that a programmer is a professional who knows what he or she is about and should be able to use powerful and dangerous tools in a responsible and professional way with the absolute minimum of built-in restrictions and expensive checks. An interesting collection of papers relating to a three-cornered comparison of Pascal, Ada and C can be found in Feuer and Gehani (1984).

A relatively recent development is the appearance of what are sometimes called *fourth-generation languages*. These offer the user an English-like set of commands and simple control structures in which to specify general data-processing or numerical operations. These programs are then translated into a conventional high-level language such as COBOL, which is passed to a conventional compilation system. Closely related are *application generators* which bear the relationship to fourth-generation languages that interpreter implementations bear to compiler implementations of conventional languages. Some vendors claim that their products make COBOL (or whatever) programming a thing of the past, but the extent to which this may be true remains to be seen.

All the languages discussed so far can be considered to be stages along a single line of development from the machine codes of von Neumann machines. Their most essential operation, assignment, arises directly from the architecture of such a machine—specifically from the fact that it has a memory in which data is stored in individually addressable locations. Their next most important operation is control transfer, which reflects the fact that instructions are fetched in storage sequence for execution. Languages whose unit operations are based explicitly on assignment and control transfer are called *imperative* languages, because of the fundamental role of statements which instruct hardware to move data from one cell to another.

The purpose of most programming, however, is to compute domain-relevant symbolic values from domain-relevant symbolic data, not to instruct computing machinery. A number of attempts have therefore been made to reformulate the whole basis of programming in ways which make programming languages and the design of algorithms genuinely independent of the hardware machines they are implemented on. These are discussed in Chapter 7 after a brief introduction to some of the necessary mathematical ideas.

Comprehensive discussions of programming language principles can be found in the books by MacLennan and Pratt (MacLennan 1983, Pratt 1984).

4.7 PROGRAM-DEVELOPMENT TOOLS

The creative aspects of programming, in the limited sense of implementing a given software design in a programming language, do not actually need more in the way of tools than pencil and paper. However, the process of converting the handwritten code into an executable representation is a tedious task which should be relegated to software as far as possible.

To start with, the text of the program must be entered into the computer system. This is normally done interactively, using a program called a *text editor*, which provides general word-processing facilities for the entry and modification of text.

Once the program text has been stored in a file it can be submitted to the compiler which will respond with error messages ('diagnostics') if any violations of the syntactic rules of the language are detected. When developing a program the quality of the diagnostic information generated by the *compiler* is far more important than the quality of the machine code generated. For syntactically correct programs the opposite is true. Since both error analysis and code optimization are very expensive operations, separate *development* and *optimizing* compilers are usually provided. A good development compiler attempts to specify the nature of each error and has good error-recovery procedures. This will allow it to pick up the next recognizable construct after an error and continue compilation so as to give the maximum diagnostic information.

Once the syntax errors have been corrected, the program will compile and can then be tested, a process which is discussed in Chapter 5. If incorrect behaviour is identified, the sections of code responsible must be found and corrected. This involves a critical inspection of the program code, comparing what it actually does with what it is required to do. If the operation of the code is traced, statement by statement, the point at which actual program behaviour starts to diverge from its intended behaviour will eventually become apparent.

A first step towards automating the debugging process is to insert output statements in the program code to force the display of data values at judiciously selected stages of execution. This is useful, but subtle errors may need every value generated in a section of code to be output. This requires an unreasonably high density of such statements.

The simplest software tool used in debugging is a *symbolic dumper*, which generates a listing of all program variables and their contents at the point in program execution where the dump is made. This may or may not contain sufficient information to identify the error, but extraction of it is very tedious for programs of any size.

More useful is a *trace facility*, where the compiler inserts code in the object program which allows it to generate information about the progress of its own execution. A typical facility allows entry and exit to subprograms, display of values passed as parameters and returned by functions, execution of source-code lines and statements and accesses to variables to be traced, and the trace information to be logged in a file for later perusal.

The most generally useful tools, which incorporate the facilities of symbolic dumpers and tracers, are *interactive debuggers*. These typically allow the user to set breakpoints at which execution of the program is halted and the user can request a selective symbolic dump, initiate and remove traces, assign values to variables, obtain information about the declarations of types and variables, inspect the source code and set new breakpoints and remove existing ones. Breakpoints and traces can often be made conditional upon variable values and the program can be executed statement by statement if required. Interactive debuggers which operate at the source-code level rather than the machine-code level are much easier to implement, and are consequently much more commonly found, for interpreter-based language implementations.

Most computer systems offer a general-purpose interface for program development which includes a file-management system, one or more general-purpose text editors, a collection of programming-language compilers and interpreters and possibly associated dumpers, tracers, and debuggers.

Some specific software tools currently being developed are known as integrated programming support environments, or IPSEs. These are directed towards the production of software in a particular language and offer the programmer a single uniform interface to a set of software facilities which share knowledge of both the program under development and of the syntax and semantics of the programming language. Each component of the system can access and modify the shared information. The basic components of most IPSEs under development are a syntax-directed editor, an interactive source-code level debugger and an execution facility which allows the program to be executed at all stages of its development. A syntax-directed editor has a knowledge base containing an internal representation of every syntactic structure in the language, including the highest level structure defining a complete program. The user gives a command specifying the syntactic structure required. The editor responds by displaying a template to be filled in (or *instantiated*) which it generates from the knowledge base. The development of a program begins with a program template and ends with a syntactically correct program. The editor maintains an internal representation of the program under construction which, at any intermediate stage, consists of a mixture of instantiated and un-instantiated templates and is always complete and syntactically correct. The user may typically move around the program representation instantiating templates in any order, but only if a particular template request is syntactically correct at that point in the program structure.

Several more or less integrated LISP programming environments have been available for some time and a number of systems for other languages are under development. The Cornell Program Synthesizer (Teitelbaum and Reps 1981), for example, was initially designed for a subset of the language PL/I and later extended to Pascal. The ambitious Gandalf project (Habermann 1982) includes an IPSE for a variant of C. However, IPSEs are still in the experimental stage and it remains to be seen whether they will displace the general-purpose programming environments in current use.

Fundamentals of Information Technology
Edited by G. G. Wilkinson and A. R. Winterflood

Chapter 5

Constructing Software Systems

5.1 THE SOFTWARE LIFE CYCLE

The term *software system* implies a program or collection of programs created to meet some perceived needs in a real-world domain, a non-trivial piece of software for which a customer is prepared to pay an economic price. A small software system is one whose development could be carried out from start to finish by a single person. A large system is one which is inherently and necessarily too complex for all its aspects to be understood by a single person rather than one implemented in more than some minimum number of lines of source code. However, it is true in general that program size increases with system complexity. The construction of large systems thus presents the problems of managing and co-ordinating the activities of groups of people in addition to the problems of constructing small systems. This chapter discusses problems common to the development of both kinds of system, consideration of the additional problems of large systems being deferred until Chapter 6.

All aspects of the development of software systems are now subsumed under the heading of *software engineering*, which originated as a distinct discipline in response to the 'software crisis' of the mid-1960s, when the industry became aware that its methods of software production were seriously inadequate for meeting the demands being made on them. The problem proved to be chronic, the cost of software continuing to escalate as the cost of hardware dropped rapidly.

The advances in micro-electronics had resulted in a rapid increase in the availability of raw computing power and hence in the complexity and size of applications which could be envisioned. The rapid rise in production costs might have been more tolerable if the software product had been serviceable, but all too often it was not. It became almost axiomatic that software would be delivered late, would cost far more than estimated, would be difficult and therefore expensive to maintain but need constant maintenance, would not accommodate apparently minor enhancements, would not meet its specifications and, worst of all, would be unreliable. This track record was dismal by the standards of any established branch of engineering precisely because, it was gradually realized, the principles and practices characteristic of the established branches were not being utilized in the production of software.

Part of the reason was the unique nature of the product. Software is abstract, intangible and shows complex dynamic behaviour. Structured programming ideas were a significant contribution to the problem of managing complexity but programming, in the limited sense of generating source code to implement a defined algorithm, is by no means the only activity involved in software production. In the *software life-cycle* model of software development it is only one of a sequence of stages through which a software system develops from an initial perception of need for its services to a point where it is rendered obsolete by changes in the environment it serves.

The simplest life-cycle model consists of:

Stage 1. Statement of needs. The customer identifies the services required of the system to the system developers.

Stage 2. Requirements specification. A detailed and definitive set of specifications of the services the system is to provide, and of the constraints it is to conform to, is established in consultation with the customer. These specifications form the basis of the contract between customer and system designer.

Stage 3. Design. A system is designed to meet the specifications produced in stage 2. The design represents the operations of the system down to a level which is independent of the features of any particular programming language, but which is detailed enough to be readily translatable into such a language.

Stage 4. Implementation. The design produced in stage 3 is translated into a programming language.

Stage 5. Testing and debugging. The executable code produced in stage 4 is tested against the specifications produced in stage 2 and the causes of any failures are traced and corrected.

Stage 6. Operation and maintenance. The system, consisting of the executable code and the documentation which informs users about its use, is delivered to the customer, installed and put into production. Maintenance, which continues for the lifetime of the system, involves the correction of faults which come to light during operation and modification of the system to meet changes in the customer's requirements. While a well-designed system will withstand a great deal of modification it may eventually become more economic to do a rewrite, i.e. go back to stage 1 and start again.

These stages are distinct in terms of the major activities they involve and form a generally accepted basis for discussions of software engineering, but in reality earlier stages may well be revisited as their consequences become apparent in later ones.

The most serious defect of this simple model is the identification of testing as a single stage following implementation. The one property that any software system must possess to be of any serious use in a real environment is reliability, and for large systems in particular, which may be required to remain in production for many years to justify their development costs, maintainability, defined as reliability over the system's lifetime, is also essential. A definition of reliability is difficult to formulate precisely but must ultimately be related to the user's expectations. The term *validation* is used for the process of establishing that a system actually does what the user wants it to do. This is difficult since the user may not be able to specify what the system should do under particular conditions until those conditions arise, a fact which the life-cycle model does not cater for. If the specifications are valid, then validation of the system reduces to demonstrating that the implemented software meets the specifications, a process referred to as *verification*. Many software engineers consider that verification of a system solely by testing it after implementation is not feasible: verification should be performed at every stage and substage of the development process and the need for verification should influence the way in which the development is conducted. The most obvious drawback to leaving testing until after implementation is that errors in the specifications and design are not detected until a point when their correction could invalidate a great deal of completed work.

Software engineering is still a very young subject and is nowhere near achieving the solid base of theory and established practice that underlies the older engineering disciplines. Many people believe that its goals of providing techniques and tools which will ensure the efficient production of reliable and maintainable software will not be achieved until a theoretical basis grounded in mathematics and formal logic is established, but in the meantime the world's appetite for software increases inexorably and the software industry must do what it can to satisfy it. At present the best software engineering practices which are at all widely used in software production are incorporated in *software development methodologies*, which offer guidelines, methods, and tools to support and organize the process of software development. Methodologies range from the highly formal, derived from some theoretical base, to the highly pragmatic, derived from bitter experience. Most of them incorporate a number of interrelated principles which have developed out of the overriding need to control complexity. These can be summarized as:

1. *Modularity*. The decomposition of a complex system into simpler entities called 'modules' which interact only through narrow, well-defined interfaces and are otherwise as independent of each other as possible.
2. *Localization*. The use of a module to realize a single, understandable conceptual unit of a system.
3. *Information hiding*. The hiding of the inner details of a module from other modules which can therefore only be dependent on its interface.

4. *Abstraction.* The explicit representation of only the essential properties of a module.

These ideas, which revolve around the use of modules to encapsulate detail at one level of abstraction into a unit at a higher one, form a persistent theme in the discussions of the following sections, which deal with each major activity identified in the life-cycle model in turn.

5.2 *USER REQUIREMENTS AND SYSTEM SPECIFICATIONS*

The formulation of software system specifications is the most important stage of the software-development process since its product, a document known informally as the 'the specifications' and more formally as the *software requirements document* (SRD), determines the activities of all of the subsequent development stages. It is also the most difficult stage, since the initial expression of needs by the user very rarely contains sufficient information to allow the construction of valid specifications.

The properties that specifications must possess can be derived from their functions in the development process. Their primary function is to specify the behaviours that the implemented system is to show. They must therefore be complete, i.e. include all the services required by the user; they must be consistent, i.e. no specification must contradict any other; and they must be precise, i.e. each specification must be unambiguous and must be sufficiently detailed to answer any subsequent questions that might arise about the responses the system is to provide. The specifications form the basis of the contract between the customer and the system developers, the basis from which the system will be designed and implemented, and the criteria for its verification. They must therefore be understandable by both the customer and the system developers and must be formal enough to allow the design and implementation to be verified. The behaviours specified must obviously be possible for a software system, i.e. the specifications must be realizable in software. The behaviours required of a software system may change during its lifetime, thus necessitating changes in its specifications. The specifications must be capable of accommodating these changes without violation of completeness or consistency, i.e. they must be modifiable.

Specifications of system behaviour are commonly called *functional specifications* since they specify the functions that the system is to perform. The specification is of what the system is to do, not of how it is to do it. The customer is not normally concerned about the inner workings of the system and the designers should not be unnecessarily constrained by having details of internal structure and operations written into the specifications. The customer may well, however, require that the system operate under various constraints and these must be specified. Typical constraints are on the amount of store required by the system, on response times, on data throughput rate, and on cost. The customer may require the system to be implemented on an existing inst[illegible] and to be compatible with existing software, possibly even to be written in [illegible] particular programming language. These constraints are usually called the *non-functional* specifications and must appear in the SRD along with the functional ones.

5.2.1 The System Model

Establishing the customer's needs requires a precise and accurate understanding of the functions that the software system is to perform and of the environment in which it is to operate. The first stage in the process is the collection of detailed information about the operations and the entities operated on, which constitute that part of the customer's business within which the proposed system is to operate and which, for convenience, we can refer to as the total system. The data must then be analysed and structured so as to reveal the significant properties of the total system. The software engineer does not usually have technical expertise in the customer's domain and is dependent upon observation of activities, products, work procedures etc. and upon information gained by questioning personnel. If the proposed system is to control some plant in an oil refinery, for example, the software engineer must rapidly acquire some familiarity with the terminologies of chemical and control engineering and some grasp of the operations performed by that plant and how they relate to the rest of the refinery so that communication with the domain experts is possible. The software engineer can then start to formulate a description of the total system in terms comprehensible to the users, who can draw upon their professional expertise to assess it. This bridging of the two domains of expertise is one of the reasons why the development of specifications is so difficult and so fraught with possibilities of error. (The analysis and definition of work structures and practices is the traditional province of the systems analyst and this part of the work may well be done by systems analysts, alone or in co-operation with software engineers.)

What is needed is a representation of the total system which is understandable by both users and the software engineer. This can then be partitioned into system and environment and used to derive the specifications. Such representations are called system models and their construction constitutes the starting point of most software-development methodologies. Yeh and Zave (1980) describe a process of *conceptual modelling* in which the construction of an explicit formal model proceeds from the beginning of the process of establishing user needs and is used to guide the collection and analysis of further data. The environment is modelled in terms of *entities* (identifiable actual objects) and *events* (happenings which involve those objects). In the patient-monitoring system discussed by these authors *patient*, *nurse* and *factors* (like *pulse rate* and *blood pressure*) are entities, while *patient-monitoring* and *factors-out-of-range* are events. The system is modelled in terms of *states*, which are data objects containing information about entities and their attributes, and *actions*, which are responses to events in the environment and which may themselves initiate further events. System and environment communicate via *messages* which are passed between events and actions. For example, the event *measure-factors* passes a message containing information about the pulse rate, blood pressure and temperature of a specified patient to the system, which triggers the action *insert factors*, causing the state *patient-factor-history* to be updated with the information in the message (Figure 5.1). Sets of interactions of this kind identify the functions of the system (the actions) and the data flows (the messages). A third component, control flow, specifying the order in which actions must occur, may also be needed. When software engineer and users agree that the conceptual model is an acceptable representation of user needs it can be used to derive the specifications.

5.2.2 Notations for Functional Specifications

The notations used for functional specifications fall into three general categories:

1. numbered paragraphs and sentences of natural language;
2. a formalized, structured subset of a natural language (both this and the previous approach may be extensively supplemented by graphical notations);
3. a fully formalized specification language with rigorously defined syntax and semantics (discussion of which is deferred until Chapter 7).

Of these the first is inherently unsatisfactory and is by far the most widely used. Its advantages are its expressiveness and the fact that its use and understanding require no special expertise. Its main disadvantage is that it is too capable of ambiguity to allow verification of consistency and completeness. The use of natural language is justifiable only where precise specifications are not possible (e.g. in the early stages of developing a completely new system) or are felt to be undesirable (e.g. when presenting a description of a proposed system to users with no experience of formal notations). In the latter case the natural-language description should be only an adjunct to a more formal set of specifications. If natural language is used care must be taken to achieve as much precision as possible. Each statement should express one and only one substantive point and those expressing related points should be grouped appropriately. Figure 5.2 shows a short extract from the natural-language specifications of a text editor. The numbering reflects the hierarchical structure of the specifications. In this hypothetical specification Section 4 is devoted to the user interface to the system and

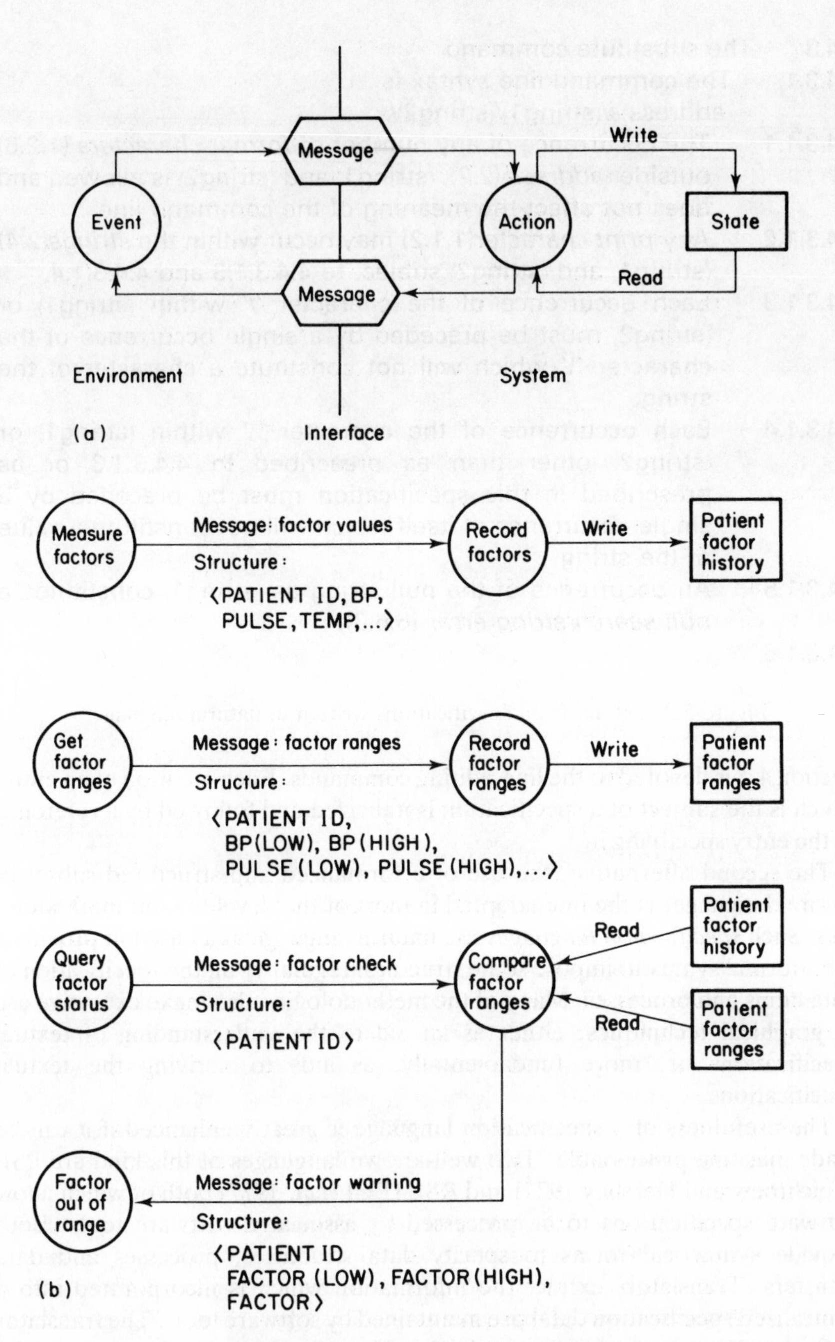

Figure 5.1 The conceptual model: (a) elements of a model; (b) modelling interactions (Adapted from Yeh and Zave (1980))

4.4.3 The substitute command

4.4.3.1 The command line syntax is
⟨address⟩s/⟨string1⟩/⟨string2⟩/

4.4.3.1.1 The occurrence of any number of *format characters* (1.2.6) outside ⟨*address*⟩(2.2), ⟨string1⟩ and ⟨string2⟩ is allowed and does not affect the meaning of the command line.

4.4.3.1.2 Any *print character*(1.1.2) may occur within the *strings*(2.4) ⟨string1⟩ and ⟨string2⟩ subject to 4.4.3.1.3 and 4.4.3.1.4.

4.4.3.1.3 Each occurrence of the character '/' within ⟨string1⟩ or ⟨string2⟩ must be preceded by a single occurrence of the character '\' which will not constitute a character of the string.

4.4.3.1.4 Each occurrence of the character '\' within ⟨string1⟩ or ⟨string2⟩ other than as prescribed in 4.4.3.1.3 or as prescribed in this specification must be preceded by a single occurrence of itself which will not constitute a value of the string.

4.4.3.1.5 An occurrence of the null string as ⟨string1⟩ constitutes a *null search string error* (6.6.3).

4.4.3.1.6 ...

Figure 5.2 Extract from specifications written in natural language

Section 4.4 is devoted to the line-editing commands. Each mention of an entity which is the subject of a specification is italicized and followed by a reference to the entry specifying it.

The second alternative, the use of a formalized and structured subset of natural language, is the one adopted in most of the development methodologies. Such *specification languages* use natural language as a base but provide a semi-formal syntax to impose some structural regularity on the specification of data items and processes. Many of the methodologies also make extensive use of graphical techniques, either as an aid to the understanding of textual specifications or, more fundamentally, as aids to deriving the textual specifications.

The usefulness of a specification language is greatly enhanced if it can be made machine processable. Two well-known languages of this kind are PSL (Teichroew and Hershey 1977) and RSL (Bell *et al.* 1977) both of which allow software specifications to be processed by associated software tools. Both provide syntactical forms to specify data structures, processes and data transfers. Translators extract the information which is incorporated into a centralized specification database maintained by software tools. The translator enforces a degree of precision on the specification and the maintenance of the database enforces a degree of consistency. Software tools use the database to generate descriptions of the composition, structure and characteristics of the system in various formats.

PSL and RSL form part of self-contained packages intended to provide an integrated set of methods and tools for the generation of system models and specifications. Many software engineers and analysts prefer to be less constrained and select techniques and notations according to the nature of the system being specified.

Data is frequently specified using structured notations, in which composite data items are represented as compositions, selections and repetitions of elementary items. An example is shown in Figure 5.3.

```
PATIENT-FACTOR-HISTORIES = [PATIENT-FACTOR-HISTORY]
  PATIENT-FACTOR-HISTORY = PATIENT-ID + FACTOR-HISTORY
          FACTOR-HISTORY = [FACTOR-RECORD]
           FACTOR-RECORD = DATE + TIME
                           + BLOOD-PRESSURE
                           + PULSE-RATE
                           + TEMPERATURE

+    denotes composition
[ ]  denotes repetition
```

Figure 5.3 Structured data specification

Access requirements may also be specified in a textual structured form, e.g.

given PATIENT_ID retrieve FACTORY_HISTORY
given PATIENT_ID and DATE
retrieve FACTORS_RECORDS with DATE

or in an equivalent graphical notation. Completeness requires that all needed retrievals of an object be explicitly specified, otherwise the designers and implementors may deliver a system which would require major, and therefore expensive, modification to provide them. Customers tend to assume that if the necessary basic items of information are held by a system, then any conceivable retrieval must be easy to provide, a frequent source of post-delivery recrimination.

Process specifications are most commonly represented using structured specification languages with syntax similar to that of high-level programming languages. The degree of formality varies from the relatively highly formal PSL and RSL to a loose 'structured English' (Figure 5.4).

Data-flow specifications are commonly represented using a graphical notation called a *data-flow diagram* (DFD) or *bubble chart* (Figure 5.5). The circles (bubbles) represent processes as data transformers and the arrows

PROCESS: COMPARE-FACTOR-RANGES

1. get FACTOR-RECORD
2. with FACTOR-RECORD,PATIENT-ID as key do
2.1 retrieve FACTOR-RANGES from PATIENTS-FACTORS
3 with FACTOR-RECORD and FACTOR-RANGES do
3.1 for each FACTOR in FACTOR-RECORD do
3.2 if FACTOR>FACTOR-HIGH or FACTOR<FACTOR-LOW
3.21 do GENERATE-WARNING-MESSAGE

Figure 5.4 Structured English process specification

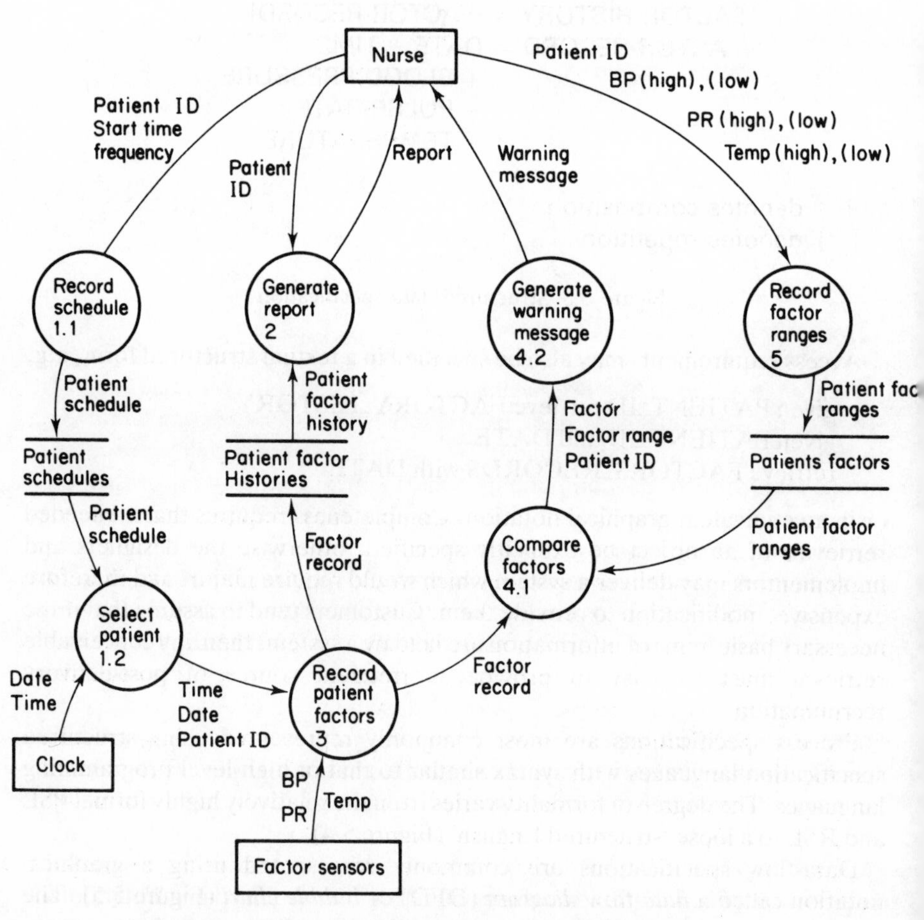

Figure 5.5 Data-flow diagram for patient-monitoring system

connecting them indicate the direction of flow of the data items whose names appear alongside them.

The specification phase of a well-known software development methodology called *structured design* uses DFDs to construct the system model. The techniques of structured design, and its specification stage, *structured analysis*, have been developed by a number of workers but have come to be associated with the company formed by one of them (Yourdon Inc.) and will be referred to here as the *Yourdon methodology*. A good introductory account, and references to the original work, can be found in Page-Jones (1980).

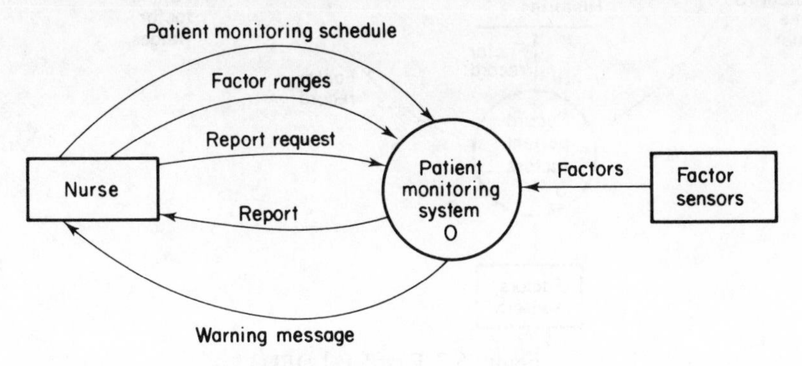

Figure 5.6 Context diagram

Construction of the model begins with a *context diagram* (Figure 5.6) and proceeds top-down. The context diagram shows the entire system as a single process transforming data input from sources in its environment into data output to 'sinks' in its environment. This single process is then decomposed into its major functional components, which appear as distinct processes on a first-level DFD (Figure 5.7). Each process identified in the decomposition should perform a single well-defined function, appropriate to the level of abstraction of the DFD, specified solely by its inputs and outputs. Data stores, denoted by pairs of parallel lines, are introduced to hold data which must be retained in the system either because it is used more than once or because it is not used in the order in which it is input. Decomposition proceeds to a second (Figure 5.5) and subsequent levels until the bubbles generated represent processes which are simple enough to be specified in detail in a single readily comprehensible unit. Constructing DFDs requires some creativity and quite a lot of practice. A number of iterations through the 'levelling' process (i.e. division into levels) may be needed before a satisfactory 'levelled set' is derived. This specifies process interfaces and the data flows between them. Process specifications are required in greater detail, but only for the bubbles in the lowest-level DFDs, called *functional*

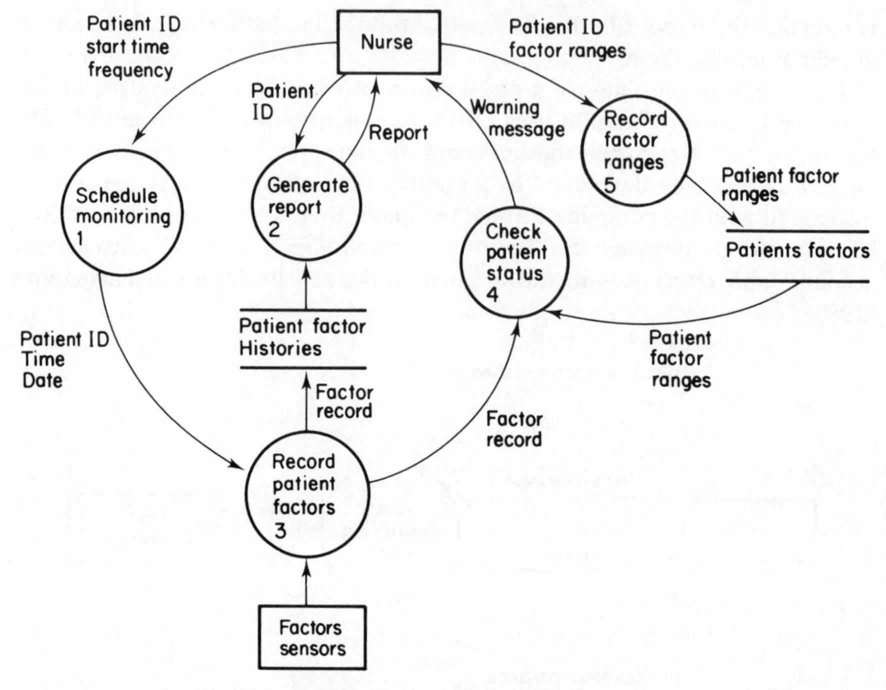

Figure 5.7 First-level DFD

primitives, since the higher-level processes are only aggregations of lower-level ones. The process specifications are written in a structured English like that of Figure 5.4.

Data specifications are collected into a data dictionary which must include all data items appearing on the DFDs and in the functional primitive specifications. The recommended techniques include those shown in Figure 5.3 and graphical versions of them.

The hierarchical set of DFDs, the functional primitive specifications, the data dictionary and the data-access specifications constitute the four components of the *structured specification* of the methodology which has a number of attractive features. The graphical DFDs are readily understandable by users and the top-down partitioning allows the system to be viewed at a number of levels of abstraction. Checking for consistency is assisted by the partioning since it is easy to check that the interface of a group of lower-level bubbles is consistent with that of the parent bubble and that the functional primitive specifications provide the interfaces required by the lowest level bubbles.

5.2.3 The Software-requirements Document

The completed specifications are incorporated into the SRD of which they constitute the major but not the sole part. This document will accompany the system through the rest of the development process and through the whole of its operational lifetime and it must therefore be made as informative and usable as possible. It should contain an overview of the system which describes the major services it provides and how these services interact with its immediate environment and fit into the activities of the user's organization as a whole.

A full explanation of the notations and technical devices used in the specifications themselves must be provided since there are many variants in use. The SRD itself should be well documented. A detailed contents list and comprehensive indices are both essential.

The final phase of the specifications stage is the validation of the SRD. For specifications in the non-formal representations described in this chapter completeness and consistency can never be assured but a high degree of confidence that they have been achieved should be aimed at. The conventional practice is to hold a series of reviews of the specifications in which they are examined systematically and in detail by users and developers. The responsibility for the consistency and realizability of the specifications must lie with the developers but completeness can only be decided by the users. Although the developers must attempt to explain and justify the detailed specifications to the users—an activity which is valuable in uncovering errors, inconsistencies and omissions—the users will almost invariably rely on the higher-level representation of the system model. They must be satisfied that they understand precisely what services the system will provide and be sure that these are the services they need. When they are so satisfied the SRD is 'signed off' and the development stage of the life cycle begins.

5.2.4 Prototyping

One way of increasing the chances of obtaining valid specifications is to provide a prototype system which simulates the services to be provided by the final production system. A prototype obviously allows the user to gain a clearer idea of the nature of the services as understood by the developers and to assess their effect on the environment. Missing, unnecessary and inappropriate services may be identified more easily and inconsistencies in requirements will come to light more quickly when the prototype is given a period of test use.

The main disadvantage of prototypes is the cost of their development, which is usually countered by building a very rough approximation as quickly and cheaply as possible and discarding it when it has served its purpose.

This is designed to operate on correct inputs only, removing the need for error detection and recovery, which normally account for a significant proportion of system code, and has much simpler and much less carefully designed and implemented modules than are required for production software.

For new systems, which cannot be specified in detail since the user's needs are necessarily ill-defined, prototyping may be the most efficient way to proceed despite the associated costs.

5.3 SOFTWARE DESIGN

The design stage of the software life cycle transforms the representation of the user's requirements embodied in the SRD into a representation of the software which is to meet those requirements.

The design process is traditionally seen as a problem-solving activity in which the representation of user needs is the problem and the design specification, embodied in a document which we can call the *system-design specification* (SDS), is the solution. The actions and entities of the high-level system model and the functional units and data objects derived from them constitute a partitioning of the problem and we can regard the problem as solved when each part of it has been mapped by a design specification into a software module. These modules thus constitute a partitioning of the solution which reflects the partitioning of the problem. But the solution is only complete when the modules are organized into a control structure. This organization is referred to as the 'structure' of the software solution and its derivation constitutes the first phase of the design process.

5.3.1 Structural Design

Design methodologies can be roughly partitioned into those based on top-down functional decomposition and the rest. Top-down methodologies have been in use for at least twenty years and virtually all production systems of any size have been designed using some variation on this theme. The rest includes the more recent data-structure-oriented methodologies and the very recent object-oriented approaches.

Functional Decomposition

Functional decomposition is not feasible without a fairly detailed decomposition of the problem and if this has not been included in the SRD it must be performed as the first phase of the design stage.

The notation most commonly used to represent a hierarchical system structure is the *structure chart*, an example of which for part of the archetypal payroll system is shown in Figure 5.9 (the symbols used are shown in Figure 5.8). The structure chart shows the hierarchy of control in a system design but contains no information about the sequencing of module activations nor about the processing and data structures within the modules. These are specified only by a data-transforming function and by control connections to other modules.

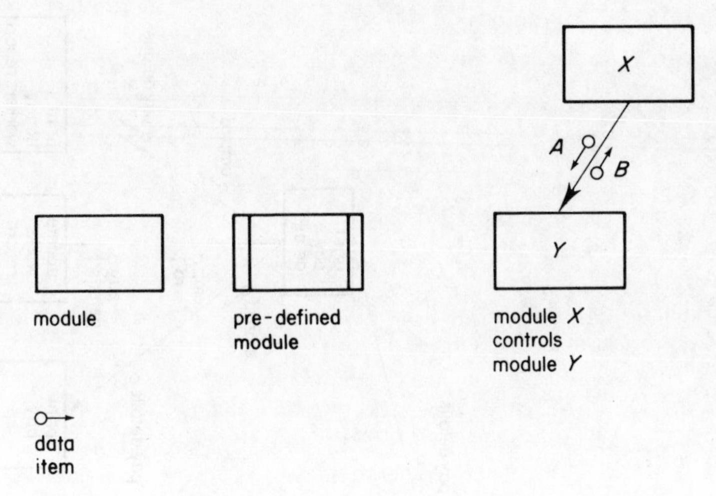

Figure 5.8 Structure chart symbols

The structure chart thus reflects the themes of localization in so far as each module implements a single logical unit of the system, information hiding in that the inner structures of the modules are not visible, and abstraction in that only the essential domain-oriented details contained in the interface are shown.

Localization, information hiding, and abstraction all contribute to the independence of modules. Independence allows the internal structure of a module to be specified and tested without reference to the rest of the system. It contributes strongly to maintainability since modules affect system behaviour only through narrow well-specified interfaces, so that the effects of adding new modules and replacing existing ones can be understood and specified precisely.

Independence is assessed using the related criteria of cohesion and coupling. Cohesion refers to the strength of the logical association of the components within a module. The ideal module has *functional cohesion*, each and every element contributing to the performance of a single problem-related function. Coupling refers to the degree of inter-relatedness between a module and the rest of the system. The ideal module has *data coupling*, being connected to the rest of the system only through the transmission of simple data values.

A number of less than ideal types of both coupling and cohesion can be identified and placed in an approximate order of decreasing desirability, as shown in Figures 5.10 and 5.11. There is a rough correlation between the two measures, modules with high cohesion generally showing a low degree of (or 'loose') coupling and modules with low cohesion generally showing a high degree of (or 'tight') coupling.

Sequential cohesion arises when a logical sequence of operations on the same data item, the output of one operation forming the input to the next, is incorporated into a single module. The main penalty incurred is that a

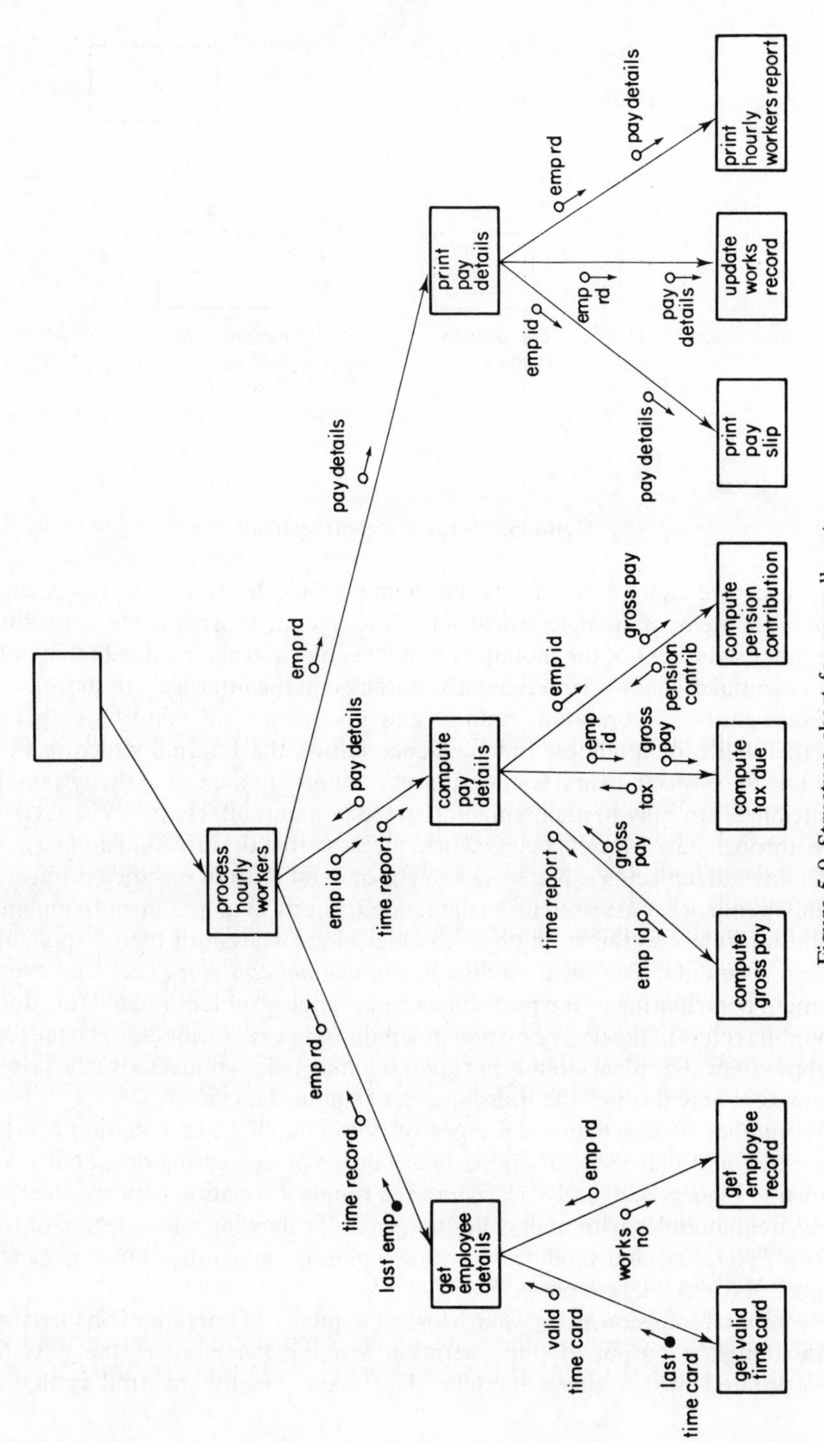

Figure 5.9 Structure chart for payroll system

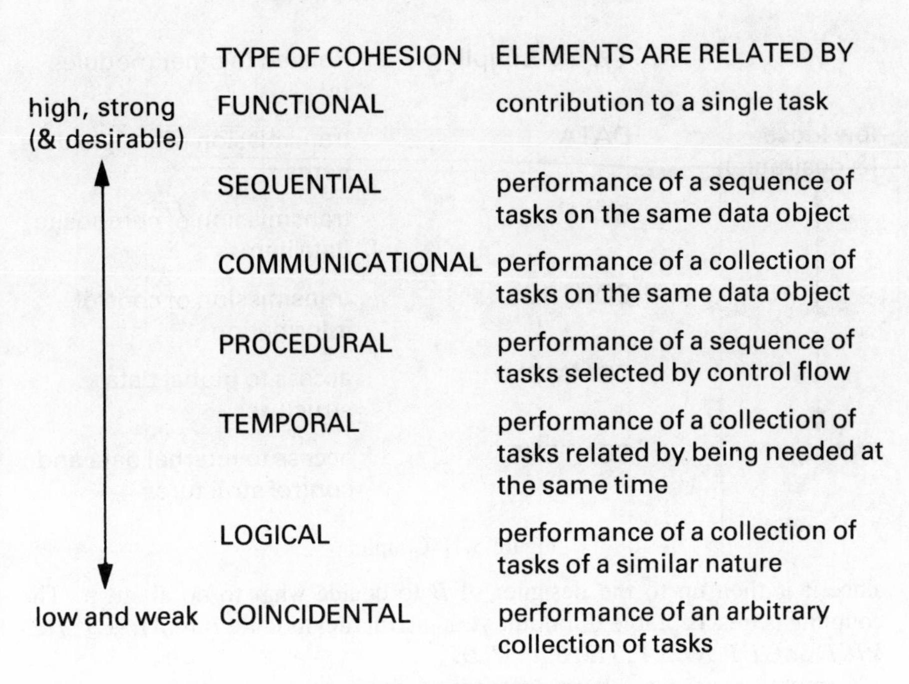

	TYPE OF COHESION	ELEMENTS ARE RELATED BY
high, strong (& desirable)	FUNCTIONAL	contribution to a single task
↑	SEQUENTIAL	performance of a sequence of tasks on the same data object
	COMMUNICATIONAL	performance of a collection of tasks on the same data object
	PROCEDURAL	performance of a sequence of tasks selected by control flow
	TEMPORAL	performance of a collection of tasks related by being needed at the same time
↓	LOGICAL	performance of a collection of tasks of a similar nature
low and weak	COINCIDENTAL	performance of an arbitrary collection of tasks

Figure 5.10 Types of cohesion

sequentially cohesive module may be less re-usable than a functionally cohesive one.

Communicational cohesion arises where the order of the operations is immaterial. This can result in a wide interface, a large number of data items being passed into and out of the module, and thus tighter coupling than for a sequentially cohesive module.

The remaining types of cohesion shown in Figure 5.10 are increasingly unacceptable and should be refined out of any structure in which they occur.

Stamp coupling is less desirable than date coupling because modules which need to access only part of the composite data structure have to be given unnecessary access to its other components. This allows the possibility of corruption of the unneeded component values, requires the other modules' interfaces to be changed if the data structure is changed and makes them less re-usable in other contexts where the unneeded components are not bundled with the needed one. The problem may be due to bad data structuring as well as bad module design, and the necessity of grouping the data items should be examined.

Control coupling usually occurs in the form of data being passed from module *A* to module *B* to specify some aspect of the operation of *B*. This is acceptable if it describes the state of the computation resulting from *A*'s activities, e.g. *DEVICE_MALFUNCTION* or *INVALID_TIME_CARD*,

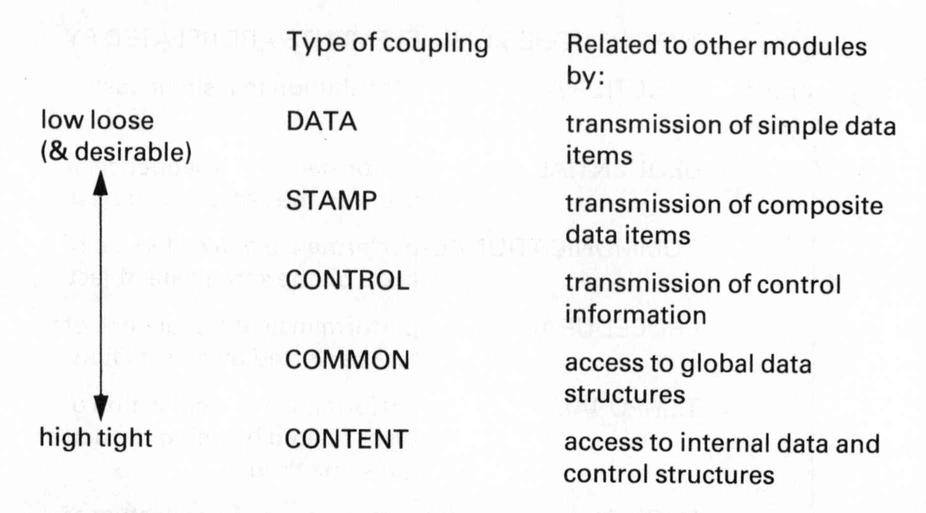

Figure 5.11 Coupling

since it is then up to the designer of *B* to decide what to do about it. The coupling is unacceptable if module *A* is instructing module *B* to *RESET_DEVICE* or *GET_NEXT_TIME_CARD*.

Common coupling, where different modules access the same global data structure, is both very useful (and in fact essential in low-level languages) and very dangerous. It may be acceptable but must be implemented very carefully. The basic problem is that an access by module *A* can corrupt data used by module *Z* which can lead to *Z* failing long after the access by *A* and after a number of intervening accesses by other modules. A change in any module accessing the global structure necessitates checking the effect on all the other modules which do so.

A number of additional criteria related to coupling and cohesion can be applied to a structure-chart representation of a system design.

The *fan-out* of a module means the number of lower-level (subordinate) modules it is directly connected to. High fan-out from a module can indicate that it is performing a number of different tasks each requiring the services of different lower-level modules or that a functionally cohesive module has been unnecessarily decomposed into subtasks with little claim to independence. In the former case the design will probably be improved if the module is decomposed (or *factored*) into a number of smaller functionally cohesive modules. In the latter case the subordinate modules are candidates for *unfactoring*, i.e. absorption back into the higher-level (superordinate) module. Most designers would look critically at a module with more than about six or seven immediate subordinates.

The overall shape of the system can be a useful criterion of design quality. Many systems of the *transform* type, 'input data—process data—output data'

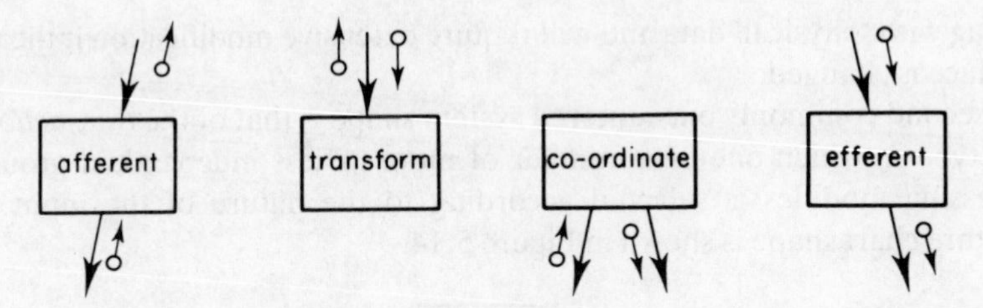

Figure 5.12 Module activities

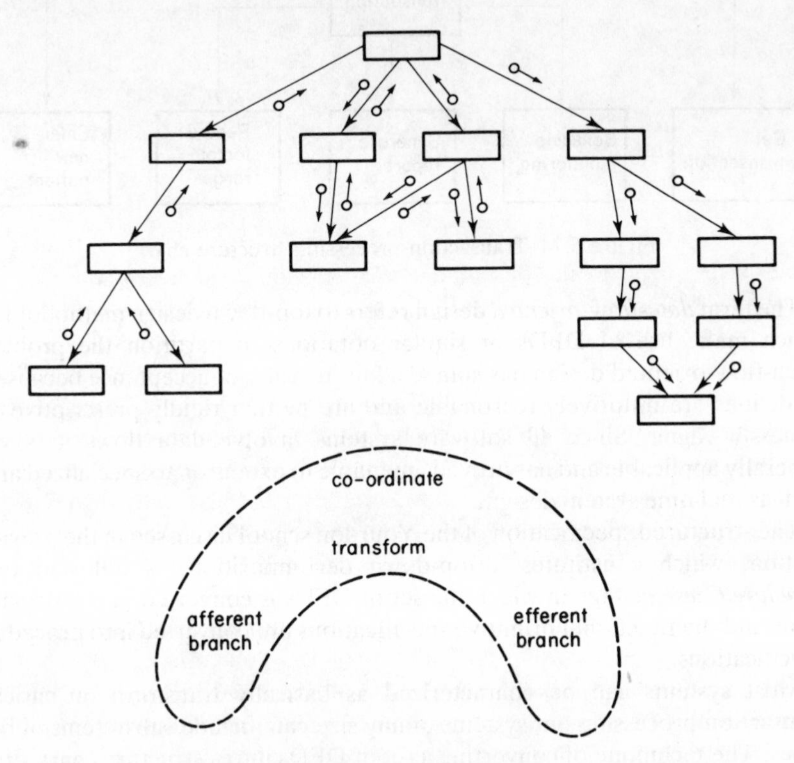

Figure 5.13 System shape

show a similar grouping of the basic module types of Figure 5.12, giving a system shape like that of Figure 5.13. The input or *afferent* arm takes in physical data and transforms it into a logical form before passing it to the central processing region which is called the *central transform*. After processing, the transformed logical data is converted into a physical form suitable for output as it passes down the output or *efferent* arm. Any chart for a transform type system which deviates markedly from this general shape should be examined critically. A short afferent arm, for example, may indicate that the central modules are dealing with 'physical' data and will require extensive modification if the input interface is changed.

A second commonly encountered system shape is that of the *transaction-system* type in which one of a number of more or less independent groups of processing modules is selected according to the nature of the input. The structure chart shape is shown in Figure 5.14.

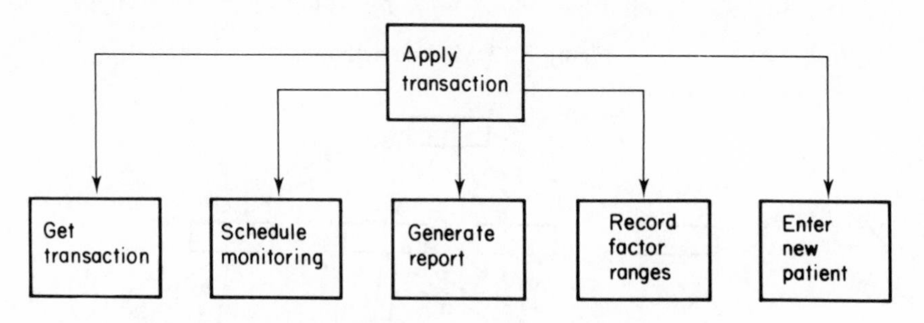

Figure 5.14 Transaction-processing structure chart

The term *data-flow-oriented* design refers to top-down design methodologies which make use of DFDs or similar notations to partition the problem. Data-flow-oriented design has gained a fair measure of acceptance because its guidelines are intuitively reasonable and are neither rigidly prescriptive nor uselessly vague. Since all software systems involve data flows it is very generally applicable and has proved amenable to extension to specialized areas such as real time system design.

The structured specification of the Yourdon school discussed in the previous section, which constitutes a top-down decomposition, is followed by a *structured design* stage in which the set of DFDs is converted into a structure chart and the functional primitive specifications are converted into procedural specifications.

Most systems can be characterized as basically transform or basically transaction processing but systems of any size can include subsystems of both types. The technique of converting a set of DFDs into a structure chart differs in the two cases and is called *transform analysis* or *transaction analysis* accordingly. These techniques are described in outline only here; for full details the reader is referred to Page-Jones (1980).

The first stage in transform analysis is to identify the collections of bubbles corresponding to the central transform and to the afferent and efferent arms. Individual bubbles on the DFD are then mapped into structure-chart modules. Graphically, the round bubbles become rectangular modules and arrows representing data flows become arrows representing control (e.g. procedure calls). The detail of this *first-cut* structure chart depends on the level of the DFD used. This should be low enough for all the major functions of the system to be represented by distinct modules, but the choice is not crucial since the entire levelled set of DFDs is available to guide subsequent factoring.

The structure chart is then refined using the criteria discussed above. Modules are factored or unfactored, using the DFDs and functional primitive specifications as guides, to give modules with high cohesion and low coupling and a system with a balanced shape. Aspects not normally shown on DFDs must be considered, modules possibly being needed to deal with error processing, with low-level I/O and with initialization and termination procedures.

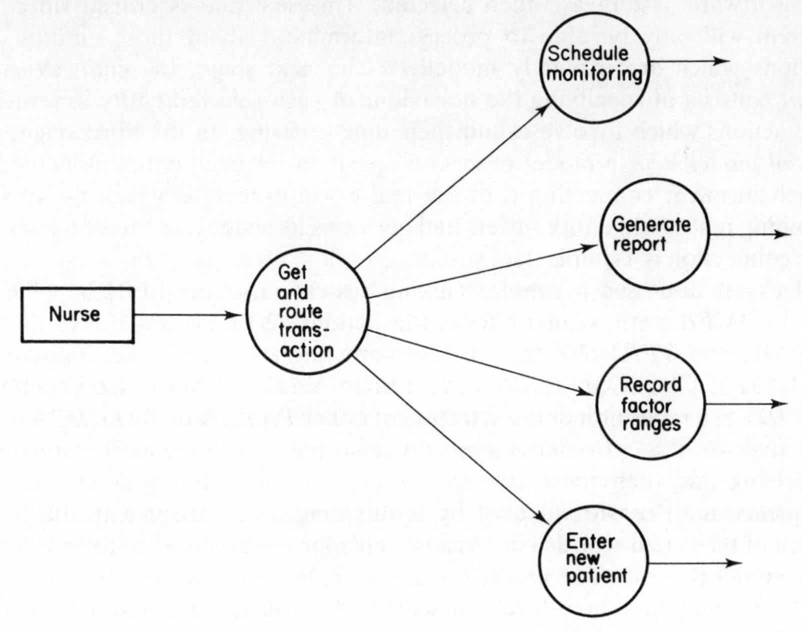

Figure 5.15 Transaction processing DFD

The first-cut structure chart for a transaction-processing system is usually a straightforward mapping of the corresponding DFD (Figure 5.15) into a top-level module which inputs transactions and invokes one of a number of second-level modules to perform the processing (Figure 5.14). In complex systems some or all of these could be full-blown transform systems themselves.

Data-structure-oriented design

Data-structure-oriented design began to make an impact in the mid-1970s, particularly as a result of influential publications by Jackson and Warnier. Both developed methods for program construction (Jackson (JSP) (Jackson 1975), Warnier (LSP) (Warnier 1974)) and later extended their ideas to system design

(Jackson 1982), (Warnier 1981). A brief introduction to Jackson's system-design methodology (JSD) is given here.

JSD has no design stage as conventionally understood, the basic idea being to construct an executable system specification by developing a model of a real-world system and then implementing it in software with functions added to display its states to the user. The first stage, called the *entity/action step*, is to define the elements of the total system. These comprise real-world entities, the real-world actions which are performed on or by them, and the orderings of those actions in time. The entities and actions which are to be modelled in the software system are then selected. This selection is crucial since the system will only be able to process information about those entities and actions which are explicitly modelled. The next stage, the *entity/structure step*, consists of specifying the behaviour of each selected entity in terms of the actions which involve it and their time-ordering. In the third stage, the *initial model step*, a model process is specified for each entity along with a mechanism for connecting it to the real-world process in which the corresponding real-world entity suffers and performs its actions. In the simplest case the connection is a simple data stream.

Jackson discusses a simple banking system (Jackson 1982) in which a *CUSTOMER* entity can perform the actions *INVEST*, *PAY_IN*, *WITHDRAW*, and *TERMINATE*. The time-ordering specified is the composition *INVEST*, *CUSTOMER_BODY*, *TERMINATE*, where *CUSTOMER_BODY* is a repetition of the selection of either *PAY_IN* or *WITHDRAW*. In the real world a customer comes into existence by making an investment in the bank and then repeatedly makes deposits or withdrawals in arbitrary sequence until ceasing to exist by terminating involvement with the bank. Each of these real-world actions causes an appropriate message to be input to the model process. The model-process specification is written in a 'pseudo-code' resembling a high-level language and is called a *structure text* (Figure 5.16).

In the next stage, the *function step*, the simulation is enhanced by giving it the ability to produce outputs when specified actions or combinations of actions occur in the real world and the model can be elaborated by incorporating attributes of actions and processes. In the banking example, for instance, the *INVEST*, *PAY_IN* and WITHDRAW actions can be given the attribute *AMOUNT* ad the *CUSTOMER* process given the attribute *BALANCE*. It is then possible to add functions, for instance to output a report if a *WITHDRAW* action makes *BALANCE* negative and to output the state of the attribute *BALANCE* on user request. The request facility requires the specification of a new process which can connect to each *CUSTOMER* process. The final stage in the specification process is the *system-timing step* in which the necessary synchronization of the model with the real world is specified. In the banking system, for example, the minimum response times

```
CUSTOMER Process;
begin
        read(message);
        INVEST;
        read(message);
        while (message = pay_in)
                  or (message = withdraw) do
                  begin
                           case message of
                                     pay_in    : PAY_IN;
                                    withdraw  : WITHDRAW
                           end;
                           read(message)
                  end;
        TERMINATE
end;
```

Figure 5.16 Structure text for the customer process

required for the current-balance and negative-balance outputs must be specified.

Object-oriented design

The modelling of real-world entities in JSD is taken a stage further in the third category of design methodologies, *object-oriented design*, where the primary components of a software system are viewed as communicating discrete objects. This approach was used in the design of the Smalltalk programming environment (Goldberg and Robson 1983). The fundamental entities of Smalltalk programs are objects which can contain information, can perform operations in response to messages received and can send messages to other objects. Smalltalk has been used in a number of applications including electronic offices and graphics processing and has shown that direct software simulation of domain objects could be a feasible basis for software-system construction. An object-oriented approach associated with the use of the language Ada as a structured specification and design language is described by Booch (1983).

5.3.2 Procedural Design

The second phase of the design stage consists of the detailed specification of the internal structures of the software units defined in the first phase. In the vast majority of systems developed to date these units have been functional modules destined to be implemented in a conventional imperative programming language; hence the commonly used term *procedural specification*. The stage at which procedural specification occurs varies widely in different methodologies. In JSD it is effectively part of the specification stage, but some authorities regard it as essentially part of the implementation stage.

Stepwise Refinement

As for system design, the commonest method of deriving the detailed design of a module from the high-level description produced in the first design phase is top-down functional decomposition. In the stepwise-refinement method (Wirth 1971b) widely adopted since the advent of structured programming and the languages like Pascal which support it, the transformation from the high-level description to executable programming language code is a continuous process with no clear demarcation between design and implementation. The process can be illustrated by deriving a specification of a module whose high-level design specification is:

```
1. Sort the character sequences in components 1 to max of array names
   into alphabetical order within the array.
```

There are many ways of sorting values into order. We shall try to specify a method based on passing repeatedly through the array and exchanging the values of adjacent array components if they are out of order. This can be written as:

```
2. repeat
     pass through the array exchanging the values of each adjacent pair
     of components if they are out of order
   until components are in order
```

'Passing through an array component by component' is naturally represented by a **for** loop so we can introduce the required array explicitly in the next stage.

```
3. repeat
     for i:=1 to max do
       if name[i] is alphabetically after name[i+1]
       then exchange values
   until components are in order
```

The logical structure of the required software is now clear except for the test following the **until**. Testing for order requires passing through the array comparing each component with the next, but this is exactly what the body of the **for** loop does. The addition of a flag to be set to indicate that an exchange has been necessary will allow the test to be specified. The two remaining operations, the boolean function 'is alphabetically after' and the operation 'exchange values' are both quite specific and readily implemented. Writing them as subroutine calls we have

```
4. repeat
     flag:= true;
     for i:=1 to max do
        if not inorder(name[i], name[i+1])
        then begin
              swap(name[i], name[i+1]);
              flag := false
          end
   until flag
```

This, along with details of the data objects used and specifications of the two subroutines, is sufficiently detailed to make the designer's requirements unambiguously clear to the implementor and is very close to executable code.

The Data-structure-oriented Approach

An alternative to functional decomposition is the data-structure-oriented approach as advocated by Jackson and Warnier. Jackson's structured programming method (JSP) (Jackson 1975) is based on the idea that the control structures of a program are determined by, and can be derived from, the structure of the data it is required to consume and generate. Data items which are structured by composition, selection and repetition will require the corresponding control structures in the program which processes them. Jackson's book (Jackson 1975) contains a full discussion of the method with many examples. A good tutorial exposition can be found in King and Pardoe (1985). JSP is of proven worth in the commercial data-processing domain where it has found most of its applications and is worth considering for any problem in which the input and output data items are highly structured.

Graphical Notations

Graphical notations for detailed design specification were used by programmers long before the advent of either of the above methodologies. The oldest, and at one time almost universally employed, notation is the much abused flow chart. Figure 5.17 shows the basic components, from which flow charts are constructed by connecting them with arrows to show flow of control. Flow-chart representations of the basic control structures are shown in Figure 5.18 and the flowchart representing the bubble-sort algorithm used in the example programs of Chapter 4 is shown in Figure 5.19. Process boxes are used for subprogram calls and the graphical equivalent of the **goto** statement is the arrow, which can be drawn from any point on a flowchart to any other point, allowing control structures of arbitrary complexity to be specified. Flowcharts constructed using only the basic control structures are reasonably comprehen-

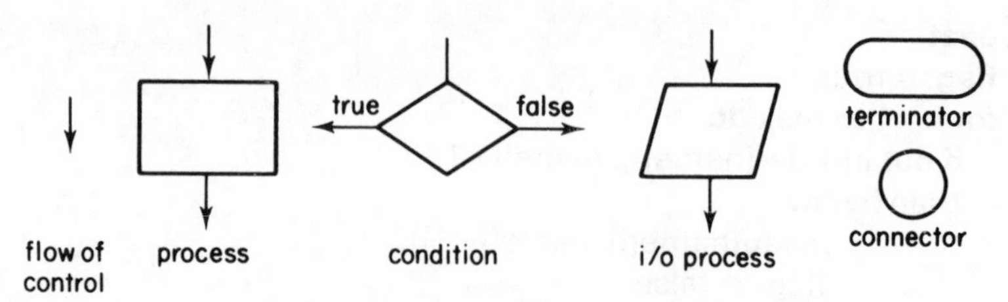

Figure 5.17 Basic flow-chart elements

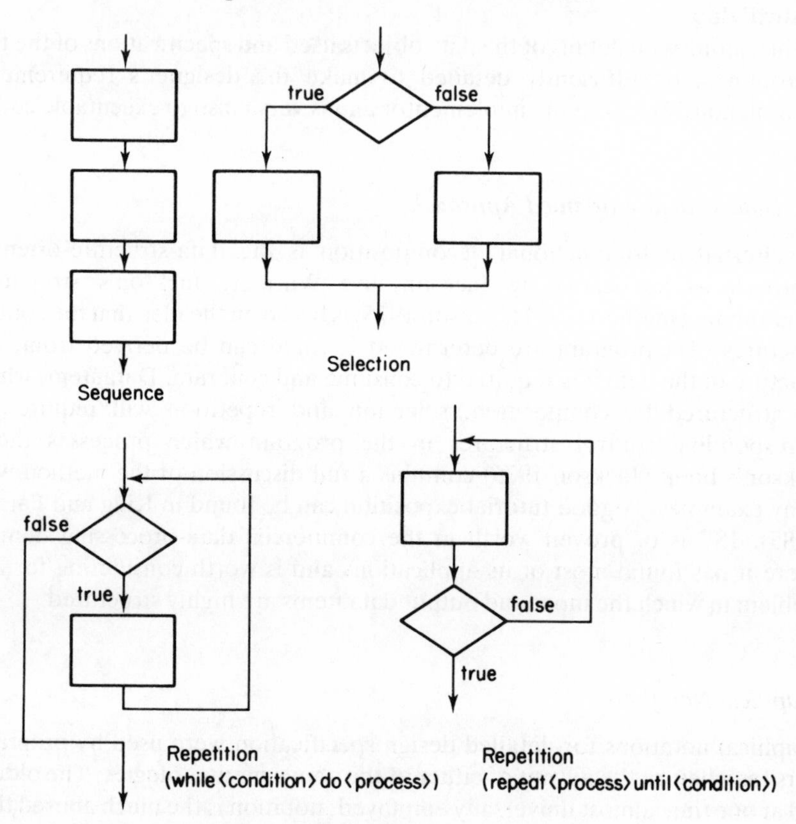

Figure 5.18 Basic control structures

sible, but the notation can be, and often has been, used to produce the graphical equivalent of 'spaghetti code'.

Design-structure diagrams (DSDs) (Bothon 1979) are also constructed from elements representing the basic control structures, some of which are shown in Figure 5.20. Control flow is represented by arrows, but control structures can be represented directly without resorting to a **goto**. A node is a branch point for control flow which has one input path and right-hand and left-hand output

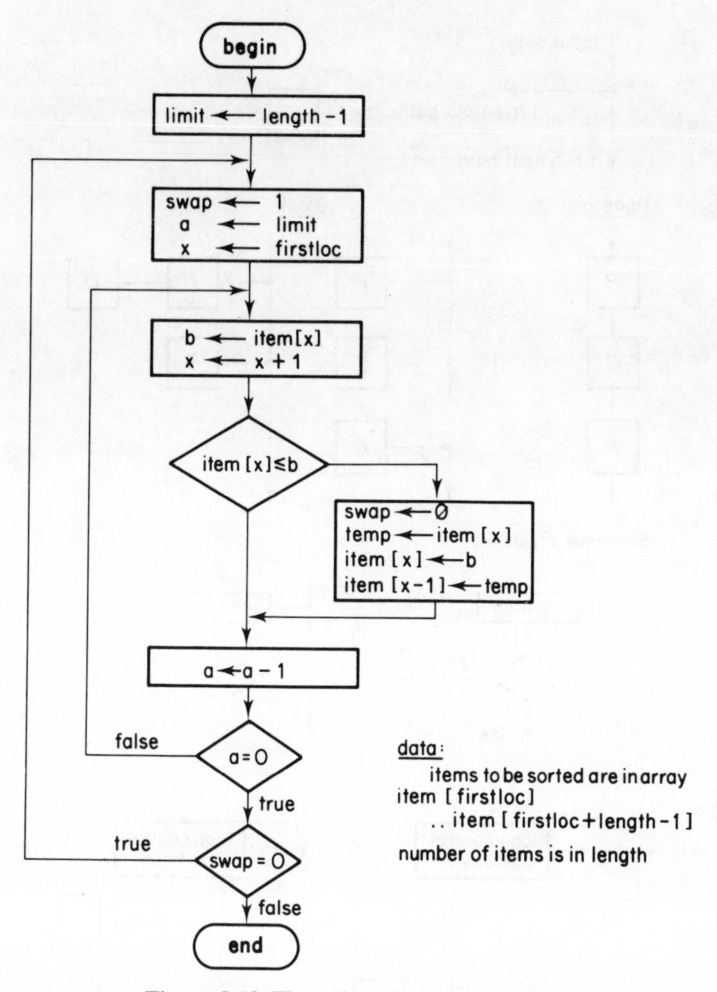

Figure 5.19 Flow chart for sort procedure

paths as defined in the figure. The left-hand path is always taken first and when control comes to the end of that path it undergoes *fall-back*, i.e. returns directly to the node at which the path originated. This is shown in the second and third versions of the sequence construct in the figure. Both are equivalent to the first which uses only the conventional rules. A comprehensive set of basic structures is defined, including some for synchronization and communication between concurrent processes and some for data structures. A DSD representation of the sort program is shown in Figure 5.21.

5.3.3 The System-design Specification

The final phase of the design stage is the production of its documentation, the

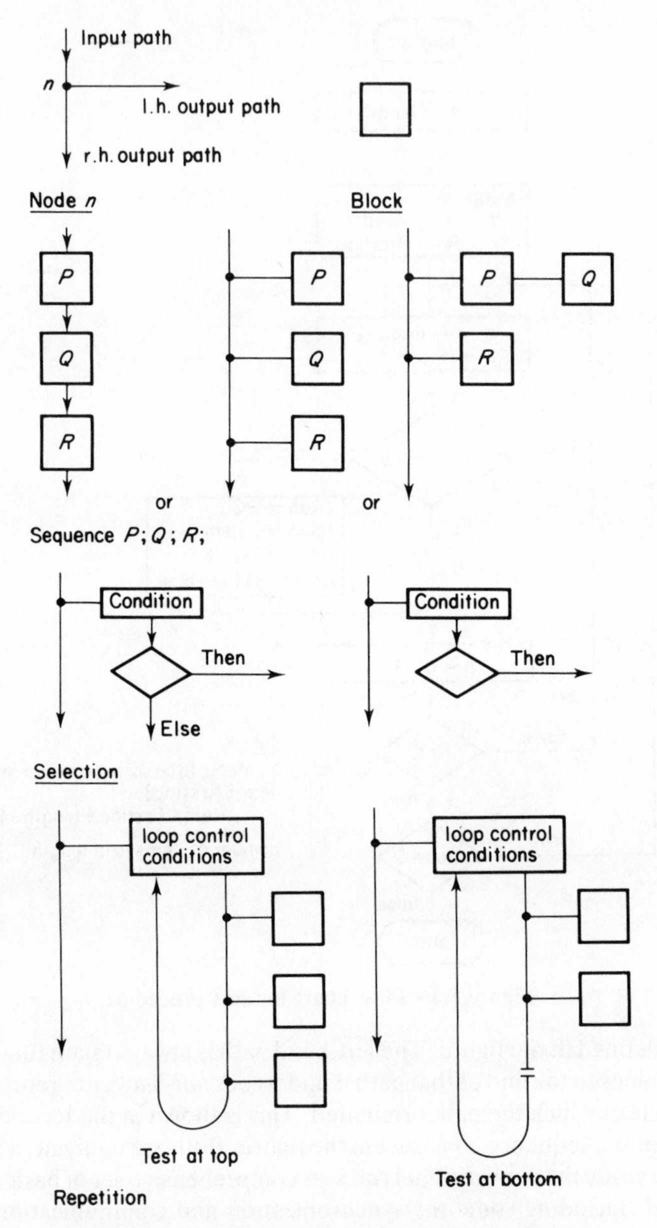

Figure 5.20 Elements of the design structure diagram

system-design specification (SDS) and its validation. The SDS must contain the complete design specification, consisting of the structure specification and the detailed specification of each module in the structure. The derivation of the

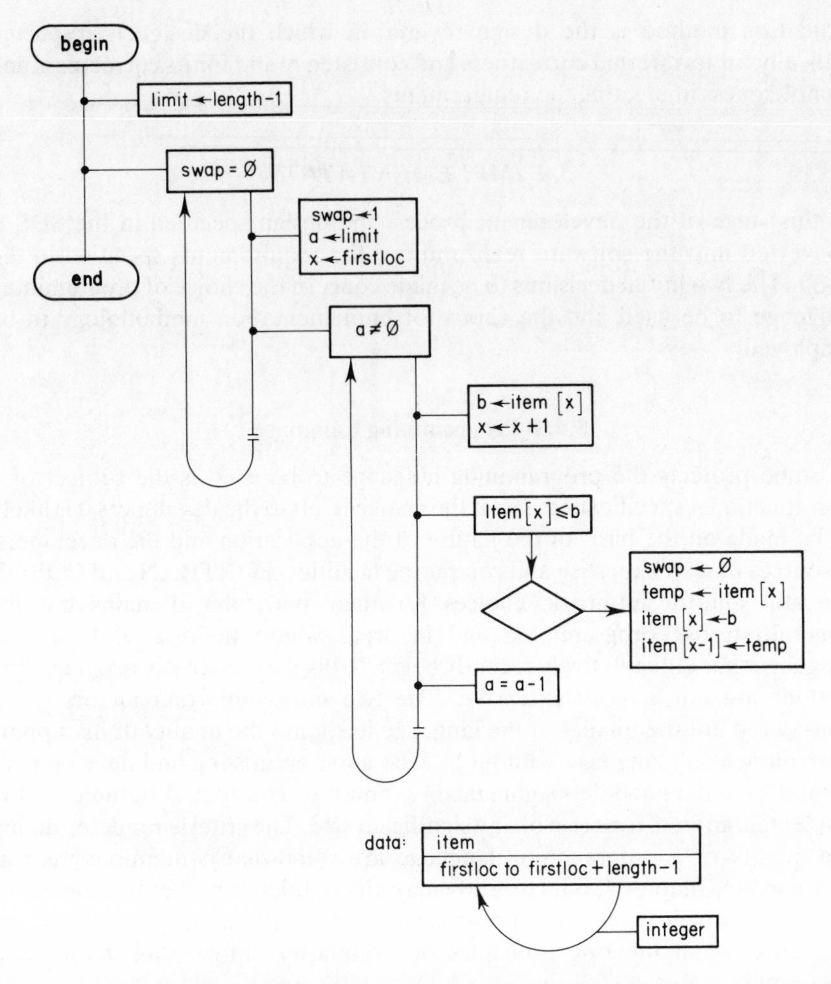

Figure 5.21 Design structure diagram for sort procedure

structure specification should be included along with the data-flow diagrams or data-structure analyses on which it is based. A full specification of external files and other global data structures should accompany the structure specification and each module specification should include specifications of all local data used. A comprehensive data dictionary should be provided both for subsequent reference and as an aid to consistency checking within the design specification. Completeness and correctness checking require that the SDS be checked against the requirements specification in the SRD. Systematic cross-reference tables should be drawn up in which the components of the design that satisfy each separate requirement are identified. The basic validation method is the design review, in which the design is inspected critically for its internal correctness and consistency and for its correctness and completeness in meeting the requirements.

5.4 IMPLEMENTATION

In this stage of the development process the design specified in the SDS is converted into the software realization of the requirements specified in the SRD. The two initial decisions to be made concern the choice of programming language to be used and the choice of implementation methodology to be employed.

5.4.1 Programming Language

In some projects the programming language to be used is the subject of a non-functional specification, but if the choice is left to the developers it is likely to be made on the basis of the nature of the application and the developers' resources of staff expertise and computing facilities. FORTRAN and COBOL are still almost automatic choices for their particular domains but for general-purpose programming and in areas where the use of high-level languages has only relatively recently begun to displace assembly language, the options are much more extensive. The two most important factors to be considered are the quality of the language itself and the quality of its support environment. A language without at least good optimizing and development compilers and a good debugging facility cannot be considered suitable for the implementation of a system of any significant size. The criteria for determining the quality of a programming language are somewhat contentious, as was discussed in Chapter 4, but currently majority opinion is probably in favour of languages which explicitly support structured-programming techniques and the software-engineering principles of modularity, information hiding and abstraction.

The language which goes furthest to meet these requirements is Ada, which was designed at the instigation of the US Department of Defense to be the standard language for embedded system software. The history of its development is outlined in the book by Barnes (1984) which contains a detailed and readable account of the language. In embedded systems, the computer is part of a larger non-computational system (such as a cruise missile or a warship or a chemical-plant control system).

It interacts directly with this system to perform monitoring and control functions, has all the characteristics of any large software system, along with special requirements for concurrent programming, real-time operation, direct interaction with hardware interfaces to the controlled system and the responsibility of dealing with error conditions (or 'exceptions') without human intervention. Ada has facilities to satisfy these special requirements. It is also a general-purpose high-level imperative programming language based on Pascal but providing more powerful and flexible forms of data and control structuring facilities as well as a major extension for the support of data abstraction.

An Ada program consists of one or more program units each of which can be compiled separately. There are three kinds of program unit: subprograms, packages and tasks (for concurrent programming), all of which consist of two parts, a specification and a body, which are themselves separately compilable. The general principle is that the specification of a program unit defines its interface and the resources it offers to other units, while its body contains the implementation of the resources, hiding it from other units. Modularity and information hiding are thus built in to the basic structure of the language.

5.4.2 Implementation Methodologies

There are two systematic methods of implementing a system design: top-down and bottom-up. The top-down method parallels the top-down derivation of a design by functional decomposition. The module at the top of the hierarchy is implemented first with the second-level modules it controls incorporated as *stubs*. The function of a stub is to simulate, in a simple way, the behaviour of the fully implemented module whose place it is holding. Once the top-level module executes correctly, the second-level stubs are replaced by the full modules with the third-level modules in place as stubs. The process continues in this way until the implementation is complete.

The advantage of top-down implementation is that the whole system is kept in an executable form right from the start, which allows it to be viewed as an entity and its modules to be viewed and tested in context. The system is tested after each stub has been replaced by its full module both for correct operation of the new module and for the continued correct operation of the previously incorporated modules. This allows early detection of design errors in the interconnections and functionality of the modules, which is essential since late detection means a great deal of wasted programming effort and hence wasted money. The major problem is that devising stubs to simulate the functions of lower-level modules can be very difficult. The usual methods are to return constant or randomly generated values or to request values to be input interactively. Low-level modules which interact directly with system interfaces may have to be implemented in full early on and provided with routes to higher-level modules to allow the system to communicate with its surroundings.

Bottom-up development involves implementation of the lowest-level modules first, then the next lowest and so on until implementation of the highest-level module completes the system. As the structure hierarchy is ascended the lower-level modules are combined into the higher-level ones. The individual modules are tested separately using *drivers*—programs which are specially constructed to provide inputs for them. Testing itself is easier with this method since it is easier to simulate the environment of a low-level module than that of a high-level one, but it has the prohibitive disadvantage that the correct working of the combined modules is not tested until implementation is complete and if high-level design errors are present they will not be detected until a late stage. As this is unacceptable for systems of any size, pure bottom-up implementation is not practicable.

In practice the lowest-level modules are usually implemented and tested separately and high-level modules with a hierarchical structure are implemented top-down, pre-implemented lower-level modules being incorporated as needed.

A great deal of wasteful duplication of programming effort can be avoided if modules providing commonly needed services are made available in subroutine libraries. In practice, even when working in languages which are regarded as having good subroutine libraries, most programmers probably expend a significant amount of their effort programming modules which in all essential respects have been programmed thousands of times before. This state of affairs contrasts sharply with hardware development, where maximum use is made of standardized components with flexible interfaces and the expense of one-off custom-designed components is avoided as far as possible.

The idea of establishing collections of re-usable software components is an attractive one and the extensive subroutine libraries of languages like FORTRAN can be seen as going some way to implement it. The trouble is that such libraries are restricted to subroutines, that the services they provide are only of the most basic and universally useful kind and, most seriously, that such libraries are not easily programmer-extendable in block-structured languages.

Ada is based on the idea of a software system as a main procedure which makes use of the services provided by units in a program library which are implemented and compiled beforehand. Separate compilation is built into the language without restriction on the use of language facilities and with full type-checking across separately compiled units. The programmer or group of programmers working on a large system or within a particular application domain can build up customized libraries which are maintained as a permanent part of the programming environment.

The restriction of software libraries to subprograms is removed by the introduction of the package, a construct which allows the implementation of abstract data types. The package shown in Figure 5.22 implements a pushdown stack which is a *last-in–first-out* queue of elements which can be added to (by *PUSH*ing an element on) and subtracted from (by *POP*ping an element off) at one end only, conventionally called the top of the stack. The package exports only the operations *PUSH* and *POP* and a function which tests whether there are any elements on the stack. The way in which the stack is

```
package STACK is
        procedure PUSH(E: in INTEGER);
        function POP return INTEGER;
        function IS_EMPTY return BOOLEAN;
end STACK;

package body STACK is
        MAX: constant POSITIVE := 100;
        S: array(1..MAX)of INTEGER;
        TOP: INTEGER range 0..MAX := 0;

        procedure PUSH (E: in INTEGER) is
        begin
                TOP:=TOP+1;
                S(TOP):=E;
        end PUSH;

        function POP return INTEGER is
        begin
                TOP:=TOP-1;
                return S(TOP+1);
        end POP;

        function IS_EMPTY is
        begin
                return TOP=0;
        end IS_EMPTY;
end STACK;
```

Figure 5.22 Ada package STACK

implemented, as an array in this case, is completely hidden in the package body. The data structure can only be accessed via the operations provided by the exported subprograms and the data abstraction is fully enforced. This is impossible in Pascal or FORTRAN where units have either no access to a data structure or total access to it. If an array is used to implement a stack in these languages a unit with access to the stack can read and write values of any array component, not just the one at the 'top', thus subverting the intended abstraction.

The package of Figure 5.22 implements a single stack object only. If a stack type is required, the limited private type facility of Ada can be used as shown in Figure 5.23. This package specification exports a *STACK* type, declared as private, along with the subprograms which provide the allowed operations. The private section of the specification includes the implementa-

```
package STACKS is
        type STACK is limited private;
        procedure PUSH(S: in out STACK; E: in INTEGER);
        procedure POP(S: in out STACK; E: out INTEGER);
        procedure IS_EMPTY(S: in STACK; B: out BOOLEAN);
private
        MAX: constant POSITIVE := 100;
        type STACK_ARRAY is array(1..MAX)of INTEGER;
        type STACK is record
                TOP: INTEGER range 0..MAX :=0;
                S: STACK_ARRAY;
                        end record;
end STACKS;
```

Figure 5.23 Ada package STACKS

tion of the type for the benefit of the compiler, but the implementation is not accessible to other program units. The only operations which can be performed on objects of type limited private are those implemented as subprograms declared in the visible part of the package specification; *PUSH*, *POP* and *IS_EMPTY* here. With a package of this kind units that use it can declare objects of type *STACK* but perform only the intended operations upon them.

These implementations provide a stack object and a stack type for stacks of integers only. Stacks of many other types are frequently required, however, and with only the facilities described so far a separate package would have to be implemented for each different type of stack element. This kind of situation has long been a great irritant to programmers in connection with both subprograms and data structures. The sort program discussed in Chapter 4, for example, must have different implementations for sorting integers and for sorting strings of characters, although the algorithm is the same in both cases. Ada provides a solution for this problem in the form of generic program units which serve as templates for the creation of actual units with the same logical structure.

5.4.3 Coding Style

The designers of Ada recognized that the code of a software system is read very much more often than it is written and that the readability of code is a vital factor in its understandability, which in turn exerts an important influence on its development and subsequent maintainability. Ada was designed to be easily readable, and if the code is well laid out to reflect its logical structure and uses meaningful identifiers for program entities it succeeds very well. These requirements for coding style are even more important when using languages which are less inherently readable.

The provision of comments within the system code constitutes an internal documentation of the system which can make all the difference between code which is relatively easy to understand and code which requires a great deal of detective work to discover what it does. Commenting should not be necessary to explain the operation of well-written code but rather to provide a map of the design structure of the system such that the function and context of each module and submodule of the system can be readily ascertained. Each unit should have a comprehensive *prologue* comment describing its function, interface, calling units, called units, component units and, in due course, its maintenance history. If a formal specification or design language has been used it is often incorporated into the code as comments.

5.5 TESTING AND DEBUGGING

The simple life-cycle model of software development requires verification of the implemented software system by subjecting the system to a systematic test regime embodied in a test plan. The test plan consists of sets of test cases devised so that if the system responds to each test case as specified it can, with a high degree of probability, be certified as meeting its requirements specifications.

Testing during the implementation stage is concerned with establishing the correct functioning of individual modules (a process usually called unit testing) and with establishing that the modules continue to perform correctly, and interact in the required way, as the system is built up (integration testing). The same process is performed on a smaller scale at the submodule level, testing being performed at suitable stages during the construction of a module. Unit and subunit testing are usually performed by the programmer as an integral part of the coding process with reference to the design specification for the module rather than the formal test plan. The test plan specifies the integration testing and the testing of the assembled system which constitutes this stage of the life cycle. In principle the purpose of testing is to demonstrate that the system (or module) under test responds correctly to all possible sequences of all possible inputs, but since the number of possible inputs is effectively infinite, this exhaustive testing is not a feasible proposition. It is therefore necessary to devise a finite set of test cases which will provide a high degree of probability that the system responds correctly to any sequence of inputs if it responds correctly to that set.

The immediate purpose of a test is the converse of the ultimate purpose of testing, a successful test being one which demonstrates erroneous behaviour of the software. Testing is essentially destructive, test cases being devised to find errors, and the test plan should ideally be devised and implemented by personnel unconnected with the design and implementation of the system, although the co-operation of designers and implementors is essential, since detailed knowledge of the software is often necessary for the design of test cases.

A module can be tested at two levels, a lower, procedural level at which the detailed internal working is tested and a higher, functional level at which the transformation of inputs to outputs is tested without reference to the internal operations which implement it. Testing at the procedural level is appropriate to the unit and subunit testing performed during implementation. Exhaustive testing at this level requires that every possible logical path through the piece of software be traversed and shown to operate correctly, but again this is rarely feasible. Testing at the functional level is appropriate to the integration and validation testing phases, where the correct transformation of input to output data, the appropriate handling of invalid inputs and the integrity of global and external data structures under operation of the system is examined.

A test case consists of a specification of input data, a description of the modules or logical paths exercised by it and a specification of the response it should invoke. Test cases for integration and validation testing, which are normally functional, constitute part of the formal test plan and should refer to any relevant requirement of the SRD for the input and response and to the design specification in the SDS for the parts of the system exercised. Implicit in all response specifications is a requirement that global and external data structures are not corrupted by the exercise of the function being tested.

The formulation of test cases for procedural testing depends on the skill and experience of the tester, usually the programmer, who will devise tests to execute the most important logical paths, to check that local data structures are correctly initialized and used, to check that the interface handles input and output correctly and that invalid inputs are dealt with correctly. There are characteristic errors associated with particular control and data structures (e.g. loops being executed $n+1$ or $n-1$ times instead of n times) which must be looked for. Errors are particularly associated with *boundary values* and *boundary conditions*, e.g. when the first or last component of a file or array is processed, when a loop is executed zero times or just once, when an empty file or a file containing just one item is accessed. Such errors should be looked for by the test cases and are also detectable by *code inspections*, in which the programmer conducts a group of colleagues or independent testers, who have read the relevant design specifications beforehand, through the code. Perhaps surprisingly this is a well-tried and productive technique for the detection of procedural errors.

Test cases at the functional level are most commonly selected on the basis of partitioning the set of all possible inputs into equivalence classes whose members have properties in common such that, if the system responds as specified to one member of the class, it could reasonably be expected to do so to all members of it. Equivalence classes are identified from the requirements and design specifications by the testers and again the process requires skill and experience. Test-case inputs are selected from the equivalence classes and, as with testing at the procedural level, cases at the boundaries of the equivalence classes should receive particular attention. To achieve maximum coverage of classes, and of combinations of them, test cases should be devised in which the inputs fall into as many classes as possible. The number of equivalence classes, even for a small program, can be large so that efficient formulation of test cases is important. It is also necessary to consider procedural details at the level of connections between modules, combinations of inputs being selected on the basis of the inter-modular connections they exercise. Outputs can also be partitioned into equivalence classes and the set of test cases should include those which generate typical and boundary values of each of these.

A number of software tools are available to assist testing. *Test-data generators*, which automatically generate large volumes of data for input to a system under test, are of limited use since they cannot generate the corresponding specified outputs.

Profilers are useful when testing at the procedural level. These tools insert *software sensors* into the source code to record the number of times statements are executed and the values of relevant variables when the system is exercised. This information is analysed after execution and used to construct a profile of the execution which shows how many times each sequence of statements has been executed. Logical paths which have not been executed can thus be identified and further test cases devised accordingly. Since profilers require a syntactical analysis of the program they are normally provided as compiler options or combined with a static syntax analyser in a pre-processor which operates on the source code before passing it to a compiler. A number of so-called *automatic-validation* systems have been constructed on the latter basis, some of which will generate test data to exercise paths not exercised by the current set of test cases (Saib 1984). Others, like the *program evaluator and tester* (PET) system, provide an assertion-checking facility whereby the programmer can insert logical statements about the state of the computation, in terms of the values that specified variables should have, at strategic points in the source code and have these assertions checked when the program is executed (Stucki 1977).

File comparators, general-purpose tools for detecting differences in the contents of two files, are useful for comparing test outputs which should be identical and for checking memory dumps for corruption of global data.

The errors uncovered by testing are corrected by debugging, an activity discussed in Section 4.6. Testing and debugging are continued, ideally, until the developers are satisfied with the reliability of the system, although deadline and cost overruns have been known to force a premature closure which simply defers error detection and correction to the maintenance stage, at which time it is very much more expensive.

As in the previous stages of the life cycle the testing stage must be adequately documented. An overview of the test plan identifying the system functions and associated modules to be tested should be followed by a detailed description and justification of the test cases used. The test results themselves must be recorded since this information can be essential for system maintenance.

A further stage of testing occurs after installation of the system. Called *acceptance testing*, it is performed in conjunction with the users so that they can familiarize themselves with the operation of the system and satisfy themselves that it meets their requirements. When, and if, so satisfied they take delivery of the system, including the documentation described in the next section, and the final stage of the life cycle, operation, and maintenance begins.

5.6 DOCUMENTATION, MAINTENANCE AND OPERATION

Documentation, an essential component of any software system, consists of system documentation for use in maintenance and user documentation for use in operation.

System documentation consists of the documents produced in each stage of the development process: the SRD from the specification stage, the SDS from the design stage, a description of the implementation including a data dictionary and the test documentation. These documents must be organized and comprehensively indexed for maximum ease of use during maintenance and the labour involved in their preparation and maintenance makes on-line storage and management with software tools almost mandatory.

Maintenance activities are conventionally classified as corrective, adaptive and perfective maintenance respectively. Corrective maintenance consists of the correction of errors discovered by users during system operation. The frequency and severity of such errors depends on the quality of the system. A system which has been developed on good software-engineering principles should not have errors beyond the implementation level, or at worst the detailed design level. The ease with which such errors may be safely corrected depends on the modularity of the system and the extent to which the maintenance programmers understand it. In the early stages of its operational life it will probably be maintained by its developers, or at least by personnel with access to them, so that understanding should not be a problem. Within a fairly short period of time, however, it is quite probable that all of the development team will have moved on and ease of maintenance is then crucially dependent on the quality of the system documentation, including the internal documentation of the code.

Similar considerations hold for adaptive maintenance, modification of the system to meet changes in its environment, and perfective maintenance, enhancement of system services. The whole motivation of the software-development principles discussed in this chapter is to produce understandable systems composed of modules which are as autonomous as possible and interact only through well-defined interfaces. If this structure is well-documented, the effect of a proposed modification and the ease with which it can be implemented can be assessed with a minimum amount of detective work.

For practical purposes, as far as the users of the system are concerned, the quality of the documentation provided with the system is as important as the quality of the software itself. User documentation normally consists of a *System Reference Manual*, a comprehensive and detailed description of every service the system offers, and one or more *User Manuals*. The reference manual must be complete and definitive, providing the answer to every question that an expert user of the system might ask. It can assume professional computing expertise on the part of its readers and make free use of standard technical notations and terminology. It will include an *installation guide*, describing how to bring the system up on the target machine and an *operator's guide* describing the necessary activities for day-to-day system operation and management. This documentation is aimed at the computing professionals who will keep the system going.

The user manuals are for the end users of the system who are not, in general, trained computer personnel and whose use of the system may well be a relatively minor part of their work. The major requirements for these manuals are comprehensibility and accuracy. Computing jargon must be avoided and each description of a system function should be accompanied by examples which are correct with respect to the current state of the system. There is nothing more demoralizing to a user than to be told that the system will respond in a certain way to a certain input and to find that it does not. Designers of man–machine interfaces stress the importance of providing the users with a domain-oriented conceptual model of the system and the user documentation should reflect this model. The user manuals normally consist of at least a *beginner's introduction*, which explains how to enter and leave the system, how to get started on using the major functions and how to escape if the system starts to behave in an unexpected way (e.g. when a typing error generates a valid but unintended input) and a *standard user's manual* which covers all the functions of the system in sufficient detail for normal routine use. A large system offering many services may well require a number of such manuals covering different aspects of its use. The quality of user documentation is so important to the successful operation of a system that some software producers involve users in assessment of preliminary versions, using the feedback to improve subsequent versions, and make extensive use of technical authors and graphic designers in the production of the final version.

Fundamentals of Information Technology
Edited by G. G. Wilkinson and A. R. Winterflood

Chapter 6

Project Management

6.1 PROJECT PLANNING

This chapter is concerned with the problems that arise when the efforts of more than one or two software engineers are necessary for the development of a system. Large projects can involve very large numbers of people: Brooks (1975), for example, estimates that the development of the infamous IBM OS/360 operating system involved some 5000 man-years of effort over a three-year period. As we have seen in Chapter 5 the problems presented by the development of small systems are far from trivial, so we can expect those encountered with large systems to be formidable indeed. Without formal procedures for planning and controlling large projects there is little chance of their producing anything useful at all, let alone a product which shows any profit for its makers.

Large software systems are normally developed within organizations large enough to require a formal management structure which is likely to be the conventional hierarchy where personnel at one level are directed by and report to the level above. The details of the structure vary from one organization to another but usually there are three fairly distinct levels of staff directly concerned with a software-development project. The lowest consists of the software engineers and analysts who actually perform the technical operations of system development. They are usually grouped in teams of between six and ten individuals and one or more such teams are allocated to a particular project, or a stage of a particular project, under the direction of a project manager (or similarly titled individual) representing the second level of the hierarchy, who may be responsible for more than one project. The third level, the senior management or *organizational* level, provides overall control of software-development activities within the context of the resources, objectives and policies of the organization as a whole.

The basic approach to the management of any project is to formulate a plan, arrange for the provision of the resources necessary to carry it out, including personnel, then to direct and co-ordinate the activities of those personnel to ensure that the plan is correctly implemented. The project plan is the responsibility of the senior management level and is produced after an analysis

1. System Definition
2. Software Development Plan
3. Quality Assurance Plan
4. Documentation Plan
5. Training Plan
6. Installation and Operation Plan
7. Costing Plan
8. Organisation and Staffing Plan
9. Scheduling Plan

Figure 6.1 A software project plan

of the proposed system in which technical and economic feasibility has been assessed, preliminary assignment of functions to software and hardware has been made and approximate constraints of cost and delivery data have been established. A typical contents list for a project plan is shown in Figure 6.1, which serves to identify the major considerations involved in planning the development of a software system. These reflect the five basic planning concerns of 'what?' (1), 'how?' (2–6), 'how much?' (7), 'who?' (8) and 'when?' (9). A brief discussion of these subplans provides an overview of management activities, some of which is then discussed in more detail.

The *system definition* specifies the functions, interfaces and performance requirements for the system to the extent that these have been established by the initial analysis. It is essentially a preliminary version of the software-requirements document (SRD) discussed in Chapter 5, and provides the context for the formulation of the remainder of the project plan.

The *software development plan* defines the technical tasks to be performed during the development process in terms of the life-cycle stages through which development is to proceed, the monitoring procedures to be applied and the tools and techniques to be used for development and monitoring. Monitoring procedures are based upon specifications of system status at a series of points during development, called *milestones*, which also serve as the basis for scheduling. Milestones at the end of each stage of the life cycle can be used as *baselines*, points where the system status has to be validated before development can proceed to the next stage. Standards and techniques for system configuration control and change control are also specified.

The *quality assurance plan* specifies procedures designed to provide assurance to both the organization and the customer that each task described in the software-development plan has been properly planned, managed, carried out, monitored and documented. These procedures are applied by a group independent of the development teams which acts on behalf of the organization as a whole. In some kinds of contract work it is usual for the customer to have his own quality assurance specialists attached to the group.

The *documentation plan* prescribes the nature, scope, structure and format of the documents to be produced in the course of the project and specifies the relationships between them. Most of these are 'deliverables'—specified outputs of life-cycle stages and contractually required documents such as user and system manuals.

The *training plan* deals with the scheduling and nature of the training required for development personnel and the eventual end-users of the system.

The *installation and operation plan* details the procedures to be followed when the system is delivered to the customer and includes specification of installation and acceptance testing.

The *costing plan* consists of estimates of the resources required for the project including time, personnel, facilities, materials and equipment and estimates of their costs, and describes the procedures by which the estimates have been arrived at.

The *organization and staffing plan* describes the organizational structure of the project staff in terms of activities, responsibilities, and authority. It includes estimates of staffing requirements and prescribes how the composition of the organization changes as development proceeds through the life-cycle stages.

The *scheduling plan* specifies the rate at which development should proceed by assigning dates to the milestones defined in the *software development plan* and specifies the techniques used to prepare and represent the schedule. Scheduling is closely related to costing and resource provision and is complicated by the need to schedule development tasks to be carried out in parallel where possible to achieve competitive completion times.

6.2 RESOURCE ESTIMATION AND COSTING

The accuracy with which delivery date and total cost can be estimated for a proposed software-system development is obviously a crucial factor in the profitability or otherwise of the project. The estimates of these two key quantities depend on estimates of the resources needed to carry out the development and their associated costs. Resources can be divided into human resources and the rest, where the rest includes such things as computing facilities, training, and office accommodation and services. The crucial distinction is that whereas the amount and cost of the latter per unit time period can be predicted with reasonable certainty, the amount of human effort which is required to actually create the software is extremely difficult to estimate. This means that the time necessary to complete the project is difficult to predict, which in turn affects all the other estimates, although this effect may be of secondary importance since the cost of the personnel is normally by far the greater proportion of the total.

The first problem is to find some useful measure of the productivity of people engaged directly in the technical activities of software development. Ideally this requires separate measures for each of the distinct activities in the life cycle, but in practice overall measures of beginning-to-end productivity are usually used, the simplest and by far the most popular of which is the number of validated lines of source code produced per person-month averaged over the entire duration of the project. (Hence development personnel are generally referred to as *programmers* in this context, regardless of their actual activities). This value obviously depends on what constitutes a line which in turn depends on the language being used and the programmer's style: a line of C generally represents more effort than a line of FORTRAN, for instance. An alternative measure is the number of machine-code instructions produced per person-month, but this depends on the efficiency of the compiler used and on the machine the object code is generated for. These considerations make comparison of productivities from different sources difficult, but if a consistent policy is followed within a given organization it is possible to use these measures in resource and cost estimation and in estimation of the effect of various factors upon programmer productivity. A well-known study (Walston and Felix 1977) attempted to identify the effect of about 70 factors on productivity, measured by lines of code per person-month, in the course of an assessment of the impact of techniques such as structured programming, inspections and top-down development methodology on a collection of about 60 projects of widely varying type. They identified some 30 factors as significant, and while some of their findings confirmed intuitively obvious effects, such as productivity increasing with the programmer's experience of the language used, machine used and type of application, others were less predictable. Complexity of the user interface and the degree of customer involvement in requirements definition both had a strong negative effect on productivity, for instance.

The *lines-of-code* (LOC) costing technique (Pressman 1982) uses productivity data from previous projects to estimate costs. The system definition is functionally decomposed until an estimate of the number of lines of code required to implement each function can be estimated from historical data for similar functions. An average value and a variance are calculated from 'optimistic', 'most likely' and 'pessimistic' estimates and used to calculate effort in person-months and hence cost from historical productivity data for similar functions and current pay rates.

The *effort-per-task* costing technique (Pressman 1982) requires more information, being based on establishing effort (i.e. number of person-months) for each life cycle stage of each function. Cost per unit effort is then used to estimate the cost for each function and hence the total cost. Results derived from the two techniques should be in reasonable agreement if either is to be given much credence.

A number of mathematical models of the software-development process have been devised to predict data for use in planning. The simplest ones estimate a *resource requirement* R as a function of an estimated *software characteristic* C, such as number of lines of code, according to an equation of the form

$$R = a\,C^b,$$

where a and b are constants whose values depend on the type of system being developed and on the environment it is being developed in and are derived empirically from historical data.

In the *basic COCOMO model* (Boehm 1981) equations of this kind are used to calculate effort from the estimated number of lines of code and to calculate duration from effort. The number of people required can then be calculated from effort and duration. Three levels of complexity of product (relative to the developers' experience) are provided for with different equations (i.e. different values of a and b) for each level. The *intermediate model* takes account of other factors affecting the effort required for a project by providing multipliers to be applied to the 'basic' estimate. There are four classes of factors, as shown in Figure 6.2, with multipliers for each of a set of levels of the

Product Attributes:
- (i) reliability required
- (ii) size of database
- (iii) complexity of product

Computer Attributes:
- (i) execution speed required
- (ii) storage limit
- (iii) likelihood of host system change
- (iv) turnaround time on development system

Personnel Attributes:
- (i) capability of analysts
- (ii) experience with type of system
- (iii) experience of host system
- (iv) capability of programmers
- (v) experience of implementation language

Project Attributes:
- (i) use of modern programming practices
- (ii) use of software tools
- (iii) required development duration relative to basic model estimate

Figure 6.2 COCOMO development effort factors

estimated contribution of each factor. Estimates derived from this and similar models can never be accurate because of the subjective selection of level for each factor, because many factors are not considered and, most significantly, because the whole edifice rests on a necessarily imprecise estimate of the number of lines of code the system will require. The models are nevertheless useful in assessing the effects of changing attributes e.g. of increasing the use of software tools or of making the required duration a closer match to the estimated one.

More elaborate 'dynamic' models provide for resource estimation with time as an explicit variable. The Putnam estimation model (Putnam 1978), for example, uses an equation derived from a graphical relationship (called a Rayleigh–Norden curve) between effort expended and point reached in the life cycle which relates development effort to lines of code and development time. An equation of this type allows duration to be calculated from effort estimates from simple models which do not include it as an explicit factor. Automation of costing can be based on these techniques; the SLIM system (Putnam 1980), for example, is based on the Putnam model.

6.3 PROJECT SCHEDULING

Any software-development project must be scheduled to meet a fixed delivery date which is, ideally, a consequence of scheduling considerations. In practice it is not unusual for the schedule to have to be devised after the data has been set. Accurate scheduling is probably more important than accurate cost estimation, since excess costs may be recoverable through increased sales or increased prices but late delivery is irrecoverable and likely to result in missed markets and lost customers.

Scheduling is a difficult planning activity requiring correlation of staff organization with effort under constraints of resource availability, cost and time to achieve an optimum distribution of tasks over time and personnel. The basis of the schedule is the set of activities defined in the software-development plan. The life-cycle stages through which software development proceeds are essentially sequential, but within these stages many tasks can be performed in parallel. Once the structural design phase is complete, detailed design of modules can proceed concurrently as can tasks within the implementation and testing stages. The schedule must incorporate these parallel activities, take account of their necessary interdependencies and ensure that they are co-ordinated with resource availabilities and with sequential progress through the life cycle. It defines the milestones which mark this progress and the monitoring activities to be performed at, and deliverables associated with, each milestone. The schedule interacts with all the other components of the project plan: it includes quality-assurance activities, training activities for development personnel and installation activities. It must be consistent with the organization and staffing plan and is partly determined by cost considerations.

The *program evaluation and review technique* (PERT) and the *critical path method* (CPM) are related project-scheduling methods (Wiest and Levy 1977) which are commonly applied to software development. They provide techniques for determining the task sequence on which the project duration depends (the *critical path*) and duration estimates for individual tasks and time windows within which particular tasks must be completed. The schedule is represented by a (formal) graph in which nodes represent completion points and arcs represent tasks. Each arc is labelled with the task name and its duration in time units, usually weeks or months. Traversal of an arc represents completion of the associated task and arcs leaving a node cannot be followed (i.e. the corresponding tasks started) until all arcs entering it have been traversed. The scheduling graph shown in Figure 6.3 has a critical path consisting of the task sequence T1–T5–T10–T15 which takes 10 time units. If the schedule is accurate this is the minimum duration of the collection of tasks represented and delay in completion of any of these will delay overall completion, whereas some slippage on other paths may be accepted providing it does not place any of them on a new critical path. Actual PERT charts are more complex than this since they allow for different estimates of task durations. This makes the derivation of information from them more complicated and the method is usually automated. (One such method forms part of the SLIM automated costing system mentioned earlier.) The schedule depends on the resources available and in particular upon the human resources. The task-duration estimates depend on the staffing of each task and the way in which the members of staff are organized. This aspect of project management has been the subject of a good deal of study and discussion, some of which is summarized in the next section.

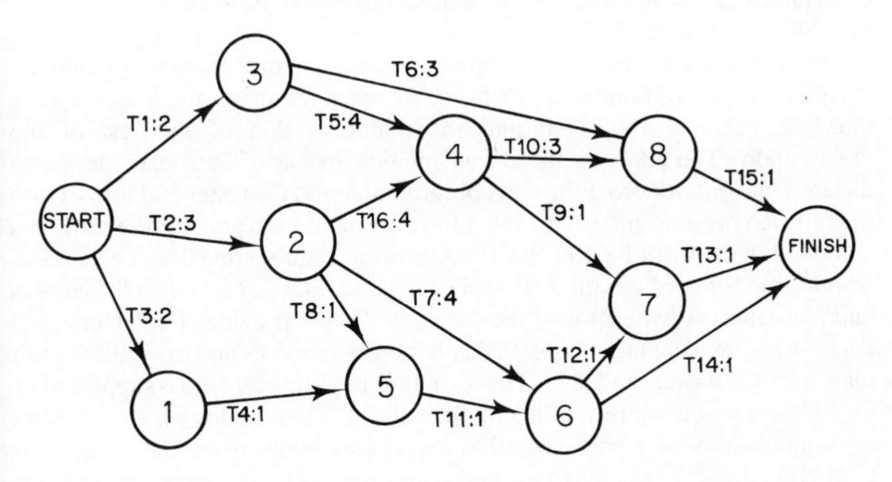

Figure 6.3 Scheduling graph

6.4 ORGANIZATION AND STAFFING

There is a great deal of practical experience to suggest that the duration of a project is not simply inversely proportional to the number of staff working on it; thus a project duration cannot be halved by simply doubling the number of staff assigned to it. The basic reason for this is that the number of communication paths between N individuals increases roughly as the square of N rather than in direct proportion to N and each new path increases the non-productive work of co-ordination and communication. The apparently obvious remedy for schedule slippage, adding more staff, is generally accepted as being counter-productive (in accordance with Brooks' Law (Brooks 1975): 'Adding manpower to a late software project makes it later.') both because of the increased number of communication paths and because the existing staff have to spend time familiarizing the newcomers with the work in hand. The only sensible response to slippage is to reschedule, which makes it all the more important to schedule realistically in the first place.

Current practice in development staff organisation has been strongly influenced by the *chief programmer team* idea of Mills which is described by Brooks (1975) and Baker (1972). In Brooks' version the team has seven technical members, two secretaries and an administrator and is designed to strike an optimum balance between the effort advantages and communication disadvantages of multiple staffing. The chief programmer who heads the team is responsible for all the technical operations of software development and should be a senior software engineer (designer/analyst/programmer) of high ability and with great experience in the application domain. The *co-pilot* or backup-programmer works closely with the chief programmer, represents the team to him or her and should be able and experienced enough to take on the chief-programmer role if necessary. The *administrator* is responsible for resource provision and management, ensuring that money, personnel, machines and accommodation are available when required, and also acts as an interface between the team and the administration of the rest of the organization. The *editor* is the documentation manager who takes draft and dictated information from the chief programmer and the tester and turns it into the finished product and ensures that the documentation plan for the project is complied with. Both he and the administrator need secretaries. The *clerk* is responsible for configuration control (discussed later); the *toolsmith* acquires and constructs software tools; the *language lawyer* provides implementation expertise in the language being used and the *tester* devises and executes the test plan and its test cases and data. The team thus has one boss who is supported by an assistant and a number of highly specialized subordinates which simplifies communications and preserves the conceptual integrity of the project by restricting design decisions to the two senior members. For larger projects the team can be expanded by including a number of assistant programmers to handle coding and unit testing but the preferred method is to use a number of teams with each one responsible for a more or less autonomous part of the project. In this case overall control can be exercised by a second-level project manager heading a group which includes all the chief programmers and is responsible for maintaining the conceptual integrity of the system. The number and nature of the teams is likely to vary over the life cycle with only the management group active in the early stages, a full complement of programmer teams active in the detailed design and implementation stages and specialized testing and installation teams active in the later stages.

6.5 PROGRAMMER AND GROUP PSYCHOLOGY

Programmers appear to obtain their main job satisfaction from the actual technical activities of software production and regard these activities as essentially private. They seem prone to the attitudes of the self-sufficient craftsman who lives by his skills rather than those of 'corporation man' willing to subsume individuality in the organization and to find job satisfaction in climbing the corporate ladder. This has ominous implications for adherence to specifications and standards and for the co-operation and communication required on large projects. The remedies generally proposed are tight managerial control with frequent monitoring of work products and the fostering of an 'egoless programming' culture (Weinberg 1971) in which loyalty to the group (rather than the larger organization) and pride in the quality of the group's output are important to each individual and in which the group can be self-monitoring to a large extent.

In democratically organized groups of peers the group leader role is likely to be conferred on the most technically proficient member whose skills are respected by the others. Imposition of a less proficient leader by management is likely to be resented and to reduce group productivity, hence the pre-eminence given to technical competence in the chief programmer team. The problem (not confined to software production) of promoting competent people out of productive work has been explicitly recognized in some organizations which ensure that the productive have at least equal status with the administrative in terms of promotion ladders, salaries and status symbols.

Group loyalty is not an unmixed blessing, since independence of mind is a necessary ingredient of problem solving and this may be eroded if individuals are disinclined to question majority ideas. There is also a tendency for groups to conspire to conceal slippages and other problems from project management in the (usually misguided) hope of fixing them later. These factors require 'rug-lifting' mechanisms (Brooks 1975) to be applied, as discussed in the next section.

6.6 CONTROLLING SOFTWARE PRODUCTION

The preceding sections have been concerned with resource estimation, costing, scheduling and staff organization which are essentially the concerns of the top level of management. The control of software production, by procedures specified in the project plan, is typically the responsibility of the second, technical control, layer of management. The objectives are to ensure the conceptual integrity and quality of the product, to ensure conformance to the project schedule and to perform configuration and documentation management as the product evolves through the life-cycle stages.

An essential component of the project schedule is the sequence of milestones which are used as checkpoints for recording progress through the development process. The first requirement for a milestone is that it correspond to some definite and unambiguous status of the system: 'structural design complete' and 'coding complete' are suitable milestones; 'coding 50% complete' is not. In general a milestone coincides with the completion of some part of the system documentation and this is presented, along with a formal progress report, to the second-level project management. Status monitoring may be performed between milestones and those milestones which occur at the completion of major life-cycle stages may be used to baseline the system before any work starts on the following stage. All three levels of monitoring are performed by *reviews* of varying degrees of formality, the commonest kinds of which are the *walkthrough*, the *formal review* and the *inspection*. These terms can mean different things in different organizations, but the procedures described below are fairly typical.

A *walkthrough* is usually a relatively informal peer-group review of the work product of an individual member of a team. An individual's contribution to a life-cycle stage would typically be subjected to a walkthrough before being combined with the work of other members of the group. The objectives of a walkthrough are to detect errors, omissions, inconsistencies and deviations from group standards. The usual practice is to distribute the work product to be reviewed along with information about its place in the total group effort to the walkthrough participants a few days before the actual event. The participants are normally a *moderator*, who organizes and chairs the walkthrough, the author of the work, who presents it to the group, taking them through it and explaining how it achieves its objectives, a few reviewers whose function is fault detection, and a secretary to record events. The reviewers and moderator are generally chosen from within the team but if the team is a specialized one responsible for one particular stage of development only, members of teams responsible for adjacent stages may also participate. A greater degree of formality can be achieved by choosing an outsider as moderator. If faults are detected a *re-work* is necessary to correct them and the follow-up to check for correction may be a re-run of the walkthrough or just a check by the team leader or moderator. The egoless-programming attitude is important in allowing walkthroughs to be conducted without acrimony and resentment. Errors must be regarded as inevitable and not due to the incompetence of the author. The product is treated as group property and no response by the author to reviewers' suggestions of errors is allowed: the suggestion is recorded by the secretary and the walkthrough continues. (Some organizations, however, prefer an author-led discussion to this form of walkthrough). Walkthroughs are typically conducted before the formal reviews which occur at the ends of the major life-cycle stages.

Formal reviews are similar in nature to walkthroughs but typically involve the work product of an entire team for a complete life-cycle stage, require much more preparation on the part of moderator and reviewers (who may be required to submit a written assessment of the product in advance of the review) and require a fairly formal presentation with slides, display charts, etc. As with walkthroughs a non-recriminatory atmosphere is essential and no attempt should be made to solve problems during the review. The number of participants is usually considerably greater than for a walkthrough, the actual composition being dependent on the particular review but likely to include top-level management representatives and representatives from all other teams involved in the project.

Walkthroughs and reviews are an integral part of the software-development process, reviews constituting the commonest method for validating requirements and design specifications for instance, whereas inspections are usually employed as quality-assurance tools (Ackerman *et al.* 1984). *Quality assurance* (QA) is usually a top-level management function exercised by an independent specialist group with organization-wide responsibilities. The objectives of QA are to maintain product standards by preventing software and documentation defects as far as possible and detecting and removing those which are not prevented. Prevention involves the establishment and monitoring of procedures for software development—an activity which requires the collection and analysis of quantitative data about the development process.

The major sources of such data are *inspections*, which are group reviews similar to walkthroughs except for the production of a formal quantitative report on resources expended and amount and quality of product generated. An inspection consists of a reading of the work product (by someone other than the author) to a group consisting of a moderator appointed by QA, the author and a small number of the author's peers who act as inspectors. The moderator and the inspectors will normally have had training by the QA group for their roles. Defects found in the work are classified according to a scheme specific to the kind of product being inspected. Preparation for the inspection is required of both moderator and inspectors and the work must satisfy entry criteria before the inspection can take place. Some organizations use *previews* in which the author provides information about the context of the work and about any special techniques which have been used in its construction: alternatively this information is provided in documentary form along with the piece of work to be inspected. The possible outcomes of an inspection are that the work meets the exit criteria specified for it and is therefore certified and released to configuration control, or that a re-work is required, or, if the work is seriously defective, that a re-inspection is required. The follow-up in the latter two cases is the responsibility of the moderator.

The defect classification can include defects in performance of object code, in data, in module interfaces, in module functionality, in documentation and in conformance to guidelines (e.g. a requirement that every module in a structural design specification should have a one-to-one correspondence to an item in the functional requirements specification).

The data acquired from an inspection is used both locally within that particular project and also by the QA group which combines it with data from other inspections to obtain an overall estimate of the efficacy of the software development and monitoring procedures in general use by the organization. Quantitative norms can be established, such as errors per 1000 lines of code, so that departures from the norm can be identified and analysed for cause. QA data can exert a considerable influence on development practices if, for example, increased effort in design reviews at the expense of code reviews is found to improve productivity or if the use of a structured design language is found to significantly reduce the frequency of defects in procedural design. Within a project information can be fed forward to later stages: the test plan may be extended, for instance, if a significant number of logical defects is found in a code inspection.

QA activities can be extended to cover every aspect of the development process with QA personnel monitoring project walkthroughs and reviews and providing certificates for all deliverables.

A major problem in all software development projects is keeping track of the large number of individual pieces of work produced as the system evolves through the development stages. Another is ensuring that the collection of individual items which should constitute the system configuration at each baseline is correct and preserved from corruption. The process is made more difficult by the inevitable changes made to system components already produced, and possibly validated or certified, in the light of later developments. It is all too easy, especially if the development is being done on an interactive time-sharing system, to have different developers working with different versions of what should be common items or situations where the wrong version of a system component is retained in the configuration. Further complications occur when a number of different versions of the system intended for different environments are being developed in parallel or when alternative versions are being retained until a decision is made as to which one to use. Management procedures to deal with these problems constitute what is usually referred to as configuration management, which includes specific provision for change control. The basic requirements are a set of closely defined baselines, recording of system status relative to the baselines as a result of reviews and inspections and a *program-support library* (PSL) in which the official (i.e. required and validated/certified) versions of documents and coded modules are stored. Developers are allowed read-only access to the PSL, write access being strictly limited to project management. PSLs originated in *version-control* systems designed for the management of interdependent code modules, but this facility must be enhanced with documentation management and reporting facilities for configuration management purposes. PSLs can be used to enforce documentation standards and to ensure that all personnel are notified if a change is made to their contents. In a single chief programmer team, the clerk is responsible for the PSL, which in that case could just be a controlled-access file system, but large projects require extensive automation of PSL functions. In large projects change control is imposed by project management, possibly via a *change-control board* (CCB). All proposals for changes to PSL components must be formally submitted to the CCB for approval, and for implementation if approved. The board may hold formal meetings of developers to discuss and decide upon proposed changes.

Fundamentals of Information Technology
Edited by G. G. Wilkinson and A. R. Winterflood

Chapter 7

Formal Methods in Software Engineering

7.1 THE NEED FOR FORMAL METHODS

The major motivation for the development of the techniques discussed in this chapter is the prospect of being able to prove, using the established methods of mathematics and other formal reasoning systems, that a software system is a correct implementation of the requirements specification that gave rise to it.

As yet these techniques have had little effect on the industrial production of software, but large producers are showing a definite, if cautious, interest and a significant amount of research in the area has been done under their auspices. At present the amount of skilled effort required makes formal methods uneconomic, in general, but there is a significant body of opinion to the effect that the demands now being made on software in terms of extreme complexity and very high reliability will only be satisfied when they have been developed to the point where the routine use of such methods is feasible.

7.2 MATHEMATICS AND LOGIC IN SOFTWARE ENGINEERING

This section introduces some of the concepts, terminology and notation of those parts of symbolic logic and mathematics which form the basis of the formal methods of software engineering discussed in the following section. It is not possible here to do more than try to give an intuitive appreciation of the subject matter, but it is hoped that this will be sufficient to make the rest of the chapter comprehensible.

7.2.1 Logic

Logic is the study of valid reasoning. It is concerned with the form and internal consistency of arguments rather than with their subject matter. For example, if the statements

If it is cold then it is snowing.
It is not cold.

are assumed to be true, are we entitled to infer from them the truth of the statement:

It is not snowing.

The logical structure of this argument can be separated from its meteorological references by using symbols to represent each simple declarative statement or 'proposition' e.g.

let P = 'it is cold'
let Q = 'it is snowing'.

Then the argument can be stated in the form

(a) if P then Q
(b) not P
(c) not Q

A proposition is essentially a statement to which one of the two *truth values*, TRUE (or T) and FALSE (or F), can be meaningfully attached. It makes sense to say '*it is true that* it is cold' but not to say '*it is true that* is it cold?' nor to say '*it is false that* cool it!' so that questions and commands are not propositions. There are many natural-language statements whose status as propositions is debatable but this is not important in software engineering, where we are more concerned with statements like $a > b$ or $x = y$, whose propositional status is not in doubt.

As the example shows, simple or *atomic* (cannot be further decomposed) propositions can be connected to form compound propositions (or *logical expressions* or *well-formed formulas* (wffs)) by constructions like 'if ... then ...' and 'not ...'. There are five of these, called logical connectives, which are conveniently represented by the symbols shown in Figure 7.1.

P and Q	$P \wedge Q$	the CONJUNCTION of P and Q
P or Q	$P \vee Q$	the DISJUNCTION of P and Q
not P	$\sim P$	the NEGATION of P
if P then Q or P implies Q	$P \Rightarrow Q$	an IMPLICATION in which P is the ANTECEDENT and Q is the CONSEQUENT
if and only if P then Q or P is equivalent to Q	$P \Longleftrightarrow Q$	an EQUIVALENCE between P and Q

Figure 7.1 The logical connectives

Using these connectives the example can be represented by

(a) $P \Rightarrow Q$

(b) $\sim P$
(c) $\sim Q$

The precedence of the connectives is

$\sim$ (highest) $\vee$ $\wedge$ $\Rightarrow$ $\Leftrightarrow$ (lowest).

It can be overridden by parentheses (as in mathematical expressions) and these are often used to improve the readability of expressions even when their use is not strictly necessary.

P	Q	$P \wedge Q$	$P \vee Q$	$\sim P$	$P \Rightarrow Q$	$P \Leftrightarrow Q$
T	T	T	T	F	T	T
T	F	F	T	F	F	F
F	T	F	T	T	T	F
F	F	F	F	T	T	T

Figure 7.2 Truth table showing the properties of the logical connectives

The truth values of compound propositions depend on the truth values assigned to their constituent atomic propositions and on the logical properties of their connectives as shown in Figure 7.2, which defines those properties. Tables of this kind, which show the truth values of expressions for all possible interpretations (i.e. all possible assignments of truth values to their constituents) are called *truth tables* for those expressions. The truth table shows that $P \wedge Q$ is true only when both P and Q are true, that $P \vee Q$ is false only when both P and Q are false, and that negation converts true to false and false to true. An implication is false only when its antecedent is true but its consequent is false.

A truth table can be constructed for any logical expression by evaluating the expression for all interpretations using the tables of Figure 7.2.

For example, the value of the expression

$$P \wedge (P \Rightarrow Q)$$

under the interpretation $P = T$, $Q = F$ is obtained by evaluating

$$T \wedge (T \Rightarrow F).$$

Use of the truth table for implication gives

$$T \wedge F$$

and use of that for conjunction gives

$$F.$$

The complete truth table for this expression, and for several others, is shown in Figure 7.3. Expressions which are true under all interpretations, such as $P \vee$

P	Q	$(\sim P) \vee Q$	$P \vee (\sim P)$	$P \wedge (\sim P)$	$P \wedge (P \Rightarrow Q)$
T	T	T	T	F	T
T	F	F	T	F	F
F	T	T	T	F	F
F	F	T	T	F	F

Figure 7.3 Truth tables for some logical expressions

$\sim P$, are called *tautologies* or *valid expressions*. Those which are false under all interpretations, such as $P \wedge \sim P$, are called *contradictions* or *inconsistent expressions*. Expressions which are not consistent are said to be *inconsistent* and those which are not valid are said to be *invalid*. Thus an invalid expression is consistent if there is at least one interpretation under which it is true. Expressions which are neither valid nor inconsistent are said to be *contingent*.

Comparison of the truth table for $\sim P \vee Q$ with that of $P \Rightarrow Q$ in Figure 7.2 shows that these two contingent expressions have identical truth values under any interpretation. Such pairs of expressions are said to be *logically equivalent*, a relationship expressed by writing

$$(P \Rightarrow Q) = (\sim P \vee Q).$$

A set of logical equivalences (or *laws*) is shown in Figure 7.4. All of them can be verified by the construction of the appropriate truth tables. Logical equival-

1 $P \wedge Q = Q \wedge P$ } commutative laws
2 $P \vee Q = Q \vee P$ }
3 $(P \wedge Q) \wedge R = P \wedge (Q \wedge R)$ } associative laws
4 $(P \vee Q) \vee R = P \vee (Q \vee R)$ }
5 $P \vee (Q \wedge R) = (P \vee Q) \wedge (P \vee R)$ } distributive laws
6 $P \wedge (Q \vee R) = (P \wedge Q) \vee (P \wedge R)$ }
7 $P \wedge \text{TRUE} = P$
8 $P \vee \text{TRUE} = \text{TRUE}$
9 $P \wedge \text{FALSE} = \text{FALSE}$
10 $P \vee \text{FALSE} = P$
11 $\sim P \vee P = \text{TRUE}$
12 $\sim P \wedge P = \text{FALSE}$
13 $\sim(\sim P) = P$
14 $\sim(P \vee Q) = \sim P \wedge \sim Q$ } de Morgan's laws
15 $\sim(P \wedge Q) = \sim P \vee \sim Q$ }
16 $P \Leftrightarrow Q = (P \Rightarrow Q) \wedge (Q \Rightarrow P)$
17 $P \Rightarrow Q = (\sim P)\ Q$

Figure 7.4 Logical equivalences

ences can be used to transform logical expressions into equivalent ones by substituting sub-expressions with their logical equivalents.

For example, the expression

$$(P \wedge (P \Rightarrow Q)) \Rightarrow Q$$

can be shown to be valid by the series of transformations

$\sim(P \wedge (P \Rightarrow Q)) \vee Q$	(by 17)
$\sim(P \wedge (\sim P \vee Q)) \vee Q$	(by 17)
$\sim((P \wedge \sim P) \vee (P \wedge Q)) \vee Q$	(by 6)
$\sim(\text{FALSE} \vee (P \wedge Q)) \vee Q$	(by 12)
$\sim(P \wedge Q) \vee Q$	(by 10)
$\sim P \vee (\sim Q \vee Q)$	(by 15 and 4)
$\sim P \vee \text{TRUE}$	(by 11)
TRUE	(by 8)

The problem of deciding whether some proposition Q (the *conclusion*) follows logically from (or is a *logical consequence* of) a given set of propositions $P_1, P_2, \ldots, P_n$ (the *premises*) can be stated as the problem of determining whether the expression

$$(P_1 \wedge P_2 \wedge P_3 \cdots \wedge P_n) \Rightarrow Q$$

is valid (i.e. is a *theorem*) or equivalently, whether the expression

$P_1 \wedge P_2 \wedge \cdots \wedge P_n \wedge \sim Q$ is inconsistent.

For example, to decide whether, given $P \Rightarrow Q$ and $\sim P$, we can infer $\sim Q$, we evaluate the expression

$((P \Rightarrow Q) \wedge \sim P) \Rightarrow \sim Q$	
$= \sim((\sim P \vee Q) \wedge \sim P) \vee \sim Q$	(by 17)
$= \sim(\sim P \vee Q) \vee P \vee \sim Q$	(by 15 and 4)
$= (P \wedge \sim Q) \vee P \vee \sim Q$	(by 14)

which is consistent but invalid, so that we cannot conclude from the premises

If it is cold then it is snowing
It is not cold

that

It is not snowing.

Having shown already that $(P \wedge (P \Rightarrow Q)) \Rightarrow Q$ is valid we can, however, deduce from

If it is cold then it is snowing.
It is cold

that

It is snowing

using the same assignments to P and Q. Such an expression is called a *rule of inference* since once its validity has been established it can be used immediately to infer Q from P and $P \Rightarrow Q$.

The form of logic discussed so far is called the propositional calculus. It is adequate for reasoning about propositions with no internal structure but to reason about statements like

(a) **All** politicians are liars.
(b) **Some** students are clever.
(c) **Everyone** has a mother.

it must be extended to give a form of logic known as the first-order predicate calculus. In this formalism statement (a) is represented by

$$(\forall x)\, P(x) \Rightarrow L(x) \qquad (7.1)$$

where P and L are predicate symbols such that

$P(x)$ represents 'x is a politician'
$L(x)$ represents 'x is a liar'.

Predicates have truth values dependent upon the values assigned to their argument variables, e.g.

$P(\text{Machiavelli}) = T$
$L(\text{Washington}) = F$ (say)

The symbol $\forall$ is called the *universal quantifier*. $\forall x$ placed to the left of an expression means that the expression refers to all possible values of the variable x (in some universe of discourse) and is read as 'for all x'. Thus the predicate calculus expression (7.1) above is read as

'for all x, if x is a politician then x is a liar'.

Statement (b) is represented by

$$(\exists x)\, S(x) \wedge C(x) \qquad (7.2)$$

where S and C are predicates such that

$S(x)$ represents 'x is a student'
$C(x)$ represents 'x is clever'.

The symbol $\exists$ is called the *existential quantifier*. $\exists x$ placed to the left of an expression asserts that there exists an x (i.e. at least one x) such that the expression is true. Thus statement (7.2) is read as

'there exists an x such that x is a student and x is clever.'

Statement (c) can be written as

$$(\forall y)\ (\exists x) M(x, y)$$

where $M(x, y)$ represents 'x is the mother of y' and is read as 'for all y there exists an x such that x is the mother of y'.

Quantifiers are applied left to right, so the expression

$$(\exists x)\ (\forall y) M(x, y)$$

means something quite different, i.e. that every y has the same mother.

Functions can be used in predicate calculus expressions, for example if *mother*(x) returns the constant representing the mother of its argument we could have

$$(\forall x) F(mother(x))$$

where $F(y)$ represents 'y is female'.

First-order logic consists of propositional logic with the addition of constants, variables, functions, predicates and quantifiers. Quantifiers can only be applied to variables and predicates only to functions, variables and constants. Higher-order logics allow the quantification of functions and predicates and the introduction of predicates of predicates.

An atomic proposition in first-order logic is a predicate. Expressions are constructed from the same five logical connectives as in the propositional calculus and the logical equivalences of Figure 7.4 still hold. Additional equivalences involving quantifiers are shown in Figure 7.5, where $P[x]$ denotes an expression containing the variable x.

Unlike the propositional calculus there is in general an infinite number of interpretations for a predicate-calculus expression, since to establish an interpretation it is necessary to provide 'values' for predicate, function and

$$(\forall x) P[x] \lor Q = (\forall x)\ (P[x] \lor Q)$$
$$(\exists x) P[x] \land Q = (\exists x)\ (P[x] \land Q)$$
$$(\forall x) P[x] \land Q = (\forall x)\ (P[x] \land Q)$$
$$(\exists x) P[x] \lor Q = (\exists x)\ (P[x] \lor Q)$$
$$\sim(\forall(x) P[x]) = (\exists x) \sim P[x]$$
$$\sim(\exists(x) P[x]) = (\forall x) \sim P[x]$$
$$(\forall x)\ (P[x] \land Q[x]) = (\forall x) P[x] \lor (\forall x) Q[x]$$
$$(\exists x)\ (P[x] \lor Q[x]) = (\exists x) P[x] \lor (\exists x) Q[x]$$
$$\left.\begin{aligned}(\forall x) P[x] &= (\forall y) P[y]\\ (\exists x) P[x] &= (\exists y) P[y]\end{aligned}\right\}\ \text{renaming of variables bound by quantifiers}$$
$$(\forall x) P[x] \lor (\forall x) Q[x] = (\forall x)\ (\forall y)\ (P[x] \lor Q[y])$$
$$(\exists x) P[x] \land (\exists x) Q[x] = (\exists x)\ (\exists y)\ (P[x] \land Q[y])$$

Figure 7.5 Logical equivalences in the predicate calculus

constant symbols and to provide a domain of values for variables. It is thus not possible to investigate the validity of an expression by evaluating it under all interpretations.

Once an interpretation has been specified, validity, inconsistency and logical consequence can be defined as in the propositional calculus. Thus the validity of the expression

$$((\forall x)\ (MAN(x) \Rightarrow MORTAL(x)) \wedge MAN(Socrates)) \Rightarrow MORTAL(Socrates)$$

demonstrates that

Socrates is mortal

is a logical consequence of

All men are mortal

and

Socrates is a man

Proof of the validity follows from the observation that if $MAN(x) \Rightarrow MORTAL(x)$ is true for all x (in some interpretation) it is true for x = Socrates (in that interpretation). Thus we can write

$$((MAN(Socrates) \Rightarrow MORTAL(Socrates)) \wedge MAN(Socrates)) \Rightarrow MORTAL(Socrates)$$

which can be shown to be logically equivalent to *TRUE* by using the equivalences of Figure 7.4.

First-order logic is undecidable, i.e. there is no general procedure for deciding whether or not a quantified expression is valid, but the validity of every valid expression is verifiable, i.e. first-order logic is complete. Second-order logic, which is necessary to provide a logical description of arithmetic, is not complete; it has valid expressions which are not verifiable within it.

Proving first-order theorems automatically is an important topic which is beyond the scope of this introduction. A good account of symbolic logic from a computing viewpoint, including automatic theorem proving, can be found in Chang and Lee (1973).

7.2.2 Sets

A set is a collection of distinguishable objects which are called its *elements*. Sets are denoted by upper-case letters and can be defined either by listing all their delements explicitly e.g.

$$A = \{red, blue, green\}$$

or by giving a defining property for inclusion, e.g.

$$B = \{x: even(x) \wedge integer(x)\}$$

which uses predicates to state that B is the set of all even integers.

As these examples show, sets may have finite or infinite cardinality (number of elements). Membership of a set is denoted by the symbol $\in$, e.g.

$4 \in B$ states that '4 is a member of B'
$yellow \notin A$ states that '*yellow* is not a member of A'

Two sets are equal only if they have exactly the same elements:

$$(A = B) \Rightarrow (x \in A \Leftrightarrow x \in B).$$

There is no ordering of elements and no repetition of elements in a set, e.g.

$$\{a, b, b, a, c, a\} = \{a, b, c\} = \{c, b, a\} = \ldots$$

The empty set is denoted by {} or $\emptyset$ and has the same status as any other set e.g.

$$\{x: even(x) \wedge odd(x)\} = \{\} = \emptyset$$

A set A is a subset of a set B if $x \in A \Rightarrow x \in B$ and the relationship is denoted by

$$A \subseteq B.$$

A is a proper subset of B, denoted by

$$A \subset B$$

if $A \subseteq B \wedge A \neq B$.

In particular

$\{\} \subseteq S$ for any set S
$\{\} \subset S$ for any non-empty set S.

Sets may contain sets as elements, e.g.

$$A = \{1, 4, \{3, 5\}, 9\}$$

then

$$\{3, 5\} \in A$$

and

$$\{\{3, 5\}\} \subset A.$$

For most purposes it is convenient to define a universe of discourse U such that all sets considered are subsets of U. The universe U may be specified, e.g.

as the set of all integers, or undefined, in which case it serves to exclude paradoxes associated with the 'the set of all sets', e.g. the set of all sets which are not members of themselves. A specification like

$$A = \{x: P(x)\}$$

is then read as 'the set of all $x \in U$ such that $P(x)$'.

A number of operations which can be performed on sets are defined in Figure 7.6 along with *laws* which can be derived from the definitions.

UNION:	$A \cup B = \{x: x \in A \vee x \in B\}$
INTERSECTION:	$A \cap B = \{x: x \in A \wedge x \in B\}$
DIFFERENCE:	$A - B = \{x: x \in A \wedge x \notin B\}$
COMPLEMENT:	$A' = U - A$

$$\left.\begin{array}{l} A \cup B = B \cup A \\ A \cap B = B \cap A \end{array}\right\} \text{commutative laws}$$

$$\left.\begin{array}{l} (A \cup B) \cup C = A \cup (B \cup C) \\ (A \cap B) \cap C = A \cap (B \cap C) \end{array}\right\} \text{associative laws}$$

$$\left.\begin{array}{l} A \cup (B \cap C) = (A \cup B) \cap (A \cup C) \\ A \cap (B \cup C) = (A \cap B) \cup (A \cap C) \end{array}\right\} \text{distributive laws}$$

$$\left.\begin{array}{l} (A \cap B)' = A' \cup B' \\ (A \cup B)' = A' \cap B' \end{array}\right\} \text{de Morgan's laws}$$

Figure 7.6 Set operations

The Cartesian product of n sets $S_1, \ldots, S_n$ is defined to be the set of all possible sequences

$$(s_1 \in S_1, s_2 \in S_2, \ldots, s_n \in S_n)$$

which are called n-tuples. Unlike sets, sequences are ordered, e.g.

$$(a, b, c) \neq (b, c, a).$$

The Cartesian product is denoted by

$$S_1 \times S_2 \times \cdots \times S_n.$$

Cartesian products can be constructed from a single set S, in which case

$S \times S$ is denoted by S^2
$S \times S \times S$ is denoted by S^3, etc.

7.2.3 Relations and Functions

A binary relation **R** on sets A and B is a subset of the Cartesian product $A \times B$.

The two objects $a \in A$ and $b \in B$ are related by **R** if and only if the ordered pair $(a, b) \in \mathbf{R}$. Thus **R** associates an element in B with an element in A. The set A is called the domain of the relation and B its co-domain. In $(a, b) \in \mathbf{R}$ b is said to be the image of a. The set of all images is called the **range** of the relation and is a subset of its co-domain. If $A = B$ a subset of $A \times A$ is said to define a (binary) relation on A.

Relations as so far described have some use in defining data structures but relations which satisfy certain additional properties are more generally useful. These are more conveniently discussed using alternative notations:

$$a\rho b$$

or $$b \in \rho(a)$$

instead of $(a, b) \in \mathbf{R}$. (The Greek letter is used instead of the upper-case Roman letter when set aspects of relations are not being emphasized).

The most important properties a relation ρ on a set A may have are:

1. reflexive $(\forall x \in A) x\rho x$, irreflexive $(\forall x \in A) \sim(x\rho x)$
2. symmetric $x\rho y \Rightarrow y\rho x$, asymmetric $x\rho y \Rightarrow \sim(y\rho x)$
3. antisymmetric $(x\rho y \wedge y\rho x) \Rightarrow x{=}y)$
4. transitive $(x\rho y \wedge y\rho z) \Rightarrow x\rho z$

For example the relation $\leqslant$ on the natural numbers $N = \{1, 2, 3, \ldots\}$ is

reflexive $(\forall x \in N)\ (x \leqslant x)$
antisymmetric $(x \leqslant y \wedge y \leqslant x) \Rightarrow (x{=}y)$
transitive $(x \leqslant y \wedge y \leqslant z) \Rightarrow (x \leqslant z)$

whereas the relation $<$ on N is transitive, irreflexive and asymmetric.

A partially ordered set is defined to be a (non-empty) set with a relation defined on it which has the same properties as $<$ on N. (Some authors use $\leqslant$ on N as the definition; the important property which both have is transitivity.) A well-ordered set is a partially ordered set which has no infinitely decreasing sequence, where sequences are defined using the order relation, so that every non-empty subset of it has a 'least' element.

n-place relations on sets $S_1, \ldots, S_n$ are defined analogously to two-place (binary) relations as subsets of the Cartesian product

$$S_1 \times S_2 \times \cdots \times S_n$$

Such relations are important in database theory where the n-tuples belonging to the relations constitute records and their elements constitute fields.

A relation ρ is called a function from set A to set B if for each $x \in A$ there is at most one $y \in B$ such that $x\rho y$. More formally ρ is a function if

$$(a\rho b \wedge a\rho c) \Rightarrow (b = c).$$

Functions are conventionally denoted by

$y = \rho(x)$ rather than $x \rho y$

and in mathematics lower case Roman letters or names are used, e.g.

$$y = f(x)$$
$$y = \sin(x).$$

The sets involved are specified using the notation

$$f: A \rightarrow B$$

and if $x \in A$ and $y = f(x)$ this is denoted by

$$f: x \mapsto y.$$

A function $f: A \rightarrow B$ is called a total function if its domain is the whole of A. If there are elements of A for which it is undefined it is called a partial function. (Some authors use the term *mapping* as synonymous with function, others as synonymous with total function. Users of both conventions refer to $f: x \mapsto y$ as a *mapping of x to y*. Others again reserve the term function for cases where the relation is specifiable by some general rule, e.g.

$$\text{square}: N \rightarrow N$$
$$\text{square}: x \mapsto x*x$$

and the term mapping for cases where the relation is specified by listing pairs of y and x in $y = f(x)$ explicitly, e.g.

$$A = \{\text{sue, mary, fay}\}$$
$$B = \{\text{logician, mathematician}\}$$
$$f: A \rightarrow B$$
$$f = \{(\text{sue, logician}), (\text{mary, mathematician}), (\text{fay, logician})\}$$

A function is said to be *onto* if its range and co-domain are equal, *one-to-one* if every element of the range comes from a unique element of the domain and *bijective* if it has both properties.

Thus for $x \in \text{Int}$, where $\text{Int} = \{x: \text{integer}(x)\}$

$f(x) = x*x$ is neither onto nor one-to-one
$f(x) = 2x$ is one-to-one but not onto
$f(x) = -x$ is bijective

7.2.4 Mathematical Induction

Induction is a basic proof technique which is used to prove statements about the natural numbers N or non-negative integers and can be generalized to prove statements about any well-ordered set.

If $S(n)$ is some statement about $n \in N$ and we can prove that $S(1)$ is true and can prove that if $S(n)$ is true then $S(n + 1)$ is true, we can obviously construct a proof that $S(n')$ is true for any $n' \in N$.

An inductive proof thus has the form

$$S(1) \triangle (n \geqslant 1 \triangle S(n) \Rightarrow S(n + 1)) \Rightarrow (\forall n \in N)S(n)$$

The proof that $S(1)$ is true is called the *basis* of the induction and the assumption that $S(n)$ is true is called the inductive hypothesis.

As a simple example we can prove that the sum of the first n' natural numbers is given by $n'(n' + 1)/2$.

The basis is $S(1) = 1(1 + 1)/2 = 1$, which is obviously true.

The induction hypothesis is that $S(n) = n(n + 1)/2$.

If this is true, then $S(n + 1) = n(n + 1)/2 + (n + 1)$; i.e. we can just add on the next number, which is $n + 1$.

Now this expression can be simplified as follows:

$$\begin{aligned} n(n + 1)/2 + (n + 1) &= (n*n + 3n + 2)/2 \\ &= (n + 1)(n + 2)/2 \\ &= (n + 1)((n + 1) + 1)/2. \end{aligned}$$

But this expression is obtained by substituting

$$n' = (n + 1) \text{ into } S(n') = n'(n' + 1)/2.$$

Thus if $S(n)$ is true, so is $S(n + 1)$, and since $S(1)$ is true the proof is complete.

There is a very large number of books available which provide introductory accounts of the areas of mathematics that have been touched on here. Cooke and Bez (1984) may be recommended as assuming little prior knowledge, yet providing a thorough coverage up to a fairly advanced standard with a strong computing orientation.

7.3 FORMAL METHODS OF SPECIFICATION, DESIGN AND VALIDATION

A specification of software-system requirements should be restricted to the behaviour the system is required to show and not specify how this behaviour is to be achieved. This means that specifications should be abstract and not presented in terms of particular entities and operations of some particular (virtual) machine. The basic reason for this restriction is that the purpose of a specification is to communicate requirements to customers, designers and implementors and must therefore be concise and understandable, providing only essential information unobscured by inessential detail. This allows designers and implementors freedom in devising an optimum realization of the specifications.

Demonstration that a realization does in fact satisfy the specification should be an essential part of the development process and to be convincing this demonstration should utilize established methods of reasoning such as those of formal logic and mathematics. This requires specifications to be written in a formal language, i.e. one whose syntax and semantics are fully mathematically defined, and it also requires that the syntax and semantics of the implementation be fully and formally defined. If both languages are defined in terms of the first-order predicate calculus, for example, a complete and consistent set of inference rules allows proof that a correct program is logically equivalent to its specifications. Unfortunately, first-order logic is too weak to provide a semantics for imperative programming languages and too low level to be at all convenient for writing specifications of any complexity.

7.3.1 Formal Definition of Programming-language Semantics

The problem of providing formal semantics for programming languages is a long-standing one which, despite a considerable and continuing research effort, is by no means comprehensively solved. Since the problem is closely related to that of specifying program behaviour, a brief indication of the three main approaches is given below. For a fuller account the reader is referred to McGettrick, 1980.

The earliest approach has come to be known as *operational* (or *computational*) *semantics*, since it defines the meaning of statements in the programming language in terms of operations of (i.e. changes in the state of) a hypothetical machine. It originates in the work of McCarthy who in the late 1950s invented the conditional expression

IF(⟨boolean_expression⟩ ⟨expression1⟩, ⟨expression2⟩)

whose value is ⟨expression1⟩ if ⟨boolean_expression⟩ evaluates to *TRUE* and ⟨expression2⟩ otherwise, and used it in conjunction with some simple recursive functions to develop a theory of computation based on a universal function which constitutes an interpretive abstract machine capable of evaluating any other function. The language in which the universal function was written was the first version of what turned out to be the programming language LISP. The function interprets LISP functions and thus defines the semantics of LISP.

McCarthy made use of a formalized calculus of functions called the lambda calculus, which was later extended with constructs to describe the state of an abstract machine with a store and other computer-like attributes. These ideas formed part of the basis for the work of IBM's Vienna Laboratory on a formalization of the semantics of the imperative programming language PL/I in terms of the intepretation of PL/I programs by a hypothetical computer. The methods used effectively constitute a specification language called the *Vienna definition language* (VDL) which can be used to provide formal definitions of other imperative languages.

A second approach, associated with the names of Strachey and Scott and developed at Oxford, is to formalize the semantics of a programming language by associating a well-defined mathematical entity (such as a set or a relation or a function) with every basic entity and operation of the language. The mathematical object is said to be the denotation of the language component; hence the term *denotational* (or *mathematical*) *semantics*. A denotational semantics requires the definition of semantic functions (again making use of the lambda calculus) which map from the language constructs to their denotations. The development of the theoretical basis of this approach involved a good deal of fundamental mathematical research which has given it a somewhat forbidding reputation. Nonetheless it has been applied successfully to a number of languages and forms the basis of what is probably the best known and most successful formal software development methodology, the *Vienna development method* (VDM) (not to be confused with VDL, with which it has nothing in common except geography) which is discussed later.

Both operational and denotational semantics are based on models of programming-language constructs. The third approach, associated particularly with the names of Floyd and Hoare, defines the semantics of a programming language by a collection of axioms and rules of inference with the specific aim of providing proofs of assertions about programs using only the 'uninterpreted' program text, i.e. without reference to any underlying model of the language. This approach has been extensively used in program verification and forms the basis of most of the automatic *program verifiers*. We shall see a simple example of its use below.

7.3.2 Formal Specifications

The specification of programs requires specification of the transformation to be performed on its inputs to generate its outputs and consequently requires specification of the input and output data items themselves. The requirement of abstraction applies just as much to data specification as it does to procedural specification: we require only the essential characteristics to be represented, not the details of any particular implementation. A module specification is therefore that of a function whose domain and range consist of abstract data types, where an abstract data type consists of a set of values and a set of operations which manipulate those values. These operations are themselves program modules and conversely a program can very often be regarded as an abstract data type: the choice of viewpoint is dictated only by conceptual convenience.

Before discussing the languages which might be used to express these specifications it should be noted that although the prospect of being able to prove a program correct is an important motive for devising formal specifications it is by no means the only one. Liskov and Berzins (1979) give as advantages of formal specifications:

1. the possibility of proving alternative specifications to be equivalent;
2. the possibility of automatic detection of some forms of inconsistency and incompleteness;
3. the possibility of actually executing the specifications;
4. the absence of ambiguity and imprecision, which is important in an SRD to be used by designers and implementors.

The major objections to the use of formal specifications are that they are difficult and expensive to construct (and to debug) and that they can only be understood by people with some mathematical training. The usual defences to these objections are that informal specifications are easier to construct only because they leave a great deal unspecified and that designers and implementors ought to be mathematically trained (some real enthusiasts think that customers ought to be mathematically trained as well).

The languages which are used to write specifications range from those of more or less pure operational, denotational or axiomatic semantics through various mixtures of formal logics and discrete mathematics to high-level special-purpose specification languages of which a large number are currently under development. These specification languages generally provide support for structuring specifications in much the same way as high-level programming languages like Ada and Pascal provide support for structuring programs. They have a defined syntax and semantics but, ironically, in most cases the definitions are informal. A notable exception is the specification language CLEAR (Burstall and Goguen 1981) which has fully formalized algebraic semantics.

It is not possible in the limited space available here to do other than give an idea of some of the approaches to the specification of procedural and data abstractions by looking at some very simple examples starting with the specification of well-known functional abstraction, the factorial of a non-negative integer.

The commonest type of specification of a procedural abstraction is derived from axiomatic semantics and is called an input/output or pre-/post-condition specification. It consists of an input constraint (or pre-condition) and an output constraint (or post-condition) which is a predicate of the function arguments and its result. The meaning of the specification is that outputs are guaranteed to satisfy the output constraints if and only if the corresponding inputs satisfy the input constraint. (For functions with side-effects and procedures we must include all logical inputs and outputs.) There are various possible formats for this type of specification; the one used here is similar to that used in VDM, where the syntax of the function is given with its name on the first line and the symbol *r* is used to represent the function value.

```
FACT: INTEGER → INTEGER
pre-FACT(n):    n ≥ 0
post-FACT(n,r): r = n!

axioms:         0! = 1;        n! = n*(n−1)!
```

Figure 7.7 An input/output specification for factorial

Such a specification for a factorial module is shown in Figure 7.7 and makes use of an axiomatic definition of the (mathematical) function to provide the output constraint.

A second input/output specification for a function *gcd*(i, j) which evaluates to the largest integer which exactly divides both of its integer arguments (their greatest common divisor) is shown in Figure 7.8. This uses a previously specified function to provide the post-condition. Since *IS_DIVISOR* is a predicate, *post-GCD* can be defined as its result.

```
GCD: INTEGER, INTEGER → INTEGER
pre-GCD(x,y):        (x>0) ∧ (y>0)
post-GCD(x,y,r):is_divisor(r,x) ∧ is_divisor(r,y)
                 ∧ ∀ i ∈ INTEGER{is_divisor(i,x) ∧ is_divisor(i,y)
                            ⇒ is_divisor(i,r) }

IS_DIVISOR: INTEGER, INTEGER → BOOLEAN
pre-IS_DIVISOR(x,y):           (x>0) ∧ (y>0)
post-IS_DIVISOR(x,y):∃i ∈ INTEGER{y = x*i}
```

Figure 7.8 An input/output specification for GCD

The important thing to note about these specifications is that they do not define an implementation. (The axioms for factorial could be regarded as defining a recursive implementation, but that is not much help to a FORTRAN programmer.)

A second way of specifying procedural abstractions uses operational semantics. Operational specifications describe the transformation from input to output explicitly by giving an implementation in a language for a hypothetical machine. This differs from a real implementation only in that the hypothetical machine need not exist. Operational specifications for *FACT* and *GCD* are shown in Figures 7.9 and 7.10 respectively. They use the conditional function defined previously in a LISP-like functional language which permits recursion.

A great variety of methods has been used to specify data abstractions, most of which can be classified as using either an abstract model or an implicit definition in terms of relationships between operations. In the abstract model (or

```
FACT: INTEGER → INTEGER
FACT(n) = IF(n<0, ERROR('NEGARG),
                 IF(n=0, 1, MULT(n,FACT(n-1)))

where  MULT(x,y) returns x*y
       ERROR('⟨id⟩) writes ⟨id⟩ on the standard output
```

Figure 7.9 An operational specification for factorial

```
GCD: INTEGER, INTEGER → INTEGER
GCD(x,y) = IF( OR( LE(x,0), LE(y,0)), ERROR('NONPOSARG),
                 SEARCHFROM(x, y, MIN(x,y)))

SEARCHFROM: INTEGER, INTEGER, INTEGER → INTEGER
SEARCHFROM(x,y,z) = IF(AND( ZERO( MOD(x,z)), ZERO( MOD(y,z))), z,
                                       SEARCHFROM(x, y, z-1) )

where     LE(x,y)  returns    x ≤ y
        AND(a,b)  returns    a ∧ b
       ZERO(x)     returns    x = 0
        MOD(x,y)  returns    x mod y
         MIN(x,y)  returns if x ≤ y,x,y
```

Figure 7.10 An operational specification for GCD (Adapted from Liskov and Berzins (1979))

operational) approach an abstract data type is modelled in terms of an existing data type (e.g. list) or mathematical entity (e.g. set) or abstract machine language (e.g. VDL). Figure 7.11 shows a specification of the data type *STACK* (an Ada implementation of which was discussed in Chapter 5) adapted from a VDM specification discussed by Jones (1980). The example differs from the Ada version in that the *POP* operation has been split into *TOP*, which returns the element at the top of the stack without removing it, and a new *POP*, which changes the stack but does not return a value and in providing an explicit initializing operation which creates an empty stack. *STACK* is modelled using an abstract data type called a list, which is an ordered sequence of elements represented here by

$$\langle \text{elem1}, \text{elem2}, \text{elem3}, \ldots, \text{elemn}, \ldots \rangle$$

The empty list is represented by $\langle\rangle$.
Examples of applications of the *LIST* operations used in the specification of *STACK* are given in Figure 7.12 to assist understanding of both specifications. Figure 7.11 is essentially a recipe for the construction of a stack object. If we

STACK: X-list

CREATE: → STACK
pre-CREATE(): true
post-CREATE(s'): s' = ⟨⟩

PUSH: X STACK → STACK
pre-PUSH(n,s): true
post-PUSH(n,s,s'): s' = ⟨n⟩||s

POP: STACK → STACK
pre-POP(s): s ≠ ⟨⟩
post-POP(s,s'): s' = tail(s)

TOP: STACK → X
pre-TOP(s): s ≠ ⟨⟩
post-TOP(s',n): (n' = head(s)) ∧ (s = s')

IS_EMPTY: STACK → BOOLEAN
pre-IS_EMPTY: true
post-IS_EMPTY(s,s',b'): (s = s') ∧ (b' = (s' = ⟨⟩))

Figure 7.11 An operational specification of Stack

⟨list1⟩ = ⟨list2⟩ returns TRUE if both lists have the same elements in the same sequence

⟨x, y, z⟩||⟨a, b, c⟩ returns ⟨x, y, z, a, b, c⟩
⟨a, b, c⟩||⟨x, y, z⟩ returns ⟨a, b, c, x, y, z⟩
this operation is called concatenation and in general ⟨list1⟩||⟨list2⟩ is not equal to ⟨list2⟩||⟨list1⟩

head⟨x, y, z⟩ returns the element x

tail⟨x, y, z⟩ returns the list ⟨y, z⟩

unit(x) returns the list ⟨x⟩
this is a coercion of an element to a list

Figure 7.12 Some list operations

have an implementation of *LIST* we can immediately construct an implementation of *STACK* from it. The recipe is not prescriptive, however. Any implementation, such as one using the array type, can be used providing it can be shown to be equivalent to the specification using the list implementation. List is extremely useful for modelling data types and would be a good choice for a built-in data type in a programming language. It is, in fact, one of the two built-in types of LISP (a LISt Processing language), the other being a primitive unstructured element for making lists. This accounts for the ease with which complex data structures can be constructed and manipulated in that language. VDM, which has been used to specify and develop large systems, makes do essentially with sets, lists and mappings to model new data types.

In the most widely used implicit definition methods the data abstraction is defined by listing the operations which can be performed on values of the type and stating axioms which relate the operations. The most extensively developed approach is the algebraic one, where the axioms are equations. This has been subjected to an extensive theoretical analysis which provides a proof system allowing consistency between implementation and specification to be demonstrated. Algebraic specifications of *STACK* and *LIST* are shown in Figures 7.13 and 7.14. (The reader will find it interesting to compare Figures 7.12 and 7.14). They consist of interfaces (or *signatures*) which name the operations of the type and specify their syntax. They also give the types of their arguments and results and include a list of equations each of which specifies two expressions which have the same value in any valid implementation of the type. For example,

$$\text{POP(PUSH (S,I))} = \text{S}$$

states that

$$\text{POP(PUSH (PUSH (PUSH (CREATE, 3), 5), 4))} = \text{PUSH(PUSH (CREATE, 3), 5)}$$

or using the model of Figure 7.11

$$\text{POP}(\langle 4, 5, 3\rangle) = \langle 5, 3\rangle$$

The specifications of Figures 7.13 and 7.14 are deficient in that they do not define the meaning of expressions such as *POP*(*CREATE*) and *HEAD*(*EMPTY*). Two possible ways to deal with this are to define error values, such as *UNDERFLOW* of type *STACK* and *INTEGER_ERROR* of type *INTEGER*, which are returned by the above expressions or to apply pre-conditions so that *POP* is not applied to an empty stack and *HEAD* is not applied to an empty list. The theory underlying algebraic specifications has in fact been extended to provide a consistent mechanism for error handling, which is one of the great advantages of the algebraic approach, but consideration of this is well beyond the scope of this brief introduction. For a full treatment of the algebraic approach the reader is referred to Goguen *et al.* (1978).

The main drawback to algebraic specifications relative to abstract model specifications is that the algebraic ones are more difficult to construct. There are many pitfalls, even for the experts, and proof of completeness and

```
OPERATIONS
        CREATE:         STACK
        PUSH:           STACK INTEGER → STACK
        POP:            STACK → STACK
        TOP:            STACK → INTEGER
        IS_EMPTY:       STACK → BOOLEAN
EQUATIONS
        TOP( PUSH(S,I)) = I
        POP( PUSH(S,I)) = S
        IS_EMPTY(PUSH(S,I)) = FALSE
        IS_EMPTY(CREATE) = TRUE
END
```

Figure 7.13 An algebraic specification of Stack

```
OPERATIONS
        _||_:   : LIST LIST → LIST
        UNIT    : X → LIST
        HEAD    : LIST → X
        TAIL    : LIST → LIST
        EMPTY:  LIST
EQUATIONS
        (L||M)||N = L||(M||N)
        EMPTY||L = L
        L||EMPTY = L
        HEAD(UNIT(I)||L) = I
          TAIL(UNIT(I)||L) = L
END
```

Figure 7.14 An algebraic specification of list

consistency of the axiom sets is far from trivial. On the other hand algebraic specifications have less of an implementational bias and are preferred for the specification of types which are not easily modelled by existing entities. A good discussion of these and related matters can be found in Liskov and Zilles (1977).

7.3.3 Proofs of Program Correctness

Verification of a program requires that it be demonstrated to be consistent with its specification. A method which takes a given program and a specification of what it is supposed to do and attempts to construct a proof of consistency (i.e. *correctness*) is called a static method. Experience has shown that this approach is prohibitively difficult for all but very small and simple programs. In general, to have any realistic chance of proving the correctness of a program it is necessary to construct that program with verification in mind. Verification methods based on this idea are called constructive methods and constitute formal development methodologies when applied to large systems. The best-known such methodology is the VDM one mentioned above in connection with specification methods. As might be expected VDM is too complicated to be discussed in any detail here, but a brief indication of its approach will be given below after an introduction to the most widely used static method which is based on Floyd–Hoare-type axiomatic semantics of the programming language used.

In this method the specification of a program S is written as an *inductive expression*

$$\{P\}S\{Q\}$$

in which P and Q are predicates called *assertions*. P is called the input assertion or pre-condition and expresses a constraint on the input data. Q is called the output assertion or post-condition and expresses requirements on the results computed by S. The inductive expression states that if P is true before S is executed, then if S is executed, and terminates, Q will be true. Proof of the inductive expression constitutes proof of what is called the partial correctness of S: a proof of total correctness requiring proof that S does terminate. The distinction is necessary since if S contains loops it could execute forever.

Proof of the inductive expression is performed by what is known as the *method of inductive assertions*, which requires that assertions about the relations between program variables be inserted at points in the program text such that every loop is cut by at least one assertion (see Figure 7.16). Each assertion is an invariant, i.e. a claim that the relationship stated is true whenever control reaches it during execution of the program on any data which satisfies P, and proof of correctness requires proof that the program text makes each claim true. A *path* between two assertions A and A' is defined to be the set of phrases (language constructs including statements and declarations), bracketed by A and A' and containing no other assertions, which is executed when the program is run on inputs consistent with P. Since every loop contains at least one assertion, there is only a finite number of paths in a program containing a finite number of phrases. (If there is a loop not cut by an assertion the number of paths could be infinite, corresponding to the infinite number of different times the loop body could be executed.) The method of inductive assertions then requires proof that the inductive expression $\{A\}S\{A'\}$ is true for each path S bracketed by assertions A and A', i.e. that if execution reaches A with A true, then if execution reaches A' then A' will be true. Note that for a loop A and A' could be the same. By an induction argument, the proof follows that if the method of inductive assertions is carried out, then each time execution reaches a point in the program that has an assertion attached to it the assertion is true, and hence that if execution ever reaches the output assertion Q that assertion will be true. The basis of the induction is that the first point reached with an assertion attached is the start of the program and the input assertion is true by assumption. The induction hypothesis is that the assertion A attached to the nth point with an assertion attached to it reached during execution is true. Then we need to prove that if execution continues to the $(n + 1)$th point with an assertion A' attached to it, then A' will be true. But there must be a path between these two points and in performing the method of inductive assertions it must have been shown that if execution is at the nth point with A true, then when execution reaches the $(n + 1)$th point the assertion A' will be true, Thus given the inductive hypothesis the assertion at the $(n + 1)$th point is true. This completes the proof by induction, which gives the method its name.

```
program factorial (input,output);
var
    fact,number,count:integer;
begin
        read(number);
        fact :=1;
        count:=0;
        while count <> number do
        begin
                count:= count+1;
                fact := fact * count
        end;
        write (fact)
end.
```

Figure 7.15 A Pascal program for factorial

To illustrate the method we consider the proof of correctness of the Pascal program shown in Figure 7.15, which computes the factorial of a non-negative integer. The treatment is adapted from that in McGettrick (1982), which gives a good introduction to (Ada) program verification. Anderson (1979) is also a good introduction with many examples and exercises. Two relatively informal ways of performing the proof will be considered first, followed by a brief consideration of the requirements for a fully formal proof. To shorten the treatment we consider only the section of the program shown in Figure 7.16, which excludes the declarations and the I/O statements. The paths in this program are delimited by the assertions shown, one of which cuts the while loop as required. The choice of assertions is reasonably obvious in this

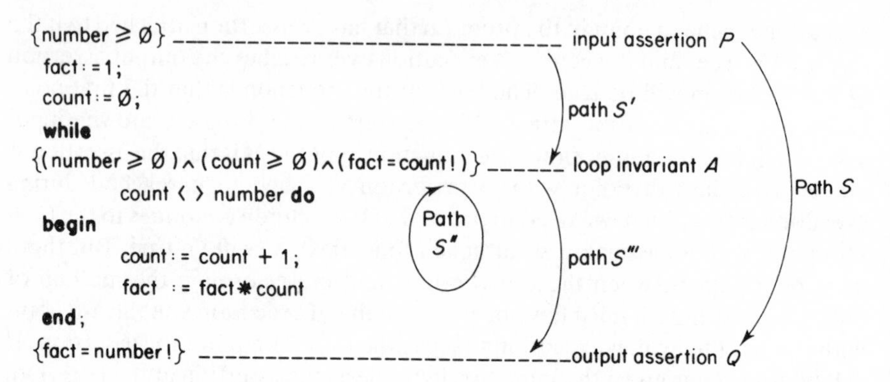

Figure 7.16 Assertions for the proof of correctness

example, but in general the formulation of suitable assertions, particularly assertions cutting loops (*loop invariants*), is one of the most difficult aspects of constructing a proof.

The method of *back substitution* involves transforming the assertion at the end of a path to that at the beginning by a process of replacing variables by the expressions assigned to them. For the first path the substitution of 0 for *count* and 1 for *fact* in the loop invariant:

$$\{(\text{number} \geqslant 0) \wedge (\text{count} \geqslant 0) \wedge (\text{fact} = \text{count}!)\}$$

gives

$$\{(\text{number} \geqslant 0) \wedge (0 \geqslant 0) \wedge (1 = 0!)\}$$

so that we need to show that

$$\{\text{number} \geqslant 0\} \Rightarrow \{(\text{number} \geqslant 0) \wedge (0 \geqslant 0) \wedge (1 = 0!)\}$$

Since $0 \geqslant 0$ is trivially true and $1 = 0!$ is true by definition of the factorial function this reduces to

$$\{\text{number} \geqslant 0\} \Rightarrow \{\text{number} \geqslant 0\}$$

which is true since the antecedent is true by assumption.

Proceeding similarly for the second path (when the loop assertion is true) we need to show that

$$\{(\text{number} \geqslant 0) \wedge (\text{count} \geqslant 0) \wedge (\text{fact} = \text{count}!)\} \wedge (\text{count}\langle\rangle\text{number})$$
$$\Rightarrow \{(\text{number} \geqslant 0) \wedge (\text{count} + 1 \geqslant 0) \wedge (\text{fact}*(\text{count} + 1) = (\text{count} + 1)!\}$$

where the initial assertion and the condition for loop execution are required to imply the final assertion, in this case the same as the initial assertion, transformed by back substituting according to the statements on the path. Since

$$(\text{count} \geqslant 0) \Rightarrow (\text{count} + 1 \geqslant 0)$$

from the properties of integer addition and

$$(\text{fact} = \text{count!}) \Rightarrow [(\text{fact}*(\text{count} + 1)) = (\text{count} + 1)!]$$

from the definition of factorial, the initial assertion implies the transformed final assertion as required.

The third path, followed when the loop assertion is false, requires that

$$\{(\text{number} \geqslant 0) \wedge (\text{count} \geqslant 0) \wedge (\text{fact} = \text{count!})\} \wedge (\text{count} = \text{number}) \Rightarrow \{(\text{fact} = \text{number!})\}$$

which follows immediately since

$$(\text{fact} = \text{count!}) \wedge (\text{count} = \text{number}) \Rightarrow (\text{fact} = \text{number!}).$$

and completes the proof.

The second method is called symbolic execution and is more natural in that the proof proceeds forwards through the program text rather than backwards. The values of variables at the beginning of a path, treated as algebraic variables, are transformed into their values at the end of the path by performing the operations indicated by the statements on the path. The verification conditions for the first two paths can thus be written

$$\text{Path1: } (\text{number} \geqslant 0) \wedge (\text{fact}' = 1) \wedge (\text{count}' = 0) \Rightarrow (\text{number} \geqslant 0) \wedge (\text{count}' \geqslant 0) \wedge (\text{fact}' = \text{count}'!)$$

$$\text{Path2: } (\text{number} \geqslant 0) \wedge (\text{count} \geqslant 0) \wedge (\text{fact} = \text{count!}) \wedge (\text{count} \langle\rangle \text{number}) \wedge (\text{count}' = \text{count} + 1) \wedge (\text{fact}' = \text{fact}*(\text{count} + 1)) \Rightarrow (\text{number} \geqslant 0) \wedge (\text{count}' \geqslant 0) \wedge (\text{fact}' = \text{count}'!)$$

where the primes indicate updated values. Both implications are readily seen to be true by substituting appropriately for *fact′* and *count′* in the consequents. The condition for the third path is the same as in the back-substitution method since there are no statements on the path. Thus by either method the program of Figure 7.16 is shown to be partially correct.

To show total correctness the Floyd technique based on the properties of well-ordered sets can be used. It depends upon finding a loop invariant which implies that the value of some function of the program variables, which decreases each time the loop is executed, belongs to a well-ordered set and therefore cannot decrease indefinitely, so that the loop must eventually be exited. Again, for our simple example the choice of loop invariant and function are:

$$\text{invariant: } (0 \leqslant \text{count}) \wedge (\text{count} \leqslant \text{number})$$
$$\text{function}: f = \text{number} - \text{count}$$

with the loop invariant placed immediately before the test in the while loop as before. This may seem fairly obvious but is by no means generally true.

To show that the predicate is a loop invariant we can use back substitution: firstly on the path from the initial assertion which gives the verification condition

$$(\text{number} \geqslant 0) \Rightarrow (0 \leqslant 0) \wedge (0 \leqslant 1)$$

which is obviously true, and secondly on the path from the loop invariant back to the loop invariant to get

$$(0 \leqslant \text{count}) \wedge (\text{count} \leqslant \text{number}) \wedge (\text{count} \langle\rangle \text{number}) \\ \Rightarrow (0 \leqslant \text{count} + 1) \wedge (\text{count} + 1 \leqslant \text{number})$$

which is also obviously true. To show that the truth of the loop invariant implies that the value of f belongs to the non-negative integers, a well-ordered set, we need to show that

$$(0 \leqslant \text{count}) \wedge (\text{count} \leqslant \text{number}) \Rightarrow (\text{number} - \text{count}) \geqslant 0$$

which again is obviously true. The value of f does decrease on each loop traversal, since *count* is incremented by 1 each time.

We have thus shown that the loop must eventually terminate (when *count* = *number*) and since this is the only loop in the program the program itself must terminate for all input such that *number* $\geqslant 0$. The program has therefore been shown to be totally correct, i.e. for all input *number* $\geqslant 0$ it terminates with *fact* = *number*!. Its behaviour for any input *number* < 0 is undefined.

The above arguments are only semi-formal since an intuitive understanding of the semantics of the phrases in the Pascal program was assumed. To make the method fully formal it is necessary to prove an inductive assertion of the form

$$\{P_i\}S_{i+1}\{P_{i+1}\}$$

for every phrase in the sequence

$$S = S_1, S_2, \ldots, S_n, \ldots$$

constituting a Pascal program S.

Formalization of the semantics of Pascal requires that for every kind of phrase in the language an axiom, or rule of inference, relating P to Q must be devised. The axiomatic semantics of the Pascal phrases in the program of Figure 7.16 are shown in Figure 7.17, mostly in the form

$$\frac{P_1, P_2, \ldots, P_n}{P}$$

which asserts that the truth of predicate P can be inferred from the truth of P_1, $P_2, \ldots, P_n$.

The *consequence rule*, which is frequently needed in proofs, is used in two forms assignment statement:

$$\{P(y/x)\} \quad x:=y \quad \{P\}$$

where $P(y/x)$ denotes the predicate obtained from P by replacing all occurrences of variable x by variable y [This is a formalization of the back-substitution used in the example].

sequence statement:

$$\frac{\{P\}S_1\{R\} \wedge \{R\}S_2\{Q\}}{\{P\}S_1;S_2\{Q\}}$$

compound statement:

$$\frac{\{P_{i-1})S_i\{P_i\} \ (i=1,2,\text{---}n)}{\{P_0\} \ \textit{begin} \ S_1;\text{---};S_n \ \textit{end} \ \{P_n\}}$$

while statement:

$$\frac{\{P \wedge B\} \ S \ \{P\}}{\{P\} \ \textbf{while} \ B \ \textbf{do} \ S\{P \wedge \sim B\}}$$

Figure 7.17 The axiomatic semantics of some Pascal statements

$$\frac{(P \Rightarrow R) \wedge \{R\}S\{Q\}}{\{P\}S\{Q\}} \qquad \text{I}$$

and

$$\frac{\{P\}S\{R\} \wedge (R \Rightarrow Q)}{\{P\}S\{Q\}} \qquad \text{II}$$

The formal proof of the program of Figure 7.16 then proceeds as follows:

1. $\{\text{number} \geqslant 0\}$
   fact: = 1
   $\{(\text{number} \geqslant 0) \wedge (\text{fact} = 1)\}$
   by the assignment axiom;
2. $\{(\text{number} \geqslant 0) \wedge (\text{fact} = 1)\}$
   count: = 0
   $\{(\text{number} \geqslant 0) \wedge (\text{count} \geqslant 0) \wedge (\text{fact} = \text{count!})\}$
   by the assignment axiom and the definition of factorial;
3. $\{\text{number} \geqslant 0\}$
   fact: = 1;
   count: = 0
   $\{(\text{number} \geqslant 0) \wedge (\text{count} \geqslant 0) \wedge (\text{fact} = \text{count!})\}$
   by 1, 2 and the sequence rule;

4. $\{(\text{number} \geqslant 0) \wedge (\text{count} + 1 \geqslant 0) \wedge (\text{fact} = \text{count}!)\}$
count: = count + 1
$\{(\text{number} \geqslant 0) \wedge (\text{count} \geqslant 0) \wedge (\text{fact} = (\text{count} - 1)!)\}$
by the assignment axiom;
5. $\{(\text{number} \geqslant 0) \wedge (\text{count} \geqslant 0) \wedge (\text{fact} = (\text{count} - 1)!)\}$
fact: = fact*count
$\{(\text{number} \geqslant 0) \wedge (\text{count} \geqslant 0) \wedge (\text{fact} = \text{count}!)\}$
by the assignment axiom;
6. $\{(\text{number} \geqslant 0) \wedge (\text{count} + 1 \geqslant 0) \wedge (\text{fact} = \text{count}!)\}$
begin
    count: = count + 1;
    fact: = fact*count
end
$\{(\text{number} \geqslant 0) \wedge (\text{count} \geqslant 0) \wedge (\text{fact} = \text{count}!)\}$
by 4, 5 and the compound statement rule;
7. $\{(\text{number} \geqslant 0) \wedge (\text{count} \geqslant 0) \wedge (\text{fact} = \text{count}!)\}$
begin
    count: = count + 1;
    fact: = fact*count
end
$\{(\text{number} \geqslant 0) \wedge (\text{count} \geqslant 0) \wedge (\text{fact} = \text{count}!)\}$
by 6 and consequence rule I (using $(\text{count} \geqslant 0) \Rightarrow (\text{count} + 1 \geqslant 0)$);
8. $\{(\text{number} \geqslant 0) \wedge (\text{count} \geqslant 0) \wedge (\text{fact} = \text{count}!) \wedge (\text{count} \langle\rangle \text{number})\}$
begin
    count: = count + 1;
    fact: = fact*count
end
$\{(\text{number} \geqslant 0) \wedge (\text{count} \geqslant 0) \wedge (\text{fact} = \text{count}!)\}$
by 7 and consequence rule I;
9. $\{(\text{number} \geqslant 0) \wedge (\text{count} \geqslant 0) \wedge (\text{fact} = \text{count}!)\}$
while (count⟨⟩number) **do**
begin
    count: = count + 1;
    fact: = fact*count
end
$\{(\text{number} \geqslant 0) \wedge (\text{count} \geqslant 0) \wedge (\text{fact} = \text{count}!) \wedge (\text{count} = \text{number})\}$
by 8 and the while rule;
10. $\{(\text{number} \geqslant 0)\}$
fact: = 1;
count: = 0;
while (count⟨⟩number) **do**
begin
    count: = count + 1;

```
        fact: = fact*count
    end
    {(number ≥ 0) ∧ (count ≥ 0) ∧ (fact = count!) ∧ (count = num-
    ber)}
    by 3, 9 and the sequence rule;
11. {(number ≥ 0)}
    fact: = 1;
    count: = 0;
    while (count⟨⟩number) do
    begin
        count: = count + 1;
        fact: = fact*count
    end
    {(fact = number!)}
    by 10 and consequence rule II,
```

which completes the proof.

As is obvious from the example a fully formal proof of a program of any size is extremely tedious to perform, and in practice proofs are conducted by the method of back-substitution or symbolic execution as described earlier. These methods are said to be *rigorous* rather than formal. The term implies a degree of precision sufficient to allow the ready provision of a fully formal treatment of any part of the proof if required, i.e. if the rigorous version is not sufficiently convincing. This is, of course, the way in which mathematical proofs are normally performed.

The method of inductive assertions is satisfactory for any program which does not include recursive calls of procedures and functions. To deal with these a method called *structural induction* is used, which is not discussed here. The interested reader is referred to McGettrick (1982) and Anderson (1979).

Although these methods have been applied successfully to fairly sizable programs, they do not by any means remove the need for the non-formal techniques of system validation such as reviews, inspections and testing. Proofs can be, and often are, erroneous. The effort required to construct a proof can be equal to or even greater than that required to construct the program itself, which makes the process uneconomic for industrial production. Particular weaknesses of the methods are that appropriate assertions can be very difficult (if not impossible) to devise for complex systems, and the correctness proof, if constructed, is only a proof of consistency with assertions which do not specify program behaviour for data which fails to satisfy the initial assertion.

7.3.4 Formal Development Methodologies

The future of formal methods appears at the moment to lie with constructive techniques in which the software is constructed with ease of verification as a major design guideline. One of the best-known constructive techniques, which has seen some use in the industry, is based on the Vienna development method (VDM) mentioned previously, and is described in detail as a *rigorous method* of software development by Jones (1980, 1986).

It involves the top-down development of a system from an abstract specification to an executable program in a series of stages. Each development stage is subjected to a rigorous verification which is easily made formal if necessary. The specification is that of an abstract data type: a collection of objects which provide a possible set of computational states of the system and a set of operations upon those states. The abstract-model approach is adopted using a small number of primitive types plus constructors for basic objects such as sets, lists and mappings. This is preferred to the axiomatic approach as being more appropriate for objects which are actually to be implemented and as having the developmental advantage that operations upon the model can be considered singly whereas only relationships between operations are considered directly in the axiomatic approach. The operations are generally constrained by one or more predicates on the state of the system, called *data-type invariants*, which are required to remain true for all states created by the operations. The need for them arises because the real-world objects being modelled are rarely susceptible to being completely represented by the simple mathematical objects like sets and mappings which are used to create the model. To take a simple example, a state containing dates might have *MONTH* and *DAY* components modelled by sets {Jan, Feb, ... , Dec} and {1, 2, ... 31} respectively. Data-type invariants would be needed to exclude Feb 30 and Sep 31 (for example) from the set of states represented by the Cartesian product.

The abstract model is required to be minimal in the sense of incorporating only the essential properties of the real-world entities being modelled and not properties conferred by the representation. In practice this means that there should be no two distinct states which cannot be distinguished by application of the operations. A specification which meets this requirement is said to be free of *implementation bias*. Operation specifications are given in terms of pre-conditions, predicates of a single state which define the set of states over which the operation is required to terminate, and post-conditions, which are predicates of pairs of states defining the required relationship between input and output states.

The design or development phase which follows specification is an iterative process of devising successively more concrete models of the system until an executable implementation is finally produced. The two methods used are data refinement (or *reification*) and procedural decomposition. The early stages of development tend to be concerned with data refinement since operations need to be defined in terms of implementable objects before being decomposed into executable statements. A data-refinement step involves devising a more concrete representation of the objects in the specification and a new set of operations upon those objects, the representation of one step providing the specification for the next. A representation is related to a specification by a *retrieve function* which is a mapping from the states of the representation to the states of the specification. A representation generally shows more implementation bias than a specification, a number of different states in the representation corresponding to a single state in the specification, because of the need for implementation using structures with intrinsic properties. For example, sets are often conveniently implemented as arrays but the ordering intrinsic to an array is redundant as far as the properties of sets are concerned. A primary requirement for a representation is *adequacy*, the property that every state in the specification has at least one corresponding state in the representation, from which it is recovered by the retrieve function. The mapping defined by the retrieve function is thus onto, and the redundancy of the representation means that it is also many-to-one. Invariants are applied to representations to ensure that retrieve functions are total. For each operation on the abstract state of the specification there must be a corresponding operation on the representation which models the abstract one, i.e. fulfils the same function in the representation as the abstract one does in the specification. More precisely, the new operation is a model of the abstract one if

1. for any state satisfying the pre-condition of the abstract one the states of the representation which are mapped on to it by the retrieve function satisfy the pre-condition of the new one;
2. all such states of the representation when operated on by the new operation yield a state which is mapped by the retrieve function to a state which satisfies the post-condition of the abstract one.

The data-type invariants which hold in the specification must hold in the representation and the relationships between operations must also be preserved. Proof rules are provided to assist in the necessary demonstration that a representation is adequate and that its operations model those of the specification.

The other aspect of development, the decomposition of operations into executable code, is done by conventional stepwise refinement and Hoare-type rules of inference are provided for correctness proofs.

Both sets of proof rules are normally used as checklists during the development process, but if there is any query about the validity of any particular proof the transition to a fully formal proof is easily made.

The basic reference for this *rigorous method* is Jones (1980). A more theoretical account of the method, and of other forms of VDM, can be found, along with a number of case studies of system development, in Bjorner and Jones (1982).

7.4 ALTERNATIVE MODELS OF COMPUTATION

Much of the difficulty of writing correct programs in conventional imperative programming languages, and of proving them correct, is due to the presence of assignment and sequence-control statements arising from the underlying model of computation based on the physical characteristics of the von Neumann machine, as discussed in Chapter 4.

Imperative programming languages are said to be *referentially opaque* since the value of a variable can be changed within its scope, possibly as a side-effect of a function call, which can cause successive evaluations of the same expression to yield different values. Programs written in such languages cannot be reasoned about by a static analysis of the program text but must be subjected to some kind of simulation of their dynamic behaviour such as the symbolic execution described above. For this reason an alternative model of computation, not based on a sequence of changes in the state of a machine, has been developed and is known as *declarative programming* since programs consist of assertions or declarations about entities and computation proceeds by making deductions from the assertions.

The best-established form of declarative programming is known as *functional* or *applicative* programming, in which the assertions take the form of function and data-structure definitions. The oldest and by far the most widely used functional language is LISP, which originated in the late 1950s as discussed above, but it must be said at once that the LISP systems used by the AI community today are large agglomerations of both functional and imperative features which include McCarthy's small and (almost) entirely functional language as a tiny subset. As will become apparent, LISP is easily and indefinitely user-extendable, a property which has led to a profusion of dialects, two or three of which have achieved very wide use in LISP programming environments complete with syntax-directed editors, interactive debuggers and compilers (all written in LISP). A very brief indication of some of the main features of the small functional subset which is near the core of most LISP systems is all that space permits here; an account of one of the main dialects, with references to the others, can be found in Winston and Horn (1984) along with an introduction to AI programming techniques.

The sole structure in LISP is the S-expression, which is either an atom (denoted by a string of one or more characters) or a list of S-expressions. Both programs (i.e. functions) and the data they operate on are written entirely in S-expressions. The recursive definition allows lists to have lists as elements. A LISP system is traditionally implemented as an interactive loop:

READ(an S-expression)–EVAL(uate it)–PRINT(the value)

where *EVAL* is the universal function (referred to in Section 7.3.1), which interprets (i.e. evaluates) input S-expressions in the context of an environment, which is a set of bindings of atoms to values.

If a single atom is input, the value to which it is bound in the top-level (or global) environment of the system is returned. (If there is no such binding an error occurs.) In most LISP systems numeric atoms are bound to the corresponding numeric values and in all systems the two special atoms *T* and *NIL* are bound to themselves as values. If a list

(elem1 elem2 elem3 ... elemn)

is input it is interpreted as a function application. The function definition to which the atom *elem1* is bound is applied to the values of the S-expressions *elem2*, ... , *elemn* as arguments and the result of the application is returned as the value.

In a minimal LISP system five primitive functions (*CONS*, *CAR*, *CDR*, *EQ*, and *ATOM*) for operating on S-expressions as data are built in along with a function (*QUOTE*) which returns its arguments unevaluated and a pseudo-function (*SET*) which is evaluated for its side-effect of adding a binding to the global environment. (In fact *QUOTE* is what is called a *special form* in LISP as are *COND* and *LAMBDA* (discussed below), but these will not be distinguished from functions here.) Examples of the use of these functions are shown in Figure 7.18. All except *SET* are true functions i.e. have no side-effects. For example, after

(CONS 'OSLO (CONS 'MADRID CITIES))

which returns the value

(OSLO MADRID LONDON PARIS)

the value of *CITIES* is still

(LONDON PARIS).

Additional functions are defined with the aid of three further built-ins: a conditional function (*COND*), a function-defining function (*LAMBDA*) and a pseudofunction (*DEFINE*) which adds function bindings to the global environment.

Application of *COND* gives a conditional expression. The form is

(COND (P1 E1) (P2 E2) ... (Pn En))

where the P_i are predicates (function applications which return *T* or *NIL*) and the E_i are S-expressions. The predicates are evaluated in turn, in written order, until one returns *T* (otherwise an error occurs) when the corresponding S-expression is evaluated and its result returned as the value of the *COND* application.

Functions are defined by means of lambda expressions of the form

(LAMBDA (arg1 arg2 ... argn) E)

which defines an (anonymous) function of *n* arguments whose value is the S-expression *E* evaluated in an environment in which the actual–formal

```
  (i) QUOTE suppresses evaluation of its arguments
      most systems allow (QUOTE E) to be abbreviated as 'E
      (QUOTE A) or 'A returns A
      (QUOTE (A B C)) or '(A B C) returns (A B C)

 (ii) SET establishes a global value binding
      after (SET 'CITIES '(LONDON PARIS)) which returns (LONDON PARIS
      CITIES returns (LONDON PARIS)
      'CITIES returns CITIES

(iii) CONS constructs a new list from two S-expressions
      (CONS 'ROME CITIES) returns (ROME LONDON PARIS)
      (CONS '(VIENNA LINZ) CITIES) returns
                                   ((VIENNA LINZ) LONDON PARIS)

 (iv) CAR returns the first element of its list argument
      (CAR CITIES) returns LONDON
      (CAR (CONS '(A B) '(C D))) returns (A B)

  (v) CDR returns the list formed by removing the first element of its list
      argument
      (CDR CITIES) returns (PARIS)
      (CDR (CDR CITIES)) returns (), the empty list

 (vi) EQ returns T if its two atom arguments are identical, NIL otherwise
      (EQ (CAR CITIES) 'LONDON) returns T
      (EQ 'ROME (CAR '(A B C))) returns NIL
      (EQ NIL '() ) returns T, the atom NIL is identical with the empty set

(vii) ATOM returns T if its S-expression argument is an atom, NIL
      otherwise
      (ATOM 'CITIES) returns T
      (ATOM CITIES) returns NIL
```

Figure 7.18 LISP primitives

parameter bindings are temporarily added to the existing global environment. (The actual parameters must follow the S-expression, which constitutes the *LAMBDA* application.) Such a function may have a name (atom) bound to it in the global environment by means of the pseudofunction *DEFINE*. Figure 7.19 shows the definition of a function to concatenate two list arguments, *DEFINE* being used to bind the name *APPEND* to it, and examples of its use.

```
( DEFINE 'APPEND
    ( LAMBDA ( L1 L2 )
        ( COND ( ( EQ L1 NIL ) L2 )
                ( T ( CONS ( CAR L1 ) (APPEND ( CDR L1 ) L2 ))))) ))
        (a)

( APPEND  '( A B ) () )             returns    ( A B )
( APPEND  () '( A B ))              returns    ( A B )
( APPEND  '( A B C ) '( D E ))      returns    ( A B C D E )
        (b)
```

Figure 7.19 (a) Definition and (b) application of a LISP function

Since functions are S-expressions which take S-expressions as arguments and return S-expressions as results it is possible to define functions which take functions as arguments and/or return functions as results. Such functions are known as functionals. A commonly defined LISP functional is *MAPCAR*, which has the form

(MAPCAR 'F L)

and applies the function F to every element of the list L, returning a list of the results as value. For example

(MAPCAR '(LAMBDA (L) (APPEND '(Z) L))
'((A B C) (D E F)))

returns

((Z A B C) (Z D E F)).

The effect of this use of *MAPCAR* is to convert a function of two arguments, *APPEND*, into a function of one argument which concatenates a list (Z) to every list element of its single list argument.

A more convenient way to achieve this effect is to define a functional *BU* which operates upon any binary function like *APPEND* and returns as result a new unary function, e.g.

(BU 'APPEND '(Z))

which has the same effect as

(LAMBDA (L) (APPEND '(Z) L))

or, more generally

((BU FOO X) Y)

where the function being applied to Y is the result of

```
(BU  FOO  X)
```

and the net effect is that of

```
(FOO  X  Y)
```

where *FOO* is a binary function.

The definition of *BU* is

```
(DEFINE  'BU
    (LAMBDA  (F  A)
        (FUNCTION  (LAMBDA  (B)  (F  A  B)))))
```

The built-in function *FUNCTION* is necessary because (most) LISP systems use a scoping mechanism in which functions are called in the environment of their caller (dynamic scoping) and not in the environment of their definition (lexical scoping) as in imperative languages. If this occurred with a call of *BU* the lambda expression which is returned (the inner one) is returned to the caller's environment in which *F* and *A* are either not bound or are bound to the wrong values. (*B* is correctly bound to the single argument provided for the result of the *BU* application in the caller's environment). The effect of the application of *FUNCTION* is to bind the lambda expression to its environment of definition, which ensures that the *free variables F* and *A* are bound to the arguments given to *BU* when it is called. A full discussion of scoping in LISP can be found in MacLennan (1983), from where the *BU* example has been adapted.

This brief introduction to LISP gives little idea of its power as a production programming language for AI applications. Atoms can have properties attached to them which allow elaborate dynamic data structures (all S-expressions) to be built up in ways which have been found to be extremely convenient for knowledge representation and manipulation and many of the hundreds of predefined functions in the major dialects are designed to create and operate upon these structures. The fact that functions have the same form as data means that LISP functions can create and apply LISP functions giving the language enormous computational power. A complete *READ–EVAL–PRINT* loop can be written in fewer than 100 lines of LISP code, for example. Unfortunately a production LISP system implemented using only the primitives described above would be hopelessly inefficient and real systems have many functions implemented in compiled code and make heavy use of imperative features (including *GOTO*s !). There is absolutely no standardization between the dialects (one uses ALGOL-like syntax, another is totally lexically scoped, and so on) and this, combined with the referential opacity of dynamic scoping and imperative features (and other aspects of real systems not discussed here), means that in practice LISP programs are no easier to reason about than programs written in imperative languages.

In order to realize the potential advantages of functional programming a number of languages have been developed which are purely functional. In KRC, for example, one of a series of such languages developed by Turner (1982), a program consists of a set of equations which define functions and data structures. Expressions composed of these entities are then presented for evaluation. The language has all the computational power of the functional subset of LISP presented above: functions have the same status as data objects as the integers, strings and lists which comprise the data structures of the language in that they can be elements of lists and arguments and results of functions. Unlike LISP its semantics are simple and are clearly reflected by the notation, i.e. the language is referentially transparent. The equations, functions, variables and constants have the same significance as their mathematical counterparts. Expressions only denote values; there are no side effects. Variables behave like mathematical variables, their values being invariant within their scopes. Equations have the same significance as in mathematics, in particular the substitutive property that if $a = b$ then b can be substituted for a everywhere without changing the value of any expression containing a. This means that KRC programs can be subjected to a style of proof like that of methematics, which consists basically of reasoning with equations. Turner (1982) demonstrates a proof method based on structural inducation and the reader should refer to this paper for details. Being referentially transparent, functional languages are easier to write correct programs in and referential transparency combined with the high level of abstraction achieved by the use of functionals makes them eminently suitable as (executable) specification languages. (Turner (1985) describes an extension of KRC for this purpose.)

Part of the reason for the increasing interest in applicative languages in recent years is the language FP introduced by Backus (the chief designer of FORTRAN and the B of BNF) in a celebrated lecture (Backus 1978). FP emphasizes the use of functionals to manipulate functions, i.e. complete programs, rather than to manipulate conventional data objects, and was designed to make the language in which FP programs are proved correct FP itself. Since FP is essentially an algebra of functions, standard algebraic reasoning techniques can be applied directly. Discussion of FP is beyond the scope of this introduction, and the interested reader is referred to Williams (1982), one of an informative collection of papers on functional programming (Darlington *et al.* 1982).

A recent and particularly interesting language which combines the functional forms of FP with data structures supporting nested arrays is NIAL (Jenkins 1985). This has been used for a wide range of applications from database prototyping (Winterflood 1984) to logic programming (Glasgow 1985).

Logic programming languages, of which PROLOG (Clocksin and Mellish 1982) is probably the best known, are declarative programming languages in which the assertions take the form of logical implications. PROLOG uses a form of implication called a Horn clause in which the consequent is a single predicate and the antecedent is either a single predicate or a conjunction of predicates. Thus

(a) father(x,y) $\Rightarrow$ male(x)

meaning: 'if *x* is the father of *y* then *x* is male'

(b) father(x,y) $\wedge$ father(y,z) $\Rightarrow$ grandfather(x,z)

are Horn clauses whereas

father(x,y) $\vee$ mother(x,y) $\Rightarrow$ parent(x,y)

is not but can be expressed as two Horn clauses

(c) father(x,y) $\Rightarrow$ parent(x,y)
mother(x,y) $\Rightarrow$ parent(x,y).

In PROLOG these clauses are written in the form

(a) male(x) $\leftarrow$ father(x,y)
(b) grandfather(x,z) $\leftarrow$ father(x,y), father(y,z)
(c) parent(x,y) $\leftarrow$ father(x,y).

Assertions (hypotheses) are written as

father(John,Alan)
parent(Sue,John).

A simple PROLOG program might then take the form shown in Figure 7.20. It consists of a number of implications which serve to establish general relationships, a number of hypotheses and a *goal*.

$\leftarrow$ grandparent(John,x)

which can be interpreted as an instruction to find the constants, if any, which, when substituted for the variable *x*, make the assertion:

grandparent(John,x)

true.

In this example the PROLOG system will return

x = Joan.

How the PROLOG system does this does not affect the meaning of the program (although it does affect the efficiency with which the program is executed), which is referentially transparent.

This brief glimpse of PROLOG does the language no justice at all (the reader is referred to Clocksin and Mellish (1982) for a comprehensive account and to Kowalski (1979) for a thorough discussion of the principles involved)

```
        parent(x,y) ← father(x,y)

        parent(x,y) ← mother(x,y)

grandparent(x,z) ← parent(x,y), parent(y,z)

        father(John,Mary)
        father(James,Joan)
        mother(Sue,Peter)

        mother(Mary,Joan)

    ← grandparent(John,x)
```

Figure 7.20 A simple PROLOG program

and is intended simply to indicate the declarative nature of logic programs. (It is also discussed in more depth in Chapter 11.)

In practice, however, PROLOG bears the sort of relationship to pure logic programming that LISP does to pure functional programming. In order to achieve tolerable efficiency in production programs the 'how' of PROLOG has to be specified in the program text, which thereby loses its referential transparency. Pure logic languages do offer the prospect of programs which can be reasoned about simply and correctly using the standard methods of the predicate calculus, and active research to this end continues.

PART 3

INFORMATION MANAGEMENT SYSTEMS

Fundamentals of Information Technology
Edited by G. G. Wilkinson and A. R. Winterflood

Chapter 8
Conceptual Modelling

8.1 THE NEED FOR DATABASE SYSTEMS

The last three chapters have been devoted to the general techniques, problems and solutions involved in the development of general software systems. However, each class of application (e.g. transaction systems, real time systems, expert systems, etc.) will possess individual characteristics that require additional, specialized approaches to system development. One such class of application is **database systems**.

Alongside scientific computation the first application area of computers was 'business systems'. Tabulation of insurance company data and payroll computation were amongst the first programs ever written for industry. Ever since then business has used an increasing amount of expensive computing resources to perform operations previously entrusted to filing cabinets and basic calculators.

These business applications are characterized by the fact that the computations to be performed on the data are trivial (e.g. multiply number of hours worked by basic rate of pay and deduct tax) but have to be carried out on masses of data (would you want to do the payroll for a company with 400 000 employees?). As the price of computing resources fell and more and more business functions became computerized within each company, a number of problems become apparent. All the data relating to a company are unique and valuable. Is it reasonable then to have several departments all keeping separate copies (some possibly out of date) of the same information, taking up space on expensive machines and demanding more of already hard-pressed programmers?

Eventually these problems led to the realization that data in the enterprise were a resource, the acquisition and use of which had to be planned and managed on a global company scale. Data then had to be *integrated* into one or more company *databases* that would enable the elimination of redundancy, thus saving space and time and providing more consistent results. Ways also had to be found so that programs could be made independent of changes in data-storage techniques and save programmer time. Finally it was realized that if more *meaning* could be attached to the data they could be shared and re-used more easily, thus providing new or better reports for corporate management and analysis.

Implementing such a system meant creating software that would provide the *only interface* to the company's data resource, allowing data to be described and manipulated through high-level constructs, hiding all implementation details from users, controlling and monitoring usage, enabling data to be shared easily while still forbidding any unauthorized access, and above all ensuring that this mass of precious and vital data was always kept safe, secure and meaningful.

This software soon became collectively known as *data base management systems* (DBMS). More details on the origins of DBMS and their merits relative to *file management systems* (FMS) can be found in the introductory chapters of Deen (1977, 1985), and Howe (1983). (*Note.* The current trend is to use 'data' and 'base' as the single new word 'database', although the abbreviation DBMS still remains the same.)

It would be impossible in this book to devote time to DBMS implementations; instead this chapter will concentrate on the preliminary work that is necessary to the successful implementation of a database on a DBMS. Chapter 9 will review some of the definition and manipulation features that the main existing systems provide to database managers, while Chapter 10 will survey some of the facilities offered to end-users and speculate on further evolution of DBMS.

8.2 INTRODUCTION TO CONCEPTUAL MODELLING

The development of any database follows the same fundamental principles one finds in other areas of computing science. The golden thread that characterizes all engineering disciplines is that implementation must be preceded by careful analysis, design, and modelling.

In the case of databases this means analysing the subset of the real world which is deemed relevant to the task at hand (this is referred to as the *universe of discourse*). The results of this analysis must then be built into an abstract, implementation-independent model; this is known as the *conceptual model*.

The model thus produced serves several purposes. First, it is a communication tool that can be used to describe the intended scope and purpose of the project to different parties within the enterprise. Second, it can be used as a feedback device to confirm (or invalidate) information gathered during the analysis phase and prompt further requirements details out of the users. Third, it will be used as a reference document by system implementors.

It is most important that one should be able to represent the universe of discourse as exactly as possible. Checking the model for internal and external consistency can yield valuable clues to the quality of the analysis and the design. To serve as a reference document and an aid to design control, the model must be expressed in as formal a way as possible and its construction should be the object of a precise methodology. On the other hand, to serve as a communication and feedback tool the model should be as expressive and simple as possible.

Although conceptual modelling must be implementation independent, it is still difficult to find a unique set of abstract modelling concepts that would satisfy everyone. Indeed there are several different approaches to modelling, each with equally convincing advocates. Among the most publicized, special note should be made of the following approaches to conceptual modelling:

- the entity–relationship approach (detailed below);
- the interpreted predicate logic approach (described in ISO 1982);
- the semantic model (see Borkin 1980, McLeod 1978, King and McLeod 1985).

The entity–relationship (E–R) approach is the only one presented here. The interested reader may obtain details of the other approaches in the references given above.

8.3 AN OVERVIEW OF THE ENTITY–RELATIONSHIP APPROACH

The approach was first described by Chen (1976, 1980, 1985) and has since been used by a wide number of people, both in research and in practical situations. As a result several variations have appeared that either simply use another name for the same method (such as 'entity–attribute–relationship' (EAR) or 'entity–relationship–attribute' (ERA)) or introduce new conceptual restrictions and tools such as the 'binary relationship' approach (ISO 1982) or the 'extended relational analysis' (also ERA—see Addis (1983)).

The entity–relationship approach is favoured for a number of practical reasons:

1. It can quickly and easily be learned and put into use even by the most inexperienced database administrators.
2. It has been widely publicized and literature on it is easy to obtain. Much of the method is often summarized in vendors' guides to database systems.
3. It uses as its central clement a diagrammatic representation of the model that is readily understood by non-specialists.
4. Although this central diagrammatic element would be insufficient on its own as an implementation specification, it can conveniently be supplemented by additional documentation.
5. It is of a level of detail that is compatible with the facilities offered by most commonly available database management systems.

A simple methodology for using the entity–relationship approach to data analysis and modelling is summarized below. Each step in the methodology is described in detail in separate sections and individual examples will appear as appropriate.

1. Starting from either direct observation of company procedures and interviews, or from documentation provided by the analysis team, identify within the universe of discourse occurrences of the three types of objects around which the methodology is built (entities, relationships and properties). Abstract them into entity-types, relationship-types, and property-types.
(*Note.* Contrary to the general approach we find it better to use the term 'property-type' rather than 'attribute-type' to refer to the corresponding objects identified in the initial definition phase, and only call them 'attribute-types' once they have been linked with (attributed to) a particular entity- or relationship-type.)
2. Determine the complexity of the relationship-types.
3. Assemble the identified entity-types and relationship-types in such a way that they form a model of the universe of discourse.
4. Refine the model by identifying inconsistencies, redundancies, and incompleteness, and simplifying complex relationships-types.
5. Link specific property-types to specific entity- and relationship-types (properties now become attributes).
6. Clarify attribute dependencies within entity-types (normalization).
7. Throughout the process define and refine static and dynamic constraints on the database.

As in other analysis and design methodologies, completing the process is done by a series of successive refinements, each of which often implies looping back to a previous stage in the process (see Figure 8.1)).

8.4 IDENTIFICATION

The first step in the process consists in identifying those entity-, property-, and relationship-occurrences that seem to be of interest. This can only be achieved with an in-depth knowledge of the enterprise. An entity can be a concrete, animated or inanimated object, or an abstract concept of interest to the enterprise. The main characteristic of an entity is that it seems capable of existence independently from other objects encountered in the system. We tend to use substantives or short sentences to refer to entities (see Figure 8.2).

We must then abstract occurrences of entities into entity-types. This may be straightforward as, for instance, in the case of sentences (a)–(c) of Figure 8.2, which clearly denote three particular occurrences of the two entity-types, *Person* and *Car*. At this stage the particular name we give to our entity-type is not in itself important. It may indeed vary according to the application at hand and to the individual preferences of the analyst in charge. Depending on the

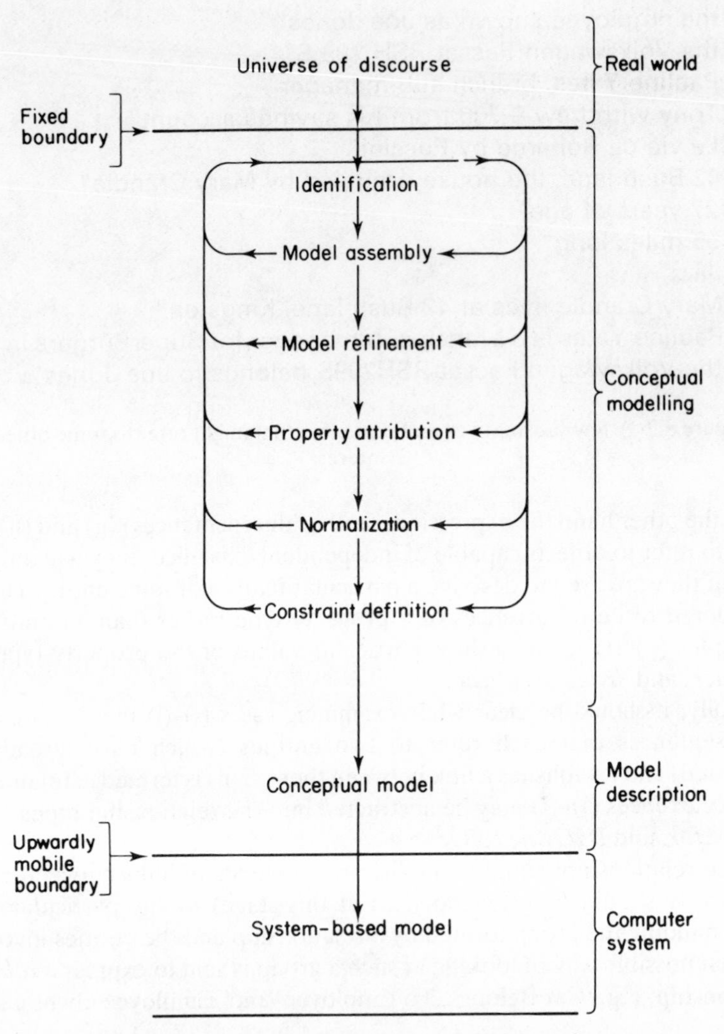

Figure 8.1 The data analysis and design cycle

circumstances of the analysis our first entity-type may well be referred to as *Employee*, or *Staff* if both people mentioned in (a) and (c) are already working with the company. If they are not, the sentences may instead refer to an entity-type *Applicant* or *Client* or *Supplier* as the case may be.

Sentences (d) and (e) also quite clearly point to particular entity-types, although this time abstract ones, which we may call *Bank_Transaction* and *Performance*. Sentence (f) requires more thought, and possibly, more knowledge of the intended use of the information: is it a reference to an entity-type *Dwelling_Category* or *Address*?

(a) "the employee known as Joe Jones"
(b) "the Volkswagen Passat RSH 299 S"
(c) "Pauline Yates, branch sub-manager"
(d) "Tony withdrew $ 700 from his savings account"
(e) "La vie de Boheme by Puccini"
(f) "42 Bush lane, the house occupied by Mary Crandle"
(g) "27 years of age"
(h) "55 miles long"
(i) "Jazz"
(j) "Mary Crandle lives at 42 Bush lane, Kingston"
(k) "Pauline Yates is a branch sub-manager for SuperBurgers in Soho"
(l) "the Volkswagen Passat RSH299S belongs to Joe Jones"

Figure 8.2 A few substantives and sentences that might refer to some objects of interest

On the other hand the expressions (rather than sentences) (g) and (h) do not seem to refer to objects capable of independent existence; they will only make sense if they are used to describe a particular feature of some entity. These are considered to be occurrences of a property-type rather than an entity-type. Examples (g)–(i) seem to show particular values of the property-types *Age*, *Distance*, and *Style_Of_Music*.

Finally, it should be clear while examining cases (j)–(l) that we are dealing with sentences that each refer to two entities (which have already been identified) and establishes a link between them. This is termed a 'relationship', and occurrences (j)–(l) may be abstracted into the relationship-types *Resides*, *Works_for*, and *Is_Owned_By*.

Since relationships simply establish the existence of links between entities, no priority should be given (at least at this stage) to any particular way of understanding the group formed by a relationship and the entities involved in it. Each possible way of looking at such a group is said to express a *role* of the relationship, e.g. 'Car Belongs_To Employee' and 'Employee Owns Car'.

Entity Relationship Diagrams

As mentioned earlier, diagrams are used as a communication device and only summarize some of the information collected during the modelling process. Because of the informal nature of the method, different authors each construct their diagrams slightly differently. The most widely used 'icons' in E–R diagrams are:

- a rectangular box to represent an entity-type;
- a diamond-shaped box to represent a relationship-type;

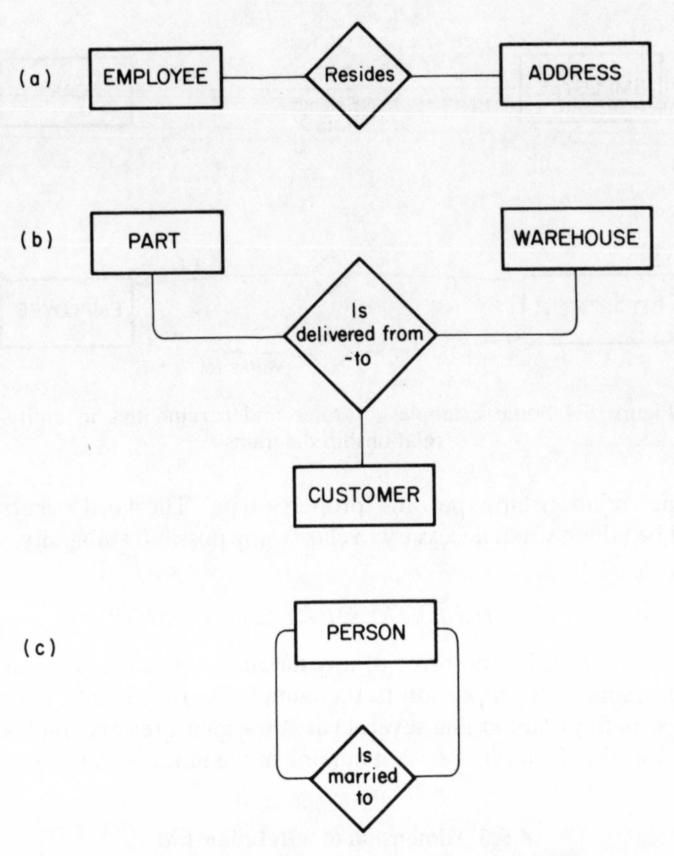

Figure 8.3 Some examples of entity–relationship diagrams

- non-directed lines to connect explicit the entity-types involved in each relationship (see Figure 8.3).

The boxes are labelled with appropriate terms which tend to be a singular substantive for an entity-type, and a verb (third-person singular, present tense) for a relationship-type. Layout should be ordered in such a way as to enable a sentence to be formed when the diagrams are read in the normal left-to-right top-to-bottom manner (remember this is a communications tool). When it seems necessary to make different roles explicit, these can either be put onto different arcs between the entities, or in different areas of the relationship-type box (see Figure 8.4).

The identification stage finishes when it seems that the entity-, property-, and relationship-types defined so far could be used to represent any possible occurrence of data in the enterprise. In the remainder of this chapter, we will use the words 'entity', 'relationship', and 'property' as synonymous to

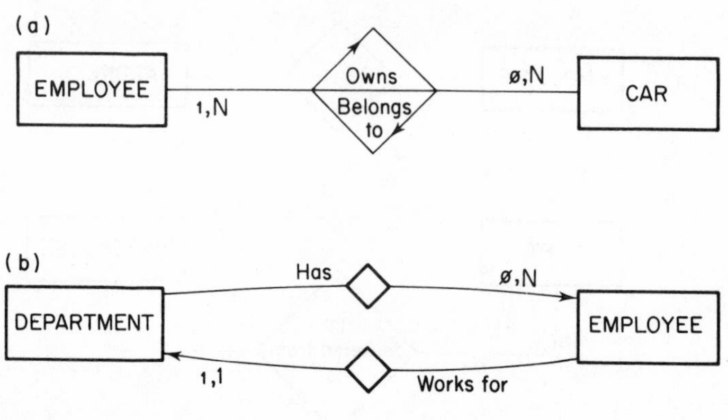

Figure 8.4 Some examples of roles and cardinalities in entity–relationship diagrams

'entity-type' 'relationship-type', and 'property-type'. The word 'occurrence' or 'type' will be added when necessary to clarify any possible ambiguity.

8.5 COMPLEXITY OF RELATIONSHIPS

Relationships are really the pivot of any database since the difficulty of the query processing is in proportion to the complexity of the links between the data. It is with this in mind that several yardstick measures of complexity have been developed to facilitate decision making in the model-refinement stage.

8.5.1 Dimension of a Relationship

The three relationships in our last example each involve two entities and are therefore of *dimension two* (one may also use the expression 'binary relationship'). Relationships of this type are amongst the most frequent to be found in the modelling process and the simplest to implement. For this reason some approaches actually require all modelling to be done in terms of relationships of dimension two only. However, the entity–relationship approach is general enough to express all degrees of relationships.

In the context of a stock management database, for instance, the enterprise might want to maintain a record of shipments made to all customers. There are many parts in the catalogue, and several warehouses where stocks are kept. The relationship *Delivery* abstracted from the sentence 'a part is delivered from a warehouse to a customer' would then be of *dimension three* (or *ternary*) since it involves three entities (see Figure 8.3(b)).

One occasionally finds examples of relationships which may seem of *dimension one* (*unary*), such as that abstracted in 'employee is married to Employee'. This view of things is not strictly correct since one can also consider

Married-To as a binary relationship in which both entities happen to be the same (Figure 8.3(c)).

(*Note*. Obviously, if what we are defining is a measure such that connectivity = dimension − 1, then a unary relationship cannot exist.)

8.5.2 Cardinality

A second fundamental measure of the complexity of a relationship is its *cardinality*. The cardinality of a set is the number of elements in that set. Although a relationship-type is the set of all possible relationship occurrences, this simple measure would be of little interest. Instead the total cardinality of a relationship R is worked out by calculating partial cardinalities for each entity E_1, E_2, ..., E_n involved in R. This is done (as for instance, with partial derivatives) by considering fixed values for all entities but one, and calculating the cardinality for that 'free' entity. However, it is the range of possible cardinalities for an entity that is interesting more than a particular value. We will then vary the fixed values chosen for, say, entities E_2 to E_n until we can establish the *minimum* and the *maximum* cardinalities for E_1 in its relationship with E_2, ..., E_n. The process is, of course, repeated for each of the other entities in turn.

Suppose, for example, that Joe Jones has two cars. Our universe of discourse accordingly contains the two sentences 'Joe Jones owns the Volkswagen Passat RSH299S' and 'Joe Jones owns the Austin Mini C402AKH' and both refer to occurrences of the relationship *Employee Owns Car*. The cardinality of the entity *Car*, with respect to its involvement in the relationship 'Owns' and the particular value of *Employee* (*Joe Jones*), is 2. We must now imagine other possible (rather than actual) occurrences of the relationship in order to determine the maximum and minimum cardinalities for *Car*. We may happen to know that Mr Doyle does not have a car at all; so it is easy to see that our minimum cardinality is 0.

We must be careful, however, to remember that these cardinalities define what database entries are acceptable (rather than which ones already exist). Hence even if every employee had a car we would still keep a minimum cardinality of 0 rather than 1 (unless it was company policy to refuse hiring pedestrians!). We must then stretch our imaginations in a similar way when we look for the maximum cardinality. Though we may not personally know of a member of staff who owned more than three cars, we would not want to deprive our company of the possibility of retaining the services of Lord Montagu, owner of the Beaulieu Motor Museum, so we must set the maximum cardinality to N!

Having finished with the *Car* side of our relationship we must continue with the *Employee* entity. We may have heard of the rather bizarre Potts family who all work here: they share everything, only have one car (a battered old Citroën

2CV), and all drive to work in it. By extension we say the maximum cardinality of *Employee* will be *N*. Our last case will be better illustrated if we imagine that the *Car Belongs_To Employee* relationship is used by the company's car-park services to determine whether cars are rightfully parked in front of head office, or whether they should be towed away. This means that any car in the car park must be recorded in the attendant's file as belonging to at least one employee. The minimum cardinality for employee in the relationship *Car Belongs_To employee* is then 1.

It is good practice to keep track of this information both in written descriptions of the relationships and in entity–relationship diagrams. Again different authors have slightly diverging views on the notation to be used for cardinalities. This can be very confusing for beginners. It also seems important in view of the use of cardinalities in determining relationship functionality and entity constraints (see below). We have chosen the notation that seems most logical to us: since cardinalities are always related to a particular entity in the relationship they are noted next to the name of that entity (this notation is consistent with that of Tsichritzis and Lochovsky 1982). We would then write *Ownership (Employee(1,N), Car(0,N)* which we would read as 'the ownership of any car (in the car park file) must be traceable to at least one employee, but any employee may own zero or more cars (of those mentioned in the car park file).' The notation adopted for use in the entity–relationship diagrams is kept consistent with the one above (see Figure 8.4).

(*Note.* Entity-types and relationship-types can be viewed as forming sentences that can be likened to propositions in predicate logic. Any combination of terms may form a proposition, but we will only incorporate into our conceptual model those that correspond to a proposition that is deemed to be true. Cardinalities can be likened to logical quantifiers. Data can then be thought of as instantiations of logical variables.)

8.5.3 Functionality of Relationships

The maximum cardinality of each entity enables us to establish the *functionality* of the relationship. Three main types of functionalities of special interest are generally found in any model:

1. *One-to-one* relationships, e.g. *Teaches (Lecturer(1,1), Topic(1,1))*'. This indicates that the departmental policy is that each lecturer must lecture on at least one, but not more than one, topic, that each topic must be taught, but that teaching of a topic may not be shared. Another, more flexible, departmental attitude, which enables staff occasionally to take a research year during which they do no teaching and allows options to figure in the prospectus even if they are not to be taught that particular year, would be summarized by *Teaches (Lecturer(0,1), Topic(0,1))*. It is easy to see that

the general pattern of the links between the *Lecturer* and *Topic* entities is the same in both cases. We refer to each as a 'one-to-one relationship' (see Figure 8.5(a) and (b)).

2. *One-to-many* relationships where any one occurrence of entity E_i of a relationship R may be linked to several occurrences of the entity E_j, although any occurrence of E_j may only be linked to one E_i. For instance *Teaches (Lecturer(0,1), Topic(0,N))* describes a departmental policy whereby a lecturer (who is not away from teaching) will lecture on one or more topics. However, we still have the specification that not more than one lecturer will teach a topic. As in the first type of functionality, we do not take the minimum cardinalities into account, so that *Teaches (Lecturer(1,1) , Topic(0,N)), Teaches (Lecturer(1,1) , Topic(1,N))* and *Teaches (Lecturer(1,N) , Topic(1,1))* are referred to as *one-to-many* relationships (see Figure 8.5(c)).
3. *Many-to-many* relationships, where any one occurrence of entity E_i of the relationship R may be linked to several occurrences of the entity E_j, and any occurrence of E_j may also be linked to several occurrences of E_i. This corresponds to the case where each lecturer in the department may teach on any number of course units and each unit may be taught by several lecturers. For instance 'Teaches (Lecturer(*0*,*N*) , Topic(*0*,*N*)) (see Figure 8.5(d)).

8.6 MODEL ASSEMBLY

Identifying all individual relationships effectively binds all entities into a complex network that we hope to use to model (represent) the universe of discourse. So we now need to re-examine each of our definitions in the light of the whole model and weed out any inconsistency, ambiguity or redundancy that we may find. It is at this stage that a diagram representing the assembly of all the relationships often proves the most useful.

A simplified view of the world of estate agencies specializing in property rental will now be used as a database development example for the coming sections. A short textual description of this particular universe of discourse appears as Figure 8.6. We recommend that you break off your reading at this point and try and use that description to build your own lists of entity-types, property-types, and relationship-types. Work out the associated minimum and maximum cardinalities using the indications given in the text. When these appear insufficient, use your knowledge of the real world and your common sense to reach a decision. Represent a first assembly of the whole model on a single diagram. Once you have done this you can compare your answer with the model in Figure 8.7.

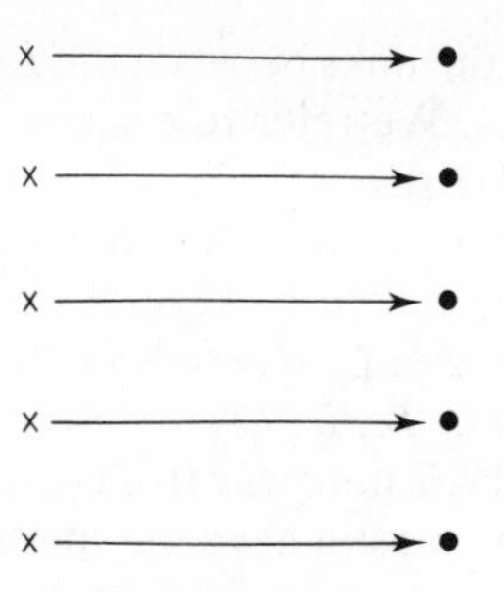

(a) "Teaches (LECTURER (1,1), TOPIC (1,1))"

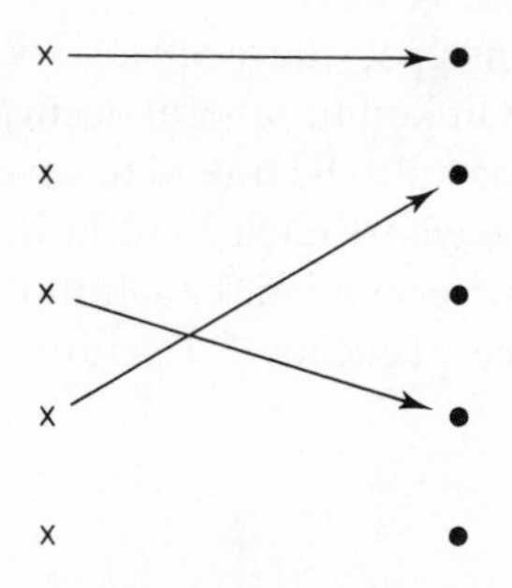

(b) "Teaches (LECTURER(0,1), TOPIC (0,1))"

8.7 MODEL REFINEMENT

We must now carry out a detailed review of the model, checking it for errors (Vasta (1985) gives full details on this). The measures required to eliminate the most common awkward or erroneous features of a design can be classified into the categories of Sections 8.7.1–4.

8.7.1 Identification of synonymic or homonymic entities or properties

Synonyms would be, say, two or more identical entities which have been given a different name during the analysis process (possibly because they appear in the data environment of two disjoint departments, each having its own terminology which naturally became reflected in the interviewer's report). An example of this may be found in a large company, where the personnel division functions in terms of 'employee records', a particular department may talk about its 'members of staff', and the medical service

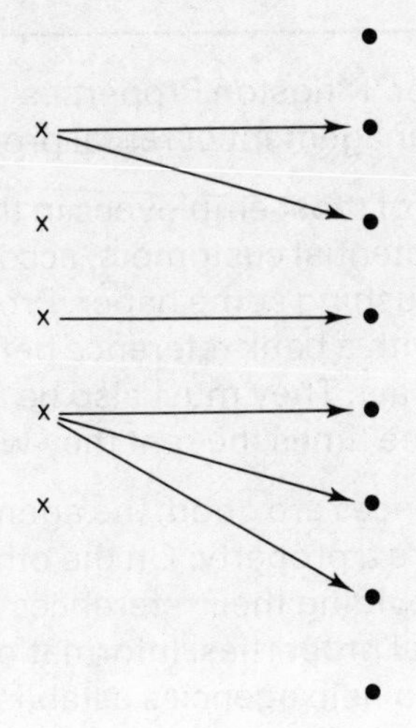

(c) "Teaches (LECTURER (o,1), TOPIC (o,N))"

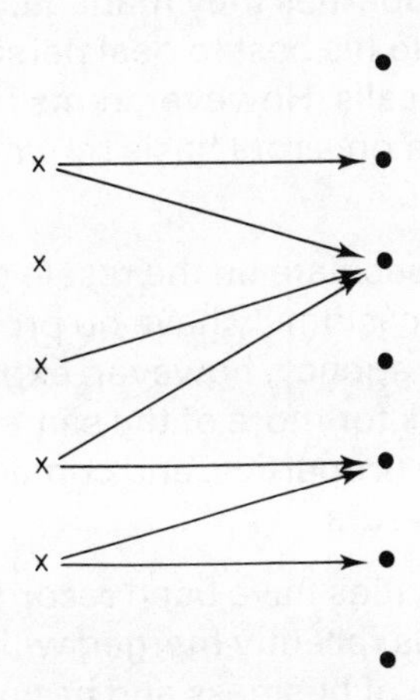

(d) "Teaches (LECTURER (o,N), TOPIC (o,N))"

Figure 8.5 Occurrence diagrams for different types of relationship functionalities: (a) Teaches (Lecturer (1,*1*), Topic (1,*1*)); (b) Teaches (Lecturer (ø,*1*), Topic (ø,*1*)); (c) Teaches (Lecturer (ø,*1*), Topic (ø,*N*)); (d) Teaches (Lecturer (ø,*N*), Topic (ø,*N*))

mentions only 'Patients'. All three are in fact referring to the same *Employee* entity.

Homonyms occur when two or more entities or properties are referred to by

Julian Avery works for 'Kingston Properties', an agency which handles sales and management of rental properties.

Julian's job is typical of most employees in the agency: his time is spent interviewing potential customers, accompanying them on property visits, and pushing some paper. Prospective tenants must provide the agency with a bank reference before they can be invited to sign a contract. They must also be able to show a regular income of at least three times the rent they will have to pay.

Providing their references are good, the agency will let several personal tenants share a property. On the other hand, only companies (again providing their references are good) will be allowed to rent several properties. Information on tenants is kept on file for four years to help agencies establish credit records on tenants.

The agency insists on providing a friendly personalised service to the landlords whose properties they manage, so Julian, for instance, must always do his best to deal personally with Mr. Patterson whenever he calls. However, rents from, and repairs to, properties are dealt with on a rota basis by whichever employee is on office duty at the time.

Since a few landlords speculate on the resale price of their properties, they may occasionally have no property under management at all. The agency, however, expects that these landlords will come back for more of the same service as soon as they have acquired new properties, and contact is kept with these landlords for up to two years.

Up to now all these activities have been recorded manually, but 'Kingston Properties' has recently merged with 25 other agencies involved in a similar line of business and has now become a branch office of 'United Property Rentals' (UPR). UPR has decided that this is a good time to modernize its operations and computerize all its property management data. In view of the new Data Protection Laws, however, they will not keep any record concerning past tenants on the computer.

Figure 8.6 A description of the universe of discourse for the property rental agency

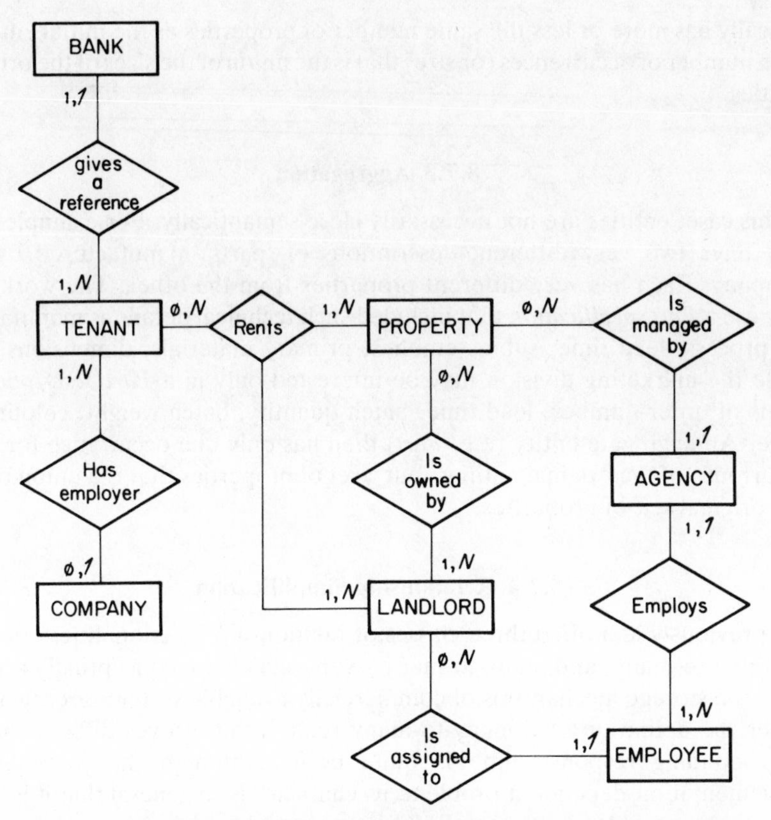

Figure 8.7 The assembled model for the property rental agency example

the same name but really correspond to different concepts. For instance both the managing director and an administrative officer may describe their data as relating to an 'office', but one may be referring to a particular company sub-division (as in 'the London office of Bloggs and Co.') and the other to a room within a building (as in 'the ground floor offices').

8.7.2 Generalization

There are also cases where entities or properties are semantically close but are not synonyms. It may still be advantageous to create a new 'higher-level' entity or property that will aggregate those. For instance analysis of the structure of some academic institution may have identified the three entities *Lecturer*, *Administrator*, and *Librarian*. Depending on the use to be made of the data, there may be good reason to redefine the three as occurrences of a more general entity *Staff* which simply has an extra property *JobTitle*. The new entity typically has more or less the same number of properties as the initial entities, but a number of occurrences (or size) that is the union of the sizes of the original entities.

8.7.3 Aggregation

In this case, entities are not necessarily close semantically. For examples, we may have two very different descriptions of 'parts' manufactured by the company. Each has very different properties from the other. The workshop may use a *PartSpecification* that included such technical details as manufacturing process, lead time, sub-assemblies, primary materials, dimensions, etc. while the marketing division may be interested only in a *PartDescription* in terms of order-number, lead time, batch quantity, batch weight, colour and price. An aggregate entity (e.g. *Part*) then has only one occurrence for each occurrence of the original entities, but a set of properties that is a union of the two original sets of properties.

8.7.4 Relationship Simplification

We previously identified three classes of relationship functionalities– one-to-one, one-to-many, and many-to-many. Although all are conceptually acceptable, the storage mechanisms of commercially available systems are such that either the definition of a many-to-many relationship proves difficult or the corresponding response time is quite poor. Although this is really an implementation-dependent problem, its character is so general that it is often preferable to tackle it at the level of the conceptual model.

The solution adopted is the replacement of any many-to-many relationship by two one-to-many relationships, the combination of which provides the same level of information. This implies identifying a new entity that joins the two relationships together. It is often found that this new entity does in fact have attributes of its own that would have been difficult to attach elsewhere. A typical example is the relationship *Registers_For (Student(5,50) , CourseUnit(4,7))*. This is a many-to-many relationship representing the school rule by which a student must choose to take at least four, but no more than seven, course units every year towards his/her degree. It also indicates a unit is cancelled when less than five students register but that no more than 50 will be catered for. We may replace this by two one-to-many relationships: *Takes_Diet (Student(1,1) , S-C-Link(4,7))*; *Has_Enrolment (S-C-Link(5,50), CourseUnit(1,1))* (see Figure 8.8). With a little more observation we can see that rather than creating a 'dummy', meaningless linkage entity like *S-C-Link*, there are some useful data (entity or property) that had not yet found their place in the model, e.g.: *Takes_Diet (Student(1,1) , ResultReport(4,7))*; *Has_Enrolment (ResultReport(5,50) , CourseUnit(1,1))*.

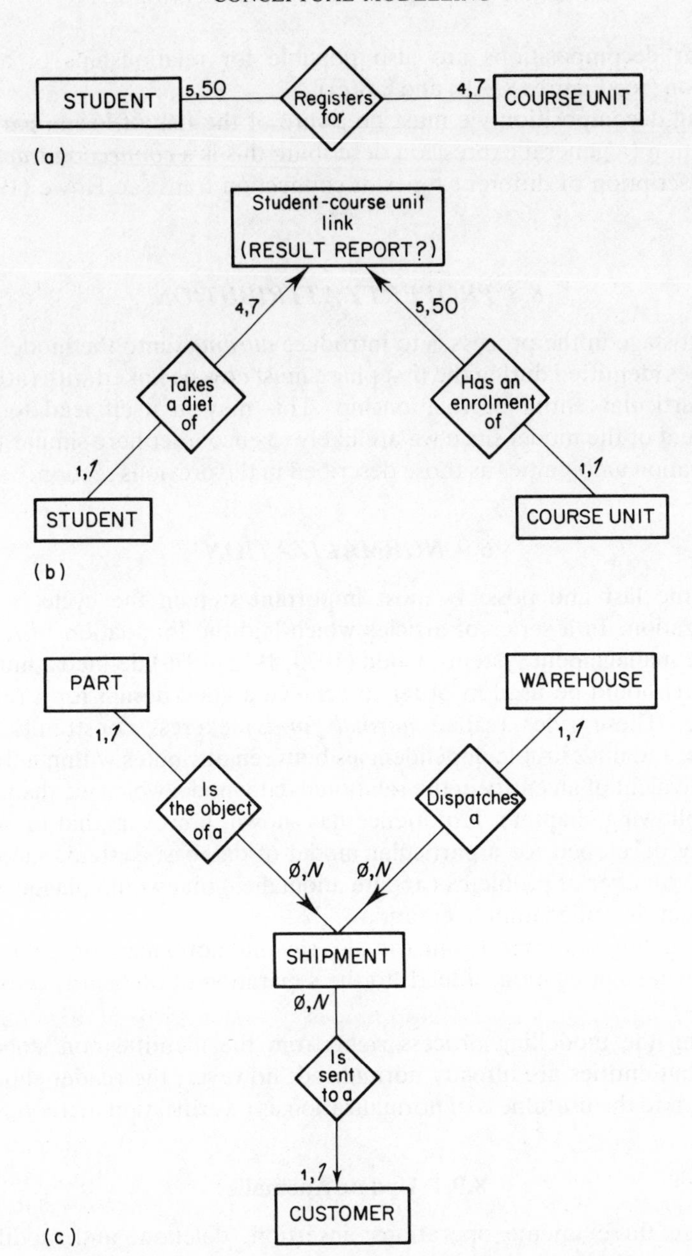

Figure 8.8 Simplification of many-to-many relationships: (a) The many-to-many relationship 'Registers_for'; (b) The two one-to-many relationships chosen to replace 'Registers_for'; (c) The three one-to-many relationships chosen to replace the complex relationship 'Is_delivered' shown in Figure 8.3 (b)

Similar decompositions are also possible for relationships of a higher dimension (see Figures 8.3(b) and 8.8(c)).

During decomposition we must be aware of the risk of losing part of the information (a general expression describing this is a *connection trap*). For a good description of different types of connection traps see Howe (1983, pp. 113–25).

8.8 PROPERTY ATTRIBUTION

The next stage in the process is to introduce *attributes* into the model: all the properties identified during the first phase must now be linked with (attributed to) a particular entity or relationship. This may in itself lead to further refinement of the model since we are likely to encounter here similar types of identification ambiguities as those described in the previous section.

8.9 NORMALIZATION

Finally the last and possibly most important step in the cycle is that of normalization. In a series of articles which laid the foundation of *relational* database management systems, Codd (1970, 1972, 1979) defined a number of rules that should be used in order to achieve a good design for a relational database. These rules (called *normal forms*) express constraints on the desirable and undesirable dependencies between attributes within a 'relation' (the equivalent of an entity in the relational data model which we shall present in the following chapter). Experience has shown, however, that these rules, originally developed for a particular model of database system, successfully tackled a number of problems (update anomalies) that would plague a model whatever its intended implementation.

Viewing things differently one can also say that normalization is the inverse process from aggregation: it leads to the separation of one entity into two or more.

Starting the modelling process right from the identification stage often means that entities are already normalized; however, the reader should still keep in mind the usefulness of normalization as a verification method.

8.9.1 Update Anomalies

There are three update operations: insertion, deletion, and modification (which can always be reduced to a delete/insert combination). In certain (unnormalized) databases carrying out these operations may have certain unwanted side effects. An insertion anomaly occurs when we wish to insert into the database some information that seems incomplete in terms of the model in its present state. This is the case for an entity which has wrongly been defined as

Department	Date of request	ItemOrdered	ItemSupplier	Quantity
Planning	06/04	Pencils	W. H. Smith	200
		Erasers	W. H. Smith	100
		Rulers	Cartier	8
		Aspirin	Boots	55
Sales	07/05	Diaries	W. H. Smith	15
		Shoes	Marks & Sparks	12
Production	07/06	Robots	Boots	6
		Tea (lb)	Marks & Sparks	450
		Pillows	Simpsons	12
		T.V. sets	W. H. Smith	2

(a)

ItemOrdered	ItemSupplier	Quantity
Pencils	W. H. Smith	200
Erasers	W. H. Smith	100
Rulers	Cartier	8
Aspirin	Boots	55
Diaries	W. H. Smith	15
Shoes	Marks & Sparks	12
Robots	Boots	6
Tea(lb)	Marks & Sparks	450
Pillows	Simpsons	12
T.V. sets	W. H. Smith	2

Department	Date of request
Planning	06/04
Sales	07/05
Production	07/06

(b)

Figure 8.9 Transformation of entities into first normal form: (a) The entity "supplies_on_order"; (b) the two 1NF entities "supplies_on_order" and "origins_of_order"

part of another. A deletion anomaly is similar to this. It corresponds to the case where the deletion of one piece of information cannot be carried out without resulting in some other, unwanted deletion. Finally a modification anomaly corresponds to the case where data is arranged in such a way that what is conceptually the modification of a single value actually requires N physical modifications to be effected. For example, suppose we have entity occurrences similar to the following:

- Prof Jarreau teaches Economics to H. James of 54 Aberdeen St, Esher
- Prof Jarreau teaches Economics to J. Sommers of 22 London Rd, Kingston
- Dr Smith teaches Computing to H. James of 54 Aberdeen St, Esher
- Dr Smith teaches Computing to J. Sommers of 22 London Rd, Kingston
- Prof Tar teaches Maths to J. Sommers of 22 London Rd, Kingston

A change of address for any one student requires at least four physical modifications to the data (the minimum number of course units a student must take).

The advantage of having these normal forms to assist in model refinement is that they provide a *tool* for detecting faults rather than relying solely on personal judgement.

8.9.2 First Normal Form

The canonical rules for having an entity in first normal form (1NF) requires that there be no repeating groups of attributes in any entity occurrence. In most cases, such properties correspond to parts of another entity that have wrongly been attributed to the present one. The repeating groups can usually simply be removed and formed into a new entity. For instance the entity *Supplies_On_Order* comprising the attributes *Department*, *Date*, *ItemOrdered*, *ItemSupplier*, *Quantity* may conceptually have been thought of as having occurrences such as those in Figure 8.9(a). The figure clearly shows the repeating group formed by the properties *ItemOrdered*, *ItemSupplier*, *Quantity*. Transforming *Supplies_On_Order* into an entity in 1NF requires forming those properties into a separate entity (see Figure 8.9(b)). To preserve the information contained in the original entity we must also create a new relationship *Ordered_For* to link the two new entities.

In other cases (see Figure 8.10) removing the repeating group is not desirable since it leaves a single attribute in the entity. The preferred solution is then to define the entity as having no repeating group and replace the group occurrence by corresponding occurrences of the whole entity (see Figure 8.10(b)).

Each new normal form adds new restrictions onto the ones defined by the previous normal form. So we must ensure that all the entities in our model are in 1NF before progressing any further.

Course number	Student number	Student name	Grade
SE-010	KPCS010	T. Barrow	A
	KPCS009	S. Charles	A
	KPCS014	E. Signel	B
	KPCS017	J. Andrew	C
	KPCS002	M. Thorper	D
IP-030	KPCS009	S. Charles	A
	KPCS014	E. Signel	A
	KPCS010	T. Barrow	B
	KPCS002	M. Thorper	C

(a)

Course number	Student number	Student name	Grade
SE-010	KPCS010	T. Barrow	A
SE-010	KPCS009	S. Charles	A
SE-010	KPCS014	E. Signel	B
SE-010	KPCS017	J. Andrew	C
SE-010	KPCS002	M. Thorper	D
IP-030	KPCS009	S. Charles	A
IP-030	KPCS014	E. Signel	A
IP-030	KPCS010	T. Barrow	B
IP-030	KPCS002	M. Thorper	C

(b)

Figure 8.10 Another first normal form transformation: (a) the entity "Courseresults" un-normalized; (b) the entity "Courseresults" in 1NF

8.9.3 Functional Dependencies

The rules for establishing normal forms other than the 1NF require an understanding of the concept of functional dependencies between attributes of an entity. As we have seen before (Chapter 7) there exists a mathematical object known as a *relation* which simply expresses a series of connections between two sets. A characteristic of a relation is that given an element from one set, we can always determine the corresponding element (or elements) of the other set (if they exist). A relationship R is therefore a relation between, say, entities E_1 and E_2. A relation expresses a very general kind of correspondence. We can apply several types of restrictions to relations, but probably the most useful one is to limit to one (at most) the number of images made to correspond to a single element from the origin set (see Figure 8.11). This is what is called a *function* (Figure 8.11). If every element in the origin set has an image, then the function is said to be *total*. If some but not all of the elements in the origin set have an image, then the function is *partial*.

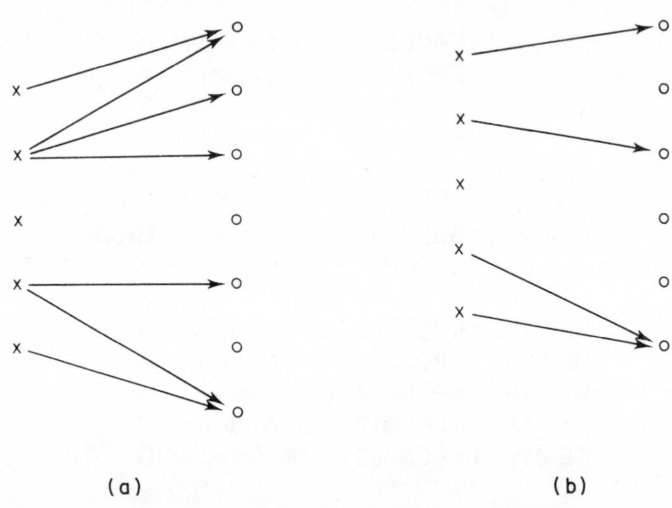

Figure 8.11 Relations and functions: (a) a relation; (b) a function

Transforming a many-to-many into two one-to-many relationships effectively transforms a relation into a function. To apply the same concept to entities we need to distinguish two sets (origin and image) within the attributes that constitute them. We refer to these as the *set of determinant attributes* (also called the *entity key*) and the *set of dependent attributes* (all the non-key attributes). We can then view the entity E as a relation between K (the entity key) and D (the dependent attributes). We must also be able to identify each element of one set (the origin set) and link them to specific elements of the other set (the image set). That is, we need a 'key' to enable identification of particular occurrences of the entity.

Any attribute (or set of attributes) that uniquely identifies an entity occurrence is called a *candidate key*. Amongst those candidate keys we will select one that we will designate as the *primary key*. If a key is made up of a combination of more than one attribute, we will say it is a *composite key*.

Transforming an unnormalized entity into one in first normal form establishes the rule that one and only one dependent group may correspond to one key. That is, it transforms a relation into a function. We can then say that in an entity in first normal form, the non-key attributes are functionally dependent on the key attributes. Of the two examples above, functionality was achieved in the first case by removing some attributes to another entity, but in the second case it was done by implicitly redefining the entity identifier to be the key composed of the two attributes *Course Number* and *Student Number* rather than *Course Number* alone.

Dependencies are conveniently represented in diagrams such as those in Figure 8.13. Each attribute is written in a cell, with a bolder box drawn around some of them to represent the key grouping. Full lines stand for the dependency(ies) that should be present in the normal form, and go from a key group to a non-key group. Dotted lines represent spurious dependencies that should be removed.

Item	Quantity	Administration Officer	Department
Chalk	100	June Roberts	Mathematics
Notepad	50	Joe Carsons	Personnel
Pen	25	Joe Carsons	Personnel
Computer paper	1000	Mary Miller	Computing

Figure 8.12 Entity "StationeryRequest"

The rules for characterizing further normal forms rely directly on the observation of functional dependencies to detect and correct deviations from the norm. The general idea is that a well-formed entity should only exhibit one kind of functional dependency: that of the non-key attributes on the key attributes. Any other dependency detected between attributes corresponds to a design fault. Second and third normal forms deals with the removal of attributes that exhibit a dependency other than that on the primary key (the primary dependency).

8.9.4 Second Normal Form

An entity may only need reduction to 2NF if it has a composite primary key. By extension this means that any entity which is in 1NF and has a single primary key is also in 2NF. The 2NF restrictions aim to remove the dependency of any non-key attribute on a particular key attribute rather than on the whole key. This is often described as making the non-key attributes *fully* dependent on the key attributes. Consider an entity taken to represent details of various stationery requests put forward by different departments. Items may be recorded as presented in Figure 8.12: description of item, quantity requested,

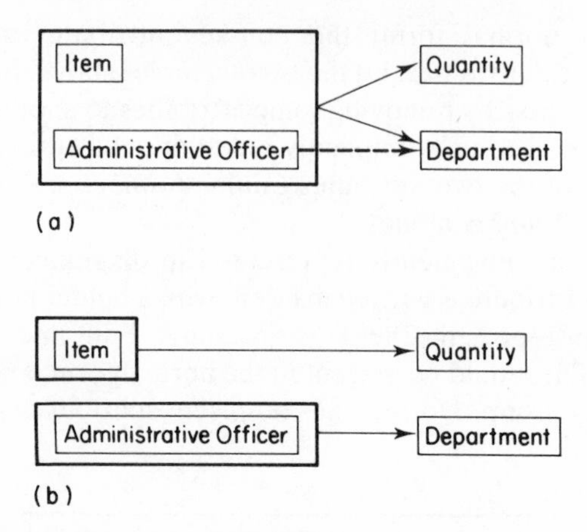

Figure 8.13 Functional dependency diagram and transformation to second normal form: (a) For entity "StationeryRequest"; (b) For the two resulting entities "StationeryRequested" and "AdministrativeOfficer"

administrative officer responsible for the request, department to which the administrative officer belongs. If there is only one administrative officer per department, we can represent the functional dependencies for that entity as in Figure 8.13(a), which shows a non-full dependency between *Administrative Officer* and *Department*. Deletion anomalies are particularly clear here: deletion of the *Computing Paper* request would deprive us of the information that Mary Miller was affiliated to the computing department. Removal of this non-full dependency results in the two entities *StationeryRequested* and *AdministrativeOfficer* linked by the relationship *RequestedBy* (Figure 8.13(b)).

8.9.5 Third Normal Form

All 2NF entities must then be checked for conformity with third normal form rules. They aim at removing any dependency between non-key attributes. These are called transitive dependencies and usually correspond to the erroneous inclusion of a sub-entity within the main one. Take for instance the entity *Book* pictured in Figure 8.14(a). Although the attributes *Title* and *AuthorName* are dependent only on the single key *ISBN*, the attribute *AuthorAddress* is also a function of the non-key attribute *AuthorName*. These can be formed into a new entity *Author* (Figure 8.14(b)), linked to a new *Book* entity by a relationship *Written_By*.

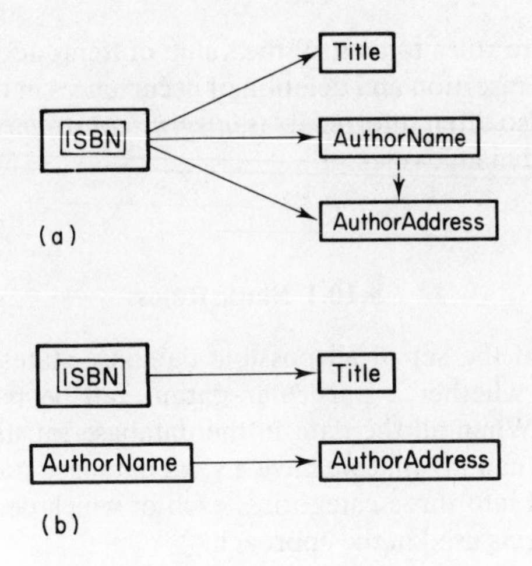

Figure 8.14 Reduction to third normal form: (a) the entity "Book"; (b) the entities resulting from the 3NF transformation

8.9.6 Higher Normal Forms

Normal forms restrict the domain of all possible relations while tackling specific logical and practical problems. As designers gain more experience in the use of these techniques and as database analysis and design comes of age, further unresolved problems come to light and new normal forms are established to help achieve the corresponding correct design decisions. Thus there are now several forms that are more recent and more restrictive than the first three. These are, however, outside the scope of an introductory text. The interested reader should consult the following references: Codd (1972), Date (1981), Fagin (1977), Howe (1983) and Lien (1985).

8.10 INTEGRITY RULES

We have so far described the logical structure we wish to give to the data in our model of the universe of discourse. We have said nothing about the values of the data that might be inserted into this structure. As would be the case for a single variable in abstract data typing, a domain of possible values should be associated with our model. Since we are dealing with a structure that is large and complex there can be no question of enumerating its domain or even mapping it onto existing sets. Instead we try to apprehend this domain by defining all the rules that are necessary and sufficient to construct it. In particular there are rules to control the value of items added to the database and to restrict the insertion and deletion of occurrences in the database. These rules, which are also often referred to as *integrity constraints*, are best classified first as static and dynamic rules.

8.10.1 Static Rules

Static rules govern the set of all possible database states. They enable the determination of whether a particular datum can be part of a particular database (state). When all the data in the database satisfies all of the static integrity rules, we can say that we have a valid database state. Static rules can be further divided into three categories, each of which deals with one of the three kinds of objects used in the approach.

Rules on attributes

They are often called *domain integrity rules* and appear at the lowest level as *type* definitions such as one finds in most programming languages, e.g. *integer*, *double-length integer*, *string of maximum length 25 characters*, etc. They are supplemented in many systems by range constraints or enumerations, e.g.

'AGE must be less than 129'
'Employee-Age < 65'
'Salary ≥ $1000'
'NAME only includes {'a' . . 'z','A' . . 'Z','-'}'
'MODEL is in {'Mini','Metro','Maestro','Montego'}'

Rules on entities

Regardless of the acceptability of a value as an instance of a particular attribute, some rules will establish logical connections which must be respected between attributes within the same entity. For instance, given an entity *Employee* with attributes *Name*, *Employee Number*, *Sex*, *Age*, *Home Address*, *Phone*, we can imagine that the following would apply:

- we do not want to record an employee's address or phone number without knowing that employee's name;
- since there may be employees with identical names, each employee must be given a different employee number;
- it is not acceptable to record an employee's name but not his/her age and sex;

- we may want, as a temporary measure, to record information on an employee who, having just moved to town, does not yet have a home address;
- we certainly will have, as a permanent feature, employees who do not have a telephone in their home;
- if however, an employee does have a phone number to give us, we then expect an address to go with it.

The following rules are necessary and sufficient to enforce the above restrictions:

1. no entity occurrence may have empty values for *Name*, *Sex* or *Age*;
2. values for *Employee Number* must be unique;
3. if *Phone* has a value, then *Home Address* must have one too.

Rules on relationships

These define logical dependencies that must be respected in links between relationships. Suppose for instance that we add to our previous example the entity-type *Medical Record*. It would not be acceptable to store medical information without the knowledge of whom this information related to. We must then have a rule requiring a link to exist between any occurrence of *Medical Record* and an occurrence of *Employee*. Some of these rules (often called *referential integrity rules*) have already been defined in a different way as the minimum cardinalities mentioned in Section 8.5.2.

8.10.2 Dynamic rules

Dynamic rules govern the set of all possible transitions between two (or more) specific, valid database states. The rules enable the determination of whether a particular datum can be part of a particular database state given the previous state(s) of the database. When the data in the database satisfies all of the dynamic integrity rules, we can say that we have a valid database.

Dynamic constraints also can be attached to the same categories of objects as static rules. These constraints should, in principle, require knowledge of both the previous and the new, intended database state. This appears clearly in the following two examples:

1. Imagine that our *Employee* entity is specified to contain the property *Marital Status*. Changes to this attribute over time can only be made if they are one of a number of legal cases. We have summarized those in Table 8.1 (this supposes a certain continuity in the recording of the information).

Table 8.1

	Marital status	TO Single	Married	Divorced	Widowed	Unknown
FROM	Single	N.A.	Yes	No	No	No
	Married	No	N.A.	Yes	Yes	No
	Divorced	No	Yes	N.A.	No	No
	Widowed	N.A.	Yes	No	N.A.	No

2. Another example of rule requiring knowledge of both 'old' and 'new' states is simple to state (although it may be more difficult to implement): 'no employee may be given a rise that would make him earn more than his/her manager.'

In other cases, dynamic constraints govern the way in which the database can evolve over time, and can be enforced by rules that carry out checks on single states or even that are independent from any database state. For instance the rule 'No publication may be deleted from the catalogue' (see ISO 1982, Chapter 2 for more examples).

8.10.3 Authorization Rules

Finally we must mention that in addition to the above rules that describe possible states of the database, further rules are needed that would define the interactions permissible between the information (database) system and its users. Most present commercially available systems, however, only enable the definition of one category of rules of this type: those that grant access privileges (or bar access) to certain categories of users.

Once this final step in the specification of the model is done and no more refinement seems necessary, conceptual modelling is finished. The next stage in the construction of a database (system) then involves defining a data model that could appropriately be used to represent our conceptual model (in the same way that in software engineering one must choose the language and constructs most appropriate to represent abstract data types). To be able to do this we must first obtain an understanding of the most common data models we are likely to come in contact with. This is the object of the next chapter.

Fundamentals of Information Technology
Edited by G. G. Wilkinson and A. R. Winterflood

Chapter 9

Logical Database Models

9.1 DATA MODELS

A database management system (DBMS) is a collection of computer programs that provides the services required to manage a database. In general a particular implementation of a DBMS will support data structures and operations to maintain one particular type of logical data model.

The three logical data models most commonly supported by database management systems are the hierarchical model, the network model, and the relational model. The hierarchical and network models are formatted models in which a variety of data structures are used to represent the relationships identified in the conceptual model. In these the access paths which will be required to maintain logical associations within the stored data have to be explicitly pre-defined. In relational databases, however, data is represented by a single class of object: two-dimensional tables known as relations. In this case logical associations within the stored data are achieved by having common information within two different tables.

A study of the historical development of databases gives an interesting insight into the driving forces behind the evolution of database management systems based on each of these three data models. Deen (1977) and (1985) summarizes the development of databases and database management systems from their beginning in the early 1960s. The first database management systems were developed as a solution to data-processing problems in parts management and inventory applications and were closely tied to the applications for which they were produced (hence the ubiquity of the parts-supplier example in texts on database systems). Hierarchical data structures were thus the first to be supported. The need to represent more complex relationships soon encouraged the production of new software (in particular supporting network data structures). By 1970 interest groups had been formed to nurture the development of *generalized* DBMS.

9.2 THE HIERARCHICAL MODEL

In the hierarchical model data are represented in a hierarchical or tree structure. The highest level in the hierarchy is known as the root node. It has no

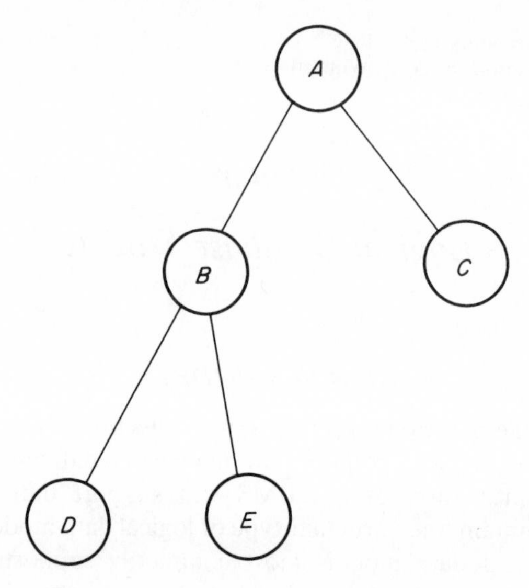

Figure 9.1 A simple hierarchical structure

parent node above it. Apart from the root node all other nodes must have one and only one parent node, but any node can have more than one dependent or *child* node related to it at a lower level in the hierarchy. In Figure 9.1 node *A* is the root node, node *B* is the child of node *A* and the parent of node *D*. A hierarchical file is one in which the relationship between records is represented by a tree structure.

An aspect of the property-rental agency example (see Chapter 8) can be used to illustrate this. Consider the situation in which landlords, properties and tenants are of interest. Figure 9.2 shows a hierarchical model in which one landlord can be associated with many properties and can equally be associated with many tenants.

Using this model it is not possible to associate properties with tenants other than via their parent landlord without violating the rules for constructing a tree structure. However if, say the prime interest in tenants were to be in the context of the history of occupation of a property, the hierarchy of Figure 9.3 might be

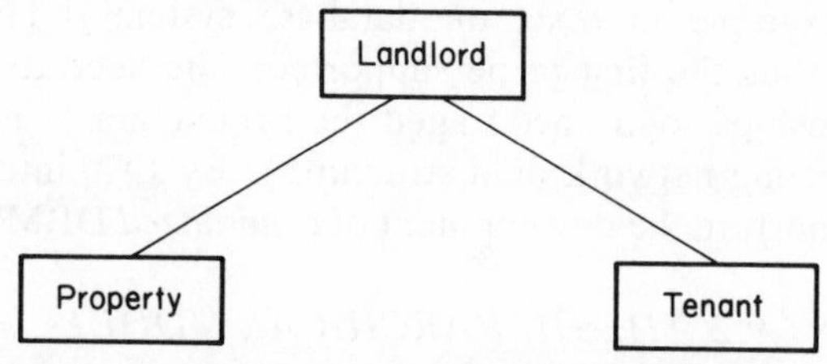

Figure 9.2 Two-level hierarchical structure for the property rental agency

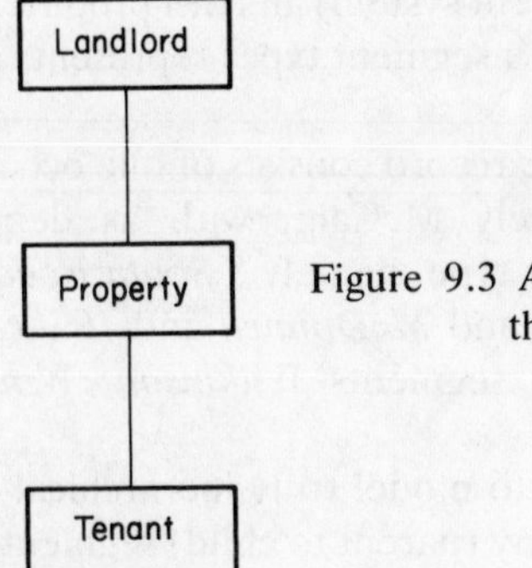

Figure 9.3 A three-level hierarchical structure for the property rental agency

considered suitable. In this instance a three-level tree structure can be used to represent landlords' ownership of many properties and occupancy of property by many tenants.

A physical database record modelled on the hierarchy of Figure 9.3 is shown in Figure 9.4.

The major commercial implementation of a DBMS based on the hierarchical

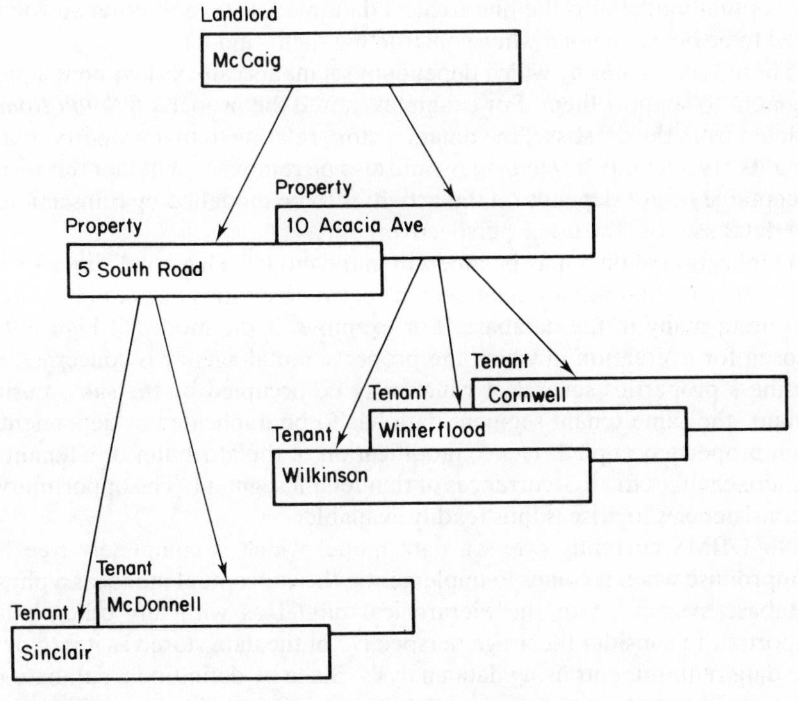

Figure 9.4 Physical database record for the three-level hierarchical structure for the property rental agency

model is IMS (information management system) an IBM product. In IMS each heterogeneous node type (known as a segment type) represents an entity and its attributes.

In Figure 9.4 the physical database record consists of one occurrence of the root segment type landlord, namely McCaig, with as dependents two occurrences of the property-segment type, namely *5 South Road* with its two dependent tenant segments *Sinclair* and *McDonnell* and *10 Acacia Avenue*, which has three dependent tenant segments *Wilkinson*, *Winterflood* and *Cornwell*.

Tree structures are a natural way to model truly hierarchical relationships from the real world when one-to-many (parent to child) segment types can be defined to represent successive levels in a tree structure in order to relate entities to one another.

However, in many situations relationships do not naturally fit into this model. For instance it is not easy to directly represent relationships between segment types at the same level in the hierarchy, nor is it possible without introducing data duplication to represent many-to-many relationships between entities.

Apart from the problems which may be encountered in trying to 'squeeze' a conceptual model into the hierarchical data model, several other restrictions need to be borne in mind when constructing such a model.

There is no means by which dependent segments can exist without a parent segment to support them. For example, should the property *5 South Road* be deleted from the database, the tenant history relating to that property, namely tenants *Sinclair* and *McDonnell*, would also be removed. Whether this result is acceptable or not depends on the activities to be modelled by transactions on the database, i.e. the usage perspective.

Duplication of data may be inherent in the model. This usually arises where real-world many-to-many relationships between entities have to be modelled as one-to-many in the database. For example, if the model of Figure 9.3 is chosen for a situation in which the property-rental agency is concerned with business properties several of which may be occupied by the same business tenant, the same tenant segment data has to be duplicated as dependents of each property occupied. Hence modification of the attributes of a tenant will require changes to all occurrences of that tenant segment. The opportunity for inconsistencies to arise is thus readily available.

No DBMS currently offers a data model which is completely free from compromise when it comes to implementig the conceptual model as a physical database system. With the hierarchical model as with any other it is as important to consider the usage perspective of the data stored as it is to define the data requirements using data analysis. Since by definition a database is to be shared by many users, each with different and, very likely, conflicting data and data-processing requirements, it is not easy to decide which data model within a DBMS will provide the best representation for the users as a whole. Fortunately, however, the designers of DBMS acknowledge these problems and facilities are often provided within DBMS to permit reorganization of the database throughout its lifetime.

A more detailed discussion of the hierarchical model and IBM's IMS in particular can be found in Date (1981). Those wishing to explore how tree structures are physically represented in storage will find abundant detail in Cardenas (1985) and also in Martin (1977).

9.3 THE NETWORK MODEL

A hierarchical model such as the one presented in the last section is based on a special case of the more generalized *network* or *plex* structure. In the network model any node can be connected to any other node in the structure. The nodes consist of groups of data usually representing an entity and its attributes, whilst the connection between the nodes represents the existence of a relationship between the two nodes (entities). Figure 9.5 shows a network model of the landlord, tenant, and property entities of the property-rental agency example.

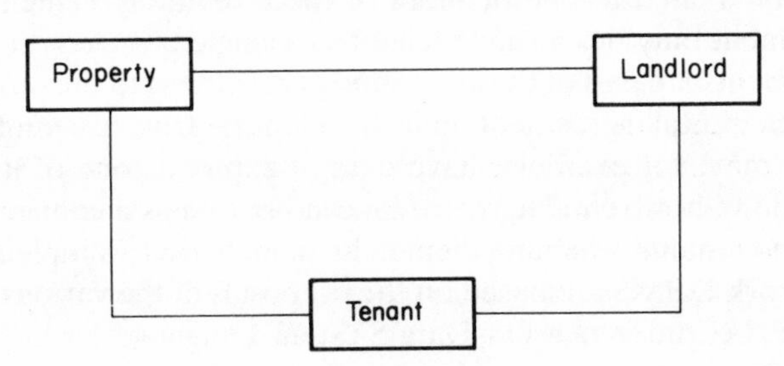

Figure 9.5 A network structure for the property rental agency

If the property-rental agency is concerned with an environment in which one landlord may own many properties and the property-to-tenant relationship is one-to-one, the network of Figure 9.5 is said to be a *simple plex* structure, since only one-to-one and one-to-many relationships are involved. If, however, the situation is such that a business tenant may occupy many properties, and some properties, e.g. a block of offices, may be occupied by many tenants, the relationship between property and tenant becomes many-to-many. Such a network is then known as a *complex plex* structure. In general, DBMS based on the network model do not support complex plex structures directly therefore a conceptual model which involves many-to-many relationships between entities needs to be modified (or *flexed* as it is sometimes termed) in order to produce a network data model which is a simple plex structure.

A many-to-many relationship between two entities can be transformed into

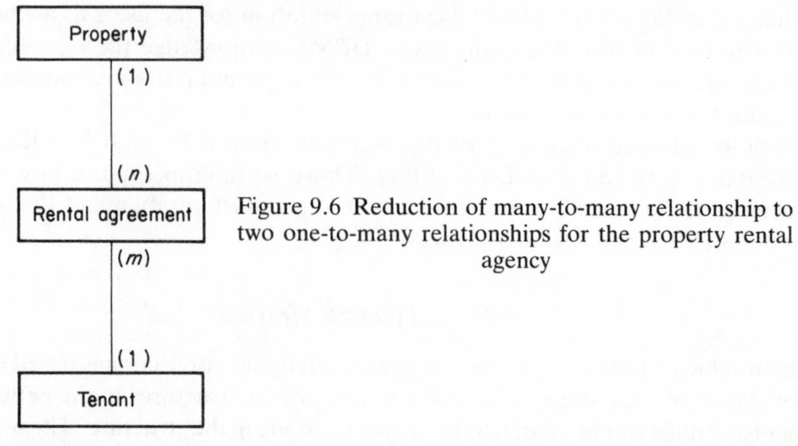

Figure 9.6 Reduction of many-to-many relationship to two one-to-many relationships for the property rental agency

two one-to-many relationships if an intervening connection node is established (cf. Section 8.7.4). In the property–tenant example an intervening connection could be established as shown in Figure 9.6.

In this situation each tenant is party to one or more rental agreements and each property is cited in one or more of these rental agreements, but each rental agreement only ties a single tenant to a single property. It may be that rental agreements are part of the environment of interest to the property-rental agency. Each rental agreement may be identified by a rental agreement number and may, for example, have date of expiry as one of its attributes. Figure 9.7 shows how rental agreements can be used as a connector between properties and tenants, enabling them to be modelled as a simplex plex.

Most network DBMS are based on the proposals of the various committees of CODASYL (Conference On Data SYstem Languages) which have been concerned with the systematic development of ideas on many aspects of

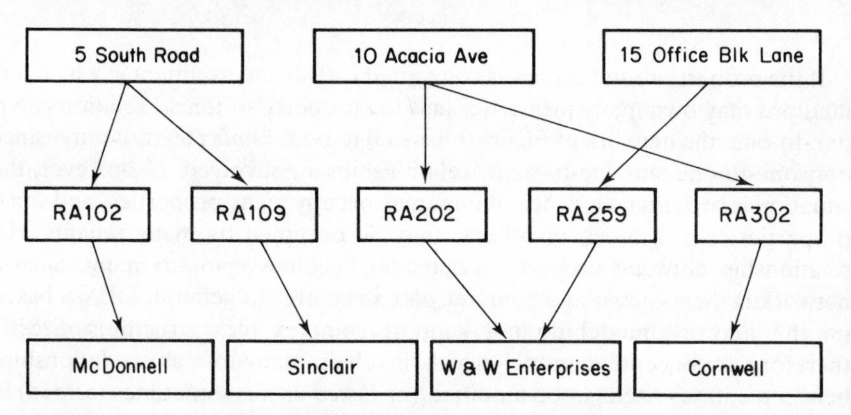

Figure 9.7 Connection between properties and tenants through rental agreements for the property rental agency

database systems, database architecture, data description and in particular data-manipulation languages and data structures. The salient feature of their proposals with respect to network data structures is the concept of sets often referred to as *DBTG sets* after the particular committee which developed them.

Each entity-type and its attributes forms a *record type* within a network database. Different record types are linked together to represent relationships by the definition of *set types* within the network. A set type consists of an *owner* record type and one or more *member* record types. Thus a set type defines a two-level hierarchical relationship between the owner record type and its member record types. For example the relationship *rents-to* between landlord and tenant (Figure 9.5) could be defined as a set type with owner record type *landlord* and member record type *tenant*. A physical set of the set type *rents-to* with owner record type *landlord* and member record type *tenant* is shown in Figure 9.8.

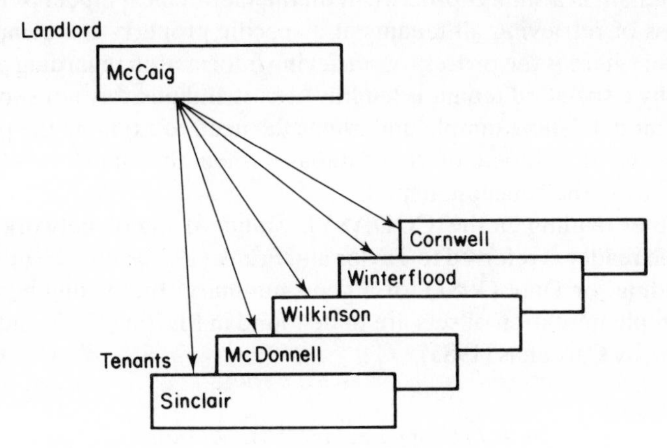

Figure 9.8 Physical set of the set type 'Rents-To' for the property rental agency

A record type may be defined as the owner of more than one set type so landlord (e.g. Figure 9.5) could also be defined as the owner record type in a set type representing the landlord–property relationship. Similarly any record type may be defined as a member of one or more set types. Furthermore, any record type may be specified as both an owner in one or more set types and a member in one or more different set types. However, the possibility of being both owner and member in the same set type is not supported.

From this it can be seen that a set consists of one owner record occurrence and as many member record occurrences as exist in the particular instance of the relationship. Note that a record cannot be included in more than one occurrence of the same set type, i.e. many-to-many relationships are not supported by these sets.

Network structures offer more scope to represent conceptual models directly than hierarchical structures do, albeit at the expense of simplicity, at least with respect to the physical storage structure. The need to transform many-to-many relationships by the construction of a network model which uses connectors does mean that more or less irreversible decisions have to be made about the nature of relationships between entities when the data model is designed.

It should be noted that the use of connectors in the network model, whilst permitting a representation of many-to-many relationships without introducing duplication of the participating record occurrences, does make retrieval of data through the connectors a symmetrically laborious process. If, for instance, it is a requirement to retrieve a list of all tenants at a specified property, then access to those tenants has to be via the connecting rental agreements through whatever data structures (pointer chains, etc.) are used to physically maintain logical links between the record entities. To retrieve properties occupied by a specified tenant is a similar process. With the hierarchical model of Figure 9.3 the process of retrieving all tenants at a specific property is a comparatively simple one, whereas the process of retrieving information regarding properties occupied by a specified tenant is lengthy at best and possibly not supported at all by the model. This example underlines the need to examine the processing which will be demanded of the database when the data model is being developed from the conceptual model.

For further reading on the 'CODASYL' standard and on network database systems the reader is referred to Taylor and Frank (1976) and Olle (1978) for in depth reading, or Date (1981) for a good summary. Interesting notes on the physical implementation of sets are to be found in Martin (1977) and specially in the book by Cardenas (1985).

9.4 THE RELATIONAL MODEL

In the relational model entities, relationships and attributes are represented in the form of two-dimensional tables. These are known as *relations* from the branch of mathematics, set theory, on which truly relational database systems are based. Records can be assimilated to the rows of the table and each set of attributes forms a column. Each row in a table is known as a *tuple* and consists of a fixed number of distinct attributes. Figure 9.9 shows a relation representing property occurrences. The column headings *PR-ADDRESS*, *PR-RENT*, etc., which are automatically displayed by the DBMS, are not part of the relation. Attributes are drawn from a domain which is the set of all possible values for the attribute. Several attributes may be drawn from the same domain. For instance if a property had the additional attribute *PR-MIN-NOTICE-PERIOD*, this would be drawn from the same domain (namely months) as *PR-MIN-LEASE-PERIOD*. Domains provide a means of ensuring valid processing in a relational system since associations between

PR-ADDRESS	PR-RENT	PR-MIN-LEASE -PERIOD	PR-NO-OF -ROOMS
10 Acacia Ave	300	6	7
5 South Road	250	12	6
7 Oak Lane	150	6	4

Figure 9.9 Relation representing property entities for the property rental agency

tuples are made by comparison of attribute values drawn from the same domain. Within a truly relational table each tuple must be unique, and the tuples are unordered, that is no information should be lost if the tuples are shuffled. Similarly there should not be any information implicit in the arrangement of the attributes.

In a relational database entities can be stored totally independently. That is to say the existence of a relation or a tuple in a relation is not dependent on any other relation or tuple, nor is access to a tuple reliant on explicitly pre-defined access paths through complex data structures as it is in the formatted hierarchical or network models. Instead logical associations among the stored data are exploited through relational operations on whole relations, requests for information being made by reference to data values of attributes drawn from the same domain. Three basic relational operations can be used to create new tables, namely *select*, *project* and *join*.

Select operates on a relation to produce a new relation consisting of tuples which satisfy some specified selection criteria expressed in terms of attribute names and values. For instance the new table in Figure 9.10 can be created by selecting tuples from the table of Figure 9.9 by specifying that *PR-MIN-LEASE-PERIOD* must have a value 6.

Project operates on a relation to produce a new relation in which a sub-set of the original attributes is retained for each tuple. The projection of

PR-ADDRESS	PR-RENT	PR-MIN-LEASE -PERIOD	PR-NO-OF -ROOMS
10 Acacia Ave	300	6	7
7 Oak Lane	150	6	4

Figure 9.10 Relation resulting from selection of properties with a PR-MIN-LEASE-PERIOD = 6 for the property rental agency

PR-ADDRESS	PR-NO-OF-ROOMS
10 Acacia Ave	7
5 South Road	6
7 Oak Lane	4

Figure 9.11 Relation resulting from the projection of PR-ADDRESS and PR-NO-OF-ROOMS from the property relation for the property rental agency

PR-ADDRESS and *PR-NO-OF-ROOMS* from the table of Figure 9.9 would result in the table of Figure 9.11.

Join is an extremely powerful operator, which provides universal access to logically related data stored in the physically separate two-dimensional tables of a relational database. Join creates a new table from two existing tables. The simplest join, called a natural join, is achieved by matching attribute values from two columns (one in each table) which are drawn from the same domain. Figure 9.12 shows the property table of Figure 9.9 together with another table representing tenants. The join operation results in the table of Figure 9.13.

The application of any (relational) operation produces an object which is itself a relation (which can be stored as a new table in the database). Thus any number of operators and relations can be combined in a 'relational expression' used to answer almost any query. For instance subsequent operations on Figure 9.13 using select and project could result in a table showing, for instance, tenants who pay monthly rents of $250, i.e. relating data items not physically linked by any embedded data structure. These relational operators together with the operators union, intersection and difference from set theory form the basis of languages based on 'relational algebra' and are used to manipulate the data stored in relational databases.

As with other models, the manner in which relations are organized in storage depends on the usage perspective, that is on the data-processing requirements imposed on the database. A relation may be stored as a serial file of tuples, usually known in this context as a *heap* or the relation may be indexed or accessed through hashing. Indexes and hashing techniques are generally applied to a key attribute identified for the tuples in a relation, but secondary indexing on other non-key attributes is sometimes supported by relational DBMS (RDBMS). As with formatted data models a compromise storage organization has to be determined after weighing up the often conflicting processing requirements of the database users. However, the storage structure of individual tables can often be modified quite simply

PR-ADDRESS	PR-RENT	PR-MIN-LEASE -PERIOD	PR-NO-OF -ROOMS
10 Acacia Ave	300	6	7
5 South Road	250	12	6
7 Oak Lane	150	6	4

Property relation

T-NAME	T-ADDRESS	T-PREV-ADDRESS
Mc Donnell	5 South Road	119 Elm Street
Sinclair	5 South Road	19 Brigden Street
Cornwell	10 Acacia Ave	20 Lake Ave
Winterflood	10 Acacia Ave	82 Old Ave
Wilkinson	7 Oak Lane	65 Ship Street

Tenant relation

Figure 9.12 Property and tenant relations for the property rental agency

during the life of the database using DBMS utilities provided for the purpose. Readers seeking more detail of relevant storage organizations should consult Epstein (1977).

In contrast, the division into sets of the attributes selected to form the tuples in separate relations in the database is not so readily altered during the lifetime of the database. The entities, attributes and relationships produced from the conceptual model can often be modelled directly as relations in a relational database model.

The importance of the relational model is widely acknowledged and the development of RDBMS is progressing rapidly and enthusiastically. Emphasis is now being placed on thorough data analysis for database design. The use of the relational model rather than formatted models is seen to demand less compromise in transforming the real-world model of the conceptual model, although the processing overhead it requires is still often a serious deterrent to its use for many applications.

Date (1981) has been a standard reference textbook for many years and is still excellent on the relational model in general and IBM's relational database system 'System R' in particular. The series of papers by Stonebraker and various associated authors as well as those by Epstein are well worth looking into. They describe various aspects of the RDBMS 'Ingres' which is usually of

PR-ADDRESS	PR-RENT	PR-MIN-LEASE	PR-NO-OF-ROOMS	T-NAME	T-ADDRESS	T-PREV-ADDRESS
10 Acacia Ave	300	6	7	Cornell	10 Acacia Ave	20 Lake Ave
10 Acacia Ave	300	6	7	Winterflood	10 Acacia Ave	82 Old Ave
5 South Road	250	12	6	Mc Donnell	5 South Road	119 Elm Street
5 South Road	250	12	6	Sinclair	5 South Road	19 Brigden Street
7 Oak Lane	150	6	4	Wilkinson	7 Oak Lane	65 Ship Street

Figure 9.13 Relation resulting from join of property and tenant relations over domain address (PR-ADDRESS and T-ADDRESS) for the property rental agency

special interest to students since it is distributed with the Berkeley–Unix operating systems, and therefore, can generally be made available to those eager to get some hands-on experience of database systems.

Fundamentals of Information Technology
Edited by G. G. Wilkinson and A. R. Winterflood

Chapter 10

The User's View of a Database Management System

10.1 MODEL UNDERSTANDING

In the last chapter we presented the differences between, and the evolution of, DBMS in terms of their underlying data models. These have changed from fairly primitive and inflexible structures that only experienced programmers could handle successfully (the hierarchical model) to the more general, dynamic (relational) structures that end-users understand well. Although we may have now reached a plateau in the development of data models, it is by no means the end of their evolution. The relational model will probably not be the ultimate one.

For instance, while the normalization rules for 2NF and 3NF presented in Section 8.9 correspond to conceptual modelling errors which would result in update anomalies, it is not always the case with the 1NF. First Normal Form essentially corresponds to the inability of present systems to efficiently process variable-length stored-data records. Once advances in hardware and/or software have obviated this inefficiency it is probable that the 1NF rule will be reformulated and the relational model will make way for new ones supporting nested tables that will offer the user even more modelling power. The flavour of these new models can be discovered in, for instance, Shipman (1981).

10.2 DATABASE INTERROGATION

Many changes in the area of DBMS have paralleled those that have taken place in software engineering. In early DBMS logical data structures had to be defined in terms of segments, records, and fields. Field values had to be defined in terms of 'integer' or 'real' contents or of length of a character string. Today's relational systems offer the users the possibility of describing their conceptual models directly in terms of high-level concepts of entities, relationships and attributes. Attribute values can be defined by reference to *domains*, some of the predefined by the system (for instance, *number*, *text*, *money*, *data*, *postcode*); others can be created just like a user-defined type, stored in a dictionary and later referenced by some other user in some other application.

In earlier systems the modification of the structure of a database, even in a small way, meant modifying its programming-language-like declaration, recompiling the whole database description, and reloading all of the data into the new structures. This, of course, took hours and had to be performed off-line. Today, relational systems are equipped with the equivalent of an *incremental compiler* and minor modifications to an existing database can usually be carried out by simply amending the relevant system dictionary entries (which describe the model in high-level terms) and/or initiating the corresponding (on-line) restructuring utilities. Creation of new relations can even be done interactively, often by the end-users themselves.

Similar changes have also taken place with the *data manipulation* operations. Early systems did little more than add data storage and retrieval commands to existing programming languages. Creating new applications would still require the services of specialized application programmers who would *embed* in a program written in, say, COBOL some special database commands of the same ilk as the following (imaginary) statements:

```
SELECT DATABASE LANDLORD
FOR EACH RECORD IN LANDLORD SEGMENT
    GET NEXT LANDLORD RECORD
    IF LANDLORD NAME = 'McCaig' DO
        WITH DEPENDENT SEGMENT PROPERTY
        FOR EACH LINK IN CHAIN
            FIND NEXT LINK
            GET PROPERTY RECORD
            WITH DEPENDENT SEGMENT TENANT
            FOR EACH LINK IN CHAIN
                FIND NEXT LINK
                GET TENANT RECORD
                PRINT TENANT RECORD
            EXIT AT END OF TENANT CHAIN
        EXIT AT END OF PROPERTY CHAIN
    END IF-BLOCK
EXIT AT END OF LANDLORD SEGMENT
```

The relational systems corresponded to a leap forwards: not only were operations more compact, but their domain of applicability was a whole entity at a time rather than a single record. Using the relational algebra presented in Section 9.4, it would be possible to replace the set of imperative statements presented above (which had the object of printing a list of all tenants living in all the properties owned by "McCaig") by a declarative sequence of statements similar to:

```
JOIN LANDLORD and PROPERTY on "PR-Address"
SELECT form RESULT1 tuples WITH "L-Name = "McCaig""
```

Join RESULT2 and TENANT on "T-Address"
PROJECT from RESULT3 "T-Name, T-Address"

Although these high-level statements were much easier to use, they still required more knowledge of the system than average users had at their disposal. Possibly as a result of that designers decided to equip these relational systems with front-end software that would embody the algebra in a single multi-parameter construct that would provide end-users with a language which, although structured, might be close enough to natural language to make them feel comfortable. These *query languages*, as they became known, would then enable the sequence of declarative statements last presented to be replaced by a 'sentence' of the form:

SELECT TENANT.T-Name, TENANT.T-Address
WHERE TENANT.T-Address = PROPERTY.PR-Address
WHERE PROPERTY.PR-Address = LANDLORD.PR-Address
WHERE LANDLORD.L-Name = "McCaig"

A little thought will show this to be a structured form of the natural language query 'Give me a list of names and addresses of tenants, whose address is the address of a property owned by the landlord whose name is "McCaig".'

The original (and probably still best-known) relational query language was *SQL* (structured query language)—the reader should explore Date (1981) to get a more complex account of the facilities it offers.

Others have since adopted a similar structured language as interface, e.g. the language QUEL used on the Ingres DBMS (see Epstein (1977a)). Indeed, the approach has been so successful in recent years that query languages of this type have been produced to allow easier interaction with DBMS based on the network data model.

Finally it is also worth mentioning that the guidance of novice users has been facilitated even more by incorporating relational query semantics in systems like QBE (query by example—again see Date (1981)). These display form-based screen templates which the user is invited to fill in, thus helping proper query structuring.

10.3 APPLICATION GENESIS

Relational DBMS and query languages may have given the end-user (and the programmer) the ability to create and interrogate databases with unparalleled ease (even though this may weigh heavily on processing resources). However, easy as they may be, these queries still have to be embedded into large programs in conventional languages to build complete applications. Until recently this still meant resorting to specialized programmers.

On the other hand a number of products known collectively as *application program generators* (APG, also called fourth-generation languages) have recently been in use, enabling applications (specially 'traditional' business ones) to be defined in fairly high-level terms. They would typically allow users to easily define data and files, input- and output-screen formats, and links between stored data and displayed data, often in an interactive way. These definitions could then be used to automatically generate code (COBOL or otherwise) that would normally have required a large programming effort. The limitations of these tools are that they often do not provide very efficient ways of storing and retrieving data and do not usually facilitate the enforcement of security, integrity, and sharing which were mentioned in the introduction to Chapter 8 as the recommended way of managing data resources.

In recent years, however, some of these products have been merged with DBMS. New commercial relational systems like Relational Technology's 'Ingres' or Oracle Corporation's 'Oracle' now offer integrated systems which combine together a data dictionary system, screen generation facilities, a fourth-generation language (4GL), a DBMS, some graphics functions, etc. These can be regarded as forming tools which are of a more general scope than previous 4GLs. We shall call these *systems development environments* (SDE) to distinguish them from the 'IPSE' referred to in Chapter 7. The former are at present oriented more towards providing increased productivity and the latter increased reliability.

These systems facilitate the development of database implementations: by using them a database administrator can describe a conceptual model in exactly the same terms as those presented in Chapter 8, using the same concepts of entities, relationships, attributes, domains, minimum and maximum cardinalities, etc. He/she may also add constraints (though still only in a limited way) to ensure the integrity of the data thus defined; or specify, for instance, the maximum, minimum, and expected patterns of usage and growth for each entity. The whole model description is held in one or more dictionaries which can be made accessible (or even modifiable), in whole or in part, to (by) a specifiable selection of database users. When the model description is judged to be complete, it can be used to automatically create the (relational) database with all its domains and relations, and its associated integrity-checking procedures that will be triggered in the conditions specified. In addition, individual users may specify their own data and/or their own local views of the shared data. They may also use the application generation tools to 'paint' their own application screens and defined specific data entry and checking procedures.

These tools can also facilitate the development of other software systems: the dictionaries can be used to hold descriptions of the data (again in terms of entities, etc.) and definitions of 'events' (processes) and the design tools can be used to prepare and link input and output screens. The difference in this case is that database implementation is not the finality of the exercise any more. Instead the DBMS appears more like a set of highly sophisticated data-storage and retrieval functions that are there to relieve the programmer from the tedious task of coding file-handling procedures yet again.

Current DBMS can thus be seen from two different (though converging) points of view: Is your system a DBMS with a fourth-generation front-end, or is it an application generator with DBMS back-end?

10.4 DBMS EVOLUTION

10.4.1 Data or Information?

Coming back full circle to considering a DBMS as a tool also leads us to another point: maybe the emphasis should now be put on the words '-base-management system' rather than on the word 'data'. Certainly these systems started off with data as the objects they were to manage. Data were the digits and characters that were stored in the files, but it was the application programs that contained all the built-in (and by definition static) knowledge of what the data meant. So it was only the application programs that 'gave life' to the data, i.e. changed the data into *information*. Without an application program the data just became (or remained) useless.

As DBMS matured, the system rather than the application program was made to keep more and more information on the semantics of the data. So now, not only is that meaning safeguarded if the application is destroyed, but rather than simply storing *occurrences* of events relating to the company, the system holds an 'abstract' image of the company's place in the world (its conceptual model). Hence DBMS have evolved to the point where they are now becoming '*information* base systems'.

10.4.2 What Kind of Information?

Separate systems had traditionally been built to store and retrieve information that did not fit into the insurance data/payroll categories of early DBMS. A particularly good example of this can be seen in 'information retrieval systems'. These are systems where the stored objects are of textual nature. They may be simple bibliographic references consisting typically of attributes such as *Author*, *Title*, *Publisher*, *Year* etc., or they may be more sizable, i.e. incorporate an abstract of the work. In some cases the information stored *is* the actual work, i.e. the whole text of the journal paper, the legal statute, or the news feature is kept in computerized files. Retrieval of these objects is later done either by using indexing terms that were associated with it during its computer entry, or by performing some form of textual scanning and pattern matching.

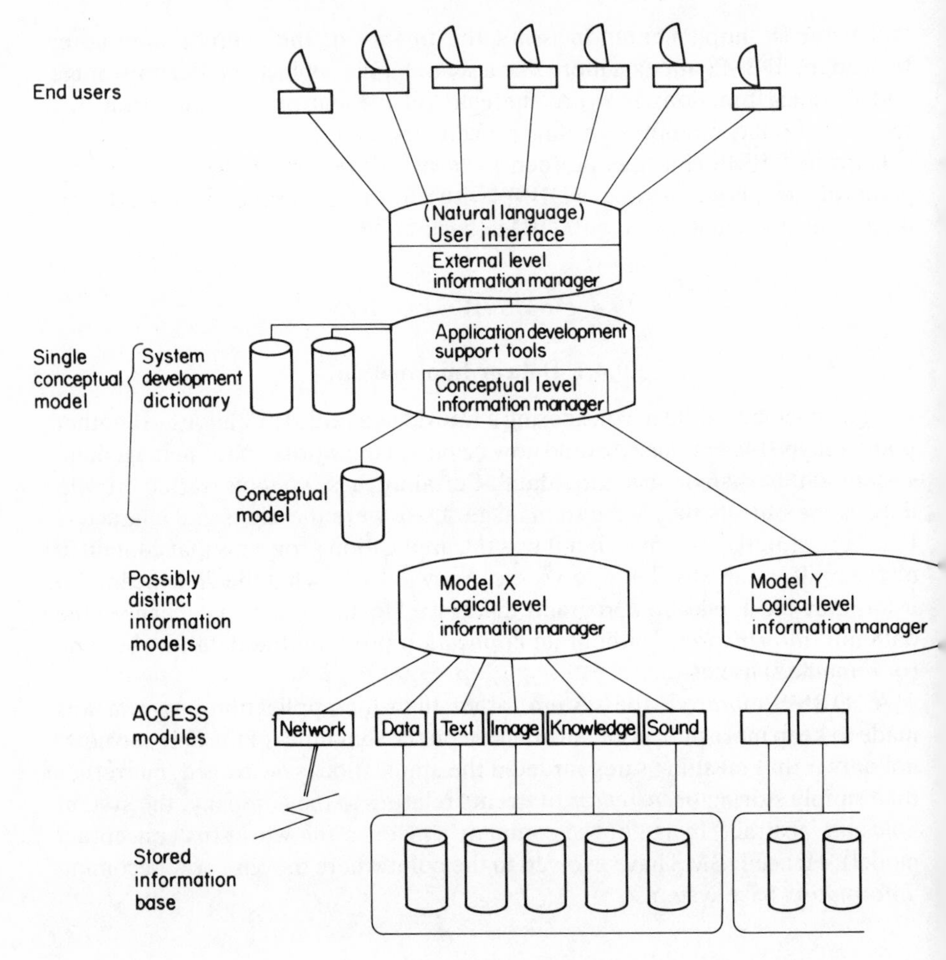

Figure 10.1 A possible architecture for a first-generation integrated information-base management system

It was originally felt that this was a problem totally separate from 'conventional' databases. Not only the information but also the indexing, the search techniques, the type of users, indeed everything, was different. Hence a number of separate (and successful) systems were developed, using their own techniques, their own models, and their own query languages (see Salton and McGill (1983) for details).

Since, however, DBMS essentially provide a means of hiding implementation details, couldn't they somehow be used to store and retrieve text? Since the query language was the most external layer of the system, couldn't a DBMS be used also to understand bibliographic queries? A number of information-retrieval systems using ordinary DBMS have been explored, and although all the problems have not yet been solved, it seems certain that they will soon be successful. An added incentive in that direction comes from 'traditional' database application areas which are now starting to handle less numerical data and more and more textual data. Information-retrieval techniques are increasingly relevant to, say, office automation systems, which have to store and find such objects as standard letters to clients or suppliers, legal contracts, particular sections of policies, newsletters etc.

There are also two types of information objects (which will be mentioned in more detail in the next chapters) which have so far been managed according to their own rather limited domain-specific principles: (rules of) 'knowledge' and digital 'images'. Again there is growing realization that although the internal structures needed to store the data corresponding to say, the last American census, the *Oxford English Dictionary*, the rules of chess, an understanding of Japanese No theatre, or a map of France may be quite different, it is likely that we could perform queries in a similar way in each case. Perhaps even in the form:

```
"Select ...... { feature }
      From ...... { object }
            Where ...... { criteria }"
```

We are already beginning to see experimental DBMSs where a number of systems using different data models (possibly in a distributed manner) are unified under a single user interface (see Atkinson *et al.* (1984) and ISO (1982)). It can not be long before similar attempts are successful in building a common interface to several 'information models'. A possible architecture for such a system is shown in Figure 10.1.

PART 4

INTELLIGENT SYSTEMS

Fundamentals of Information Technology
Edited by G. G. Wilkinson and A. R. Winterflood

Chapter 11

Introduction to Artificial Intelligence

11.1 THE DISCIPLINE OF ARTIFICIAL INTELLIGENCE

The subject of artificial intelligence is very young. A symptom of this youth is the absence of any accepted core of theory or practice, or even of vocabulary, of a body of knowledge which all or most researchers and workers in artificial intelligence (AI) would consider central and indispensable.

This point is alluded to by O'Shea and Eisenstadt (1984), who suggest that the value of a particular piece of work in AI is difficult to assess since

- systems are written to operate in domains, and to solve problems, where the success or failure of the system is inherently difficult to decide;
- the programs written tend to be very large and are usually not themselves published: it is then very hard to separate success of the conceptual framework being tested from its implementation.

There is, then, firstly a difficulty in being critical about AI work. Secondly there is a lack of such critical appraisal in the literature itself. However, such (self) critique is a valuable, indeed indispensable feature of all hard science (Newell 1984).

The aim of the present chapter is to provide a subject overview. This is no easy undertaking, particularly in a book of this size. Treatment of topics is necessarily extremely brief, but we have included pointers to the literature for further reading. Though brief, there will be an attempt to be critical, often implemented simply by choice of material included or ignored.

11.2 WHAT DO WE MEAN BY ARTIFICIAL INTELLIGENCE?

If you read six different books or articles on AI, you will end up with at least six different definitions of what is meant by the term. 'At least' because some authors give several, as this one is about to do!

Rich (1983) suggests a 'moving-target' approach:

- if people are presently better at doing something than machines then that something comes within the purview of AI.

which seems to mean that, once a machine has been programmed to a level of competence equal to or greater than that of people, its subject matter is no longer an AI topic.

She also suggests another definition, which, at first sight, appears very different:

- Artificial Intelligence is the study of techniques for solving exponentially hard problems in polynomial time by exploiting knowledge about the problem domain.

A suitable paraphrase of this somewhat mathematical statement is perhaps the following: AI techniques provide solutions, which are, on the average, *satisfactory*, to problems which are so hard that there is no algorithm which can provide an *optimal* solution in an acceptable amount of time. A little observation of his/her own behaviour should convince the reader that we humans are also happy with satisfactory, rather than optimal solutions; moreover, considering the ever-changing world in which we live, and of which we only have partial information, it is not even clear how to define *the* optimal solution in many situations.

It is important to note that AI systems deliver solutions by exploiting *heuristics*, or rules of thumb, which are specific chunks of knowledge in some problem domain. To find satisfactory solutions to globally intractable problems, they use such rules locally to generate the solution. As a classic example, consider the 'travelling-salesman problem':

A salesman must visit each city in a set of cities once, and do so over the minimum distance route. That is the problem. The difficulty with this problem is that there is no way of finding this route which is significantly quicker than simply considering each route in turn and comparing the distances covered by them, and that the number of possible routes goes up exponentially with the number of cities. (Hence the 'exponentially hard problems' above). A heuristic solution is to visit whichever unvisited city is nearest to the present location. On the average this provides a satisfactory solution, but there is no guarantee that it is the optimal one. In a sense, the problem has been made tractable by altering the specification.

Physicists, who spend all their time modelling the world and its behaviour, have been realizing over recent years that many (if not, even, most) complex problems are intractable, a fact which they ignored for decades.

There are certainly also those who would argue that there is nothing new in AI, that it is 'just' a style of programming, that new vogue words have been invented to attract funding. Firstly it is true that the AI bandwagon is rolling and a good one to jump onto at the moment, and, secondly, AI programs are, in the end, just that—programs, which presently run on the usual Von Neumann style computers. The approach to programming is what makes AI different. It is a way of solving problems about the world which accepts that the world is not closed, so that you can analyse it and write neat algorithmic solutions, but is open, requiring solutions resting often on partial knowledge incrementally acquired.

So far the word 'intelligence' has been used without definition. Whilst the meaning intended was that understood by a native speaker of the English language, the word resists more formal definition. As a consequence we must be wary of attempts to measure intelligence of either humans or machines.

As a final suggestion for a definition of AI, consider the following:

- to permit the design and construction of machines that exhibit intelligent behaviour;

and

- to elucidate the nature of (human) intelligence.

The two aims clearly feed on each other. The more we learn about the second the better we can do the first; and it is the very attempt to build intelligent machines which distinguishes AI from more traditional approaches to the enigma of intelligence, such as philosophy, psychology or the humanities, and which generates its specific insights. This definition will be referred to later as the 'two thrusts' approach.

11.3 OVERVIEW OF THE AI FIELD

Eight subject areas commonly covered in books on AI are identified and introduced below. The last topic, expert systems, is treated further in Chapter 12; the fifth, sixth and seventh topics are surveyed in greater depth in the remaining sections of this chapter.

11.3.1 Game Playing

The ways of getting a program to play an acceptable game of draughts, chess, backgammon, etc. were widely investigated and written about in the 1950s and 1960s. Even when successful this work did not arouse much interest in the outside world. The turning point occurred in 1972, when work began on the first 'expert system', MYCIN. Earlier ideas from game-playing programs were important in having prepared the way with 'production systems', a concept which is explained below, particularly in Section 11.3.3. The rules of a game are well-defined—there is, if you like, a well-understood theoretical framework for the game: i.e. the game mini-world is closed. Slightly older texts (e.g. Rich (1983)) still have chapters on such work; more recent ones (e.g. Charniak & McDermott (1985)) do not. This indicates the way the centre of gravity of the subject has moved.

11.3.2 Vision

This subject and the next one of natural-language understanding are often grouped under the heading of perception. Particularly with vision, we are dealing with an ability which we humans share with much of the rest of the Animal Kingdom. The way in which we, or they, can extract meaningful patterns from light or sound stimuli is not really known. Some of the processing is no doubt hard-wired into the optical system and probably amounts to a sort of biological number crunching. Whatever is happening is at levels of abstraction remote from our conscious minds. Here we see the principle of information hiding at work: the details of lower-level 'calculations' are not (and should not be) available at the higher levels. This leaves the researcher in the curious position, ubiquitous in AI research, of trying to discover what is going on in his own brain, but which is hidden from his mind.

Some of the current approaches in machine image understanding are covered in greater depth in Chapter 14.

11.3.3 Natural-language Understanding

From the earliest days of the computer era attempts have been made to get machines to do automatic translation. The attempts were such dismal failures in the earlier decades that funding was stopped and projects abandoned. The mistake has been to tremendously underestimate the complexity of natural-language understanding. The example everyone gives, which may be apocryphal, but fun, is of the machine which 'translated' English to Russian, and which was given the task of translating:

'The spirit is willing, but the flesh is weak'

from English to Russian, and then back again. It is reported to have returned the sentence,

'The meat is rotten, but the vodka is fine.'

The crux of the problem of natural language understanding is the meaning of the word 'understanding', which seems to be a word of the ilk of 'intelligence'. As with the proposed 'two thrusts' definition of AI work, research into natural language understanding may be said to be, ultimately, the attempt to unravel the secrets of this word through experiments on machines. The situation is analogous to that with icebergs: the tip of the iceberg corresponds in some manner to what goes on in the conscious mind, the great bulk of the iceberg to the rest of Man's linguistic ability, processing and, even, history. Early attempts at machine translation foundered on the submerged portion of the iceberg.

You often come across salesmen who will tell you that their product has a natural-language interface. Be assured that you will not be able to converse with that machine as with another human, and, one suspects, not for a long time to come. Remember, the iceberg is huge and each piece is, maybe, by a roundabout, even submerged route, connected to every other piece.

The interested reader is urged to dip into books such as Charniak and McDermott (1985), O'Shea and Eisenstadt (1984), and Winograd (1983).

The present author's feeling is that more notice should be taken of the work on situation semantics (Barwise and Perry (1983)). The stress there is on the fact that those attuned to the constraints on the behaviour of their environment, be they natural ones, such as laws of motion for falling bodies, or conventional ones, such as particular sounds to refer to particular objects, can extract meaning from events they see, or hear, about them. A theory of language must consequently be embedded in a more general theory of meaning and information flow. It cannot be pursued in isolation.

11.3.4 Learning

As with the last two topics, this is an area of intense interest and research activity, and also one in which success has been less than hoped for. Most existing systems essentially learn by being told, i.e. by the programmer explicitly adding new code, albeit indirectly in cases where there is, say, a natural-language interface. In particular, the MYCIN system, which is described in the next chapter, only learns in this fashion, with a system called Teiresias to facilitate the process.

There are also systems which learn by example: learning by induction. The book by Naylor (1983) describes simple programs for doing this; there are commercial products which incorporate the same idea (Harmon and King 1985) and Alexander and Burnett (1983) may be seen as subscribing to the same philosophy.

Another approach might be described as learning by discovery, and is exemplified by Lenat's AM and EURISKO programs (Lenat 1982). The former was given the basics of set theory and discovered 'new' concepts, which it labelled as interesting, such as prime numbers, and refound conjectures. Eventually it ran out of steam, which Lenat ascribed to its domain-dependent heuristics becoming inappropriate as the program explored new domains. The follow-up program EURISKO was given the ability to alter the heuristics with which it generated new possible discoveries, and could consequently produce new heuristics for new domains. In really new domains such as VLSI, it has generated concepts and rules that no human had yet arrived at.

11.3.5 Problem Solving, Production Systems, Search and Pattern Matching.

All living things make decisions. They are required to do so by a hostile environment. Each decision made is a sort of *mini-problem solved*. The greater the 'hit rate' of making a good decision, of finding a satisfactory solution, the more likely the organism is to survive. Intelligence is something to do with the art of making the right decision at the right time, of filtering the mass of incoming information for *patterns* which inspire an action which is to the organism's benefit. Intelligence involves having and being able to access and employ *knowledge* of what to do in a given *situation* in order to perform an *action* so as to change that situation favourably. Moreover, a correct action is possibly useless if it comes too late, so the *search* for and *application* of the knowledge must be efficient, and, also, errors which were not fatal should be recognized as such and the store of knowledge changed, deleted from or added to.

The *production system* framework is a way of organizing the decision-making/problem-solving process such as to parallel (much of) the discussion above. It was for this reason that we highlighted certain words as we went along.

Whilst this topic is pursued in greater detail in Section 11.4 a simple totally non-technical example is given now to make sure that the reader has understood what is going to be done there. Animals are capable of classifying some situations as 'those in which smoke is present' by processing visual and oral data and matching to learnt or in-born patterns in their brains which mean smoke is present. Similarly, they can recognize situations in which there is fire present. One might say, contentiously, maybe, that the animals 'know' when they are in a 'smoky' or 'fiery' situation. The animal 'knows' more if it behaves according to the rule that 'smoke means fire'; by running away from a smoky situation even before it actually sees the fire, for example.

The production system models the above by having sets of situation–action rules, such as, IF in a smoky situation THEN deduce in a 'fiery' situation, and, IF in a 'fiery' situation THEN deduce in a dangerous situation, and, finally, IF in a dangerous situation THEN run away from the danger. It also needs somewhere to store the present situation, as perceived and as deduced, and a mechanism for finding and executing rules which apply to the present situation.

11.3.6 Predicate Calculus and Logic Theorem Proving

Physicists, engineers and others are used to employing mathematics to describe the world and its behaviour. Mathematical structures are themselves defined using the language of logic. It is ultimately some logical calculus, then, which is capable, apparently, of describing the world and its behaviour, of describing situations and entailments between them.

Sentences in logic such as

$$\text{(it is raining)} \rightarrow \text{(the street is wet)} \qquad (1)$$

capture the rule by which a person could deduce that the street *is* wet if it happens to be raining. That is to say that from the two sentences (1) and (it is raining) the sentence (the street is wet) follows logically. Alternatively, sentence (1) and the sentence (the street is *not* wet) allow the inference that (it is *not* raining).

A set of sentences, which may be simple facts like (it is raining) or rules like (1), are often used to describe situations in the world. If other sentences follow logically from the set, then they capture new information which may be deduced about the situation. Such sentences are technically theorems of the set of axioms, which is the set of sentences. Consequently, AI systems which have been built to handle deduction are often referred to as logic theorem provers. The fact that logic is well understood (even in terms of its limitations) with, in particular, well-founded rules of inference, has made this a popular and successful area of research. The whole of Section 11.5 is devoted to this topic.

11.3.7 Knowledge Representation

In a certain sense, there is never any need to look beyond predicate calculus for ways of representing the world, not if the idea is accepted that theories of the world are all described using mathematics, itself defined using logic. The sense in which this is true is one of ultimate power for representation of knowledge of the world and deductive activity. The trouble is that there must also be a concern for the organization of the storage, access and manipulation mechanisms. It is not sufficient, for example, to know that some sentence is a theorem of a set of axioms and that a machine has both a representation of the axioms and an inferencing mechanism; it must also be known that the machine has sufficient storage to prove the theorem and that it can do so in an appropriate period of time.

There has consequently been much interest amongst the AI community in knowledge representation. To some extent workers have reinvented the wheel, and only now are data storage and management people and AI people beginning to talk to each other. This should prove a very valuable dialogue. In Section 11.6 several so-called structured forms for knowledge representation are discussed.

11.3.8 Expert and Knowledge-based Systems

An expert system is variously defined as having some or all of the following properties or capabilities:

- has the knowledge of an expert in some domain;
- can lead a consultation session as would an expert in some domain;
- can be interrogated as to why and how it reaches its conclusions;
- operates in an unstructured or semistructured problem domain;
- can replace a (highly paid/mortal) human expert.

Although there is no universal acceptance of the distinction between expert and knowledge-based systems, a suggestion of Harmon and King (1985) is that 'expert' be reserved for systems which satisfy the last requirements, whereas 'knowledge-based' is the more general term.

11.4 BASIC PROBLEM SOLVING

Section 11.3.5 introduced the idea of a production system. It is composed of three modules (Nilsson 1980)

1. the knowledge base, or (production) rule base;
2. working memory, or global data base;
3. the inference engine, or control system, or executive.

The knowledge base contains rules which are variously known as if–then rules, production rules, or situation–action rules. It may also contain simple facts.

As indicated by the discussion previously, the argument is that the necessary knowledge can be described by a set of productions of the form

IF ⟨situation is of some type, type 1, say⟩
THEN ⟨take an action of type 1 appropriate to this
particular situation of type 1 ⟩

We are not arguing that an animal is aware it has such rules, and therefore somehow decides to follow such rules, merely that it behaves according to those rules (Searle 1984).

The machine knowledge base in the classic production system is entered in advance of the first problem-solving activity. The machine may then be presented with an initial situation or start state in working memory. The job of the executive is then to find IF parts of rules in the knowledge base to which (part of) the situation in working memory is a fit, and if there are several such rules, to decide which to use and to apply the corresponding action. The action changes the state of working memory and the cycle recommences. The machine has solved the problem if it can change the state of working memory so as to satisfy some condition.

When there are several rules which are simultaneously applicable, the selection process is known as *conflict resolution*. The executive requires rules to perform such resolution. Such a rule is known as a heuristic. In an amusing, recursive manner, one may regard such rules as themselves being a knowledge base which the conflict-resolving part of the control system uses to solve the problem of which rule to apply next. Production systems within production systems!

Returning to organisms, suppose our animal finds itself in a situation in which only the rule

'IF there is lots of food available and hungry THEN eat'

is activated (in AI jargon 'fires'). It will then dig in. Now suppose it also looks up and notices smoke. Then both those rules indicating that it should flee *and* this rule fire. For the animal's survival it is fairly clear which rules should take precedence. It is also fairly clear how its selection could be arranged. The rules are stored in sequence so that rules with higher priority for the case of simultaneous applicability are stored earlier in the sequence. A cyclic sequential scan of the knowledge base performed by the executive, attempting to match present situations/states to IF parts as it goes, should now stop at and apply the first rule to which it finds a match. The problem with this is the case where you have rules A, B and C such that A takes precedence over B, B over C, and C over A. What ordering do you then use?

So far it has sounded as if animals react to their environment in a spontaneous, intuitive way without any planning of sequences of actions. There is no reason that this should be taken to be the case. Just as the production system we spoke about searches for a sequence of rule applications to achieve some goal, so may animals plan sequences of actions. Man does this consciously; whether other animals do is a matter of debate. But the reader should certainly entertain the idea that some production rules alter the 'internal state' of either organism or machine, so that the effect of their application is not immediately obvious, if ever. We are indeed preaching a sort of behaviourism, but a much more subtle and deep sort than many might understand by the word. It should no longer be considered pejorative to say that organisms, including even we humans, are machines. For the major realization of 40 years of playing with computers is probably that of just how complex machines can get.

When we reason out a plan of action, we may start from the initial situation and attempt to find a sequence of actions which will achieve our desired goal; this is the approach outlined above and referred to as *forward chaining*. An alternative is that we start from the goal situation and consider THEN parts of rules which could create that situation. For those rules we ask under what circumstances (i.e. in what situations) would those rules be applicable—we undo the actions. For the newly found states (situations) we repeat the process, and keep on repeating the cycle until we have *backward chained* to the initial situation. Which direction we chain in depends on the sort of problem we are trying to solve, but backward chaining strikes most people as the most natural way to reason most of the time. The choice of forward or backward chaining—or a combination of both— is referred to as the search strategy.

It is time an example was given of a production system being used to solve a problem. The one chosen is the so-called eight-tiles problem which may be found in, for example, Nilsson (1980). It is an example from the work in game playing.

Consider a three by three board of squares with eight tiles numbered 1 through 8 on the board. This leaves one blank square. A situation, or state, of this miniworld is described in terms of the arrangement of tiles on the board. The problems which the production system must solve are of the type: Given a start

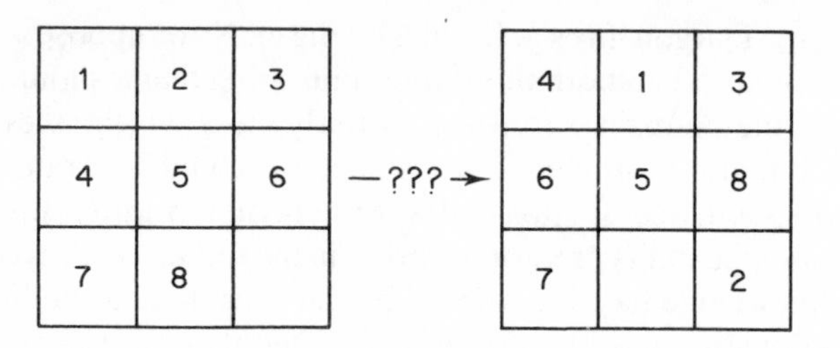

Figure 11.1

state, find a sequence of tile movements which will lead to a certain goal state (or states) (see Figure 11.1). Tile movements consist of sliding a tile into the blank square.

A first attempt at writing rules might be as follows,

IF the tile numbered 1 is to the left of the blank
THEN slide tile numbered 1 to the right
IF the tile numbered 1 is to the right of the blank
THEN slide tile numbered 1 to the left
IF the tile numbered 1 is directly above the blank
THEN slide tile numbered 1 downwards
IF the tile numbered 1 is directly below the blank
THEN slide tile numbered 1 upwards

{ And similar rules for tiles 2, 3, 4, 5, 6, 7, 8 }

A little thought shows that this is an inefficient way of representing our knowledge of this miniworld and its rules of behaviour. Better is the set of just four rules,

IF the blank is not in the top row
THEN move the blank up one square
IF the blank is not in the left-hand column
THEN move the blank to the left
IF the blank is not in the right-hand column
THEN move the blank to the right
IF the blank is not in the bottom row
THEN move the blank down

The transition from the first set of rules to this improved version is part of the art of knowledge representation.

Note that a simple problem like this has an easily enumerable *state space*, i.e. there are 9! possible arrangements of tiles on the board, each of these arrangements is a possible state, and these states exist in their very own space. Imagine each state corresponding to a light bulb on a wall. When the board is in the state, the light is on. As you slide tiles around the board, so the position of the light which is on moves around the wall. This state space has a natural structure. Draw an arc from one state to another just when there is a legal move which can take the board between those two states. The structure is thus that of a graph whose nodes are the states; it is possible to make moves to get from one state to another if and only if there is a path between the corresponding nodes along arcs. Figure 11.2 shows the complete graph for the smaller three-tile problem.

Given both the storage space required and the time to draw this graph, any given problem becomes easy to solve. You use any method you wish to find paths on this graph leading from one node to another, or to declare that no such path exists. If you only want to know whether a path exists or not, i.e. whether a given eight-tile problem is soluble or not, in our case, then you just need to work out all the paths in the graph. This approach is that of the conventional programmer. He analyses the problem until he can write an algorithm which is guaranteed to either solve the problem or tell him it cannot. The method works because our miniworld is closed: the graph can be explicitly displayed.

If the state space is too large to construct explicitly for searching for solutions to problems, and particularly if there is an infinity of possible states, then the search for solution paths through the graph must be done implicitly by constructing the relevant portion of the graph. Even this is not enough, however. In the eight-tile world at least three moves are always possible, i.e. at least three arcs leave any node. Each leads to a node from which at least three arcs leave, and so on. The number of nodes visited by all the paths of length N from some node goes up exponentially with N. This explosion of possibilities which we must consider for solution paths is referred to as the combinational explosion. It is obviously even more severe in those problem spaces in which (on the average) more than three rules are applicable to given situations.

To combat the combinational explosion we use heuristics, or rules of thumb, to prune the state space, inasmuch as only certain portions of it ever get constructed and, consequently, examined, and/or to control the order of its construction such that a solution, if it exists at all, is likely to be found efficiently.

In the eight-tile problem, a typical heuristic might be,

- Only search the state space along arcs from a node leading to nodes corresponding to less tiles out of place.

Such a heuristic on its own could lead to failure to find solutions by pursuing dead ends. Others are needed which have lesser precedence, such as,

- Search along arcs which lead to nodes corresponding to the same number of tiles out of place.

Or, even,

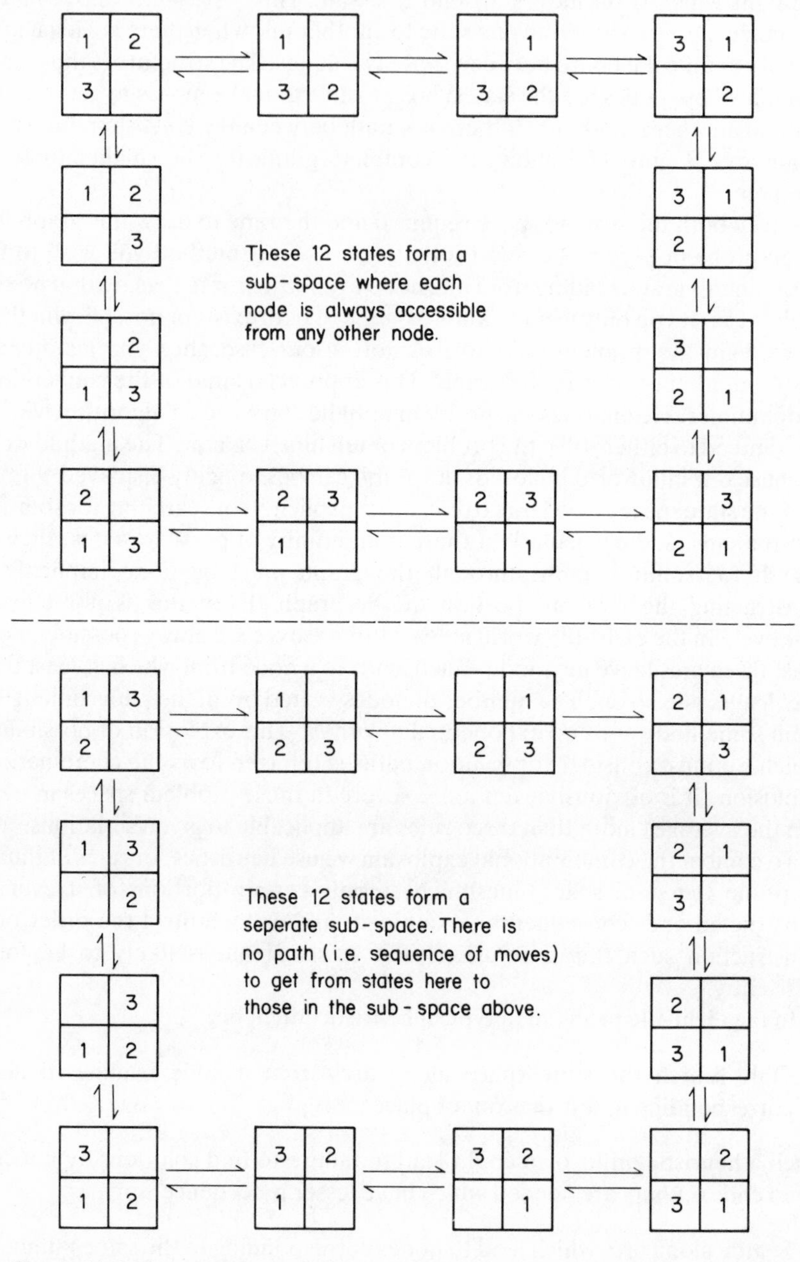

Figure 11.2 The complete state space for the three-tile problem. It is apparent that the space divides into 2 sub-spaces

- Continue the search along the arc which increases the number of tiles out of place by the least amount.

Moreover, there should be rules which govern the return of the search to a node which has already been visited, with the aim of taking another arc exiting from it. Such an idea is known as *backtracking*. If backtracking is only allowed when a dead end has been reached, one speaks of *depth-first search*. *Breadth-first search* is the opposite extreme: all arcs from a given node are considered before pursuing any one of them further.

Another example is now presented to clarify some of the terms introduced above. On arrival in a new town and not being in possession of a street map, getting from one place to another is an essentially trial and error matter, though heuristics may be immediately applicable: e.g. if you are trying to get to a church and can actually see its spire, then take any road (that you may legally enter) that goes in the direction of the spire.

In production system terms, consider each place to be a node of a graph, and each one-way street to be a directed arc between the nodes representing the places it joins; a two-way street is then just like having two one-way streets directed oppositely. The initial, groping search for a route from place to place involves an exhaustive (and, no doubt, exhausting) search for a path on the graph from corresponding start node to finish node.

As more experience is gained of the structure of the town, so more planning may be involved in getting from place to place. Once the whole street plan is in one's head, then routes may be planned totally in advance. In this situation there is the forward/backward chaining choice: forward chaining amounts to finding a sequence of one-way streets such that they may be taken in flow direction starting from the present position such as to end up at the desired location; backward chaining involves considering a route from the desired location to the start location along streets against traffic flow.

The whole street plan being in one's head amounts to having a production system which has the entire search graph available to it. The executive may still use an exhaustive search of this graph to find a path between two nodes: it is the same as studying a map and considering all possible routes. An example of a depth-first variant of this is always taking the right exit at any place (which is a junction for present purposes), backing up if a dead-end is reached, and taking the next rightmost exit on visiting the same place again. An example of a breadth-first variant is one in which all streets exiting from the start place are explored, one after the other, and only to the end of the street. If none of them leads immediately to the finish place, only then are streets exiting from the places just visited pursued.

Figure 11.3(a) shows a graph corresponding to a street plan which is not given, but which the reader could easily reconstruct. (Note, though, that no distances are indicated on the graph, which is something which would interest

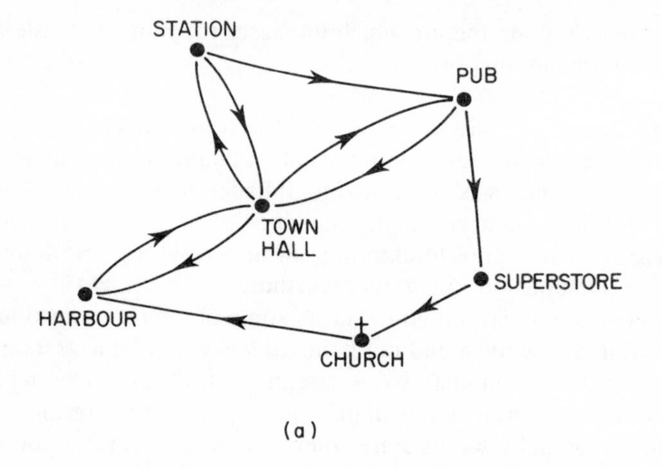

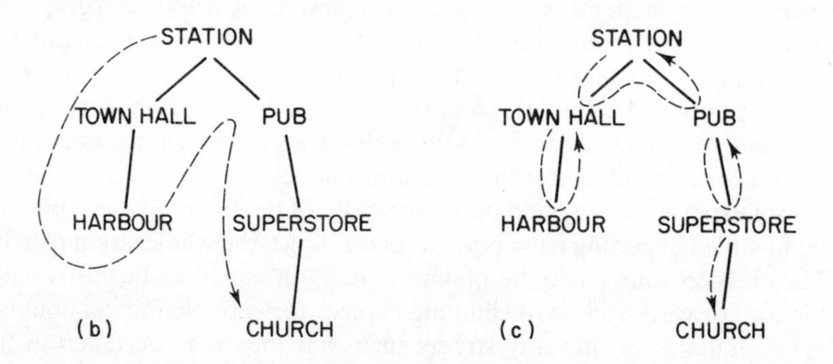

Figure 11.3 Direction-finding in a new town: (a) graph; (b) tree representation of depth-first search; (c) tree representation of breadth-first search

us in practice and which could be included on the graph. Such considerations are beyond the scope of the present introduction). A route from the station to the church found by forward chaining in the depth-first manner suggested above would be found by considering the nodes in the order

⟨STATION, TOWN HALL, HARBOUR, {BACKTRACK}, TOWN HALL, PUB, SUPERSTORE, CHURCH⟩

whereas the breadth-first approach would give the order

⟨STATION, TOWN HALL, PUB, {NEXT LEVEL}, HARBOUR, SUPERSTORE, {NEXT LEVEL}, CHURCH⟩

At this point this introduction to production systems will be concluded. Rich

(1983) also has considerable discussion of them, their classifications, and their association with various categories of problems.

11.5 PREDICATE CALCULUS AND LOGIC THEOREM PROVING

11.5.1 Resolution Refutation

A favourite subject matter for AI programs has always been the 'blocks world' which contains blocks, maybe of different sizes, shapes, colours, etc. It is a nice closed little world which is easy to describe using the predicate calculus. Consider the following situation and associated state description written in the predicate calculus,

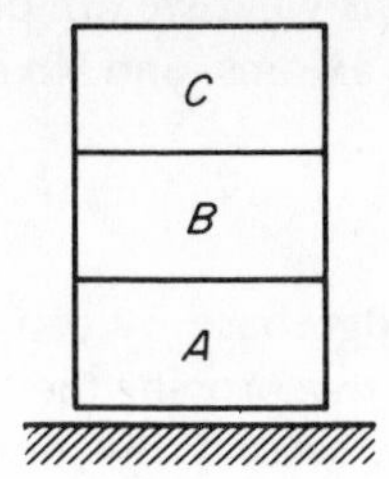

State description: on (C, B) $\wedge$ on (B, A)
The idea of the state description is, C is on B AND B is on A. We now add a rule,

Rule
on (C, B) $\wedge$ on (B, A) $\Rightarrow$ over (C, A) (r)

This rule is actually rather stupid. It really just tells us that we can use the word 'over' as further description of one particular situation. In a moment we shall redefine rule (r) using variables to increase its applicability. As it stands it still enables us to answer queries about this situation in the blocks world. For example,

Query I: 'Is C over A?'

We shall use the method known as resolution refutation. This is further discussed in Nilsson (1980) and Rich (1983), for example. As preliminary to the use of this method, we must rewrite rule (r) in so-called conjunctive normal form (see later); that is, we employ standard logical equivalences to write (r) as

$\sim$on (C, B) $\vee$ $\sim$on (B, A) $\vee$ over (C, A) (r*)

(This disjunction of terms constitutes a *clause*.)
We now take the conjunction of *facts* of the state description, and the rule (r*) to represent our state of knowledge of the blocks world.

The idea of resolution refutation is to add the denial, i.e. the logical negation, of the query expressed in conjunctive normal form, to the knowledge base, and then to demonstrate that this combination is contradictory. This proves that the sentence expressing the query *is* true whenever the knowledge base is. For, if KB is the knowledge base and Q the query, to show that KB $\wedge$ $\sim$Q is contradictory is to show that it cannot simultaneously be true that KB is true and that $\sim$Q is true. So, whenever KB is true, Q must also be true, i.e. it is a theorem.

Let us do this.

The query sentence is,

over (C, A)

The theorem prover, for that is what we are describing, should reply, Yes, if this sentence follows from the axioms, and No otherwise.

The denial is,

$\sim$ over (C, A)

which we add to the knowledge base by conjoining with the other clauses. Figure 11.4 shows a *refutation tree* proving the theorem. Along the top row are boxes, one for each clause. The second row shows a box suspended from two of the top-level boxes. The clause in this box follows from the clauses in those boxes from the resolution principle:

$$(p \vee q) \wedge (\sim p \vee r) \Rightarrow (q \vee r)$$

Note how easy this principle is to formalize for a machine: it must search for a p in one clause, and a corresponding $\sim p$ in another, and then add a new clause which is the disjunction of the remainders of the two clauses.

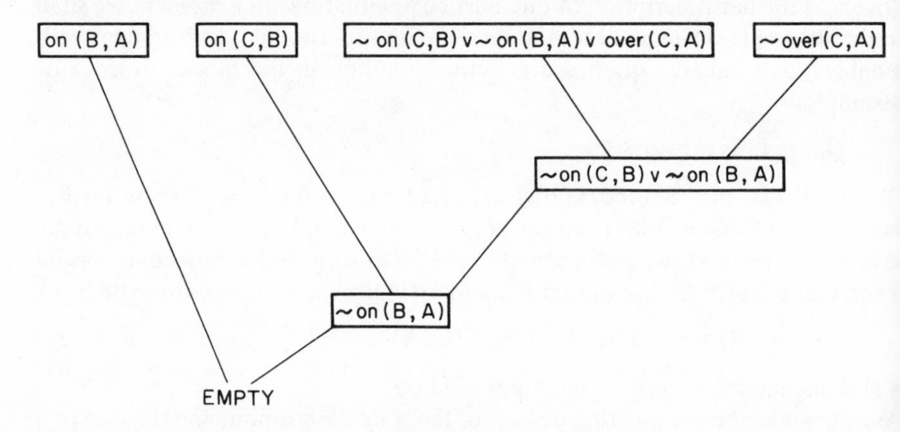

Figure 11.4

Looking at Figure 11.4 again, from the newly deduced sentence and one of the initial set of sentences hangs the sentence '~ on (B, A)', which is also a result of resolving its two parents. At this point we have both the sentence 'on (B, A)', which we have had all along, and the sentence '~ on (B, A)', which shows that the initial set of sentences was inconsistent, as we set out to prove. In fact the reader will note that the process of resolution is taken one stage further in resolving these two offending clauses to reach an *empty* clause. Its presence indicates to an automatic theorem prover that it has succeeded.

Before proceeding, it is necessary to say what is meant by conjunctive normal form. Any sentence of the predicate logic can be uniquely (hence *normal*) written as the *conjunction* of clauses, each of which consists of a disjunction of terms, each of which is simply a predicate or the negation of a predicate. It is the uniqueness and standard way of writing of this form which makes it computationally interesting. Note that an example of conjuctive normal form is provided by the conjunction of the four clauses at the top of Figure 11.4.

We said above that rule (r) (or (r*)) was pretty stupid. What we really want is a more general rule not tied to specific objects (instances):

IF something1 'is on' something2
  AND something2 'is on' something3
THEN something1 'is over' something3

This is easily done using the full apparatus of predicate calculus as

$$\mathsf{A}x,y,z\,(\,\mathrm{on}(x,y) \wedge \mathrm{on}(y,x) \Rightarrow \mathrm{over}\,(x,z)) \qquad (\mathrm{r}^*)$$

which in normal form is:

$$\mathsf{A}x,y,z\,(\,\sim\!\mathrm{on}(x,y) \vee \sim\!\mathrm{on}(y,z) \vee \mathrm{over}(x,z)\,) \qquad (\mathrm{r}\$)$$

The previous query may be answered affirmatively again, this time using the refutation tree of Figure 11.5. The following points should be noticed:

1. The 'For all' sign $\forall$ is understood with expressions containing variables in conjunctive normal form sentences.
2. A clause containing variables *holds* for every possible *instantiation* of those variables, i.e. for those variables taking on any possible values in their domain.
3. Such a clause may therefore be considered as representing the conjunction of all possible clauses which can be generated by variable instantiations.
4. When such a clause is resolved with another clause variables are instantiated as required for the resolution, and this is apparent in the child clause, as well as being noted on the tree.

So far little has been said about the way in which a machine would construct

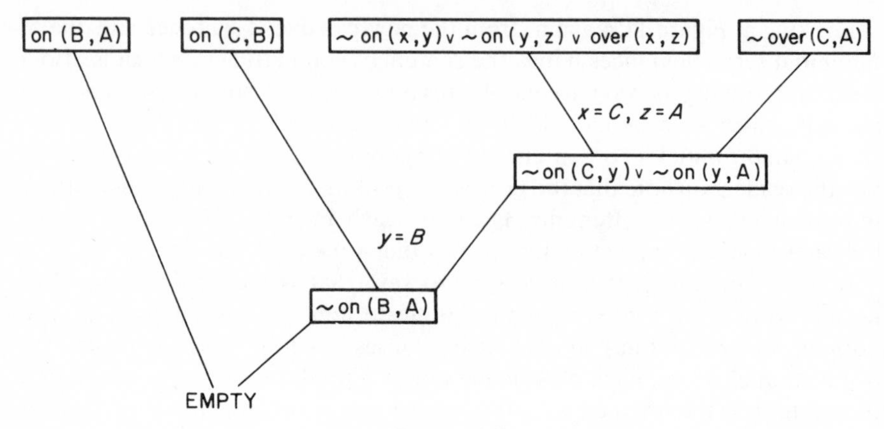

Figure 11.5

this refutation tree. The algorithm being used is as given in Nilsson (1980),

RESOLUTION REFUTATION

Start with a set of clauses, *S* ;
  until EMPTY is a member of *S* ;
  begin
  select two distinct resolvable clauses *c*[*i*] and *c*[*j*] ;
  compute the resolvant *r*[*i*,*j*] of *c*[*i*] and *c*[*j*] ;
  add *r*[*i*,*j*] to *S*
  end
(written in a Pascal-like notation).

What we are talking about here is an example of a production system: the set *S* represents the state of working memory; there is one production rule, which says that two resolvable clauses may be resolved together and their child added to *S*; the executive finds resolvable pairs and decides which of many possible pairings to do next.

Notice that child clauses are only ever added to the set of clauses. The number of clauses in *S* increases steadily, or monotonically. Not surprisingly, then, this is an example of a monotonic production system. In a certain sense, if the executive takes a dead end when searching towards the goal of adding the empty clause to *S*, it does not matter. Since the parent clauses were not deleted, any action which was previously possible is still possible. Pursuing dead ends only matters in terms of efficiency, though that is a very important 'only' in practice—machines and organisms have restricted memories and reaction times. Nilsson (1980) gives a number of heuristics which the resolution refutation executive can use to guide its search. There is, for example, the idea of resolving using the query denial or a direct descendant as one of the new parents each time—an approach which smacks of backward chaining, although it is not, since the goal here is to get the empty clause into S.

We continue this section with further queries of increasing complexity in order to expose further points of interest.

Query II: Is anything on B?

1. Translate into a sentence of the predicate calculus,

   $\exists x$ on(x,B) { Here $\exists$ means "for some" }

   i.e. if the state description and (r$) imply this sentence, then the answer to the query is 'Yes'.
2. Negate, and use the standard logical equivalence indicated to produce,

   $\sim\exists x$ on(x,B) $\Longleftrightarrow$ $\forall x \sim$ on(x,B) { Duality }

3. Add this clause to the set {state description,r$}.
4. Run the resolution refutation theorem prover on the expanded set.
5. We do not bother with drawing the refutation tree. The clauses

   on(C,B) and $\sim$ on(x,B)

   clearly (i.e. using the wonderful in-built human pattern-matching apparatus) resolve to the empty clause, with the instantiation x = C.
6. Thus we can not only answer the query with Yes, but also say, There is something on B, and it is C.

Query III: 'Is there anything which is on something which is itself on block A?'

1. Query: $\exists x,y$ [on(x,y) $\wedge$ on(y,A)]
2. Denial: $\forall x,y$ [$\sim$on(x,y) $\vee$ $\sim$on(y,A)] {Duality + De Morgan}

3, 4. As above.

5. The refutation tree is shown in Figure 11.6

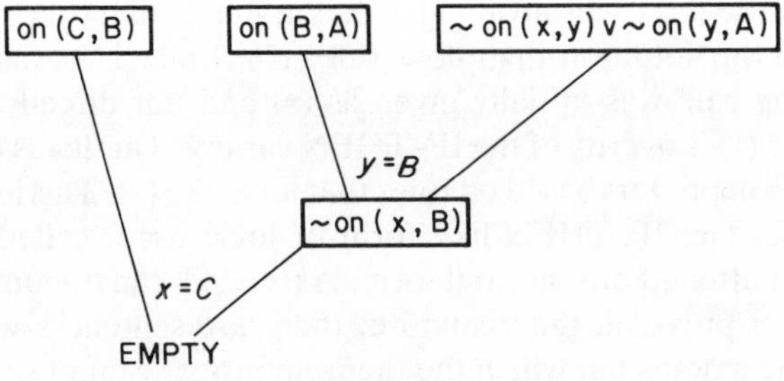

Figure 11.6

   (Clause (r$) is not used and not shown)

6. The answer is: Yes, x=C and y=B , ie C is on B, which is itself on A.

For our final example, which illustrates the fact that there are often situations where several valid alternative answers exist to a query, we change the state

description by adding a block D on top of C. This alteration is explicitly shown at step 3 below.
Query IV: "Is there anything which is over anything else"

1. Query: $\exists x,y$ over(x,y)
2. Denial: $\forall x,y$ ~over(x,y)
3. S is the set,

$$\{ \text{on(D,C)}, \text{on(C,B)}, \text{on(B,A)}, \sim\text{on}(x,y) \vee \sim\text{on}(y,z) \vee \text{over}(x,z), \sim\text{over}(u,\text{v}) \}$$

where it is to be noted that we have avoided a confusing name clash by altering the bound variables of the query to u and v.

4, 5. A refutation tree is shown in Figure 11.7(a) and another, which in no way excludes or is excluded by the first, in Figure 11.7(b). Remember this is a monotonic system. If there are several ways of getting the empty clause into S, then each leads to an answer to the query, though those answers need not be different.

The reader is encouraged to make sure that he can see the way a *machine* could perform resolution refutation. Most students seem to readily grasp problems such as the one presented, yet fail to understand abstract ones. The trouble is that our own inferencing mechanisms make the solution of concrete problems obvious, masking the fact that we are meant to be understanding how a machine can do symbol manipulation.

A machine can prove any theorem (which actually *is* a theorem) using resolution refutation. Writing everything out in conjunctive normal form has 'flattened' everything down to a standard, normal form. This has its advantages; it also has its disadvantages. It is arguable that rule (r) corresponds much more to our intuition than does rule (r*). Indeed, it was for that very reason that the rule was initially given as (r) and not directly as (r*), and, moreover, rule (r) is overtly of the IF–THEN variety. This leads us to naturally consider theorem provers based on rules that look like (r). This is the subject of Section 11.5.2. The IF–THEN-like form of logic used, called Horn clause form, is not a flattened out, normal form. As a result the 'theorem prover' we consider *cannot* prove all theorems; i.e. there are sentences which logically follow from the axioms but which the theorem prover cannot get at. This may seem damning, and it would be if we were playing pure games of logic and not worrying about such practical matters as resource management. The tables are turned on resolution refutation *because* it can go everywhere and do everything; on the other hand heuristic information is built into the very rules you write in Horn clause form, and remember, it is the heuristics which prune, or, at least, order the search of the state space and are so characteristic of AI.

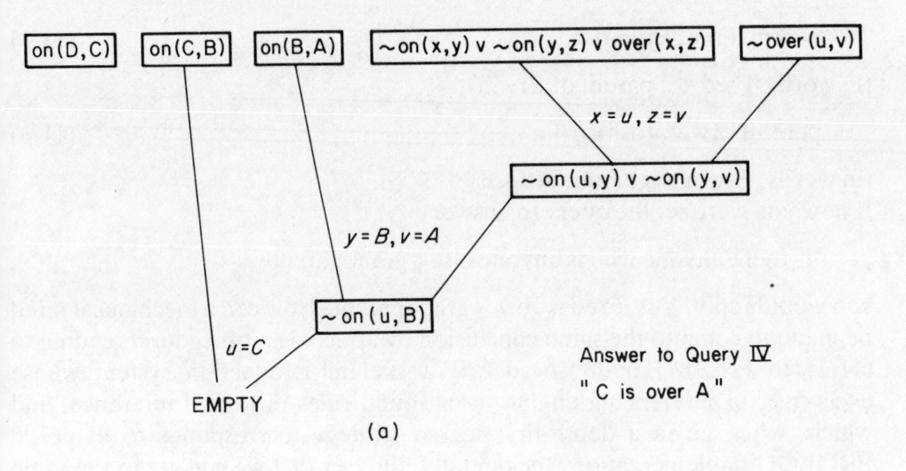

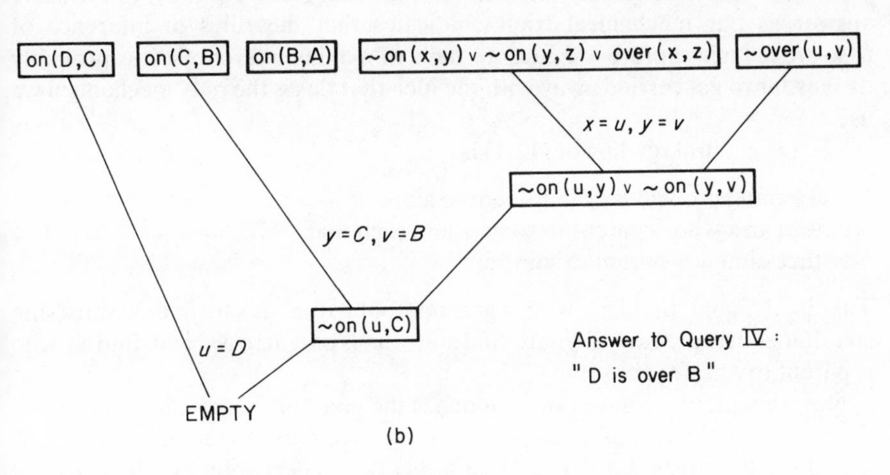

Figure 11.7

11.5.2 Horn Clause Form

We begin with an example again. Suppose you were asked to give a rule, or rules, to express the way the concepts of parents and grandparents are related, and that the rule or rules should be expressed as sentences in the predicate calculus. Consider the following,

$$\forall x,y,z\{\text{parent}(x,y) \wedge \text{parent}(y,z) \Rightarrow \text{grandparent}(x,z)\} \quad (11.1)$$

(in words, For all people x,y,z, if both x is a parent of y and y is a parent of z, then x is a grandparent of z).

Given 'in words' is what is described as the declarative reading of (11.1). Suppose further that you are given

$$\text{parent(Fred, Erwin)} \tag{11.2}$$

(in words, Fred is a parent of Erwin),

$$\text{parent(Erwin, Josh)} \tag{11.3}$$

(in words, Erwin is a parent of Josh).
If now you were set the query to answer

'Is there anyone who is anyone else's grandparent'

you would reply, Yes, Fred is Josh's grandparent. How can a mechanical mind be made to come to the same conclusion by attaching a procedural reading to (11.1) to (11.3)? To do so, define a skeletal production system whose executive, or inferencing engine, uses sound rules of logical inference, and which, when given a depth-first search strategy, corresponds to a typical PROLOG implementation. Incidentally, the fact that we can get to the same answer as our mechanical friend indicates that the rules of inference of first-order logic capture a means we have of making inferences; it is probably dangerous to get carried away with the idea that this is the only mechanism we use.

The procedural reading of (11.1) is

To find an x who is grandparent to a z,
find an x who is parent to some y and such that
that same y is parent to some z

That is, the goal 'find an x who is grandparent to a z', is satisfied by satisfying simultaneously the two subgoals 'find an x who is parent to a y' and 'find a y who is parent to a z', for the same y.

Now the query we have posed matches the goal (or, head) of rule (11.1). If we can satisfy the two subgoals, then we will have satisfied the query. But they are directly satisfied by (11.2) and (11.3) respectively by the variable instantiations x=Fred, y=Erwin, z=Josh.

Before defining a skeletal production system, it is necessary to say what is meant by Horn clause form. We lose little by using propositional logic for illustration purposes. The following are in Horn clause form,

$$\sim Y, A, A \wedge B \wedge C \Rightarrow D, \sim A \wedge D \Rightarrow \sim E, F \wedge G \Rightarrow \text{false}$$

whereas the following are not,

$$A \vee B, C \wedge D \Rightarrow E \wedge F, A \vee \sim B \Rightarrow G, H \Rightarrow I \vee J$$

That is, Horn clauses are propositional symbols or their negations, or they are implications whose antecedant (IF) sides are conjunctions of one or more such symbols or their negations, and whose consequent (THEN) sides are either the symbol false or a single propositional symbol or its negation. A set of axioms describing some state of the world (for our purposes) is then a set of such clauses which are (normally implicitly) conjoined. Such a set will be referred to as a knowledge base. Clauses are classified as either rules or facts dependent upon the property of having, or not having an implication sign.

To get from propositional to predicate logic involves the replacement of propositional symbols with atomic formulae in the above, and the convention that variables are implicitly universally quantified over.

Note that any sentence of the predicate calculus can be expressed in this form, just as any sentence could be reduced to conjunctive normal form. The difference is that the latter form is unique (hence the words 'normal form'), whereas the Horn clause is not. Depending upon this choice the inferencing mechanism will, or will not, be able to derive theorems. As mentioned at the end of Section 11.5.1, this is both a difficulty and a virtue of the approach.

Consider the table. On the left are a set of clauses in conjunctive normal form. On the right are Horn clause forms which are logically equivalent.

Conjunctive Normal Form	Horn Clause Form
$[p \vee q \vee \sim r]$	—(say)→ $[r \wedge \sim q \Rightarrow p]$
	—(or, say)→ $[r \wedge \sim p \Rightarrow q]$
$[\sim q \vee t]$	—(say)→ $[q \Rightarrow t]$
	—(or, say)→ $[\sim t \Rightarrow \sim q]$
	—(or)→ $[q \wedge \sim t \Rightarrow \text{false}]$

Now for the skeletal production system,

HORN CLAUSE REFUTATION

Initialize G to the [set of] top-level goals
which constitute the query;
until G is empty
begin

- select a member of G and a Horn clause in the knowledge base whose head matches it, possibly by instantiation of variables;
- remove the selected member from G;
- add to G the body (IF-part) of the selected clause;
- apply the variable instantiations required by the matching process to all members of G

end.

The initial goal (set) constitutes the start state. The finish state for the production system is the empty set. The rule base is the set of rules and facts in the knowledge base. The action of the executive is shown by the **until** block. What is *not* shown is how it handles conflict situations, nor do we mention whether its actions are irrevocable, so that a false choice leads to failure, or tentative, so that it may backtrack, say, and try again. We shall give the standard PROLOG answer in a moment. For the moment we illustrate with a simple example from the propositional calculus which enables us to make clearer our earlier comments about the exact form of rules influencing the ability of the system to reach theorems.

Below we show a set of three simple clauses written in two logically equivalent ways. The two ways are called KB1 and KB2.

KB1	KB2
$r \wedge \sim q \Rightarrow p$	$r \wedge \sim p \Rightarrow q$
r	r
$\sim q$	$\sim q$

Now we pose the query,

"Is p true?"

Translating this into a sentence of the propositional logic gives just

p

This is then the sole member of the goal set G initially. Take KB1. Scanning through the heads of rules (there is only one!) and through the facts, we find only one match—with the head of the rule. Our skeleton is sufficient to tell us what to do in this case—remove p, add r and $\sim q$ to G; no instantiations of variables are necessary in the propositional logic, so G is now the set $\{r, \sim q\}$. Let us scan through the rules and facts again trying to match something to r. That is easy—r is a fact. We remove r from G and add—what? We add nothing. A fact is to be thought of as a rule with no body. Thus G has now reduced to $\{\sim q\}$. Again, a scan through reveals $\sim q$ as a fact. So we remove $\sim q$ from G, add nothing again, and thereby reduce G to $\{\}$, the empty set. This entitles the system to reply Yes.

Take KB2. With the same query, p, there is no action which the executive can take! The system will reply, No.

Conclusion: Yes means 'I can prove it'
No means 'I cannot prove it, although it may follow from the knowledge base'

11.5.3 PROLOG

The skeletal production system described above leaves many details undefined. In particular there are two sorts of *indeterminacy*, to use Kowalski's phrase (Kowalski 1979). Firstly, a choice must be made as to which goal in G to satisfy next, and, secondly, given several clauses in the knowledge base which match this goal, a choice must be made of which one of those clauses to use. PROLOG, which stands for PROgramming in LOGic, and came originally from Marseille in the early 1970s, made the following choices in its original formulations. Firstly, the goals are placed in a linear list, rather than being in an unordered set, and they are tackled in list order; whenever a goal is matched to a rule head that goal is replaced by the list of new subgoals which are the (instantiated) body of the rule, or, if a fact matched the goal, that goal is removed and the next in line attacked. Secondly, the clauses in the knowledge base are also placed in a linear list and considered in order when looking for a match.

What search strategy does the system adopt? An exhaustive search in a depth-first-with-backtracking manner.

An example will again be used to illustrate these ideas and to introduce some new ones. Consider the following data base,

1. parent(x,y) $\wedge$ parent(y,z) $\Rightarrow$ grandparent(x,z)
2. grandparent(u,v) $\wedge$ grandparent(u,w) $\Rightarrow$ cousin(v,w)
3. parent(John, Erwin)
4. parent(Erwin, Paul)
5. parent(John, Fred)
6. parent(Fred, George)

with the following query,

'Is there anyone who is anyone else's cousin?'

Translated into predicate form this is,

$\exists r,s$ cousin(r,s)

The initial state for G is then { cousin(r,s) }, or, rather, since we now want to think of a goal LIST rather than SET, $\langle$cousin(r,s) $\rangle$.

The executive sets to work scanning through the clauses 1–6 in order. Rule 1 does not match, but 2 matches, requiring v=r and w=s. The list G is now,

$\langle$grandparent(u,r),grandparent(u,s)$\rangle$

The executive now tries to find a match for 'grandparent(u,r)'. It does so immediately matching 1 with the instantiations, x=u, z=r. Then G becomes,

$\langle$parent(u,y),parent(y,r), grandparent(u,s)$\rangle$

At this point goal 'parent(u,y)' matches not to rules 1 or 2 but to fact 3, with instantiations, u=John,y=Erwin, and the list G reduces to,

$\langle$ parent(Erwin,r), grandparent(John,s) $\rangle$

Now sub-goal 'parent(Erwin,r)' gets worked on. Neither 1, 2 *nor* 3 matches – in the last case because the constant symbol Erwin cannot be matched by the equally constant symbol John. 4 matches with r=Paul. G is then,

$\langle$ grandparent(John,s) $\rangle$; r = Paul

where we also show that the system will have noted the fact that the variable r of the query was instantiated to Paul.

The reader is now invited to 'run' the executive on G as it presently stands. What answer do you get? The correct answer according to the database given is the absurd one s = Paul. You may have thought the answer would be, s = George, and, of course, that *is* the answer we are really looking for. The reason the machine gets the wrong answer is the usual one when working with machines—we gave it the wrong data to work on! The trouble is that rule 2 is not good enough. It allows the possibility that v and w refer to the same person, which is not true of the way we think about the word cousin. What we need is something like the following,

NEW 2. grandparent(u,v) $\wedge$ grandparent(u,w) $\wedge$ not(v=w) $\Rightarrow$ cousin(v,w)

where, (a) '=' is a built-in infix binary operator which tests whether its arguments denote the same object, and (b) 'not' is a built-in unary operation which is defined such that if goal P is satisfiable, then goal not(P) is not, and vice versa.

Given NEW 2 the machine will reach the 'right' answer. The full search space and the order in which the depth first search proceeds is shown in Figure 11.8.

Actually, if you think about it for a moment, you will realize that rule NEW 2 is still not good enough. For, suppose we added a new fact

parent(Erwin, Peter)

after fact 4, say; then we would find that Paul and Peter are cousins, whereas, normally they would not be so described since they are brothers. Consider an EXTRA-NEW rule 2 to avoid this problem.

The interested reader is encouraged to look at one of the excellent books which are available on PROLOG (Clocksin and Mellish (1982)), or its micro version (Clarke and McCabe (1984), or Conlon (1985)). More details of the logical basis is to be found in Kowalski (1979). We close the discussion by pointing out that you must be very careful how you write your PROLOG programs—as in any language. It is not a panacea! In particular, watch the use of 'not'.

11.6 KNOWLEDGE REPRESENTATION TECHNIQUES

The last section investigated in some detail two production systems which employed clauses of first-order logic to represent states of the world, and which used well-understood, sound rules of logical inference to infer new facts from old. Other ways of representing knowledge of the world have been introduced into AI. In turn, the following will be considered: *semantic nets*, *object-attribu-*

State number	State, i.e. Goal-list	Rule used	Instantiations required	Comments
Ø	⟨cousin (r,s)⟩			
		2	*v* = *r* *w* = *s*	Rule 1 was not applicable; neither would be 3-6. Backtracking to this point means failure
1	⟨grandparent (u,r), grandparent (u,s), not (r=s)⟩			
		1	*x* = *u* *z* = *r*	This is the only rule applicable to the first goal in the list
2	⟨parent (u,y), parent (y,r), grandparent (u,s), not (r=s)⟩			
		3	*u* = John *y* = Erwin	Rules 1 and 2 were tried and found inapplicable. It would be possible to backtrack to this point and resatisfy using 4, 5 or 6
3	⟨parent (Erwin,r) grandparent (John,s) not (r=s)⟩			
		4	*r* = Paul	This is the only way to satisfy the first goal
4	⟨grandparent (John,s) not (Paul=s)⟩			
		1	*x* = John *z* = *s*	The only applicable rule again
5	⟨parent (John,y), parent (y,s), not (Paul=s)⟩			
		3	*y* = Erwin	The executive sets off on the wrong track, but will reverse!
6	⟨parent (Erwin,s), not (Paul=s)⟩			
		4	*s* = Paul	No comment
7	⟨not (Paul = Paul)⟩			
		Internal		FAILURE! Must backtrack and try again
8 (=6)	⟨parent (Erwin,s), not (Paul=s)⟩			
		No further rules applic-able		FAILURE! Must backtrack and try again
9 (=5)	⟨parent (John,y), parent (y,s), not (Paul=s)⟩			
		5	*y* = Fred	We resatisfy the first goal using another fact
10	⟨parent (Fred,s), not (Paul=s)⟩			
		6	*s* = George	The only applicable rule or fact
11	⟨not (Paul = George)⟩			
		Internal		SUCCEEDS! : the goal (Paul = George) having failed
12	⟨ ⟩			

Figure 11.8

te-value triplets and *frames*. These are mentioned because they are, respectively, a very commonly (mis-)used idea in AI, the basic unit in MYCIN (which we discuss at some length in Chapter 12), and a structuring concept closely allied to abstract data types in software engineering, to entity types in data analysis, and to classes in object-orientated programming systems. There is no space for consideration of other schemes. For an excellent critical review see Ritchie and Thomson in O'Shea and Eisenstadt (1984), Chapter 11.

Section 11.6.1 will introduce semantic nets as a way of pictorially representing the predicate calculus, without variables, and will then go on to consider 'extended' semantic nets (Kowalski 1979) which allow the introduction of variables.

11.6.1 Semantic Nets

The oft true saying 'A picture tells a thousand words' leads one to think of recording sentences of predicate logic in a pictorial way. This we shall demonstrate. The trouble with the idea, as pointed out in references above, is that one can become so fascinated by the pictures, using one's own intuition to add meaning and inference methods, that one fails to notice that no properly defined meaning has been given. We shall be careful not to fall into the same trap: at the end of the section a way of manipulating extended semantic nets to infer new facts from old will be presented.

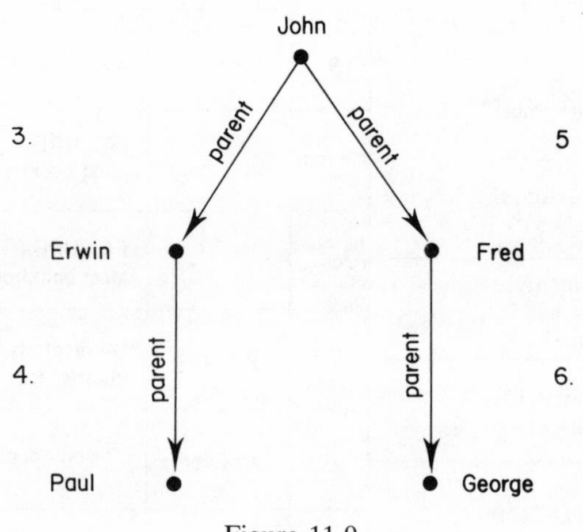

Figure 11.9

Look back at the 'cousin' database used in Section 11.5.3, Figure 11.9 gives the highly natural way of representing the facts 3–6. Nodes of the network stand for people, and directed, labelled, arcs between nodes show that those nodes stand in the relation of the label to each other.

Alternatively, consider Figure 11.10. Much of it is certainly immediately clear to the reader. But note that the node labelled 'horse' is of a different sort from 'Sandy': it stands for a class of objects of which 'Sandy' is an instance.

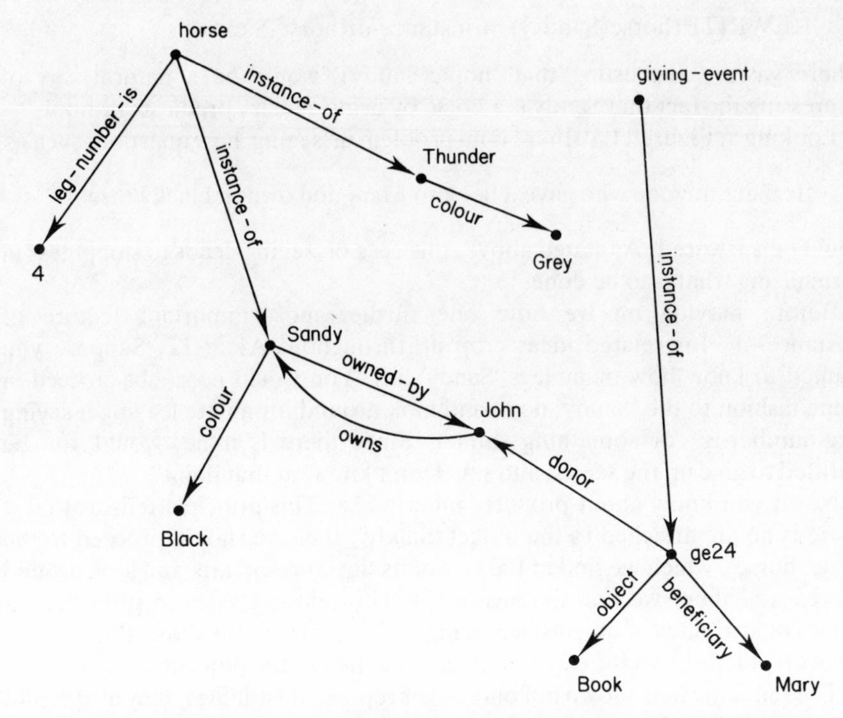

Figure 11.10 A semantic net which can answer the query "Is there anyone who gave a book to Mary and owns a black horse?"

Also, what is the strangely named node 'ge24'? It stands for a giving event, as shown by the 'instance-of' arc, and is required because we have here displayed pictorially the fact that John gave Mary a Book, which would be written in predicate logic form as gave(John,Mary,Book). Now, whilst the translation of parent(John,Erwin) was straightforward, that of gave(John,Mary,Book) is not; at least, not on two-dimensional paper. For predicate symbols are labelling arcs between two nodes, which stand for objects, but here we have three nodes. The way out is to rewrite in terms of binary predicate symbols. (Kowalski lists various advantages from doing this.) In our case

$$\begin{aligned} \text{REWRITE(gave(John,Mary,Book))} = {} & \text{instance-of(giving-event,ge24)} \\ & \wedge \text{ donor(ge24,John)} \wedge \text{object(ge24,Book)} \\ & \wedge \text{ beneficiary(ge24, Book)} \end{aligned}$$

The symbol labelling this particular giving event, ge24, was pulled out of thin air. You can imagine that it is the 24th such event that the machine has come across.

Rewriting is also the way we deal with unary predicate symbols. An example is provided by,

REWRITE(horse(Sandy)) = instance-of(horse,Sandy)

where we are suggesting that 'horse(Sandy)' would be a natural way of expressing the fact that Sandy is a horse by using a unary predicate symbol.

Looking at Figure 11.10 there is no problem in 'seeing' how questions such as

'Is there anyone who gave a book to Mary and owns a black horse'

could be answered. As stated above, this ease of 'seeing' leads to sloppiness in formalizing what is to be done.

Before moving on we note one further most important feature of 'instance-of', for related ideas crop up throughout AI or IT. Suppose you wanted to know how many legs 'Sandy' has. You would no doubt proceed in some fashion to the 'Sandy' node and look around for an arc leaving it saying 'leg-number-is', or something similar. Since there is none, would you be entitled to give up the search and say 'Don't know' at that point?

Not if you know about property inheritance. This principle tells us that if there is no arc attached to the object 'Sandy', then we should proceed to the node 'horse', which we find at the end of its 'instance-of' arc, and look around there. And there we find the answer: 4. This allows classes to store default values of attributes of objects belonging to that class; it also allows this value to be overridden in specific cases by an arc attached to the object.

The semantic nets shown not only never represent variables, they also do not show any rules. Considering once more the 'cousin' data base, how do we depict rules 1 and NEW 2? The way forward is shown in Figure 11.11. Notice that all predicates were binary already, so there was no need to rewrite any of them.

How might we describe a method of deriving new information from old, of manipulating such extended semantic nets? The following is a possibility which parallels PROLOG's way.

For simplicity, we query the extended semantic net which consists of the two nets of Figures 11.9 and 11.11 taken together with the query,

'Is there anyone who is someone else's grandparent'

Expressed as a sentence of the predicate logic this looks like,

$\exists a,b$ grandparent(a,b)

which we place into working memory as initial goal-set-net as shown in the top slot of Figure 11.12.

The manipulation rule is the following:

If an arc in the goal-set-net has the same label as a consequent (single line) arc in the semantic net, and the node labels at the arc ends can be matched, possibly by instantiation of variables, then that arc in the goal-set-net may be

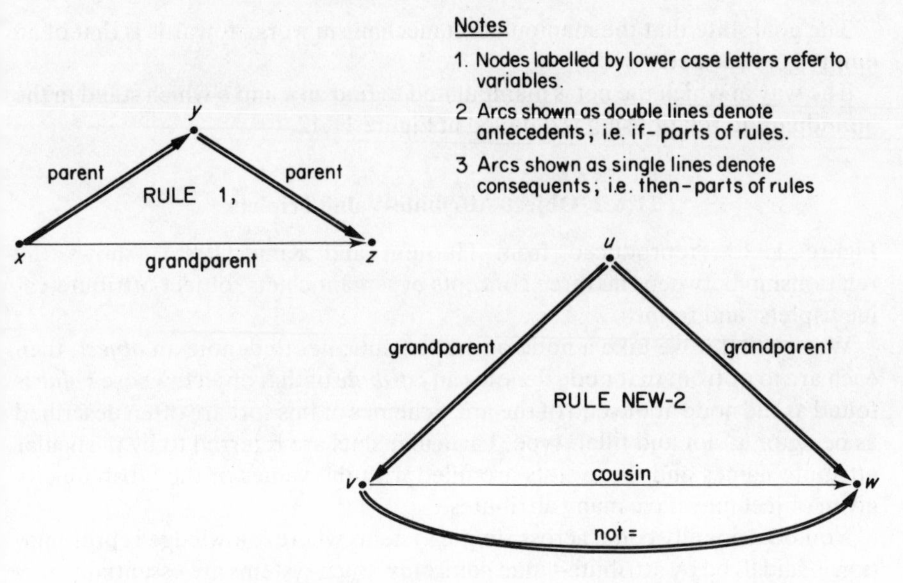

Figure 11.11 Variables and rules in extended semantic net notation

State number	STATE, i.e. GOAL-SET-NET	Semantic net subgraph used	Instantiations required	Comments
Ø	a —grandparent→ b			
		1	x = a z = b	The only applicable subgraph
1	a —parent→ y —parent→ b			
		3	a = John y = Erwin	We (somehow, not specified) choose to reduce the first arc using arc 3 of the net. Other choices could produce other answers
2	Erwin —parent→ b			
		4	b = Paul	No choice
3	EMPTY			

Figure 11.12 Reduction of a goal-set-net to the empty net showing John stands in grandparent relationship to Paul

replaced by the set of antecedent arcs (double lines) to the consequent arc, provided all variable instantiations are performed on the goal-set-net. (*Note.* A fact is represented in the semantic net by a single line consequent arc which has *no* associated antecedent arcs.)

The goal state that the manipulation mechanism works towards is that of an empty goal-set-net.

The way in which the net is manipulated to find an *a* and *b* which stand in the 'grandparent' relationship is detailed in Figure 11.12.

11.6.2 Object-Attribute-Value Triplets

Figure 11.13 (reproduced from Harmon and King (1985)) shows the relationship between the three concepts of semantic nets, object-attribute-value triplets, and frames.

We see that if we take a node of the semantic net to denote an *object*, then each arc to or from that node denotes an *attribute* of that object, whose *value* is found as the node at the end of the arc. Schemes of this sort are often described as being of a 'slot and filler' type. Particular slots are referred to by particular attribute names and those slots are filled with the values of the attributes. A given object may have many attributes.

You occasionally come across simple systems where knowledge representation is said to be by attribute-value pairs only. Such systems are essentially only considering the possibility of there being one relevant object around—hence their simplicity. Inductive learning systems have been based on this idea. For example, consider a system which is meant to decide which of several Soviet warplanes a particular plane is an example of. If the class 'Soviet warplanes' is considered to be defined in terms of a set of attributes, each of which can be assigned a value only within a certain domain (e.g. attribute: bomb load, domain of values: 0 to 1000 kg), and if the various sub-classes, such as 'Backfire Bomber', or 'Flogger', are distinguished by particular distributions of likely values amongst the attributes, then a system can be 'trained' to take a good guess at the identity of a given plane. By identity is meant the subclass to which it belongs (Naylor 1983).

More points will be made about object-attribute-value triplets and their use in the context of the MYCIN expert system in Chapter 12.

11.6.3 Frames

In the software-engineering chapters the reader has already learnt about the idea of an abstract data type and the compelling reasons for talking about and, indeed, employing such things. Not unnaturally, a similar idea is to be found in the AI world, for the problems are the same: those of modelling real world situations in such a way that the inherent complexities of the problems can be managed. The name 'frame' is used most often in AI (Minsky 1979; Rich 1983) although others are not uncommon, e.g. 'units' (Nilsson 1980).

As indicated in Figure 11.13 a frame collects together all the information about a class of objects. There is a slot for the name of a particular object of that

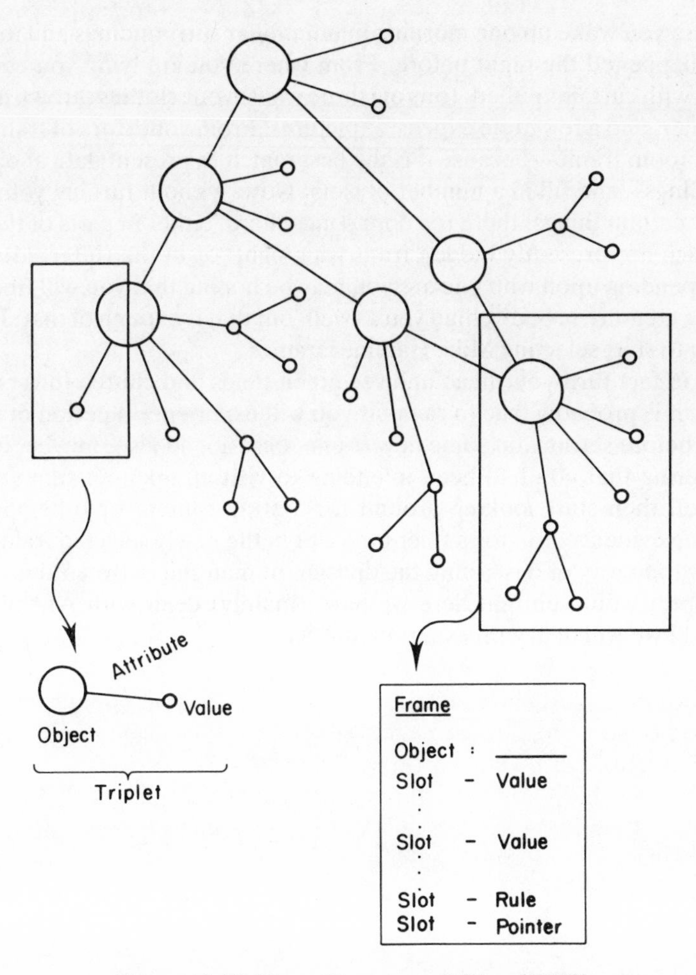

Figure 11.13 (From Harmon and King (1985))

class, and slots for values for all attributes relevant to that class. There are also slots for rules which can manipulate the frame, e.g. to derive one attribute value from others in that frame. The reader should be reminded of the data structure of an abstract data type, and the operations on that type, respectively.

It is interesting to consider a simple example of the use of frames to see the way in which inferencing can occur. For frames are structured objects, so that the very statement that some object is an instantiation of a particular sort of frame gives a lot of information. There is always a balance to be found in the representation and manipulation of knowledge (or data); a loose, unstructured representation requires more of the inferencing engine, and vice versa.

Suppose you wake up one morning in unfamiliar surroundings and forgetful of what happened the night before. From where you are lying you can see a window, with curtains pulled, (bits of) three walls, your clothes thrown untidily onto a chair, and a few quite expensive pictures. From your store of frames you choose a room frame—because it is the best match to present data about your surroundings—and fill in a number of slots. Now, without turning your head, you infer certain things; there is a door somewhere, either in parts of the three walls which are presently hidden from your sight, or in the (inferred) fourth wall. Depending upon who you arc you may be hoping that you will find some sylph-like creature in bed behind you as well, but that is enough of that; I do not want you to start selecting Mike Hammer frames.

If you in fact turn your head and see green fields and church towers in the distance, it is probably true to say that you will experience a period of mental turmoil, before settling on some new frame, occasioned also, maybe, by your remembering that you had been intending to visit an open-air film set. You might well then start looking around for a stray camera or other piece of supporting evidence, i.e. for a filler for a slot in the newly selected frame.

Finally, one way of describing the division of material between this and the next chapter would be that here we have (mainly) dealt with AI theory; in Chapter 12 we will deal with experimental AI.

Fundamentals of Information Technology
Edited by G. G. Wilkinson and A. R. Winterflood

Chapter 12

Expert and Knowledge-Based Systems

12.1 INTRODUCTION TO EXPERT SYSTEMS

The arrival of 'expert systems' has caused a surge of interest in AI in industry and commerce and amongst the public. Many would agree that the first true expert system was MYCIN, the major product of the Stanford Heuristic Programming Project, a system for interpreting medical data. The 'MYCIN experiments', as those who worked on the project like to call them (Buchanan and Shortliffe 1984), showed that a system could be written to perform at least as well as human experts in one of those fields where there is no comprehensive body of knowledge, organized into a scientific theory. The project depended on rules of thumb, on chunks of knowledge extracted from expert medical practitioners to (incrementally) build up the rule base of the system. It also did something which we have not met before, but which is obviously required of a program which should simulate our human reasoning techniques: it could handle uncertainty.

The first part of this chapter will consider MYCIN; from the comments above it is clear that we consider it to hold a pivotal position in the history of AI. Then there follows a necessarily incomplete account of other expert systems.

The experiments which produced good systems were often later exploited by taking the domain-specific knowledge out of the system to leave a 'shell' into which others could insert their own knowledge base, and thereby build their own expert. Such shells are the top end of a spectrum of AI 'languages'. At the bottom end is *the* language of AI, as it is often described: LISP. The third and last part of this chapter considers this spectrum and makes some attempt to answer the question 'Why LISP?' without actually showing any LISP code.

12.2 MYCIN

The MYCIN project brought together a multidisciplinary team to work in a real-world problem domain. They aimed to produce a machine 'capable of using both clinical data and judgemental decisions regarding infectious disease therapy' (Buchanan and Shortliffe (1984)). It should be a consultation program which practising physicians would use. This required it to be interactive, allowing the user to interject 'Why?' and 'How?' questions into the consultation session, which it led itself by asking pertinent, and only pertinent, questions of the user. The user interface should be friendly, tolerant of 'trivia' such as misspellings. It should allow its performance to be recorded, analysed and altered by changing its knowledge base.

A great advantage accrues from choosing a 'real' problem to work on. It provides the right environment for finding that elusive, correct mix of theoretical and experimental input. The purist theoretician might baulk at accepting the adopted method of handling uncertain knowledge; the experimentalist, not wishing to concern himself with abstract ideas like production systems, might never find a system structure that works. In practice, the mixture of AI and medical researchers did what we humans are so good at, as mentioned several times in the last chapter—they hit on satisfactory solutions to problems that are so hard that it is even unclear if such a concept as an optimal solution can be defined.

There are, fortunately, some excellent places from which to read about MYCIN in more depth than our book allows. We have already quoted from Buchanan and Shortliffe, which has to count as the primary reference for the serious student. There are also chapters in, say, Harmon and King (1985). All of these texts give an example consultation session, something which it is so valuable for you to see that part of that given in Harmon and King is reproduced here as Figure 12.1.

12.2.1 Structure of MYCIN

The organization of the MYCIN system is shown in Figure 12.2. It is recognizably a production system with some extra bits once the following associations have been made:

dynamic data base ↔ working memory,
static data base ↔ knowledge base, and
consultation program ↔ inferencing engine

The extras which make MYCIN more than just a production system are

- the 'explanation program', which allows the user to ask 'Why' questions, for example (such as, 'Why did you rule out the possibility of ... ?', or just 'Why?' to find out why the system just requested certain data).
- the 'knowledge acquisition program', which implies running the system in a totally different mode, in which stored knowledge can be adjusted, removed or added to, usually by a knowledge engineer (who knows the system) working with a domain specialist. A separate expert system was built for this task, named TEIRESIAS.

12.2.2 Static Knowledge, Rules

Amongst other things, the static knowledge base holds the rules of thumb which summarize in discrete chunks the expertise of the human consultants. An example is given here:

RULE 085

IF:		(1) The stain of the organism is gramneg
	and	(2) the morphology of the organism is rod
	and	(3) the patient is a compromised host
THEN:		There is suggestive evidence (0.6) that the identity of the organism is pseudomonas

The reader will agree that this looks like a pretty normal IF–THEN rule (though we need to learn how to handle the 'suggestive evidence (0.6)'). Referring back to the previous chapter, we note that the individual clauses of, say, the IF part are actually tests on the value of the attribute of some object. Thus, clause (1) tests whether the stain (attribute) of some organism (object) is gramneg (a possible value for such an attribute of such an object). Notice that clause (3) refers to a different object, namely to the patient him/herself.

Not all clauses of MYCIN rules test the value of an attribute. Some, for example, ask whether the value is known for certain.

The great advantage of having knowledge in such mind-sized chunks is that the mere statement of which rules were used to reach a conclusion constitutes an explanation as to why that conclusion is believed. Moreover, those rules can be shown to the user in just the same form and with just the same jargon which he or a colleague used when articulating them for the knowledge engineer.

We wish to emphasize this point as one central to the AI approach. To digress for an instant, we pose the question:

Why should it be a good idea to have machines which behave intelligently?

The answer is presumably, because the machine is then a better partner or replacement for Man. People and machines are different. There are things which are easy for us and difficult or impossible for them, and vice versa. It is no doubt sometimes best if we allow the machine to do the things it is good at, in the way that it can do them best.

Certainly machines are excellent at doing boring, repetitive work quickly and without making mistakes. As a result it may well be that a machine can be made to solve a problem in a way which most mortals either cannot or will not understand. This means that the result is only acceptable as an act of faith on the part of the human user. This is obviously not acceptable when the problem is the present one of how best to treat a critically ill patient, or where to sink an expensive oil well. The user may then require an explanation in terms that he or she can understand.

MYCIN begins by asking for four pieces of information about the patient—name, age, sex, and race. All are essential to any diagnosis, so they are asked at the onset of the session.

1) Please enter information about the patient.

Name	Age	Sex	Race
Sally	*42 years*	*Female*	*Caucasian*

The physician enters the information and MYCIN continues.

2) Are there any positive cultures obtained from SALLY?
No

3) Are there any pending cultures of SALLY?
Yes

4) site:	date collected:	stain examined?	method of collection: (urine, sputum only)
CSF	*3-Jun-75*	*Yes*	*N/A*

5) stain of smear: morph:
(type NONE if no organism was seen on the smear)
None

The second piece of information that MYCIN wants concerns the availability of cultures with positive readings. Rather than attempting to deduce the results of tests, MYCIN allows the physician to state what is known. In this case the physician does not have any positive cultures, and so MYCIN probes further (question 3), asking whether this patient has pending cultures. The patient does—and so MYCIN provides headings for the physician, who enters CSF to indicate that a cerebrospinal fluid culture has been taken but that no organism has yet been seen. MYCIN is unable to reach conclusions from laboratory findings, but like the physician, MYCIN continues to ask questions. Eventually MYCIN reaches this:

13) Has SALLY recently had symptoms of persistent headache or other abnormal neurologic symptoms (dizziness, lethargy, etc.)?
Yes

14) Has SALLY recently had objective evidence of abnormal neurologic signs (nuchal rigidity, coma, seizures, etc.) documented by physician observation or examination?
Yes

The CSF cultures will be considered to be associated with MENINGITIS.

MYCIN's questions 13 and 14 show a more traditional approach to the diagnosis by symptoms, and after receiving the answer to question 14, MYCIN reports its first conclusion: The CSF infection is likely to be meningitis. MYCIN then begins another line of reasoning aimed at identifying the particular organisms responsible for the meningitis infection. Further questions lead to the following:

34) Is the meningitis a hospital-acquired infection?
No

35) Is SALLY's clinical history consistent with EPIGLOTTITIS?
No

36) Is SALLY's clinical history consistent with OTITIS-MEDIA?
No

37) Has the patient ever been to an area that is endemic for coccidiomycoses?
<u>Unknown</u>

38) Is SALLY a burn patient?
<u>Why</u>

When asked whether the patient is a burn victim (question 38), the physician responds by typing WHY. MYCIN responds by restating its understanding of "why" in this context, and then explains what the information will be used for. To explain, MYCIN displays the particular heuristic rule it was considering, Rule 578, and MYCIN explains how the requested information would be useful.

[i.e. WHY is it important to determine whether SALLY has been seriously burned?]

[4.0] This will aid in determining the organisms (other than those seen on cultures or smears) which might be causing the infection.
It has already been established that
[4.1] the infection which requires therapy is meningitis, and
[4.2] organisms were not seen on the stain of the pending csf culture (CULTURE-1), and
[4.3] the type of the infection may be bacterial
Therefore, if
[4.4] SALLY has been seriously burned
then
there is suggestive evidence that Pseudomonas-aeruginosa is one of the organisms (other than those seen on cultures or smears) which might be causing the infection
[RULE578]

[back to question 38...]
<u>How 4.3</u>

The physician is curious about how MYCIN was able to conclude that the type of infection is bacterial. "HOW 4.3" is a request to explain how MYCIN established clause [4.3] of the rule it is considering. MYCIN responds with its understanding of the question, and then reports the rules it used in determining this fact. The physician can press for greater detail by asking HOW 4.5 to track down what heuristic Rule 500 is and how it was confirmed. By repeatedly asking HOW, the physician can backtrack right to the beginning of the consultation.

Notice that MYCIN has four rules that support the likelihood that the infection is bacterial, and one rule that suggests (certainty factor of .17) that the infection is not bacterial. MYCIN is considering both possibilities. Momentarily, it is following up on the more probable one.

[i.e. HOW was it established that the type of the infection may be bacterial?]

The following rules concluded about: the likelihood that the type of the infection may be bacterial

	Rule	Yes	No
[4.5]	RULE500	(.4)	
[4.6]	RULE501		(.17)
[4.7]	RULE502	(.1)	
[4.8]	RULE524	(.42)	
[4.9]	RULE504	(.28)	

Thus, it has been established that the type of the infection may be bacterial.

Figure 12.1 Sample conversation with MYCIN (From Harmon and King (1985))

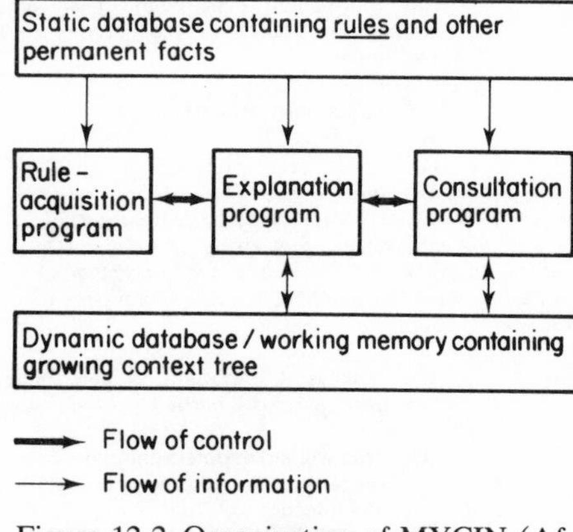

Figure 12.2 Organization of MYCIN (After O'Shea and Eisenstadt (1984))

Thus the computer may be able to solve problems in its own way, by direct frontal assault (using some cunning algorithm), as it were, yet produce correct but unacceptable answers. Even worse, the user may suspect the algorithm, or the very possibility of an algorithmic solution. (Without even seeing its output, would you accept the results of a program which decides whether Britain should buy Trident?) In such cases it is clearly preferable to program in some other way, which may be less direct, less efficient, perhaps, but which more closely resembles the human way of looking at and solving the problem, and which is then perforce more acceptable to the user, besides having other advantages, such as the flexibility and universality of human decision-making.

The rules are not all that is maintained in the static database. There is also the equivalent of a data dictionary, to borrow a term from the data analysts. That is, information is stored on the structure and properties of the objects, attributes, and domains of values. Whilst on the topic of dictionaries, note that MYCIN terminology is not that of object-attribute-value triplets but of context-parameter-value triplets, and that a class (of objects) is referred to as a context-type. We may also use our knowledge of diagrammatic techniques from data analysis to define the structure of the so-called context tree as in Figure 12.3.

12.2.3 Dynamic Knowledge, The Context Tree, Control

Every consultation session begins with the instantiation of a context of type PATIENT. This is the only context of this type which gets instantiated per session. It appears in working memory and forms the root node of a context tree. Other contexts are instantiated as and when needed.

Viewed as a production system, states are states of the dynamically growing

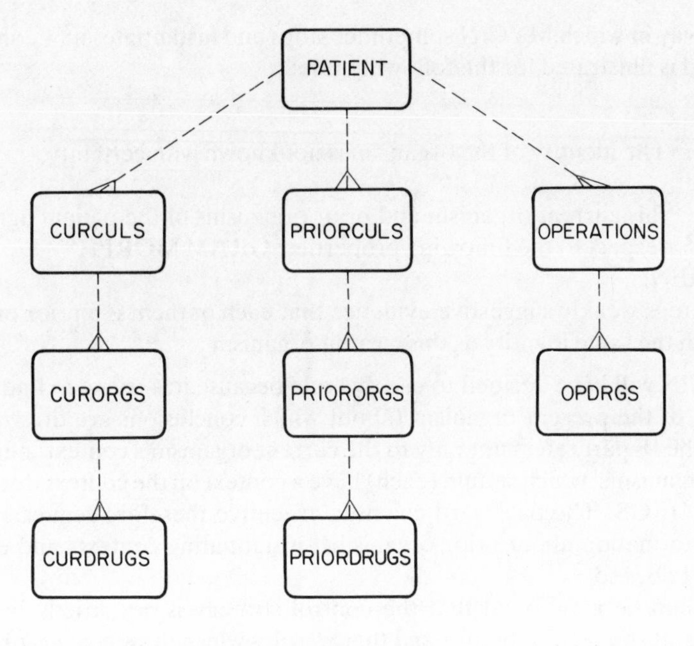

Figure 12.3

context tree, and production rule applications can either change parameter values of contexts, and/or add new contexts to the tree.

The dominant control strategy of MYCIN is backward chaining. At any given time, the system will be trying to find out the value of some parameter, 'tracing' the parameter in MYCIN terminology. The top-level goal is to trace the value of the REGIMEN parameter of the PATIENT context. This goal is pursued immediately after the system gets hold of values for the so-called MAINPROP(ertie)s of that context—the name, age, sex of the patient.

Some parameters can only have one value—the identity of an organism, for example; others can have more than one—the allergies of a patient, for example. Even when a parameter can have only one value in practice, it is often the case that the physician or, in our case, the machine, is uncertain as to what that value is. It then needs to consider the various possibilities. There may be a number of rules which draw conclusions about a given parameter. They may each suggest a different value with a particular certainty factor. In that case each possibility is recorded in the dynamic database in the context whose parameter is being considered, along with the associated certainty factor. Alternatively, it may be that several rules suggest the same value for the parameter. Their certainty factors are combined according to rules to be discussed in the next section and again recorded at their context in the growing context tree.

The way in which MYCIN sometimes stops and instantiates new contexts as required is illustrated for the following rule:

IF:

1. The identity of the organism is not known with certainty,

and

2. this current organism and prior organisms of the patient agree with respect to the following properties: GRAM MORPH

THEN:

there is weakly suggestive evidence that each of them is a prior organism with the same identity as this current organism

MYCIN will have decided to use this rule because it is trying to find out the identity of the present organism (about which conclusions are drawn by the rule). The IF part refers not only to the current organism's context, but also to 'prior organisms' which should (each) have a context on the context tree of type PRIORORGS. The backward chaining executive therefore requests (of the user) information about prior organisms, instantiating contexts and entering data as it does so.

It should be mentioned that the control strategy is not strictly backward chaining. It should also be stressed that *all* rules which draw conclusions about a parameter which is being traced are considered.

12.2.4 Handling Uncertain Knowledge

As mentioned in Section 12.2.2, the way in which MYCIN handles uncertainty may not be to the purist's taste; or, rather, he or she may find themselves pondering questions like 'Why do it that way?', which are answered neither here nor in the original literature, other than by the reply that the adopted methods were found to work in practice, sometimes after a period of experimentation and subsequent revamping. The interested reader is invited to look into Buchanan and Shortliffe (1984), especially Chapters 10 to 13.

Uncertain facts

As we have already seen, facts are represented as object-attribute-value triplets, or context-parameter-value triplets to use MYCIN terminology.

When dealing with *certain* facts, the value is simply a domain element appropriate to that attribute/parameter. When dealing with uncertain facts, a number (the certainty factor) between -1 and $+1$ is included with the domain element and more than one possible value may be given. A certainty factor of -1 implies total disbelief in the attribute taking on the suggested value; 0 implies total ignorance as to whether the parameter could have that value; and, finally, $+1$ implies total commitment to the suggested value.

We take an example from O'Shea and Eisenstadt (1984):

OBJECT/CONTEXT	ATTRIBUTE/PARAMETER	VALUE
PATIENT-1	SEX	(MALE 1.0)
ORGANISM-1	IDENTITY	((KLEBSIELLA 0.6) (HAFNIA 0.4))

Thus, the system is totally convinced that the patient is male. (As in the last section, note that SEX is a MAINPROP which gets traced at the very start of a consultation session; it is a parameter which is LABDATA, i.e. has to be asked about. The fact that it is a parameter which has the LABDATA property is known to the system by being recorded in the static data base, as mentioned in Section 12.2.2.) It is also presently of the opinion that the ORGANISM-1 could be KLEBSIELLA, that it could be HAFNIA, and that it is more likely to be the former than the latter.

The system only knows of a certain number of possibilities for organism identities. At the start of a session all possibilities are given the certainty factor of zero. It is only by the action of rules suggesting belief or disbelief in a possible value that the certainty factors change.

Combined Uncertain Facts

Let A,B,C be facts with certainty factors of $CF(A),CF(B)$ and $CF(C)$ respectively. Then,

$$CF(A \wedge B \wedge C) = \text{minimum-of}\,(\,CF(A),CF(B),CF(C)\,)$$
$$CF(A \vee B \vee C) = \text{maximum-of}\,(\,CF(A),CF(B),CF(C)\,)$$

For example, consider rule 085 of 12.2.2, and suppose that it has been possible to establish premise (1) with certainty factor 0.6, premise (2) with certainty factor 0.5, and premise (3) with certainty factor of +1. Then using the first of the rules given here, we may conclude that the certainty factor to be attached to the entire IF-part of the rule is 0.5.

Uncertain Rules

An expert may be not totally sure that certain things being true imply certain others, and he may, alternatively, know for certain that a certain combination of circumstances has given entailments with a given certainty factor. Both these possibilities are conflated into rules with attached uncertainty factors.

One of the following notations is used,

$$A \wedge B \wedge C \Rightarrow D\text{, tally } x$$

or

$$A \wedge B \wedge C \overset{x}{\Rightarrow} D$$

where x is a number in the range 0..1 in both cases.

As above, the one form of rule combines (and confuses) the two possibilities. In either case the use of the rule is the same. Firstly, suppose that A,B, and C are all known for certain. Then the rule suggests a certainty factor of x for D if it is being suggested for the first time. (The case where there already exists grounds for believing or disbelieving D, and where this piece of evidence must be combined with prior evidence, is treated in the next paragraph). Next, suppose that each factor A,B,C has itself a certainty factor attached. In this case the certainty factor which is suggested for D is given by

$$CF(D) = x * \text{maximum-of}\{ 0 , \text{minimum-of}(CF(A),CF(B),CF(C)) \}$$

The reader may well have expected to see just

$$CF(D) = x * \text{minimum-of}(CF(A) , CF(B) , CF(C))$$

arguing that the second term in the product on the right-hand side is the certainty factor one attaches to the premise, the first the certainty that one attaches to the rule, and the product, then, a reasonable idea for the certainty factor attachable to the conclusion of that rule with those premises. In fact, a close examination of the first and second formulae reveals that they yield the same value if all premise certainty factors are positive. If, however, any one (or more) of the premises is disbelieved, the certainty factor attached to the conclusion is zero. The rationale behind this choice may be more clearly seen by reference to rule 085 again. The x attached to the rule is 0.6. Suppose that the certainty factors attached to the premises (1), (2) and (3) are as given above. Then $CF(D) = 0.6 * 0.5 = 0.3$.

Now suppose that in another consultation session the same figures had been arrived at, except that it was known for certain that the patient was *not* a compromised host. The human consultant would not now wish to use rule 085 at all. It merely tells him that *if* he believes certain things, then he is entitled to infer certain other things; it tells him nothing about those situations in which he does not believe those things. In MYCIN you get the same (nullary!) effect if you do not use a rule at all, as when you use one and conclude a certainty factor of zero from it.

Combining Evidence

Suppose

RULE 1 : $A \wedge B \Rightarrow C$, tally 1.0
RULE 2 : $D \wedge E \Rightarrow C$, tally 0.75
RULE 3 : $F \wedge G \Rightarrow \sim C$, tally 0.8.

and

$$CF(A) = 0.5 \quad , CF(B) = 0.9 \; , CF(D) = 0.8$$

$$CF(E) = 0.85 \ , \ CF(F) = 0.8 \ , \ CF(C) = 0.75$$

Now, if we happen to use RULE 1 first, then we conclude $CF(C)=0.5$. Next, suppose RULE 2 is used to conclude independently that $CF(C)=0.6$. How do we combine the two pieces of suggestive evidence about C?

$$\text{combined–}CF(C1, C2) = C1 + C2*(1 - C1)$$

if $C1$ and $C2$ are both greater than zero;

$$\text{combined–}CF(C1,C2) = - \text{combined–}CF(-C1, -C2)$$

if $C1$ and $C2$ are both less than zero.
In our present case we use the first rule to see

$$CF(C) = 0.5 + 0.6*(1 - 0.5) = 0.8$$

Finally, RULE 3 suggests C is not a fact, doing so with an individual certainty factor of -0.6. How do we combine this negative piece of evidence with the positive evidence collected already?

$$\text{combined–}CF(C1,C2) = (C1+C2)/(1 - \text{minimum-of}(C1,C2))$$

whenever $C1*C2 < 0$.
Using the figures given, we then finally end up with, $CF(C)$, as the combined certainty factor using all three rules.

The combined certainty factor formula for the case where $C1*C2 < 0$ was a refinement of the previously used formula,

$$\text{combined–}CF = C1 + C2$$

which was discarded because it was found to be unrealistic in practice. The trouble was that there might be ten suggestions that some fact was true, each with certainty factor 0.9, say, and just one contraindication, with certainty factor 0.8, say. The result of combining evidence in the earlier manner was an overall certainty factor of a little under 0.2. With the formula given above the combined factor is still close to one.

12.2.5 Some Lessons From MYCIN

Buchanan and Shortliffe (1984) give some 'key questions and answers' about the MYCIN project. To the following questions a (sometimes qualified) 'Yes' answer is given:

- Is a production rule formalism sufficient for creating programs that can reason at the level of an expert?
- Is backward chaining a good model of control for guiding the reasoning and dialogue in consultation tasks?
- Is the evidence-gathering model useful in other domains?

- Is the CF model of inexact reasoning sufficiently precise for expert-level performance?
- Were we successful in generalizing the problem-solving framework beyond the domain of infectious diseases?

It is also only right to give an example of a question to which the answer is 'No':

- Can we prove the correctness of conclusions from MYCIN?

But this is such an interesting question, particularly in these days of proving programs correct, that we quote further:
'No, because the heuristics carry no guarantees. However, we can demonstrate empirically how well experts judge the correctness of a program's conclusions by using a variant of the Turing test.'
Whereby it should be known that the Turing test involves comparing the output from a machine with that of a human without prior knowledge of which is which.

This brings us back to some of our opening comments in Chapter 11, which, in some form, have remained a major theme throughout. If intelligence is an 'art', that of navigating successfully through a hostile world for as long as possible, but is resistive of more formal definition, then how do we test the intelligence of a machine other than by comparison with the human template?

12.3 OTHER EXPERT SYSTEMS

From the discussions of the last chapter the reader will recall that intelligent behaviour is to be seen as making satisfactory decisions, as solving problems using heuristic search methods. The idea was advanced that the problems that confront one are of a nature that often demands such methods. It is to be further recognized that some problems are intrinsically harder than others. It is not unreasonable to think that the harder a problem is, the more complex is the search method needed to solve it. In other words, the complexity of the structure of the expert system we use on a given problem reflects the complexity of the problem.

The inference mechanism must be organized in such a way as to make the problem solver efficient and reliable. For very simple classes of problems a very simple search process suffices. As restrictions on the search domain are lifted, and we consider more and more difficult problems, so we require more complicated search techniques.

12.3.1 Knowledge-based Systems For Simple Tasks

Hayes-Roth *et al.* (1983) suggest that as requirements for task simplicity we have

1. data and knowledge are reliable;
2. data and knowledge are static;

3. the space of possible solutions is relatively small.

where the following apply:

1. data reliability means that there is no incorrect or missing input data; knowledge reliability means that the knowledge is always applicable, without having to concern oneself with questions of consistency, and that such application does not lead to false, approximate or tentative conclusions;
2. static means that there is no concern with invalidating facts as time passes;
3. small means that the search may be exhaustive.

Given all these conditions, we can use the simplest sort of architecture: a database whose size grows monotonically as conclusions are simply added and an inferencing mechanism which follows a single line of reasoning, there being no need to develop multiple arguments in support of potential conclusions. The logic theorem prover by resolution refutation is fashioned after this architecture.

12.3.2 Handling Uncertainty With Small Search Spaces

If we lift the restriction (1) above, but retain the other two, then we have the sort of task domain in which MYCIN operated using both unreliable data and knowledge; another system which fits into this category, though with marked changes from MYCIN, is PROSPECTOR, which has been very successful in the provision of consultation facilities to geologists.

The differences are interesting enough to deserve further attention. PROSPECTOR does not use the somewhat *ad hoc* approach to reasoning with uncertainty which MYCIN does: it employs traditional probability theory, in particular, Bayes' theorem; it allows the user to volunteer information; and it updates probabilities, or belief factors, on a fixed inference net structure. There is no space available for details of statistical inference using Bayes' theorem here, but let us illustrate what is involved by an example.

Two archers are observed firing arrows at a target, which is marked by concentric rings such that scores are made of 10, 20, 50, 100 dependent upon which annular ring is hit. By observation over a long time period the probabilities of archer X scoring a 10, 20, 50 or 100, or missing altogether, may be determined. Call $P(10,X)$ the probability that X will score a 10, etc. Then

$$P(10,X) + P(20,X) + P(50,X) + P(100,X) + P(\text{MISS},X) = 1$$

expresses the fact that all outcomes of a shot have been taken into account. Similarly there is a set of probabilities $P(10,Y)$, etc, for the other archer.

Now, suppose arrows are observed impacting upon the target, but the identity of the archer is not known to the observer. There are two possible hypotheses: archer X or archer Y. Evidence as to which archer it actually is accrues as a result of the observations of arrows landing. The formula which relates evidence to hypotheses is Bayes' theorem and it involves the $P(10,X)$s, etc., above, and the so-called *a priori* probabilities $P(X)$ and $P(Y)$ that the hypothesis is true in the absence of any evidence; e.g. it may be that archer X is only at the shooting range one third as often as archer Y, so that $P(X) = 0.25$ and $P(Y) = 0.75$. (Note again that $P(X) + P(Y) = 1$, i.e. one hypothesis does have to be correct). The fact that there should be such a formula is intuitively reasonable on considering simple example situations. For example, if $P(100,X) = 0.01$ and $P(100,Y) = 0.5$ and $P(X) = P(Y) = 0.5$ (i.e. X is a rotten shot, and Y an excellent one, and they are equally likely to be at the range), then an observation of the anonymous archer hitting a bull's eye would convince most of us that it was Y shooting, and a recurrence of this event would be even more convincing evidence for this hypothesis. Bayes' theorem formalizes and confirms these intuitions.

Additional factors, additional pieces of evidence may also influence our calculations as to which archer it is. Someone else may have also observed the sort of arrow being fired (initially, when we knew which archer was shooting and we simply recorded scores for archers). They would also then have available $P(\text{white feathers},X)$, $P(\text{black feathers},Y)$, etc. Suppose in fact $P(\text{white feathers},X) = 0.99$ and $P(\text{white feathers},Y) = 0.001$.

If now a single observation is made again of an unknown archer firing and hitting the bull's eye, and with a white arrow, then this more fastidious observer would actually reverse the previous decision, concluding that it was probably X that shot (well, for a change).

The above example was particularly simple inasmuch as evidence directly supported hypotheses; sometimes evidence suggests or discredits intermediate hypotheses which themselves act as evidence for further hypotheses. In the case of PROSPECTOR, the hypotheses are such things as

'There's gold in them thar hills!'

or molybdenum, or whatever. Evidence is likely, however, to be suggestive of certain geological structures, which themselves are suggestive of the presence or absence of certain minerals.

As in the above simple example, tables of probabilities of observing certain features (evidence) when gold is present, etc. (hypotheses), as well as the *a priori* probabilities, may be used in Bayes' formulae to calculate the probabilities of hypotheses given evidence, as is required in practice.

As a final point, the reader should note that there is no intended implication that PROSPECTOR's manner of reasoning with uncertainty is to be considered superior to that used in MYCIN because it uses traditional probability theory. Bayes' approach uses certain assumptions that are sometimes not easy to justify. The interested reader is referred to Chapter 13 of Buchanan and Shortliffe (1984).

12.3.3 Real-time Experts

Lifting restriction (2) is most interesting. In particular because this is very necessary for systems which mimic the real-time behaviour of organisms—systems such as robots. The humanoid robot is no doubt still a long way off. The systems that are available now are process controllers, which can perform the same sort of function as the human operator sat at a desk, to some extent at least. A commercially available process and plant management system, named ESCORT (Expert System for Complex Operations in Real Time), 'reduces cognitive overload on operators in control rooms' (PA Computers and Telecommunications). Major points made about ESCORT in its literature are that it advises the operator (but does not bypass him), it is a real-time system, it has monitor qualities, it is priority specific, it justifies advice and it is knowledge based. The very first point is illustrated in Figure 12.4, which shows information flow.

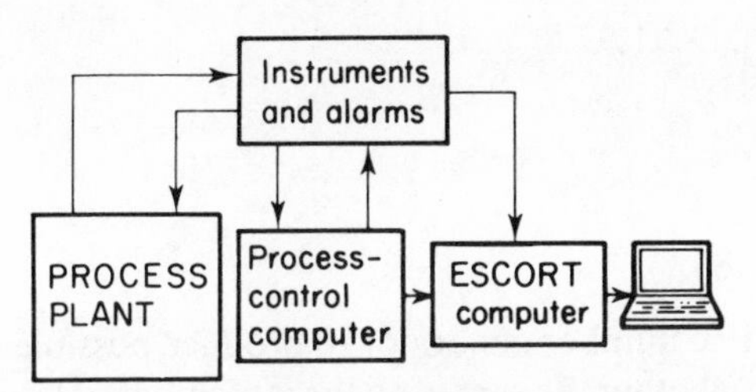

Figure 12.4 The ESCORT system (Reproduced with permission of PA Consulting Services Ltd.)

Section 12.3.4 considers the possibilities arising from the relaxation of (3) above. After looking at relatively simpler systems, where (1) and (2) still restrain the task domain, we eventually reach HEARSAY, where (1) no longer holds.

12.3.4 Systems With Large Search Spaces: Generate and Test

Some people, including members of the 'MYCIN gang', would dispute the claim that MYCIN was the first expert system, offering that place to DENDRAL, a molecular-analysis program. Certainly the latter predates the former. The argument is over what is a 'real' expert system.

DENDRAL works using the technique of 'generate and test'. The generator suggests solutions in an incremental fashion and has 'pruning rules' enabling it to evaluate and, if appropriate, reject partial solutions. Suggested complete solutions which have escaped the pruning are then tested to see if they really are solutions. Since we do not have the space to consider DENDRAL itself; we first refer you to Hayes-Roth *et al.* (1983) and the original literature, and second give a very simple example after the spirit of 'generate and test'.

Suppose you have to write a program to find all triplets of primes such that their sum is less than a certain number, 100 say. The problem might be solved as follows. Firstly, you need a prime-number generator, one that will produce all primes in ascending order starting from 1, say. You begin by setting the prime-number generator to work suggesting possible first members for the triplets.

- First pruning rule: only primes less than 100 are acceptable.

This yields candidate partial solutions such as, ⟨1,?,?⟩,⟨7,?,?⟩ ... ⟨97,?,?⟩. Next set the prime number generator to suggest second members for the triplets.

- Second pruning rule: the sum of the first two members must be less than 99.

This yields candidate partial solutions such as

⟨1,1,?⟩, ⟨1,2,?⟩, ... ,⟨1,97,?⟩
⟨7,1,?⟩, ... ⟨7,83,?⟩
⟨97,1,?⟩,⟨97,2,?⟩

but *not*

⟨7,97,?⟩ or ⟨31,83,?⟩.

Finally, get the prime number generator to produce possible third elements to the triplets and *test* whether the sum of all three elements is less than 100 for each *generated* (now) complete solution.

Generate and test is effective provided that partial solutions can be filtered for possible contribution to a complete solution (as in the example given): this reduces numbers of solutions to consider, making the scheme computationally feasible. There are, however, plenty of problems where such filtering is not possible. The way forward then is to find a 'rough', but complete, solution and to fill in the details later.

12.3.5 Abstraction

Abstraction involves the stripping away of details to get at what is essential. The art of abstraction lies in recognizing what *is* essential. The great scientist, for example, is the one who can disregard what is irrelevant to the problem at hand and concentrate on the essential. As above, problems may be such that it is impossible to say whether a partial solution is or is not part of a complete solution, yet be such that they can be solved in their entirety at an abstract level.

XCON, (formerly R1) is arguably the most successful of all expert systems. It is used to configure DEC VAX computers and has eliminated the need for human domain experts. The problem it solves is made easier by the fact that it can *always* be broken down into six subtasks, which are solved one after the other. There is, as it were, a fixed order of abstraction steps: step 1 (ensure that the customer's purchase order is not grossly in error) is performed, using its own IF–THEN rule set, followed by step 2 (put appropriate components in the CPU and its expansion cabinets), using its IF–THEN rule set, ... , followed by step 6 (do the cabling) using its IF–THEN rule set. There is no backtracking, little search: XCON operates in a highly specialized domain.

The development of XCON has an interesting history, which is given in Harmon and King (1985). The team at MIT funded the project themselves initially, such was their desire to show DEC that it was possible; they eventually wrote a package which conventional software engineers had failed to produce. A 'front-end' expert to XCON, called XSEL, is also being developed.

Many problems are not so specialized. For them an abstraction must be found for each individual variant. This is the approach you, the reader, are used to as top-down refinement.

The ABSTRIPS robot planning system uses the idea of prioritorized preconditions. It first solves a given problem (in the area of moving boxes around) at a 'high' level of abstraction, requiring only that highest priority conditions be satisfied, then drops a level of abstraction, picking up new conditions whose satisfaction amounts to filling in the next level of detail in the solution.

Top-down programming is deliberately modular. The top-level program solves the problem provided the modules from which it is built all behave according to specification. In turn, these modules are built from lower-level modules, and so on. Interaction between modules is minimized, and that between levels is eliminated. All decisions at one level of abstraction are thus taken before any at lower levels.

People often allow feedback from the problem-solving process itself, applying the principle of 'least commitment'—do not make a decision until you have to. Another robot-planning system, NOAH, which is a later product from the author of ABSTRIPS, employs this principle. See Chapter 14 of O'Shea and Eisenstadt (1984).

MOLGEN, a system for designing MOLecular GENetics experiments, alternates between least commitment and heuristic modes. For the trouble with least commitment is that you can reach a deadlock situation where several decisions are waiting upon each other in cyclic fashion. In such a situation MOLGEN takes a guess, in best heuristic AI fashion. From one branch of the MOLGEN program has emerged GENESIS, a package which includes seven different expert systems.

When explaining our successful decisions to others we are often guilty of oversimplifying those explanations. In particular, we will often present a single line of reasoning, and not recognize the fact that the decision was arrived at by a combination of several lines of reasoning.

The HEARSAY-II system (Erman *et al.*, 1980) interprets spoken requests for information from a database. Its knowledge is contained in a set of knowledge sources. The vocabularies of these knowledge sources are different, in general. Some know about acoustic signals and which phoneme or phoneme combinations a signal segment might correspond to. Some know that certain syllables combine to form certain words which exist in the language, some know that certain words are classified as adjectives and are therefore likely to be followed by either another adjective or a noun, and so on. The fact that vocabularies differ is often referred to as an example of non-uniform abstraction: at the top level the system produces a query language sentence (from the semantics knowledge source); at the next level down phrases are being suggested, etc. This is to be contrasted with top-down decomposition, where different levels can be said to use the same vocabulary, just filling in details.

The individual knowledge sources read, write and modify a global database, or working memory, called a *blackboard*, which is divided up by level of abstraction. Hypotheses are written onto the blackboard. Some may be competing, e.g. it is not possible for the same segment of signal to be two different syllables, but the system (or, rather, the knowledge source responsible) may not be sure which of two possibilities it is, so it may write both, accompanying each with a sort of certainty factor. Another source works on such syllable hypotheses, attempting to combine syllables into words. Once sufficient hypotheses have appeared on the blackboard it can start work. But which hypotheses does it use if there are several competing possibilities? Here enters the 'opportunistic scheduler'. When one of the hypotheses is more highly rated than the others it gets worked on first. If they are all equally rated, then the principle of least commitment is applied and they are scheduled to be worked on together.

12.4 LANGUAGES, ENVIRONMENTS, TOOLS, SYSTEMS

A (formal) language, for a computer scientist, is a subset of the set of all possible strings formable from some finite alphabet. The complexity of the language that a machine will accept, of the patterns in input which it can recognize and react to in some better way than crashing, is an indicator of the power of that machine. In this sense, any program running on a computer defines a language, the set of acceptable input strings for that program, whose complexity of structure is both determined by the program and an identifier of the power of the program. The computer plus program is described as a *virtual machine*.

For example, a Pascal compiler might be a program written in machine code which will accept as inputs any syntactically correct Pascal program. The power of the Pascal virtual machine is in no way less than that of the underlying machine. On the other hand, having written a Pascal program, submitted it to the compiler and started it running, that virtual machine might well have an input language as simple as the set of all pairs of integers, for the case of a program which finds the greatest common divisor, for example. Again, it is obvious in any sense of the word that the *power* of this program is not as great as that of the compiler: it can only accept an extremely limited language and do something very specific with that input.

The greatest common divisor program is a typical application program. It can be written such as to do its very specific job most efficiently, but it cannot do all sorts of other things. As with all things in life, you win on the roundabouts and lose on the swings.

Even when you do not throw away any of the underlying power of the computer, when, as in the first example, you write a compiler for Pascal or COBOL, or whatever, it is still true that you build in a certain bias in making some applications programs easier to write than others. The two languages mentioned both have the same power and can therefore both be used on any computable problem, but one will most likely be more convenient than the other for a given problem.

In the world of AI there is one dominant language: LISP. There are also challengers, such as PROLOG. Almost all of the original work in AI was written in LISP, or in a language itself written in LISP. In a moment we address the question of 'Why LISP?' more fully. For the moment let us record the fact that LISP is an extremely convenient language for doing symbol manipulation. It is a so-called 'core' language whose computational (technically, Turing machine) power can be seen in a small set of primitive functions (and functional forms, which enable us to make more complex functions from simpler ones). What you build with these core functions and provide to your LISP user is a choice which the producers of various dialects of LISP did not always agree on. A particular selection of more complicated functions, one which would usually involve such things as an editor, trace package, etc., all of which are written in LISP itself, determines an *environment*.

MYCIN, for example, was built in the INTERLISP environment (the West Coast (of the USA) version of LISP). Also note that there is a derived *tool*, in this case EMYCIN, the 'shell' of the MYCIN system with its knowledge base removed. This is suggestive of a spectrum:

LANGUAGE → ENVIRONMENT → TOOL → EXPERT SYSTEM

which is here being instantiated as

LISP → INTERLISP → EMYCIN → MYCIN

Another, historically more accurate example is

LISP → FranzLISP/MacLISP → OPS5 → XCON

where MacLISP is East Coast LISP and FranzLISP the VAX variant thereof.

Why did I say that the second example is historically more accurate? In the case of MYCIN, the expert was developed first, and then the tool. For expert-system-building tools have been a result of building an expert system in a particular domain, thereby showing that some combination of ideas about knowledge representation and inferencing mechanisms does actually work, and of then removing the specific domain knowledge to leave a 'shell' appropriate for filling with new knowledge from a domain whose problem characteristics resemble closely those of the original domain. Returning to the discussion at the start of this section, a tool defines a new 'language' in which some sorts of problems are more easily expressed, whilst others will be harder to express.

As another example, work on MOLGEN produced not only GENESIS, as stated above, but also the Xerox expert system building tool, LOOPS (using the INTERLISP-D environment).

If the reader has become worried by the profusion of dialects of LISP already mentioned, it can only add to that worry to learn that there are others (e.g. the French have Le LISP), but it must help to know that the idea of COMMONLISP (whose name should explain its purpose) has taken off to the extent that, say, Xerox have rewritten LOOPS as COMMONLOOPS.

An excellent summary of expert system building tools is given in Harmon and King (1985). Such a summary gets rapidly out of date nowadays. This is both unfortunate and unavoidable in such a fast-moving field as AI/expert systems.

We close this section with a brief discussion under the twin headings 'Why LISP?' and 'Why not LISP?'.

12.4.1 LISP as the AI Language—WHY LISP??

(A) It has the advantages common to all functional languages (provided one uses it as such).
(B) It has common (list structure) representation of data and programs.
(C) It is the *lingua franca* of the AI community.

We shall now examine each of these points in more detail.

Further to (A)

Note that words like procedure, routine, subprogram, even program, can all be forgotten. Functional languages only have functions and ways of combining them to form (and name) new functions. Programming style is naturally hierarchical, with the top-level function (*the* program) at the top of the pile. In spite of all this one continues to use the word 'program' when one could just write function. This corresponds to common practice.

(A1) Compared to the imperative style languages, LISP is already at a higher level of abstraction—closer to the thought processes of the programmer and further from the language of the machine.

(A2) Being written in (a form of) standard mathematical notation, we can apply standard, well-ingrained deductive reasoning processes to programs. In particular, program verification does not suffer from 'referential opacity' problems; i.e. (approximately!) as there are no assignment statements, variables always have the same value, they always refer to the same value within a given piece of code.

(A3) Functional languages promise a natural way of writing programs for machines which exhibit concurrent processing.

Note that (A1) and (A2) refer to two aspects of the 'software crisis' problem—longwindedness and opacity of imperative-language programming.

Further to (B)

Acceptable LISP forms are either *atoms*—strings of digits and/or letters and/or certain other acceptable symbols—or *lists*—sequences of atoms or (nested) lists, enclosed in brackets. Whether data or programs, they always have this simple form. Consequently the distinction between data and programs fades.
Thus: What is in one context a function can be used as data in another.

(B1) LISP is an interactive language. The LISP interpreter is itself written in LISP (and accessible to the user): it accepts your LISP functions as its data.

(B2) Editors, error-handlers, debuggers, steppers, etc. can all be written in LISP. Your (error-ridden) program gets treated as data by these functions. LISPers always emphasize the programming environments that they have been able to create for themselves as a consequence. In particular, and of great value in AI research, they stress the *exploratory* nature of their work and how this environment assists it.

(B3) Nobody really knows how organisms manage the amazingly complex job of classifying their surroundings and finding an appropriate corresponding action to safeguard their immediate and long-term survival, both as individual and as species. Whatever the mechanism(s) may be, some of them are probably 'hard-wired' and some of them not: even the most simple creatures 'learn'. If a program is to learn it must be able to alter itself. The program itself must be manipulable as data. In LISP it is.

(B4) LISP is important as a 'target language'. The output from LISP function evaluation is always a LISP form, which can then be a LISP program itself. It is easy to write functions which accept statements in an embedded language and return runnable LISP code.

Further to (C)

The reasons why LISP is still around (its invention having preceded that of COBOL, though not of FORTRAN) are not backing by people in high places in government or industry, but a certain 'intrinsic goodness'. The AI community were amongst the first to notice this, have worked on the language for many years (though not always to good effect), and have produced products which are possibly the major reason for the resurgence in interest in the language generally. Of course, this has also generated a certain inertia which may cause difficulties if a "better" language (no doubt more functional in character than LISP) is ever proposed.

The inventor of LISP, John McCarthy (1978), put it thus:

> LISP is now the second oldest programming language in widespread use (after FORTRAN) ... Its core occupies some kind of local optimum in the space of programming languages given that static friction discourages purely notational changes. Recursive use of conditional expressions, representation of symbolic information externally by lists and internally by list structure, and representation of the program in the same way will probably have a long life.

Whilst quoting McCarthy, it is worth mentioning in this context that he was unashamedly attempting to produce a language after the fashion of mathematical notation. This would, if nothing else, give a computer a language to express ideas clearly, concisely, precisely, etc.—as does mathematical notation. And one cannot overestimate the importance language has in aiding, or preventing, us from thinking and expressing our ideas. Again, the importance of LISP lies not only in its being a good attempt at such a language, but in the way it has become a widespread common language.

Remembering how old this language is, it is clear why LISP was chosen by the AI community. At that time the first steps were being taken towards abstraction.

> The decision about the particular data abstractions to be included in a programming language was mainly dictated by the machines for which the languages were intended (e.g. the machine provided fixed- and floating-point arithmetic) and by the spectrum of applications the languages were supposed to cover (e.g. the language was intended to cover scientific applications).

> As a result no language turns out to be appropriate for all applications, since the programmer is limited by the expressive power of the fixed set of abstractions provided by the language. . . (Ghezzi and Jazayeri 1982).

This might be unkindly paraphrased by saying that there were languages for number crunching and for file manipulation, etc., but none for the sort of general symbol manipulation which is the heart of the AI endeavour—other than LISP.

12.4.2 Why not LISP?

Barr and Feigenbaum (1982) mention the following disadvantages to LISP:

(A) Ugly syntax, which makes it hard to read. (Though 'one can conjecture that LISP owes its survival specifically to the fact that its programs are lists, which everyone, including me, has regarded as a disadvantage.' (McCarthy 1978)).
(B) There is only one data type, which prevents type checking and consequent bug finding. (However, AI researchers point to this lack of need to declare and stick to types as a distinct advantage in the exploratory mode of operation.)
(C) Inefficiency: any language executed interpretively can be slow. Most LISPs include a facility for compiling when the code is finished, and it is now nowhere near as inefficient as it is sometimes said to be. Also note again that it is a functional language, for which our present Von Neumann machines have an unfavourable architecture.
(D) Lack of a language standard.

To these might be added:

(E) A paucity of 'functional forms'. By this we mean that LISP gives rather few ways of combining functions to form new functions.

12.5 CLOSING COMMENTS

These chapters will, we hope, have given you a start in learning about the fascinating field of AI. They have also provided references to other books and publications. You may still be wondering what to read next. Whilst any answer must depend upon your personal interests, etc., the following is a suggestion. Try reading one traditional book on AI, say Rich (1983); a more modern general book, such as Charniak and McDermott (1985); the excellent essays in O'Shea and Eisenstadt (1984); and a book to help you see what is actually going on in business, industry and commerce, that of Harmon and King (1985).

It would also balance your diet a little to read Alexander and Burnett (1983), because their claim that experience has shown that the Von-Neumann machine is not a good model for certain activities which are regarded as intelligent, should be taken seriously. Weizenbaum (1976) is also useful in reminding us all not to overhype our product!

PART 5

THE MAN–MACHINE INTERFACE

Fundamentals of Information Technology
Edited by G. G. Wilkinson and A. R. Winterflood

Chapter 13

The Human Interface

13.1 INTERFACE CHARACTERISTICS

An essential function of an information system is to *communicate* and *interact* with its users, or more generally its environment, and an essential component, therefore, of the system is the *interface* between the system and its users. The *man–machine interface*, also often called the *human–computer interface* in the context of computer systems, can therefore be defined as that component of the information system which contains the processes or mechanisms by which the external world, i.e. the suppliers and consumers of information, communicate with the internal world, i.e. the processing, storage and transmission functions, of an information system.

13.1.1 The Importance Of The Interface

The implication of defining the interface as a separate component is that there is a need to consider this part of a system as a distinct and important component, in the same way as we identify the data storage or processing components of the system. This is a relatively new approach in system design and reflects a growing understanding of the critical effect the man–machine interface has on system performance within its environment. No matter how powerful the processing capabilities, how extensive and efficient the database system, the effectiveness of these functions will be considerably diminished if they cannot be easily accessed and used. The quality of the system in many other ways depends crucially on the performance of the interface, in particular on its ability to adapt to the needs of both new, inexperienced and experienced users, thus easing the problems of initial user acceptance, yet ensuring long-term performance.

The critical role played by a system's man–machine interface not only justifies identifying it as a distinct component, worthy of individual study, but also demands that the design of the man–machine interface should be considered as a major part of the overall system design. The purpose of this chapter is primarily to identify the fundamental concepts of interface design and demonstrate how these concepts contribute to a set of design guidelines, i.e. a methodology for interface design. We will also explore the technological factors which define the constraints on interface design and attempt to define criteria against which the performance of the interface can be judged.

13.1.2 Interface Technology—Hardware

Rapid technological development in recent years has dramatically increased the range of devices which can be employed in realizing the interface. The variety of devices for interaction with the external world now include the following.

- *Visual display terminals.* Mainly used for textual display of information, with input via a keyboard, but also used for the display of simple graphics.
- *Graphics displays and workstations.* Mainly used where graphics is the predominant mode of information entry and display, e.g. in computer-aided design and cartography. Interaction is via the high-resolution display of both textual and graphical information and the entry of information using both a keyboard and some form of graphical pointing device, e.g. a 'mouse'. The latter allows the user to rapidly indicate points or areas of the display so that the displayed graphics can be altered, new graphical or textual information entered in the correct location, selection made from a list or 'menu' of options, etc. Owing to the efficiency of this form of interaction over the considerably more restricted method of keyboard-only interaction, these workstations are now used extensively in other types of information systems, where text, not graphics, is predominant, e.g. office automation, but where the use of a pointing device can greatly speed up interaction.
- *Speech synthesizers and recognizers.* Recent developments in speech synthesis techniques have resulted in a range of high-quality devices which play an important role in communicating information where the use of a visual display is limited or even precluded. Such situations occur, for example, when it is necessary to supply information to people who are simultaneously carrying out tasks which require their full visual attention, e.g. pilots, vehicle drivers, machine operators. Interaction with the visually handicapped is also, of course, another important application. Speech recognition is a very complex process, requiring sophisticated techniques of signal processing to extract the relevant information from the raw electrical signal produced by the input sensor (i.e. microphone). The need to cope with the enormous range of variations in pitch, intonation, etc. in the human voice has allowed only a limited development in this area, primarily in applications where the system can be trained to recognize individual utterances of a single person (e.g. an aircraft pilot or machine operator).
- *Printers, plotters, etc.* Printing and plotting devices of various types play a major role in providing permanent or 'hard-copy' records of information, both textual and graphical, sometimes at a higher resolution or on a larger

scale than can be produced on the visual display terminal. The increasingly sophisticated technology employed in such devices, e.g. laser technology, has allowed the integration of printing and plotting operations in a single device and the use of such devices for the printing of full colour graphical images, as distinct from line drawings. Such devices are becoming increasingly important in the communication of purely visual information, e.g. image data used in satellite remote sensing, in architecture or in product design and manufacture.

- *Direct interaction via sensors and actuators.* Many sources of information in the external world can, and often must, be accessed directly, without human intervention. Examples include systems used to directly control processes, e.g. aircraft, chemical plant, nuclear reactors, or to provide information for human control of such processes. Mechanical, electronic, optical and other techniques are used to sense the information required, such as temperature, pressure, flow, etc. Likewise, direct action on such processes is usually needed, e.g. shutting off valves, switching power supplies, adjusting aircraft control surfaces. This requires mechanical, electrical, hydraulic or pneumatic powered mechanisms, e.g. motor-driven valves, relays, hydraulic rams. Since the electrical or optical signals used in controlling such interface devices are generally 'noisy', i.e. it is difficult to distinguish the information content from random variations in the signal, sophisticated processing techniques are necessary to ensure 'clean' information is passed to the information system.
- *Robots.* The most versatile device for direct interaction is the programmable robot. This provides a mechanism for carrying out, under computer control, a range of mechanical handling tasks which is limited only by the physical characteristics of the robot, e.g. reach, speed, lifting capacity, accuracy, and by the sensing devices which are required for a given task, e.g. tactile, visual, aural. The robot is now a fundamental component in the interface of most computer-based manufacturing information and control systems.

13.1.3 Interface Technology—Software

Communication of any form, whether it is between humans or between a human and a computer requires a *language* for expressing the information to be communicated. In the case of a human–computer communication, the language must be understandable to both the human user (or some form of direct interaction device) and to the computer. The ability of the computer to understand language statements made by the user is dependent on the processing capability of the interface software, in particular the availability in the computer of stored information (or knowledge) about both the language and the actions and other entities referred to in language statements. The latter is often referred to as the *domain* or *universe* of the human–computer *discourse* or *dialogue*.

Recent advantages in both software technology and in our understanding of the underlying concepts of language processing have provided a wide range of different forms of languages and language-processing methods available for use in the human–computer interface, including the following:

- *Command languages.* Simple composite statements of required action, using a command keyword to identify the basic action, optional modifier words to specialize this, and the names of entities on which the action is to be performed. Such languages are common in user interfaces to operating systems.
- *Interactive programming languages.* The extension of a simple command language to provide it with the power of a normal programming language. Such languages allow a more powerful form of interaction, whereby actions can be repeated, selected on a condition, etc. under the control of the interface software.
- *Graphical languages.* Languages in which statements can be made which refer directly to graphical entities, i.e. points, lines, drawings, and actions to be performed on these entities. The entities in such a language statement, rather than being referred to by name, may be selected by a pointing device, e.g. a statement requesting the deletion of a line of a drawing may contain a command keyword 'delete', followed by selection of the line to be deleted by the user pointing to the line on the displayed drawing.
- *'Natural' languages.* The intention in a 'natural' language interface is to allow the dialogue to take a form which closely resembles a 'natural' dialogue in the everyday language of the user. There are enormous difficulties involved in dealing with the ambiguities of such language statements, the variety and range of forms of language statement and the extent of the knowledge which is normally expected of the participants in an everyday language dialogue. There has been limited progress in this area, mainly in applications where the domain of discourse is very restricted e.g. in specific database-enquiry systems.

13.1.4 Interface Design

The development of hardware and software technology has far outpaced the development of principles or guidelines for interface design, despite the crucial nature of this component in an information system. There is a great deal of discussion of 'user-friendly' systems but there is little real understanding of what this term means or of how it relates to any of the interface technologies described above. Such an understanding, and the subsequent development of interface design principles, requires the investigation and knowledge of a wide range of concepts, many of which may not be familiar to the information technologist. Fundamental within this set of concepts are the following:

- *Concepts of human–computer communication.* The form and content of language and methods of describing and reasoning about language in terms of its syntax, semantics and pragmatics.
- *Human cognitive processing.* The abilities and limitations of humans in the process of understanding, in particular the categories of knowledge required in understanding a language, the processes involved in the use of this knowledge, and the way in which errors might occur in these processes.

A basic requirement, if a study of such fundamental ideas is to be useful, is to translate the concepts and the analysis of their application to man–machine interfaces into practical guidelines for interface design.

13.1.5 Fundamental Concepts Of Human–Computer Communication

Fundamental to man–machine interface design is the concept that the interface embodies the processes and medium for *communication* to take place between the computer system and its human user or environment. If we regard the computer system and its human user as simply two components of an overall information system, then communication between these components, as in any other system or organization, is crucial to their ability to *associate* and *co-operate*.

By focusing on communication as the fundamental process involved in a man–machine interface, we can take advantage of the substantial body of knowledge which exists in this field in order to understand the factors which might determine the performance of the interface, i.e. the quality of the communication (Cherry 1957).

The primary requirement for communication is a *language*. By this we mean

- a set of *symbols*;
- a set of *rules* for combining the symbols into *language statements*;
- a means of assigning *meaning* to symbols and statements in the language.

In order that both association and co-operation takes place between the human and machine components of the information system, it is necessary that they, at least in part, share a common knowledge of the language used in the interface. For effective communication, this goes far beyond knowledge of simply the symbols and symbol ordering rules of the language, to knowledge of the *environment* or *situation* in which the communication takes place.

These notions expressed above lead us to a fundamental *model of co-operative communication* (Figure 13.1). In this model, the *producer* begins with a set of communicative goals:

- effects to be achieved;

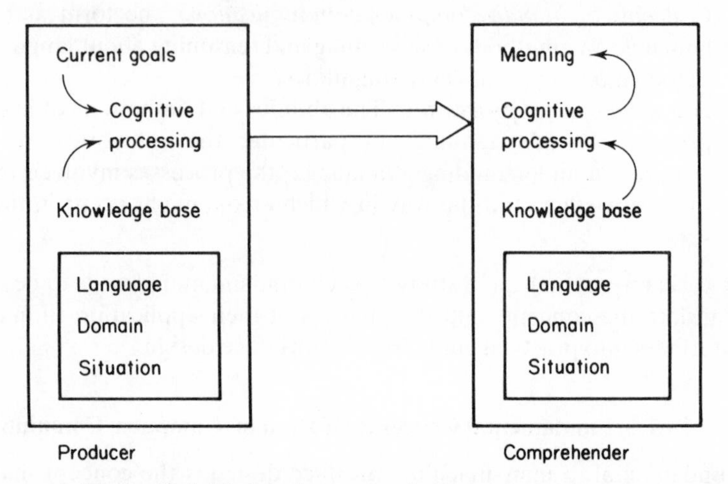

Figure 13.1 Model of co-operative communication

- information to be conveyed;
- attitudes to be expressed.

For example, these might include:

- the initiation of an action;
- causing the *comprehender* to make inferences or have reactions, either about the subject matter or about the interaction between the producer and comprehender;
- conveying information about something known to the comprehender;
- making the comprehender aware of something new known to the producer;
- directing the comprehender to some object or some property;
- establishing the context for a future communication.

The producer may have in mind a combination of more than one such goal.

Next, the producer maps these goals onto the set of available tokens (signs, symbols) that the communication medium, i.e. the language, can convey. This process

- needs knowledge of the language, i.e. symbols, rules for combination, etc., the domain of discourse and the situation in which the communication takes place;
- depends critically on the producer's expectations of the comprehender's ability to interpret the communication, i.e. the comprehender's knowledge of the language, the domain and the situation.

The value of this simple model is that it leads us to identify the major factors which determine the performance of the interface. By considering the human user and the computer system in each of the roles of producer and comprehender, we can identify a range of both *human factors* and *machine factors* which determine the quality of the interface and which can therefore be used to specify interface design guidelines.

In the following two sections of this chapter we will consider first the human factors and then the machine factors. The human component is by far the most powerful and versatile part of the interface and therefore it is preferable to be fully aware of the capabilities and limitations of the human user before we can attempt to identify those features of the machine component which are necessary for the creation of a high-quality interface, i.e. which complement, match and exploit human abilities in the most effective way.

13.2 HUMAN FACTORS IN INTERFACE DESIGN

13.2.1 Factors Affecting Human Performance

Consideration of the factors which determine human performance in an interface can be conveniently separated into a study of the *physiological* nature of the activities involved, i.e. the behaviour of the human user in relation to the physical requirements of the interface, and their *psychological* nature, i.e. the behaviour of the user in relation to the mental processing requirements of the interface. The physiological aspects of this study have been considered for many years in relation to workplace design, under the title *ergonomics*. Much of the knowledge which has been acquired in relation to other man–machine interfaces, e.g. pilot–aircraft, factory operator–process, can be applied to the human–computer interface, principally by understanding the effect of various physiological factors on human performance, such as

- visual skills, e.g. limits on level and discrimination related to size and brightness of visually displayed information;
- tactile skills, e.g. limits on keying speeds caused by lower bounds on neural transmission and muscle latency times, etc.;
- memory abilities and limitations, e.g. capacity and duration of stored information, in respect of short- and long-term memory.

The first two examples above clearly place *hard constraints* on the design of the interface, e.g. the size of displayed text, the number of displayed brightness levels, whilst the third example relates more closely to the mental processing abilities of the user, which in general leads to *soft constraints* or guidelines for design. In the following, we will concentrate on these soft factors, since it is in this area that least is known or understood and the problems which arise appear more difficult to solve. These factors also make a major contribution to the quality of the interface design.

The human abilities and limitations to be considered in this area can be gathered under the general heading of *human cognitive skills*. These cover human abilities in the *interpretation*, *processing* and *storage* of information and the *translation* of this information into some form of action, and the relationship which exists between the *knowledge* of the user and these abilities, their development, etc. The *factors* on which human performance depends include

- inherent human cognitive *skills*;
- the *activity* which demands application of cognitive skills;
- the *context* in which the required activity takes place.

The *criteria* which can be used to measure performance include

- *accuracy* of interpretation, processing, storage and translation;
- *speed* of interpretation, processing, retrieval and translation;
- *skill development*, in terms of improving accuracy and speed.

Considering first the factors involved, the cognitive *skills* required by the human user can be classified into

- perceptual skills—ability to decode information and discriminate between sorts of information;
- intellectual skills—ability to reason about and make decisions based on all available information;
- responsive skills—ability to select and activate the correct response to the information received.

All these skills are highly dependent on the availability of and access to stored knowledge, and therefore on the functional capability memory. Also they are highly complementary, i.e. perception may well involve reasoning and decision-making abilities. It is important to note that human cognitive skills vary not only between users of differing levels of experience, training, etc. but even within the individual user; they can be degraded by illness, fatigue, lack of motivation, etc. As we shall see, the guidelines for good interface design must take these apparently obvious, but often overlooked, facts into consideration. In terms of *activity*, human performance, given a particular level of cognitive skills, depends on

- the *selection* of the activity required in relation to skill (e.g. requiring a complex, multistage activity from an inexperienced user) and to skill development;
- the *combination* of activities demanded, e.g. the extent to which simultaneous application of skills is required or the effect of sequencing of activities on memory demands.

The selection and combination of activities demanded of the user is constrained ultimately by the anticipated upper and lower bounds on user skill level. It is unwise to select activities to match the 'average' user, but preferable to consider a range of user skills and to match the selection to this range, in general allowing the user more than one activity, each demanding a different skill level, to achieve a specific objective. This has the additional advantage of encouraging skill development, by presenting the user with the option of using more efficient activities which require greater skill levels, e.g. the ability to combine statements in an interface language into one composite statement. It should also be noted that under certain conditions, e.g. fatigue, it may not be possible for the user to carry out more difficult activities or sequences, and the opportunity to revert to an easier, though perhaps lengthier, method of interaction may be a valuable property of the interface.

Finally the *context* of the interactive activity can be an important factor in human performance. By this we mean not only the physical context or environment, e.g. lighting, temperature, background noise, but also the psychological context. This includes such factors as incentives and rewards, stress created by personal or organizational pressures, motivation, etc. Attention to these factors, in particular with regard to new or inexperienced users, can have a significant effect on human performance in the period of introduction of a new system.

It is clear that all the factors described above can, if not properly considered in the design of a man–machine interface lead to poor performance, resulting in loss of accuracy, slow speed of use, or lack of acceptance and skill development. Perhaps the most important consequence of poor interface design is an inability to use the system without making significant and repeated errors. Lack of speed and acceptance may be amenable to training and are often emphasized by lack of experience. In some cases of poor design, however, even the most experienced user is prone to making substantial errors on a continuing basis and often little less than a complete redesign of the interface will correct the problem. For this reason we will focus on those factors which, if not properly considered, can lead to *human error* in man–machine interaction.

13.2.2 The occurrence of human error

Errors can result in any stage of the human cognitive process, as described below.

- *Perceptive stage.* Errors occur as a result of difficulty in discrimination between information being received, by absence of essential information, or by misleading or ambiguous information,
- *Intellectual stage.* Faulty reasoning or decision-making can result from forming incorrect relationships between the information and stored knowledge in the user's memory. This may be the result of the interface

making excessive demands on memory skills or of poor design leading to otherwise reasonable decisions, either consciously or subconsciously arrived at, being invalid,
- *Response stage.* In this case the error is the result of a correct decision being translated into a faulty action or response. This can again be due to an excessive demand on memory skills or to insufficient, incorrect or misleading information, either provided by the system or stored in the user's knowledge of the system.

These general types of error can be refined to provide us with examples of very specific kinds of error which are often experienced by users of man–machine interfaces. Norman (1983) identifies a number of such errors and translates the diagnosis of their causes into design guidelines. In his classification, the various types of errors (and their relation to the cognitive processing stages described above) are broadly as follows.

- *Mode errors.* The *mode* of the system is the current state of the system and mode errors generally result from a design in which the same action results in a different effect, depending on the mode the system is in. Thus in this case poor design results in the user being unable to discriminate between modes of the system from the information available and hence the requirement is for more information identifying the mode. An alternative is not to have modes or to make actions distinct in each mode but this can result in the need to separately 'label' every action possible, resulting in, for example, a large number of special keys on a keyboard or a large set of language keywords (command names) for the user to remember. This strategy can then lead to a second class of error, the description error.
- *Description errors.* Where the number of action 'labels' is very large there is often a tendency to arrange them in similar patterns or create 'overlapping' labels, i.e. where the labels of two different actions are very similar in their descriptions. The error results from the user forming an incomplete specification of the required action and selecting the wrong label, but one which is very similar to the correct one. The problem is therefore either a perceptual one, e.g. where the labels are displayed and similar ones are not properly discriminated, or an intellectual one, where an incorrect relationship is formed between the intended action and the user's stored knowledge of the labels and their actions.
- *Derivation errors.* A common approach in any learning process is to use one's existing knowledge in new situations by forming an analogy with similar situations in order to derive the appropriate action. Errors in this case result from *inconsistency* in the design of the interface, destroying the validity of well-reasoned analogies. Such analogies can be created either consciously or subconsciously and in either case inconsistency in the design can lead to errors. Alternatively the error can result from an incorrect model

of the system being created by the user, causing erroneous analogies to be made. These errors are far more difficult to eliminate since they depend on the mechanisms which are used in the interface to build the user's knowledge of the system and the ability of the user to reason about the system using this knowledge.

- *Capture errors.* These, like description errors, result from overlap between the labels of different actions, or in the sequence of operations to be carried out to complete a specified action. In this case, however, the error does not result from the user forming an incomplete or ambiguous specification of the required action and hence selecting the wrong label or sequence, but from an unconscious selection of the wrong label due to habit. This error occurs primarily if the system is used frequently in one particular way, e.g. by an experienced user, and then a different, unusual action is called for. A radically different label for the unusual action usually results in correct activation, but similar labels or sequences of operations often lead to the more familiar label or sequence being unconsciously selected. This is clearly a case of a design fault leading to an intellectual processing error.
- *Activation errors.* Even if the information being received is properly perceived and correctly discriminated, and accurate intellectual reasoning is carried out leading to a correct decision about the intended response, an error can still occur in activating the intended response, either by failing to do so at all or by selecting an unintended response. The latter can happen because the unintended response is very similar to the intended one, as in the case of a capture error, or because an external event, e.g. an interruption, creates a delay between forming the intention and carrying it out, or because a distraction causes the unintended action to be confused with the intended one. Failure to carry out an intended action at all can also result from similar situations, in this case causing a total memory failure.

Understanding the reasons why humans make errors when interacting with a machine, and classifying the types of errors and their causes, is only useful if we can turn such information into guidelines or rules for the design of man–machine interfaces, with the intention of minimizing the occurrence of such errors. We will extract some possible guidelines from our discussion above in the next section.

13.2.3 Guidelines for interface design

Observing and analysing the causes of human error, as discussed above, is only one way of creating a set of useful design guidelines. A close examination of the features of those interfaces which experience tells us are well designed plays an important role, as does experimentation in respect of particular features of an interface, e.g. keyboard or display layout, shapes and sizes of displayed items such as menus, cursors etc. For a further discussion of design guidelines, the reader is referred to Norman (1983). To provide an example, however, of how guidelines might be created, we will consider the observations on causes of human error, as discussed in the last section, and formulate some useful design rules.

The first rule is fundamental to a number of the possible errors, in particular those which depend substantially on the user's knowledge about the system.

- *Simplicity.* The interface should present a simple, well-structured view of the system, resulting in the creation of a user's simple mental, or conceptual, model of the system.

The user's model may be structured, in relation to the view presented by the interface, in one of a number of possible ways, e.g. a hierarchical structure, where the system is divided into functionally distinct subsystems, each of which is further divided, and so on. An alternative might be a totally 'flat' structure, as in the Smalltalk system (Goldberg (1984), Tesler (1980)).

Simplicity can assist in reducing those errors which result either from excessive memory demands or from erroneous relationships existing between the actions available in the systems and the mechanisms or sequence of operations required to activate them. In particular, a system whose interface provides a large number of paths to carry out the same set of tasks can result in the formation of a very complex user model.

Simplicity as a fundamental aim also leads to the minimization of the number of alternative, similarly specified actions or labels for such actions, thus reducing the likelihood of description and capture errors occurring. Achieving simplicity is, however, not easy, and there may well be a conflict with efficiency, in particular the desire of an expert user to introduce more efficient procedures for achieving frequently used tasks. It may also lead to the need to introduce modes into the interface design, particularly if, in the interest of simplicity, only a small number of labels or keys are used to initiate a large number of actions.

- *Visibility.* A well-designed interface should make as much information as possible concerning the current activity visible to the user.

The aim here is to reduce the number of errors caused by memory overloading, especially short-term memory, where items are not permanently stored, but retained only until the current task is completed. In particular, maintaining visibility of information relating to the formation of an intention to carry out an action until that action is complete minimizes the occurrence of activation errors. A major step forward has been made by the introduction of *windowing* techniques in graphically based interfaces. These use separate, possibly overlapping areas of the screen to display related sets of information, e.g. editor menus, text to be edited, previous versions of text, glossary of terms, etc., all of which are relevant to the current activity. In some cases the number of windows required is too large for simultaneous display, in which case simple techniques are used for deleting or retrieving windows. One such technique is the use of *icons*, small graphical representation of specific sets of information, which can be maintained on the screen at all times during the task. Selection of the icon then causes the related window to be displayed, thereby giving access to the information it contains. See Figure 13.2 for example.

Figure 13.2 Icon-driven window-based interface (Reproduced with permission of Sun Microsystems Inc.)

Visibility also implies displaying information on the current status of the system. This is particularly important if the interface design makes use of system modes to interpret interface instructions. Status can be made visible in a number of ways, such as changing the screen format or background shading or altering the shape of the cursor. The aim in this case is to minimize mode errors.

For interfaces which are not graphically based, the introduction of the *history* technique has helped to increase system visibility and, in particular, reduce activation errors. This technique allows the user to retrieve information on the most recent interaction with the system, e.g. the actions requested and system responses received, thus supplementing the user's own short-term memory when this becomes overloaded.

- *Familiarity*. The view of the system provided by the interface should, as far as possible, be familiar to the user.

Several classes of errors, e.g. description errors and derivation errors, are caused by an incorrect mental model of the system being established in the user's knowledge base. One way of attempting to avoid this, and at the same time assist the development of the model, is to relate it to another conceptual model which is already familiar to the user. For example, the user of a new management information system might well expect the access to the information, and the underlying model of the information structure, to be closely related to existing non-computer-based methods for organizing and accessing information.

Familiarity can not always be achieved, and can in fact lead to errors itself, in the case where it is desirable to change significantly the components or methods of the existing system on introduction of a computer-based system. In some cases, it may be preferable to make such changes in a totally unfamiliar way to avoid errors resulting from actions formed from habit, i.e. capture errors.

- *Consistency*. The interface should provide a consistent view of the system—this applies to the syntax and semantics of the interface language as well.

First, the model of the system created by the interface should be consistent across all parts of the system, e.g. it is generally unwise to move from, say, a hierarchical structured model in one part of the system, to a flat model in another part. Similarly, operational techniques in different parts of the system should be consistent, e.g. creation by copying and editing for both text and graphics, common retrieval mechanisms for all forms of stored information.

Second, and closely related to this, there must be consistency in the interface language. This is achieved primarily in the syntax of the language, i.e. maintaining the same word-order rules, for example argument order in command languages. However it is also important that the semantics is consistent, e.g. that the meaning of, say, a 'file' of information as a structured set of data items, is maintained throughout the system, or that the action of a command, say, 'move' is the same whether it is applied to a word in a piece of text, a line in a graphical object or an item of information in a file.

- *Adaptability*. The interface should be capable of either self-adaptation or adaptation by the user to match specific user needs and abilities.

No matter how powerful or general an interface is, users will always want to tailor it to their own requirements, or to have the system recognize new requirements and modify the interface itself to meet these, e.g. increased experience of the user. Self-adaption is a difficult problem, involving the system sensing the needs of the user and correspondingly changing the form of the interface. Since little is known about how to measure human interaction requirements and what methods can be used to systematically adapt the interface to meet such requirements, it is likely to be some time before truly self-adaptive interfaces are developed.

Currently the best approach to the problem of adaption is to allow the user to access a range of different 'built-in' interfaces suited to different skill levels, e.g. the ability to switch between a menu or a command language, or to provide facilities for customizing the interface to suit individual needs. Methods used for customizing include the ability to alter graphical displays, e.g. screen layouts and icon forms, to introduce new language statements by specifying the rules for their interpretation, or to customize the form and content of system names, responses, etc. by defining 'aliases' i.e. text substitution rules.

Lack of adaptibility in an interface causes frustration and reduced motivation in experienced users and difficulty in learning about the system, i.e. creating a mental model, for new or inexperienced users. In both cases, errors in use occur. For an experienced user, the need to continually repeat a number of simple steps, more suited to the beginner, results in lack of concentration, leading to a range of activation and capture errors, i.e. wrong actions are taken due to habit. For an inexperienced user, a rigid interface usually means that complex tasks cannot be broken down into smaller tasks, for which the user is more able to predict the outcome. This leads to derivation errors, in the case where a false analogy is employed for the complex action, or to description errors, where the wrong action is taken due to the user having an incomplete understanding of what is required.

Of course, adaptability also provides other advantages, in particular improvements in efficiency of use of the system and hence greater productivity on the part of the user. This in turn can lead to greater motivation and hence better performance in other respects.

13.2.4 The Difficulty Of Using And Applying Design Guidelines

Whilst it is important to recognize that human factors must influence interface design and lead to the kind of general design guidelines discussed above, it is not always easy to apply such guidelines in practice. In particular, they almost always take the form of general *design aims* and it is often not clear how these aims can be best achieved for a specific system and in a specific application environment. There are a number of ways in which this difficulty might be overcome, including the following.

- *Development of a design methodology*. This involves the definition of a precise set of procedures to be followed systematically by the interface designer, thus ensuring that every factor is considered and, if the correct decisions taken, the aims achieved. The development of a successful methodology requires a great deal of experience of interface design from which general design procedures can be determined.

- *Development of models of human–computer interaction.* Models are used extensively to incorporate physical human factors into interface design, i.e. a particular design proposal is tested against a model for violation of any physical constraints on human abilities, e.g. vision, strength, reach. The lack of any model of human cognitive abilities prevents a similar process from being carried out in this respect. Some partial models do exist and are exploited to a certain extent. In particular, the human memory is modelled in the form of *short-term memory*, in which items are stored on a temporary basis, e.g. for the duration of a specific task, such as editing a section of text, and *long-term memory*, used for permanent storage, e.g. of the mental model of a system and its behaviour. For short-term memory, various parameters have been established. For example, it is generally accepted that such memory has capacity for only six or seven 'units' of information at any one time, where a unit may consist of any item of information which constitutes a specific entity, e.g. a message, diagram, word. This also depends on the user's familiarity with the item as an entity and on its complexity. It has also been established that the duration of the information in short-term memory depends on the number of items stored, that the serial position of items affects their accurate recollection, and that 'rehearsal' techniques, e.g. repetition, use of rhythms and patterns, improve retention of items. Using this model, interface designers can identify situations in which short-term memory is employed and can test a proposed design against the model behaviour, e.g. to determine if the number of items to be retained is too large or the period over which accurate recollection is required is too long.
- *Use of prototypes.* These are interfaces which are built to test specific design proposals, to see if they work satisfactorily in practice. They are usually built in a form which does not possess all the features or 'substance' of the eventual system interface, as is the case for an architect's cardboard model of a building, but is sufficient for testing the proposed design. Prototyping tools, to assist designers in building prototypes quickly and efficiently, have been available for some years in the form of *compiler generators*, i.e. programs which will produce a language-processing program from a set of syntactic rules defining the language. More recently tools have been introduced which extend such programs to incorporate more knowledge of the behaviour of the system in relation to language statements and to *simulate* the interactive dialogue in a human–computer interface.

Prototyping is a time-consuming, and hence expensive, activity and therefore prototyping tools must be efficient. Greater efficiency can be gained if the prototype can be directly employed in the construction of the operational system, e.g. by automatic generation of programs from the prototype description. However, there exists the danger that this can create in the designer a reluctance to throw away unsuccessful prototypes, an attitude which considerably diminishes their value.

13.2.5 Examples of good interface design

To conclude our discussion of human factors in interface design, we will briefly describe two examples of systems in which the design has been based on many of the factors discussed above.

Smalltalk (Tesler 1980; Goldberg 1984)

The design of the Smalltalk language has played a significant role in creating a new approach to the design of a human–computer interface for interactive computing. The *object-oriented* approach to programming which the language embodies provides a conceptually simple mental model of the Smalltalk system. The system is composed of a set of *objects*, which are encapsulations of both data structures and the procedures which operate on these data structures.

The objects are organized into *classes*, and objects adopt the properties of their class, i.e. are *instances* of their class. There is also a hierarchy amongst the classes, with inheritance properties between classes in the hierarchy. Interactive programming for the user of the Smalltalk system consists of creating expressions which constitute *messages* to the objects in the system, both system-defined objects, e.g. primitive objects such as integers, operators, etc. and user-defined objects, or create new classes or generate a new instance of an existing class. In principle this provides a conceptually simple mental model of the system for the user, although since all objects, both system and user defined, are available to the user, the number of objects in the system can be very large and create a complexity problem for the inexperienced user. This is alleviated by providing a number of facilities in the interface for making the system highly visible to the user, e.g. the *browse* facility, which allows the user to examine the objects in the system without prior knowledge of its exact structure. This facility makes extensive use of and depends heavily on windowing techniques.

In addition to being conceptually simple, consistently structured and highly visible, the system is easily extendable by the user. For example, new classes and objects can be created simply using existing classes and the inheritance mechanism or by the process of copying and editing existing objects. Another important feature is that the system minimizes the use of modes by making access to all classes and objects accessible to the user at a single level of interaction, thus reducing the occurrence of mode-related errors.

Xerox 'Star' (Smith et al. *1982)*

The Smalltalk language and user interface, itself derived from earlier concepts embodied in Simula, has strongly influenced the design of a number of systems, including the Xerox 'Star' Office Information System. This system is aimed specifically at the office environment and was one of the first systems to be designed with the user interface as a primary concern. The functions of the Star system include document creation, data processing, electronic filing, mailing and printing, and the system is based on an architecture which includes a processor and disk storage which are local to the user, a high-resolution *bit-mapped* display screen to facilitate the use of windows, icons and screen-based document creation, and a *mouse* device for fast user interaction, by pointing to items on the screen rather than selecting them via keyboard entries. The design principles underlying the Star user interface include all those described in the previous sections of this chapter, in particular the use of a familiar user's conceptual model, consistency, simplicity, modeless interaction and user tailorability. The design aim of a familiar user's model led to the creation of the 'physical office metaphor', in which familiar physical objects in the office, e.g. paper, folders, files, filing cabinets, etc., are represented in the system by icons displayed on the screen and selected by pointing with the mouse. Thus the system objects are made 'concrete' and visible, as are the actions on these objects, e.g. a page of a document is included in a folder by the physical movement of the corresponding icon to the icon representing the folder.

Star's universal commands provide a small set of fundamental commands, e.g. move, copy, delete, undo, etc., which each perform in the same way on any type of object. This provides both simplicity and consistency.

Several other systems have appeared subsequently to Star, based on the same user interface design concepts, including the Lisa and MacIntosh systems from Apple. More recently, similar icon/window based interfaces have appeared as additions to existing widely used systems such as the IBM PC, indicating an apparent user satisfaction with this form of human–computer interface.

13.3 MACHINE 'FACTORS' IN INTERFACE DESIGN

13.3.1 Machine understanding

As discussed in the early section of this chapter, in order that an effective dialogue takes place between the human user and the computer system, there must be a degree of commonality between their respective knowledge bases. A fundamental requirement is a common knowledge of the language used in the communication, in particular the symbols of the language and the rules which determine whether a given sequence of symbols is a valid or acceptable statement in the language. The ability to go beyond simply a statement's validity, i.e. to give it *meaning*, depends on further knowledge on the part of the human or the computer. This is so-called *domain* and *situation* knowledge. The concepts and factors involved in the machine-based language processing component of a human–computer interface can largely be separated, therefore, into two parts. The first is concerned with the syntactic analysis of the language statement, and requires shared knowledge of the symbols and rules of the languages with the human user.

The second is concerned with the semantic analysis of a valid statement, which depends on shared knowledge of the system and its components, the state of the interaction, and other aspects of the domain or situation in which the statement is expressed, and the actions or events which might be activated by the analysis of the statement.

In practice, the distinction between syntactic and semantic analysis is not so clear, since, in particular, the syntactic analysis phase of machine understanding can be aided by the availability of semantic knowledge. Similarly knowledge which is derived during syntactic analysis must be made available to the processes involved in the semantic analysis.

13.3.2 Syntactic analysis

The fundamental process involved in the syntactic analysis of most human–computer interface languages is one of *pattern matching*. This is true whether the language simply involves selection from a menu, is a formal or 'natural' language based on a set of rules for constructing statements, or is a graphically based language involving, for example, selection of objects represented by icons on a screen. The input to the process in each case is a sequence of symbols or words of the language. These may themselves have been derived, again by pattern matching, from a raw sequence of primitive characters or signals received at the machine input. The process of pattern matching requires

- *a set of rules*—these define valid patterns of symbols;
- *a dictionary*—the entries in this are the symbols and the *classes* into which the symbols fall;
- *an algorithm*—this defines the sequence of operations to be used in carrying out the matching process.

The simplest form of pattern matching is *template matching*. The rules in this case are expressed by a set of valid patterns and the algorithm simply selects each pattern in turn and attempts to match the input sequence to the pattern. The patterns themselves can be fully defined as a sequence of independent symbols, e.g. symbols referencing entries in a menu, or may let some elements of the pattern be arbitrary, i.e. free to be matched by any symbol or any symbol in a specified class, e.g. in the statement

'copy ⟨filename⟩ ⟨filename⟩'

The last two elements in this pattern can be matched to any symbol in the class ⟨filename⟩. The algorithm to carry out this process must have access to a dictionary from which the class of any symbol can be established.

In some cases, an abitrary element of a pattern might be identified by a variable name. The symbol occurring at the appropriate position is then *bound* by the matching algorithm to the variable. Further occurrences of the same variable in the pattern will then be required to match the same symbol, e.g.

'move x to y and delete x'

will match to

'move invoice to folder and delete invoice'

but not to

'move invoice to folder and delete receipt'

The result of a pattern-matching algorithm is thus simply success or failure in matching the input sequence to each of the patterns or templates and, in some cases, a binding of variables to individual symbols in the input sequence. The latter may be used in the subsequent analysis of a continuing interactive dialogue or to specify the actions which result from the statement. For example, in the ELIZA system (Weizenbaum 1966), bindings are used to create responses to user statements, e.g.

User: 'My dog is sick'
Pattern: 'My x is y'
Binding: x = dog y = sick
Response pattern: 'How long has your x been y?'
Actual response: 'How long has your dog been sick?'

Template-matching techniques are satisfactory in the case when the number of valid patterns in the language is small, which is the case in many menu-based or simple command-language-based interfaces. However, where the language approaches the complexity of any of the common programming languages, such as Pascal, LISP, etc., or takes the form of a 'natural' language, e.g. English, the number of possible patterns becomes large or even infinite. In this case, it is necessary to define the valid patterns of the language by a set of rules. From these rules all possible valid patterns of statements can be derived or produced. Hence they are often referred to as *production rules*. In order to provide for languages of different relative complexity, several formal methods of defining production rules are available.

13.3.3 Regular languages

In the definition of the simplest language, we use the formalism of *regular expressions*. To define this, consider the set A of symbols which constitute all the valid symbols in a language. We wish to define all valid sequences of symbols, i.e. statements, which constitute the language. To do this we will need to be able to denote

- *alternatives*—e.g. either symbol a or symbol b occurring at a given element in the sequence—denoted by $a + b$;
- *repetition*—e.g. the symbol a occurring an arbitrary number of times (including zero) at a given element in the sequence—denoted by a^*;
- *concatenation*—e.g. symbol a followed by symbol b in the sequence—denoted by ab.

Using this notation, we can write down expressions, composed of symbols and the operators +, * defined above, which defines a set of sequences which can be derived from the expression. For example, let a, b be two symbols. The following are examples of regular expressions and the corresponding set (possibly infinite) of sequences which they define:

Expression	*Language*
a	a
a^*	$a, aa, aaa, \ldots$
$a + b$	a, b
$(a + b)^*$	$a, b, ab, aab, ba, \ldots$ i.e. all possible sequences of *a*s and *b*s
$(a + ab)^*$	a, ab, aab, aba, ... i.e. all sequences of *a*s and *b*s which begin with *a* and do not have two consecutive *b*s.

As with template matching, we can extend the use of regular expressions as rules for defining languages by allowing the expressions to include arbitrary symbols, symbol classes and variable identifiers.

The limitation of regular expressions is clear if one tries to define an expression from which only statements of the form $a^n b^n$, i.e. a sequence of n symbols a, followed by an equal number of symbols b, can be derived.

In any case where the second half of a statement must match in size or form to the first half, this rule cannot be stated by means of a regular expression, e.g. in the English language statement 'John, Tom and George are, respectively, the butcher, the baker and the candlestick-maker.'

13.3.4 Context-free languages

In order to extend the range of languages we can define beyond regular languages, we need to introduce the concept of a *phrase*, i.e. a defined *subsequence* of symbols which forms part of a language statement. We can now define two classes of elements to be used in the rules for defining a language:

- *terminal symbols*—these can be either symbols or symbol classes;
- *non-terminal symbols*—phrases.

The language is defined by a set of *production rules*, each of which take the form

Non-terminal symbol → sequence of terminal and non-terminal symbols

We also define a *distinguished* non-terminal symbol, denoted by S, which represents the sequence of symbols which forms a language statement, i.e. S = statement.

As an example, consider a language in which we can define three phrases:

- *action phrase* (AP);
- *object phrase* (OP);
- *unqualified object phrase* (UP)

and four symbol classes:

- *qualifier*;
- *parameter*;
- *action*;
- *object*.

The production rules defining valid statements S in this language might take the form:

1. $S \rightarrow OP\ AP$
2. $OP \rightarrow$ qualifier UP
3. $OP \rightarrow UP$
4. $UP \rightarrow$ parameter UP
5. $UP \rightarrow$ object
6. $AP \rightarrow$ action
7. $AP \rightarrow$ action OP

Rule 1 states that a statement is produced by the concatenation of an object phrase and an action phrase. Rules 2 and 3 provide two alternative forms of object phrase. Rules 4 and 5 denote alternatives for unqualified object phrase. Note that rule 4 is recursive, i.e. UP appears on both sides of the rule. Thus, together with rule 5, this implies that a valid UP can be composed of a sequence of zero or more symbols in the class *parameter*, followed by a symbol of class *object*. Thus recursive definitions in production rules provide the same property of repetition as the * operator in regular expressions. Finally, rules 6 and 7 provide alternative forms for action phrase.

Assume that the following entries existed in a dictionary:

Symbol	*Class*
file, folder	object
closed	qualifier
red, blue	parameter
move-to	action

A valid language statement might then be:

'closed red file move-to blue folder'

To see this, we can represent the statement in the form of its phrase structure tree as shown in Figure 13.3. Note that the tree uses just one of the production rules from the given set to create each set of branches from a given node, the node being labelled by the left-hand side, non-terminal symbol of the rule and the derived nodes by the symbols of the right-hand side of the rule, which may

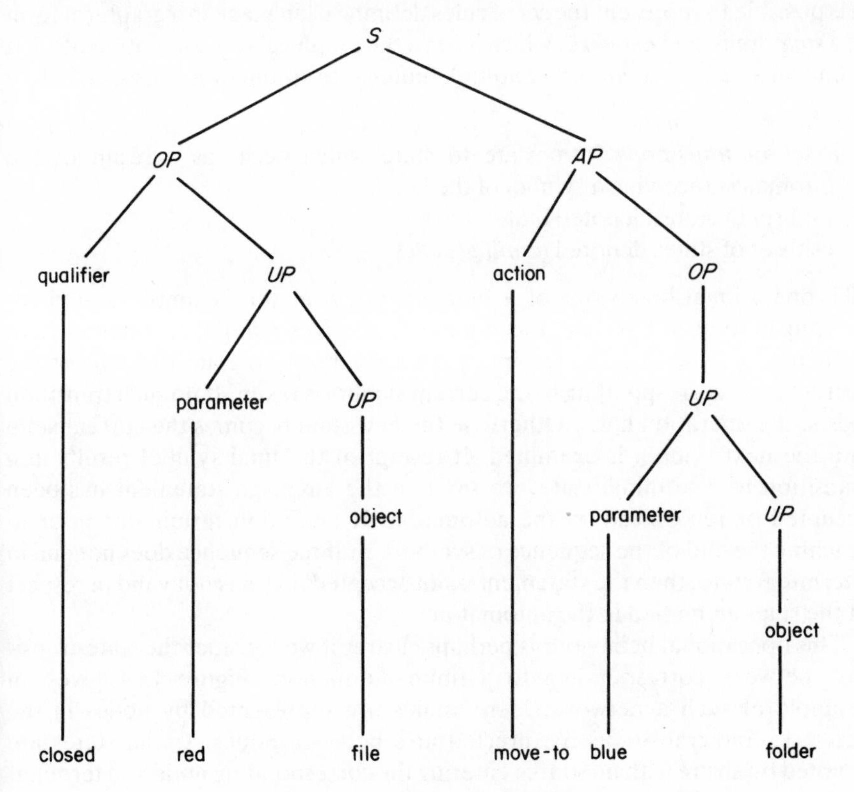

Figure 13.3 Phrase structure tree

be terminal or non-terminal. Nodes labelled by terminal symbols cannot be expanded, since only non-terminal symbols are allowed on the left-hand side of a rule.

Given a language statement, the process of deriving its phrase structure tree, by a specific application of the production rules, is known as *parsing*, and an algorithm to carry out this is called a *parsing algorithm*. The theory, design and development of parsing algorithms have been the subject of a large number of books, e.g. Aho and Ullmann (1972, 1973) and will not be considered here.

To conclude this section, it is worth noting that languages defined by regular expressions can also be defined by production rules. In this case, the rules must have one of two special forms:

Non-terminal symbol → terminal symbol
or Non-terminal symbol → terminal symbol followed by a single non-terminal symbol

13.3.5 Representation as a state-transition network

It is possible to represent the set of rules defining a language in a graphical form as a *state-transition network*, which is itself the graphical representation of what is known as a *finite-state automaton*. A finite-state automaton consists of

- a finite set of *states*;
- a set of *transitions* from state to state which occur as a result of the automaton receiving a symbol of the language;
- a subset of states denoted *initial states*;
- a subset of states denoted *terminal states*.

The operational behaviour of a finite-state automaton is simply described. Starting in some initial state, the automaton receives a language statement as a sequence of symbols. On receipt of each symbol, the transition out of the current state corresponding to the current symbol is taken. If no such transition exists, the operation halts. Otherwise the new state becomes the current state and the next symbol is examined. If receipt of the final symbol results in a transition to a terminal state, we say that the language statement has been accepted or recognized by the automaton. If operation terminates prior to reaching the end of the sequence of symbols, or if the sequence does not end in a terminal state, then the statement is not accepted, i.e. it is not valid in respect of the rules embodied in the automaton.

This operational behaviour is perhaps clearer if we consider the state-transition network corresponding to a finite automaton. Figure 13.4 gives an example of such a network. Here, states are represented by nodes in the network, and transitions by directed arcs between nodes. Initial states are denoted by an arc with no source entering the corresponding node and terminal states by a double circle at the node.

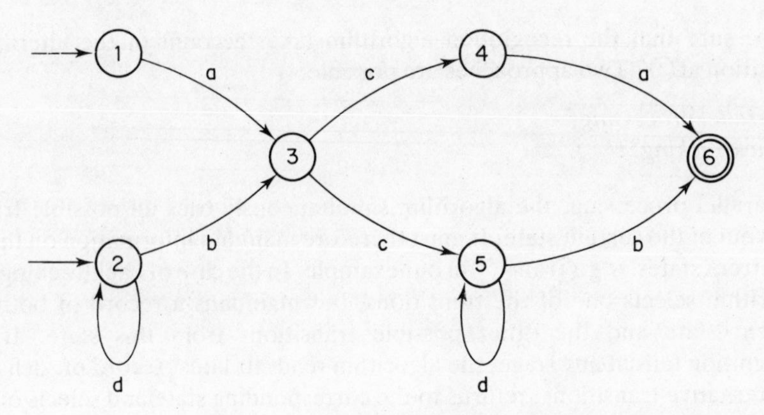

Figure 13.4 State-transition network

Each transition arc is labelled by either of the following:

- *a symbol of the language*;
- *a symbol class*.

A transition occurs from the current state if the current symbol is either identical to the label or is in the symbol class identified by the label. Note that there may be more than one transition which is possible from a current state for a given symbol. This could occur if two transitions from the state are labelled with the same symbol or symbol class (e.g. Figure 13.4), or if the current symbol can be regarded as being in more than one class, e.g. 'copy' can in English be either a noun or a verb. In such a situation the automaton and its behaviour is said to be *non-deterministic*. In such a case, an algorithm which uses the automaton to recognize a statement must incorporate a procedure to allow for each of the possible transitions to be followed, if necessary, in the recognition process.

Example: In the transition network of Figure 13.4, the arcs are labelled by the symbols from the set $\{a, b, c, d\}$. The reader should confirm that the following sequences of symbols are amongst those recognized by the automaton: *aca*, *acddb*, *dddbca*, *dbcb*. Consider now the path generated by the last sequence, *dbcb*:

→ ② —*d*→ ② —*b*→ ③ —*c*→ ⑤ —*b*→ ⑥

Clearly at state ③ it is not possible to know whether to select either the transition ③ —*c*→ ④ or ③ —*d*→ ⑤ as the next valid transition. Selecting the former will result in a failure to recognize the sequence since the operation will halt as the symbol *b* does not match any transition out of state ④. How can we be sure that the recognition algorithm takes account of the alternative transition at ③? Two approaches are possible:

- *parallel processing*;
- *backtracking*.

In parallel processing, the algorithm simultaneously tries all possible transitions out of the current state. It must therefore maintain information on the set of current states, e.g. ④ and ⑤ in our example. In the case of backtracking, the algorithm selects one of the transitions, but maintains a record of both the current state and the other possible transitions from this state. If the recognition fails at any stage, the algorithm reads its latest record of such a set of alternative transitions, returns to the corresponding state and selects one of the alternatives. The 'last in, first out' nature of creation and access to such records clearly suggests the use of a *stack* data structure for their storage. Thus we would have in our simple example:

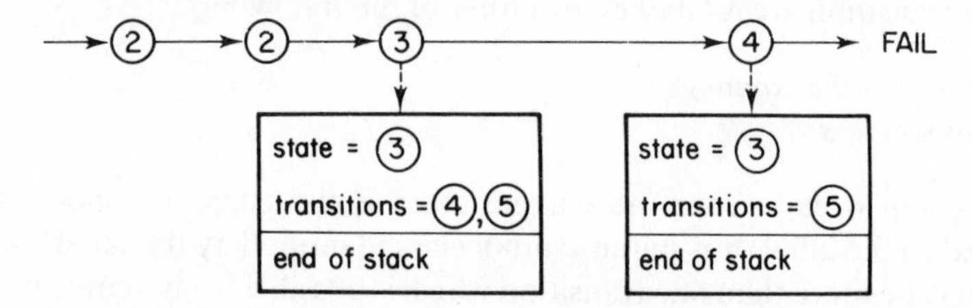

Read top of stack; backtrack to state ③ and take recorded alternative transition to ⑤:

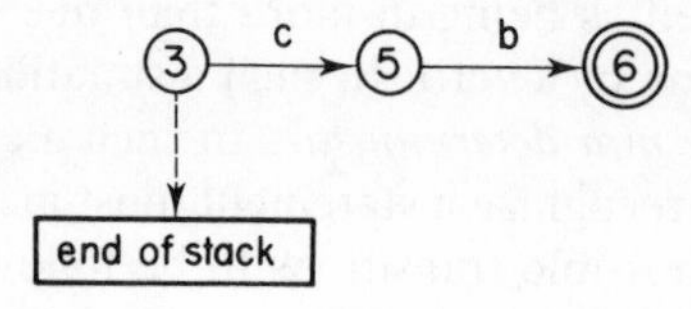

Note that a transition is deleted from the record as soon as it is taken and that a record is removed from the stack if all the alternative transitions have been deleted from that record.

The finite automaton, and its state-transition network representation, are in *one-to-one correspondence* with the class of regular languages, i.e. for any language whose rules are defined by a regular expression, we can derive a finite automaton such that the language it recognizes is identical, and vice versa.

13.3.6 Augmented transition networks

Our purpose in introducing the state-transition network representation has been twofold: first, it provides a nice basis for understanding how a regular language recognition algorithm operates, especially in the non-deterministic case; second, it allows us to consider how *semantic* knowledge might be introduced into the language understanding process. Before proceeding to the second of these objectives, we will extend the network representation to our second language class, i.e. context-free languages.

The extension is straightforward. Corresponding to our earlier development, we again introduce the notion of a phrase, i.e. a subsequence of symbols, and allow a transition in the network to be labelled not only, as before, by a symbol or a symbol class, but also by a phrase. For every such 'phrase-labelled' transition arc in the network, we then introduce an *additional* network which defines the subsequence of symbols corresponding to that phrase. Finally, we also introduce a transition labelled *jump*, which can be taken without any symbol having to be received by the network. To make these notions clearer, consider the context-free language used as an example earlier and its set of production rules. Figure 13.5 shows a corresponding pair of transition networks, each of which is headed by the phrase it represents.

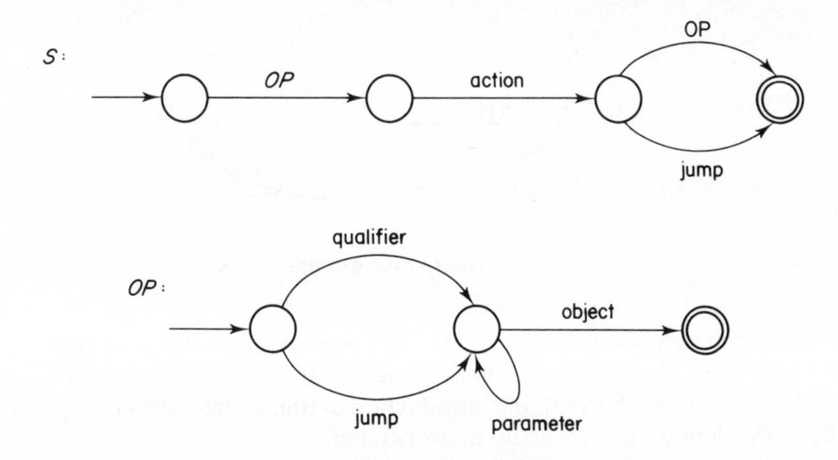

Figure 13.5 Augmented transition network

The operational behaviour of a recognition algorithm based on this pair of networks can then be described as follows. Starting in the initial state of network *S*, the first transition is labelled *OP*. To allow this transition to be taken, the network *OP* must itself be traversed from initial state to terminal state, i.e. it must recognize a subsequence of symbols in the statement starting at the current symbol. Arrival at the terminal state in *OP* enables the transition to the next state in *S*. The operation then proceeds in the same way, successful recognition corresponding to the situation where the terminal state in *S* is reached on receipt of the final symbol in the statement.

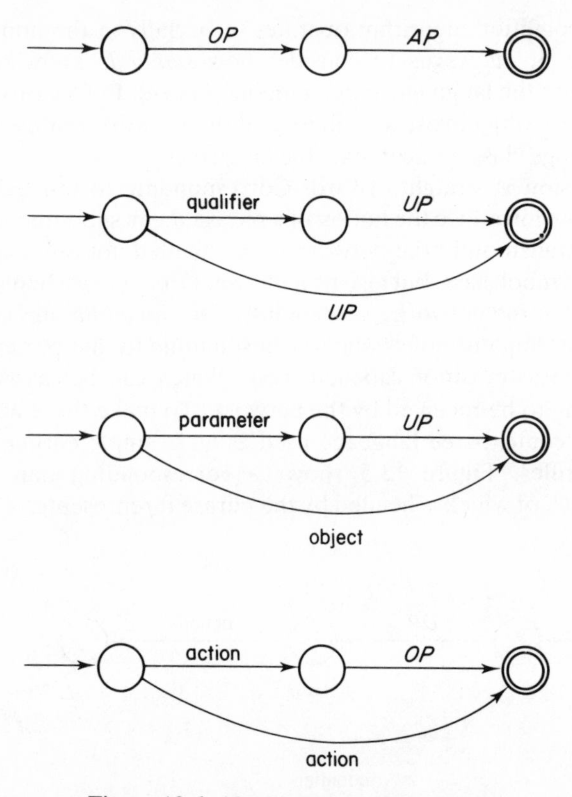

Figure 13.6 Alternative example ATN

Two points are worth noting. First, an equivalent transition network for a given set of production rules is not unique. Figure 13.6 shows another set for the example above. Second, the introduction of transitions labelled by phrases allows the definition of *recursive* networks, e.g.

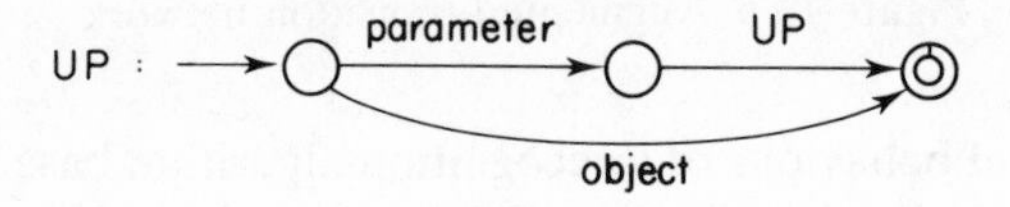

or *mutually recursive* sets of networks, e.g.

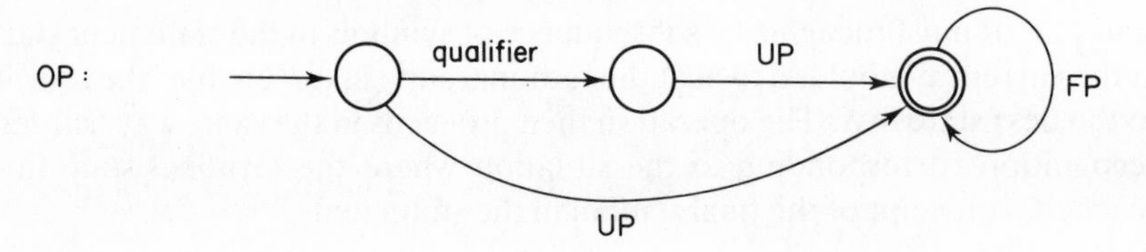

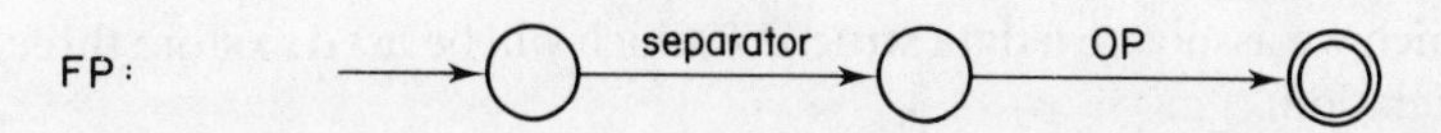

Both these constructions provide for *repetition* of symbols, symbol classes or phrases in the statement.

In view of this property, the form of representation of a context-free language is known as a *recursive transition network* (RTN).

As we said at the start of this section, the representation of language rules in the form of a state-transition graph also allows us to consider how semantic knowledge might be introduced into the language-recognition process. To do this we will extend the recursive transition-network representation of a context-free language recognizer, by associating with it a *data structure* which can be accessed by the recognition algorithm, or in this case the parsing algorithm. The operational behaviour of the algorithm is now enhanced by the following properties:

- before a transition arc is taken, the information in the associated data structure may have to satisfy some form of *condition*;
- on taking a transition in the network, some *action* may be performed on the information in the data structure.

Conditions therefore carry out the task of restricting the situation in which a transition is taken. *Actions* have the effect of creating additional knowledge from the symbols in the language statement which can be used in either the syntactic or the semantic analysis of the statement. A recursive transition network together with an associated data structure is known as an *augmented transition network* (ATN).

To study the use of an ATN for language processing, we will consider the example of recognizing and understanding a simple *move* statement in a command language, i.e. a command to move an object, e.g. a document, drawing, file, folder, from one part of the system to another.

This might have the simple form:

$$S \rightarrow \text{move}\ \langle \text{name1} \rangle \langle \text{name2} \rangle \langle \text{qualifier} \rangle$$

Here we use the angled brackets to denote symbol classes as distinct from the symbol *move*. For this command to be correctly processed we require that the two object names are compatible, e.g. we can move a document to a folder but not vice versa. The transition network might simply be

S:
move
<name 1>
<name 2>
<qualifier>
jump

with which we associate a data structure which will be used to store three items of information:

- the type of object referred to by the symbol matched to ⟨name1⟩
- a set of relationships between objects which define their compatibility
- a logical variable to denote whether or not the object requires a qualifier.

We also associate with the transition arcs in the network the following conditions and actions:

- *⟨name1⟩ arc—action:* store type of object in data structure
  —action: set logical variable = TRUE if type of object requires qualifier, otherwise set = FALSE
- *⟨name2⟩ arc—condition:* type of object must 'agree with that stored in the data structure according to the stored set of relationships'
- *jump arc —condition:* logical variable in data structure must be FALSE.

It is easy to see how the resulting ATN behaves in processing the command statement. The important concept which we have introduced is that of using knowledge of the domain in which the statement is made, i.e. knowledge of the relationship between objects in the system, to aid in recognition of the statement.

The ATN formalism has been used extensively in the development of parsing algorithms for so-called 'natural languages', i.e. languages which resemble ordinary, everyday language, as used, for example, in database query interfaces. In this case the data structure is used to store *features* of the symbols contained in a statement, such as *number* (i.e. singular or plural), *tense*, *transitivity*, and their *roles*, such as *subject*, *object*, *main verb*, etc. For further reading on the use of ATNs in natural-language parsing, the reader is referred to Woods (1970), Bates (1978) and Winograd (1983).

The ATN formalism has also found a valuable use as a tool for *specifying* the behaviour of human–computer interface, as we shall see in the next and final section of this chapter.

13.3.7 Specification of human–computer interfaces

We will end this chapter by, in one sense, returning to the beginning, that is, our major theme of the concepts and techniques for the development of human–computer interfaces. The first and perhaps the most important and difficult phase in this development is that of *requirements analysis*. In this phase, the needs of the user must be identified and a precise and complete statement made of these requirements. This statement is called a *specification* of the interface and forms the basis of both an agreement between the developer and the user that these are indeed the latter's requirements, and a 'blueprint' for the designer stating how the interface must behave if it is to meet the user's needs. The interface specification must therefore use a language which is both precise and understandable, and the ATN formalism has recently found favour as a tool for writing such a specification.

The most comprehensive approach appears to be that taken by Jacob (1983a, b). In this approach, the interface is specified by a set of ATNs, and within each ATN an arc can be labelled with

- the name of an input symbol, denoted by the prefix *i*-, e.g. *iQUIT*;
- the name of an output symbol, denoted by the prefix *o*-, e.g. *oLOGIN*;
- a non-terminal symbol, i.e. the name of another network;
- a condition;
- an action.

Figure 13.7 shows the first of a set of ATNs to specify a simple mail system.

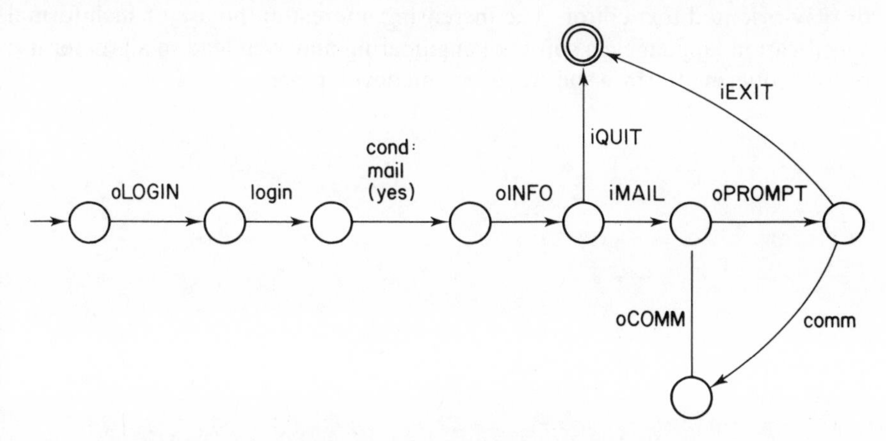

Figure 13.7 Use of an ATN for interface specification

Here the labels such as *iQUIT*, *oLOGIN*, etc. represent input and output of either symbols or specified sequences of symbols, e.g. *oLOGIN* specifies the output of a template for user entry of the logging-in information, *oPROMPT* specifies a prompt for a command name. The labels such as *mail*, *comm*, etc. are non-terminal symbols denoting another ATN which specifies the sequence to be performed at this stage of the interaction. The label *cond:* specifies a condition to be satisfied for this transition to occur. For a more detailed description of this approach to interface specification, the reader is again referred to Jacob (1983a, b). It is worth noting however, two important aspects of the approach.

- *Prototyping.* The approach lends itself to the production of prototypes by making the ATN descriptions *executable*. This can provide a significant aid in the requirements-analysis phase of development, by allowing the user to see how the interface will behave rather than infer the behaviour from the documentation.
- *Semantic specification.* The ATN formalism provides primarily a means of specifying an interface at the syntactic level, i.e. the sequence of symbols and statements occurring in a valid dialogue. However, by augmenting the network with statements regarding conditions and actions, it is possible to introduce formal specifications at the semantic level. For example, we can use the *denotational approach to program specification* to precisely define the operations referred to in the ATNs as functions on the state of the interface.

In relation to the final point made above, it is also worth noting, within the context of the use of formal techniques for interface specification, the work by Sufrin (1982) on use of the specification language Z for a simple, display-oriented text editor. The increasing interest in the use of such formal specification languages in software engineering may well lead to a greater use of such tools in interface specification and development.

Fundamentals of Information Technology
Edited by G. G. Wilkinson and A. R. Winterflood

Chapter 14

Images, Pattern Recognition and Vision

14.1 THE NEED FOR COMPUTER-IMAGE ANALYSIS

One of the most important growth areas in current man–machine interface research is the field of visual-image analysis. This has come about primarily through the considerable diversity of applications in science, engineering, medicine, industry and commerce in which visual information plays an important role and for which machine processing of such information could be of major benefit. Also it is now apparent that the information-technology revolution is creating a need for totally 'user-friendly' computers capable of accepting spoken, handwritten, and photographic input rather than alphanumeric characters typed on a VDU or read from a magnetic tape or disk. It is a fundamental requirement of user-friendly fifth-generation machines that they should be capable of *capturing*, *storing*, *manipulating* and *understanding* visual images—the latter being an extremely difficult computational problem.

Although it is clear that visual information processing is now receiving a lot of attention in the various national and international IT programmes, it is not true to say that this activity is strictly a recent phenomenon. Indeed computers have been used quite widely for handling visual images for over two decades. To illustrate the breadth of uses of computerized visual information processing we list some typical applications below. This list is by no means exhaustive:

- medical image analysis (X-rays; computerized tomography 'body scanners'; ultrasound; nuclear magnetic resonance imaging; chromosome analysis);
- industrial vision (robot vision; machine-tool guidance; quality control and visual inspection of products);
- satellite image processing (Earth resources remote sensing; weather forecasting; astronomical imaging; planetary atmosphere research);
- document processing (analysis of facsimile images, plans and engineering drawings; mail sorting by postcode analysis);
- security and criminology (signature authorization; visual recognition of faces; car-registration number identification; fingerprint matching);
- television and entertainment (TV image processing and special effects);
- weapons, aviation and naval systems (missile terminal guidance; radar-image processing; remote underwater inspection);

- subnuclear particle physics (automatic analysis of bubble-chamber photographs);
- life-science image analysis (electron microscopy; study of biological macromolecules).

Many additional applications are listed in a major UK review study carried out by Kittler (1982).

Even though computerized image analysis has many applications, it is still true to say that the potential of machine-image analysis has not yet been fully exploited.

A good example of this is medical radiology. Every day hundreds of thousands of radiographs are recorded in hospitals all over the world. Although the precise number is difficult to calculate, it has recently been estimated that in the USA alone 650 000 000 radiographs are recorded every year. These radiographs are of course essential for diagnosing serious illness and for assessing the extent of bodily injury. The majority of them, however, are recorded and stored purely in analogue form, that is as black and white photographic negatives or prints, and are not involved in any kind of computer processing. They are stored in filing cabinets and interpreted by hard-pressed radiologists. In this analogue form the images are wasteful of storage space, can be difficult to retrieve quickly from an archive and waste time—radiologists may have to inspect every one individually. Yet this need not be the case. *Digital radiography* is now a rapidly developing technology and X-ray machines are available which record and store images in digital form. They can be rapidly retrieved from a computer database and displayed on TV monitors. For some purposes they could even be analysed and interpreted automatically. For example, when mass screening programmes are carried out it would be possible for a computer to check that each X-ray picture matches a perfect image taken from a normal healthy individual. If a good match is not found, the X-ray must obviously be drawn to the attention of the expert radiologist who can give it a more detailed inspection. This would make more efficient use of the radiologist's time, allowing him to concentrate on those cases which really need his careful attention. Generally however, digital radiography is still not very widely used. The lack of digital radiography systems is partly an economic and partly a human problem. Image-processing computers are expensive, radiologists may be fearful of losing their jobs, and patients may be reluctant to trust machine diagnoses. There may also be insuperable legal problems: for example, who would be responsible if a machine failed to recognize indications of serious illness and a patient died? Such problems plague many areas in which information technology is being applied.

14.2 COMPUTER-IMAGE CAPTURE

So far we have not explicitly established what is meant by a digital image or how such an image can be captured and stored in a computer.

200	187	201	176	130	90
198	196	203	168	•	•
170	182	160	153	•	•
156	•	•	•	•	•
•	•	•	•	•	•

Figure 14.1 A typical digital image (array values indicate light intensity)

An image is essentially a flat representation of a visual scene. The contents of the scene, whether hand-written postcode, satellite view of Earth, X-ray picture, etc., are irrelevant to our purposes at this stage. The most important and distinguishing feature of an image is that it represents the spatial variation in light intensity or brightness in that scene. In analogue images this spatial intensity variation is encoded in the density of exposed silver halide grains on photographic film. In *digital* images it is represented by *arrays* of numbers indicating the brightness (see Figure 14.1). These digital values (usually integers) can be stored in computer memory in binary form. As with programs and other data they would normally reside in main memory during processing and in secondary memory (on tapes, disks, etc.) at all other times. They can only be turned into a real 'scene' for human inspection by using a *raster* display device—that is, one which displays lines of points with varying intensity like a television monitor. This is indeed the way in which computer images are normally shown to the user.

Digital images are 'captured' from scenes in a variety of different ways, depending on the nature of the application. For example, they may come from satellite radiometers, TV cameras, ultrasonic detectors, electron microscopes, etc. We do not need to concern ourselves with the 'front-end' of the camera or imaging system. We can regard it as a scanning sensor generating a continuous electrical voltage signal which is related to the brightness in the scene (see Figure 14.2).

However, a continuous electrical signal from a sensor is an *analogue*

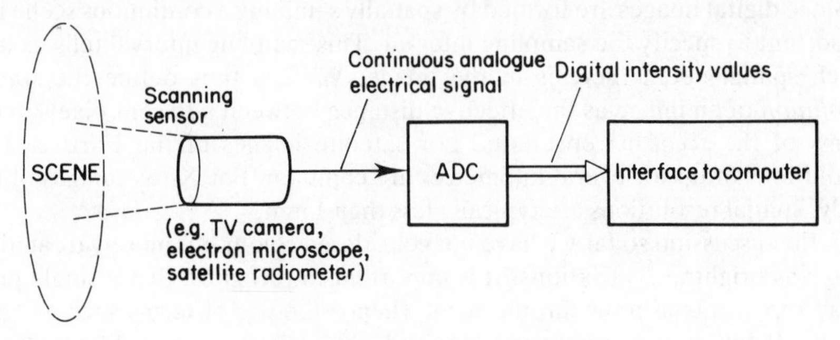

Figure 14.2 Digital image capture

representation of that scene. For computer processing this must be converted by hardware into digital format—i.e. into discrete intensity values. This is achieved by an analogue-to-digital converter (ADC) which has two primary functions: (a) to spatially sample the scene at regular points to create a spatial array, and (b) to create discrete digital intensity values from a continuous analogue electrical signal. By performing both these functions we convert a continuous scene into a digital array of intensity values, i.e. a digital image.

14.3 PARAMETERS CHARACTERIZING DIGITAL IMAGES

So far we have established that digital images are arrays of numbers representing brightness in a scene. We will now examine the parameters which characterize array-based images. (Note that although we are referring to arrays, alternative data structures are now being used for images in some situations—see Chien (1980) for example).

The individual data values in an image array represent *picture elements* (commonly abbreviated to **pixels**). Digital images can hold any number of pixels but it is fairly common to find typical image array sizes of 512 × 512 pixels. Indeed many display terminals are designed to show precisely this size of image or some integer multiple of it (domestic TV sets in the UK display 625 lines).

Pixels are usually represented by integer brightness values. Normally these values have an upper and lower limit to ensure that they can be stored in fixed-length binary words. The number of possible values allowed for one pixel is called the number of *grey levels*. It is a measure of brightness detail. Typical images have pixel values in the range 0–255, giving 256 grey levels. Each value can then be encoded by one byte (as $256 = 2^8$ eight bits or one byte are needed to store the pixel values). In some applications images have only two grey levels, i.e. 0 and 1. These are called binary images and tend to be used in simple industrial applications, e.g. machine-tool guidance. Their main advantage is their small data volume, as each pixel can be represented by only one bit.

Since digital images are formed by spatially sampling a continuous scene it is important to specify the sampling interval. This sampling interval tells us how much spatial detail there is in the image. We can thus define the *spatial resolution* of an image as the effective distance between adjacent pixels in the terms of the *scene* it represents. For satellite images of the Earth spatial resolutions of up to several kilometres are common. For X-ray images of the body, spatial resolutions are typically less than 1 mm.

In the discussion so far we have not considered colour but merely treated an image as brightness variations. It is important to recognize that a single pixel array represents a monochrome scene (hence the use of terms such as 'grey level'). If full-colour images are required, then three separate digital images (red, green, blue) have to be captured by the front-end camera system using three different spectral filters or detectors. The precise 'colour' or spectral band represented by a given pixel array is determined entirely by the spectral characteristics of the sensor system which produces it. The array does not inherently possess colour. Recent remote sensing satellites have been provided with multispectral imaging systems capable of capturing electromagnetic radiation in a number of different spectral regions from the visible to the infra-red (e.g. the Thematic Mapper scanner on Landsat-4 and -5 launched in 1982 and 1984 respectively). For more details on these and other remote sensing systems the interested reader is referred to Curran (1985). We shall not consider colour images in this book since the basic techniques of monochrome image processing are directly applicable to multiple arrays. Readers interested in the theory of colour image formation and colour vision should refer to Pratt (1978), for example. Note, however, that even monochrome images can be displayed to the user 'in colour' by assigning different colours of the spectrum to different grey levels in a display device. This is known as *false colouring*.

To summarize this section we recall the key parameters which define a digital image. They are:

- array size (no. of pixels);
- no. of grey levels per pixel;
- spatial resolution;
- spectral band (defined by detector system).

14.4 LEVELS OF IMAGE ANALYSIS

Any newcomer to the science of image processing is likely to be surprised by the large number of algorithms that have been devised over the years to extract useful information from digital images. In this chapter it would be impossible to cover any sizable fraction of the algorithms and techniques now in use in all the applications of digital image analysis. What we can do, however, is to look at typical techniques at different levels of sophistication.

It is possible to consider image analysis on three different levels:

1. *Low-level image processing*. This consists of techniques to enhance images, remove noise (corrupt data values), and to extract various image statistics.
2. *Pattern recognition*. This involves the identification of certain features in image scenes (e.g. to recognize handwritten characters).
3. *Image understanding*. This requires scene comprehension, i.e. identifying objects, their sizes, positions, orientations in three-dimensional space. This is equivalent to *vision*.

Generally speaking, the complexity of numerical algorithms required for these types of analysis increases substantially as we go from 1 to 3.

14.5 TECHNIQUES OF LOW-LEVEL IMAGE PROCESSING

Low-level image processing is aimed at computationally enhancing certain features of interest of the user. There are two broad categories of algorithms: *real space* processing and *transform space* processing. We shall deal primarily with real-space processing, as transform-space processing involves spatial coordinate transformations requiring mathematical skills beyond what is necessary for the rest of this book. There are many comprehensive books on transform-space algorithms to which the interested reader is referred. Again W. K. Pratt (1978) is a good starting point.

We shall consider some common and highly useful real-space enhancement techniques applied to digital images. All image-enhancement techniques are carried out by applying mathematical operations to pixel values.

14.5.1 Constrast Stretching

The purpose of contrast stretching is to provide a greater dynamic range in pixel values to give more visual contrast on display. This can be appreciated by reference to an image histogram. Before constrast stretching an image histogram may be narrow (Figure 14.3(a)), implying poor contrast. After applying the stretch it becomes wide (Figure 14.3(b)), giving high contrast. Note that the area under each histogram should remain constant as the total number of pixels is invariant. In general we can define any function we like to map pixel values p into new values p':

$$p' = f(p)$$

↑

constrast stretch function

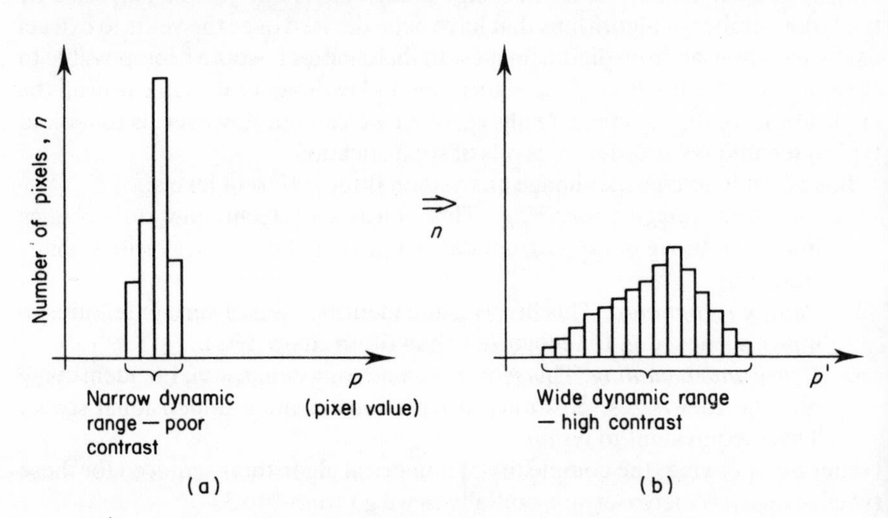

Figure 14.3 The effect of contrast stretching on image histograms

This represents a one-to-one mapping of 'old' pixel values into 'new' ones. The function f can be as simple or as complicated as we like. It could simply be $p' = 2p$, for example, doubling all the pixel values. Such a function might be appropriate when all the original scene brightness values are rather low, giving a poor dark image on display.

Usually the programmer will design a specific contrast stretch function to suit his or her own image data. Often it may be necessary to *stretch* the contrast in some parts of the image histogram and to *reduce* it in others to enhance certain brightness transitions in the original image and to suppress others. Suitable functions can be expressed as polynomials (e.g. $p' = a + bp + cp^2 + dp^3 + \cdots$) and represented in graphical form (Figure 14.4). Such functions are trivial to implement in software. (Note that contrast stretch functions can be used to achieve black/white reversal in an image amongst many other interesting effects.)

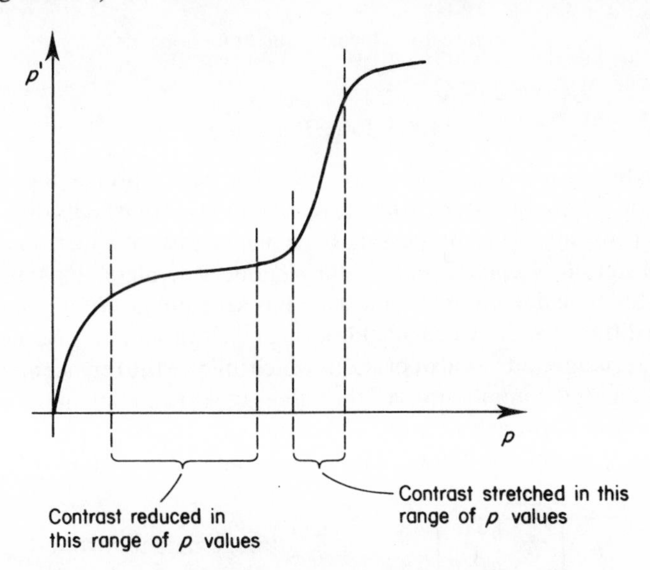

Figure 14.4 Graphical representation of polynomial contrast stretch function

14.5.2 Density Slicing

Although regarded as a separate technique, this is actually a subcategory of contrast modification functions. With density slicing all grey levels in a certain range in the original input image are set to one single value in the output image. This corresponds to a step or plateau in the pixel value mapping function (see Figure 14.5).

This kind of operation can have the effect of highlighting all areas which have roughly the same pixel values in the original image when the density slice is displayed.

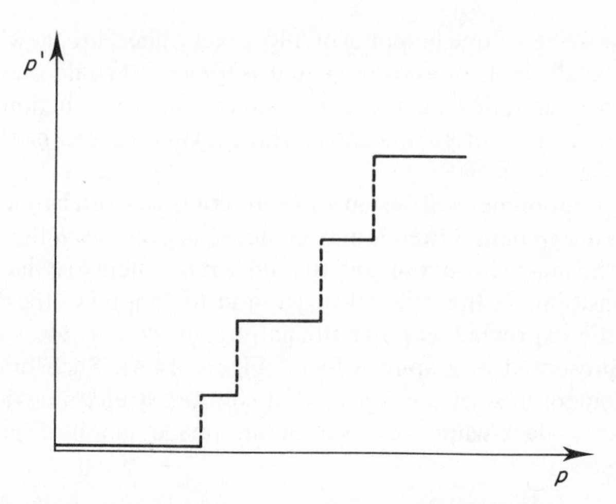

Figure 14.5 Density slice function

14.5.3 Edge Detection

Edge detection is a very important low-level image-processing technique designed to highlight the boundaries between regions of markedly different grey level. This is useful as pre-processing for machine vision, where the aim is to separate different scene objects. Many numerical algorithms have been developed for edge detection, but most are based on image *differentiation*—i.e. calculating differences between neighbouring pixels (gradients). Some schemes use local pixel neighbourhood operations which involve the replacement of pixel values by weighted combinations of the values of surrounding neighbours.

One common approach to edge detection is the 'Sobel' method based on weighted pixel neighbour values: The 'edge' value e_A at a pixel A, is given as follows:

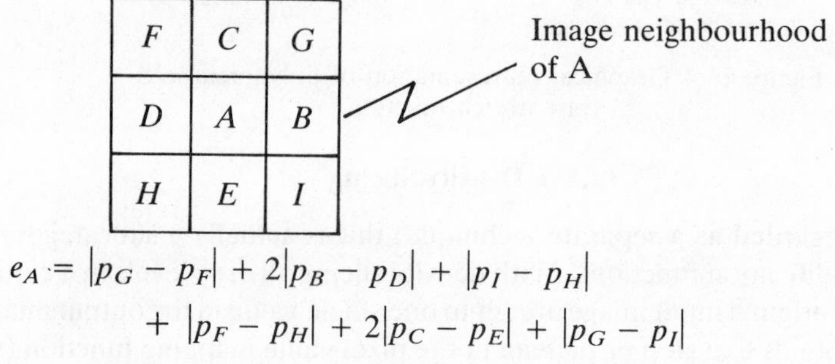

$$e_A = |p_G - p_F| + 2|p_B - p_D| + |p_I - p_H| + |p_F - p_H| + 2|p_C - p_E| + |p_G - p_I|$$

This method computes the image gradient in the vicinity of A but weights the row and column containing A more heavily. A full matrix of e_A values calculated over a full input image scene defines an edge map. Figure 14.6 shows an image from

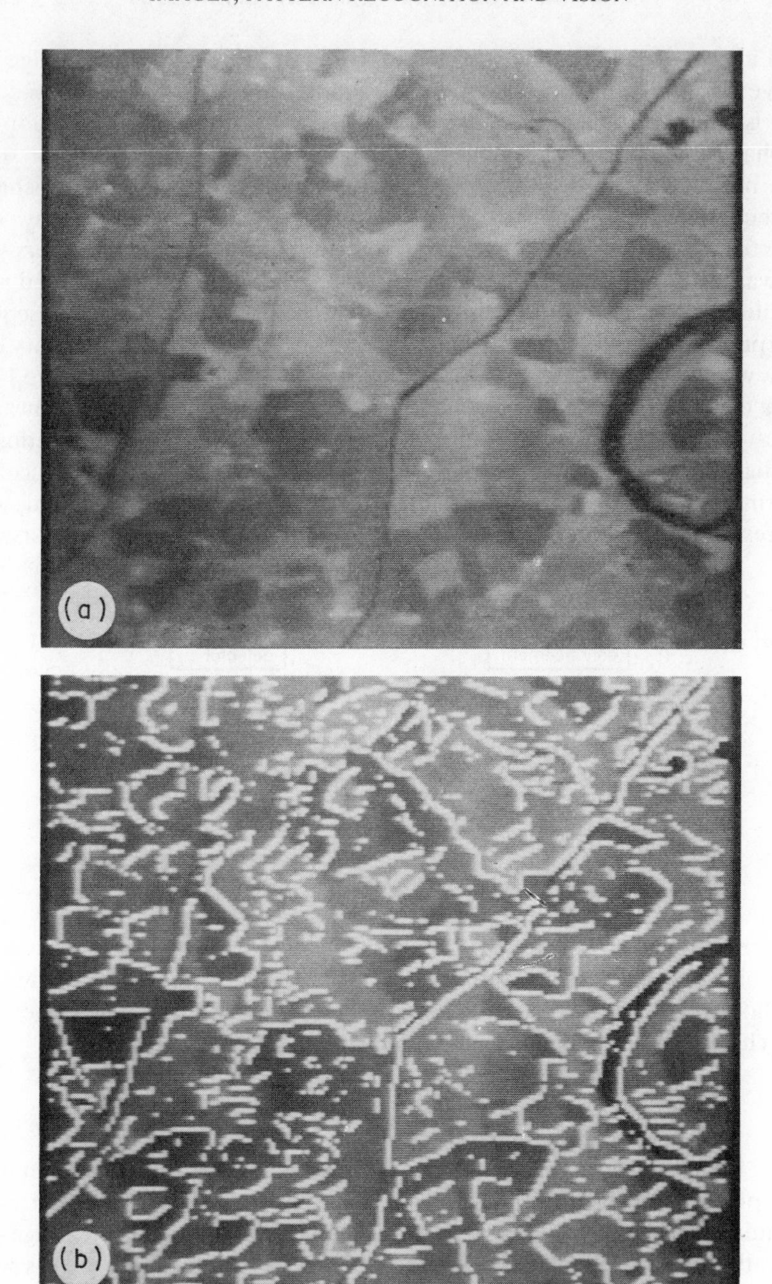

Figure 14.6 (a) Landsat-5 Thematic Mapper image of part of Gloucestershire UK; (b) Derived 'noisy' edge-map by local pixel neighbourhood computation
(Pictures kindly provided by G. Peacegood)

the Landsat-5 satellite of part of Gloucestershire (England) and an edge map derived by local neighbourhood computation.

It is important to realize that edge-enhancement by differentiation can emphasize all brightness changes in the input image whether large or small. This may lead to too many spurious edges, which would be confusing for subsequent image 'understanding' algorithms. Consequently many edge detection programs are implemented with edge *threshold detectors*—i.e. software to set edge-enhanced pixels to zero where they do not exceed some specified value. This effectively removes weak edges and helps in subsequent interpretation. Edge-detection software can be designed to create binary edge maps which are images with 1s for strong edges and 0s elsewhere (Figure 14.7). Since even threshold-based edge detection inevitably leads to some unwanted edges being emphasized, some workers have turned their attention to highlighting edges by detection at multiple resolutions and using 'coarse' information to eliminate spurious fine edge detail (e.g. Kelly 1971). This work is a result of the need for simple edge maps for automated image understanding.

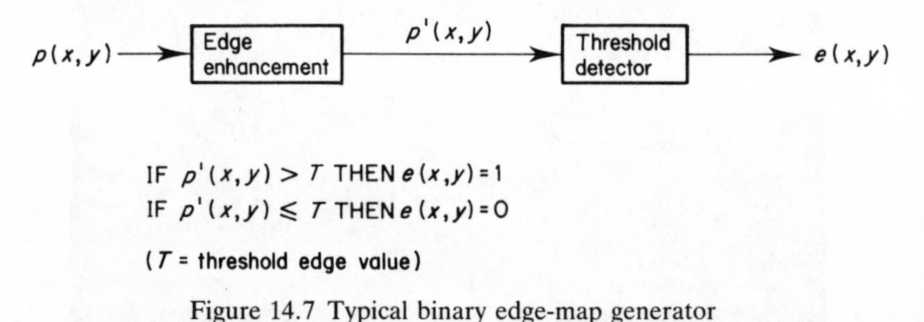

Figure 14.7 Typical binary edge-map generator

Currently there is a plethora of edge-detection algorithms. In recent years there have been attempts to find more realistic ways of simulating the psychophysical processes of human visual edge detection. Readers interested in such work should refer to Ballard and Brown (1982), for example.

14.5.4 NOISE CLEANING

Since digital images are captured from scanning sensors which may be susceptible to electronic interference it is not uncommon for electronic 'noise' to find its way into stored images. Noise can take many forms in images but typically appears as uncharacteristic pixel values in a locality (e.g. as white spots in a dark region of the image). It is quite easy to remove corrupt pixel values by examining the statistics of their neighbours. A typical algorithm is illustrated in Figure 14.8, where 'bad' pixels are replaced by averages of their neighbours.

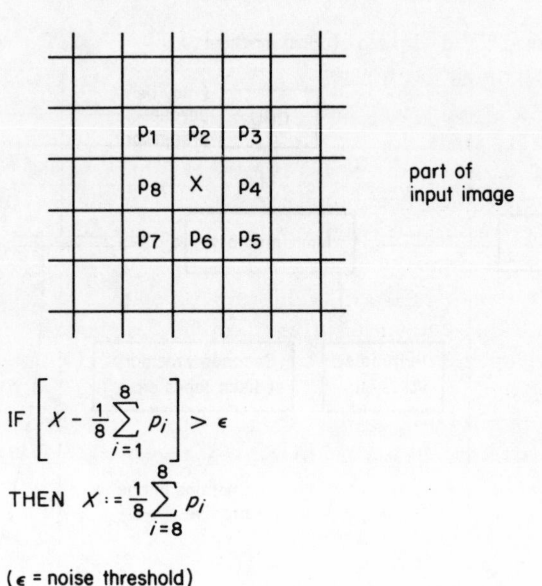

Figure 14.8 Typical image noise cleaning algorithm

14.6 IMAGE COMPRESSION

So far we have examined some simple techniques for digital-image enhancement by computer without giving any thought to the computational demands of the processing involved. Yet image processing is extremely demanding on both computer storage and processor time; the former because image arrays tend to contain large volumes of data and the latter because numerical operations or statistical manipulations of those large volumes take a long time to perform. (For example, a single image of 500 × 500 pixels and 256 grey levels contains ¼Mbyte of data—this is equivalent to over 3000 lines of high-level program source code in storage requirement). Indeed it is fairly accurate to say that one of the main limitations to current machine vision systems is their inability to process the large volumes of data involved with sophisticated algorithms in real time. The problem can essentially be tackled in two ways. In this section we shall briefly consider image *data compression*; in the next we shall discuss the use of special-purpose processor architectures to speed up image computation.

Image compression becomes necessary when it is not possible to store or transmit digital images containing their full data volume. A particularly serious problem is the transmission of large volumes of image data through communication channels or networks. Often image display hardware is located at some distance from the host computer which contains the image archive (see Figure 14.9). For example it may be desirable to allow hospital radiologists to inspect radiographs archived on one computer from a number of different

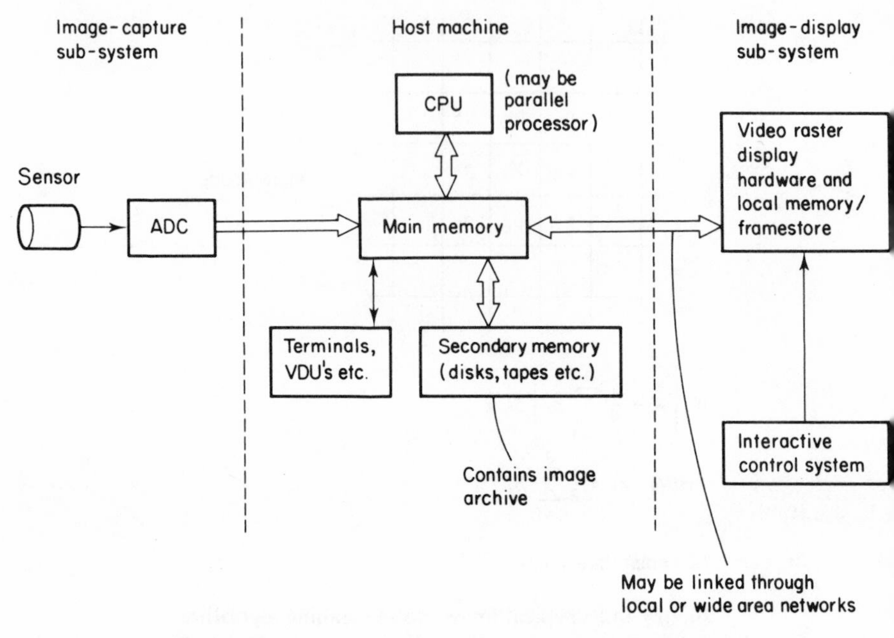

Figure 14.9 An image-processing system (simplified)

wards containing a display device linked through a LAN. Line-speed limits may prohibit rapid retrieval of full images from the host archive. This constitutes the *picture-browsing problem*.

Many image-compression techniques have been developed over the years to help solve this problem. These techniques usually involve one of the following:

1. spatial or grey-level sampling (i.e. to reduce resolution) or
2. using a transform and discarding some spatial components (equivalent to high- or low-pass filtering).

All compression schemes essentially involve the loss of information. However, the art of the game lies in discarding redundant information or in degrading the image quality in an acceptable way for the application of interest. A multitude of schemes exist, but it would not be profitable to discuss them here. The interested reader is again referred to texts such as W. K. Pratt (1978). A particularly simple and noteworthy image-archiving and -compression scheme is the PACS system developed for medical images (Meyer-Ebrecht and Wendler 1983).

14.7 SPECIAL-PURPOSE PROCESSOR ARCHITECTURES FOR IMAGE PROCESSING

Image processing, like many other numerical procedures, can be speeded up considerably by using *parallel* rather than serial computation. Since most

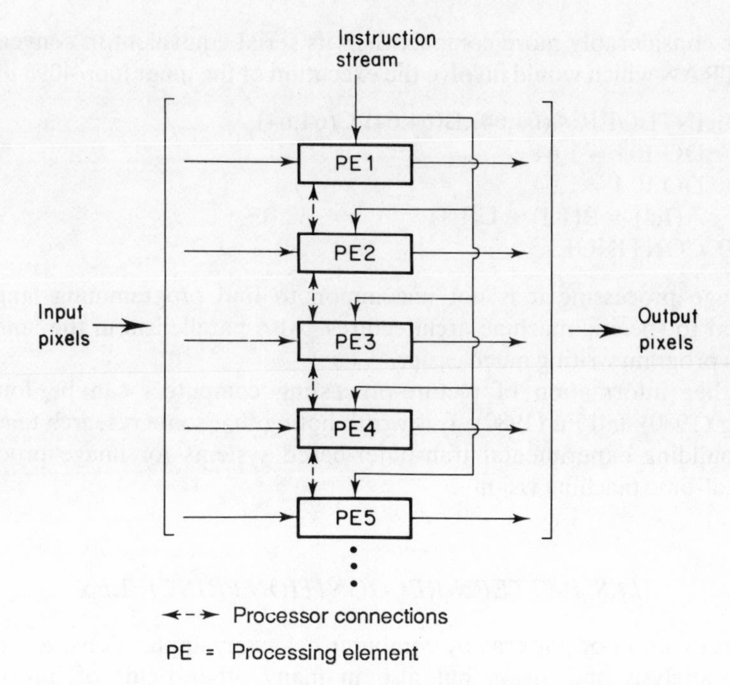

Figure 14.10 Use of SIMD architecture for pixel processing

low-level image-enhancement techniques involve the application of identical operations to each pixel in an array, the most appropriate kind of architecture is the single-instruction-stream multiple-data-stream (SIMD) type (or array-processor type—see Figure 14.10) mentioned in Chapter 2. A number of such machines are now on the market and can, in some cases, be used as 'add-ons' to conventional minicomputer hosts.

Several of these array processors have been designed and built in the UK. Three notable ones are the ICL Distributed Array Processor (DAP), the University College London Cellular Logic Image Processors (CLIP) and the National Physical Laboratory Linear Array Processor (LAP). These machines are all characterized by an array of parallel-working processors linked through a processor interconnection network which makes the interchange of data and thus local pixel neighbourhood operations easy to implement. These machines also support high-level parallel programming languages to take advantage of their inherent architectures.

For example, the ICL-DAP supports its own parallel dialect of FORTRAN, known as DAP-FORTRAN. The following DAP-FORTRAN statements would add two 64 × 64 pixel images together in parallel:

```
INTEGER A, B, C
A = B + C
```

This is considerably more compact than its serial equivalent in conventional FORTRAN which would involve the execution of the inner loop 4096 times:

```
      INTEGER A(64,64),B(64,64),C(64,64)
      DO 10 I = 1,64
      DO 10 J = 1,64
      A(I,J) = B(I,J) + C(I,J)
   10 CONTINUE
```

In image processing it is not uncommon to find programming languages tailored to specific machine architectures. Also parallelism in the languages makes program writing much easier.

Further information of picture-processing computers can be found in Huang (1980) and Fu (1980). It is worth noting that some research teams are now building experimental transputer-based systems for image processing and real-time machine vision.

14.8 PATTERN-RECOGNITION PRINCIPLES

The recognition of patterns by computer has many applications, not only in image analysis and vision but also in many other fields of information technology. Typical uses of pattern-recognition techniques are:

- identifying features in X-ray images;
- identifying land use type in satellite images;
- recognizing words in spoken sentences;
- automatically reading optical characters;
- making a diagnosis with an expert system.

Pattern recognition is a complex computational problem which is the subject of much research at present. In the last chapter we saw how pattern matching can be applied to sentence understanding in man–machine dialogue. Here we shall attempt to outline the main principles of pattern recognition in an imaging context and to identify where practical problems can arise.

Pattern recognition essentially involves the recognition of features in data, signals or images. Image-based pattern recognition is a fundamental part of machine vision and can be considered to be a higher-level problem than image enhancement. The general requirement of pattern recognition is to identify an object in an image, for example, by reference to a set of *prototype patterns* or *classification* criteria. Classification often relies on a statistical or *decision-theoretic* approach. Usually pattern recognition involves measuring certain features of an object pattern (this is known as *feature extraction*) and then using those features to perform the classification or identification.

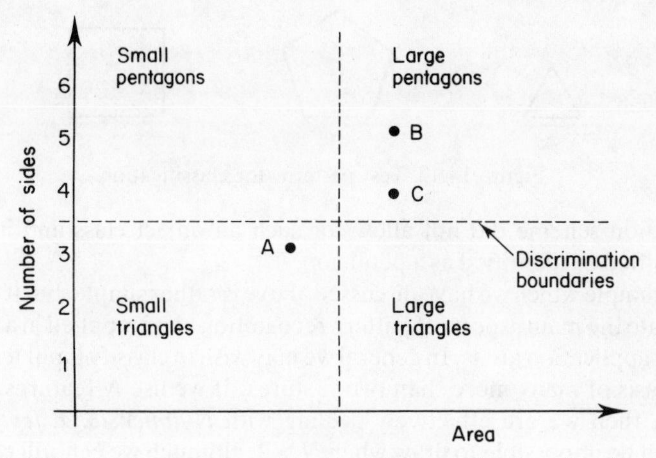

Figure 14.11 Two-dimensional feature space for the triangles and pentagons problem

We can illustrate the general principles by reference to a simple example: the triangles and pentagons problem. The objective is to identify simple polygonal objects and classify or recognize them as one of the following prototypes:

- a small triangle;
- a large triangle;
- a small pentagon;
- a large pentagon.

To perform a *recognition* we need to establish appropriate features which will enable us to classify a given polygon. The most obvious features to choose are *area* and *number of sides*—these two features should enable us to discriminate between each of the four classes of object with ease. To carry out a classification, however, we need to establish *discrimination boundaries* or values for area and number of sides which define the four prototype pattern classes. We can visualize this by referring to a diagram representing *feature space*. In this diagram the two features of interest are represented by the axes of a graph (see Figure 14.11). Any polygonal test pattern can then be represented as a point in this two-dimensional feature space. To classify such a test pattern we must simply divide the feature space into regions corresponding to the four prototype classes. When presented with an input test pattern all we then need to do is to compute its number of sides and area and locate it in the feature-space diagram. We can classify the test objects in Figure 14.12 on this basis. Their locations in the two-dimensional feature space are shown by the points labelled A, B, C in Figure 14.11. On the basis of our pre-defined discrimination boundaries A would be classified as a small triangle, B as a large pentagon and C as a large pentagon also. Clearly C is actually a square, but our

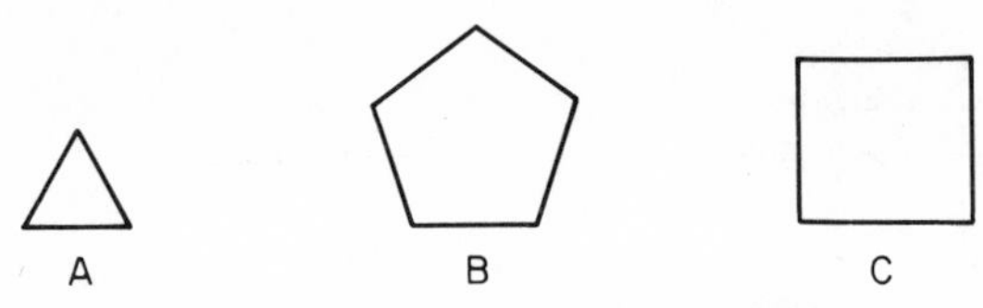

Figure 14.12 Test patterns for classification

classification scheme did not allow for such an object class and it has been mis-classified or identified as a pentagon.

The example which we have discussed above is rather simple, but it does serve to illustrate the main aspects of pattern recognition as it is applied in a number of different application areas. In general we may wish to classify input test patterns on the basis of many more than two features. If we use N features to classify patterns, then we are effectively dealing with *N-dimensional feature space*, which will be impossible to draw when $N > 2$, although we can still cope with it mathematically.

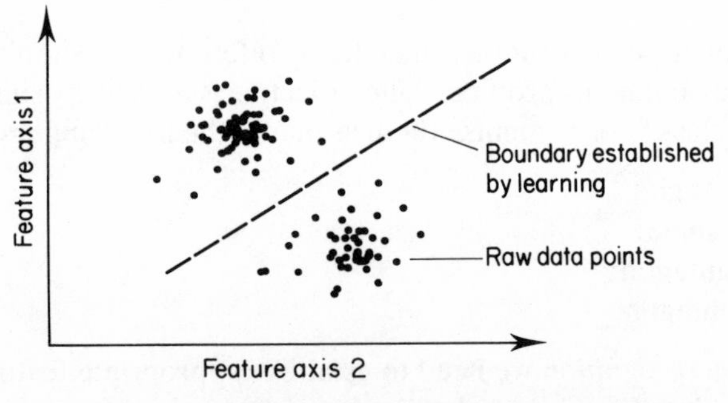

Figure 14.13 Learning

Note that in the example we used predefined discrimination boundaries to carry out the classification. In many applications the boundaries are not predefined but *learned* from lots of input test patterns (Figure 14.13). Real data points may naturally fall into distinct clusters in feature space allowing discrimination boundaries to be established. Learning may also be supervised or unsupervised. Supervised learning systems set up initial boundaries from a set of training patterns; unsupervised systems use no prior knowledge and base all classifications on earlier decisions alone.

Although we have discussed classification in terms of discrimination boundaries up to this point, there are in fact several alternative ways of doing it. Three different approaches are illustrated in Figure 14.14: the *parallelepiped* classifier, the *minimum distance to means* classifier, and the *maximum likelihood* classifier. In the latter it is assumed that all patterns in one class are distributed normally and probability contours are established. A random pattern is then allocated to the class to which it has the highest probability of belonging.

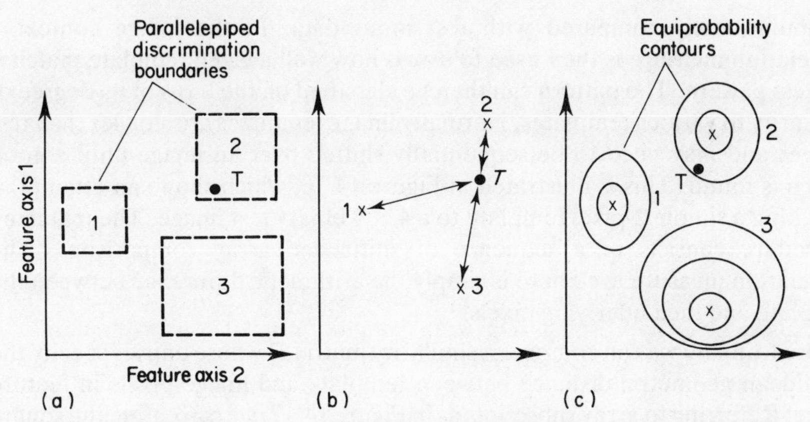

Figure 14.14 Alternative approaches to classification: (a) parallelepiped classifier; (b) minimum distance to means classifier; (c) maximum likelihood classifier
(Test pattern T is allocated to class 2 in each case)

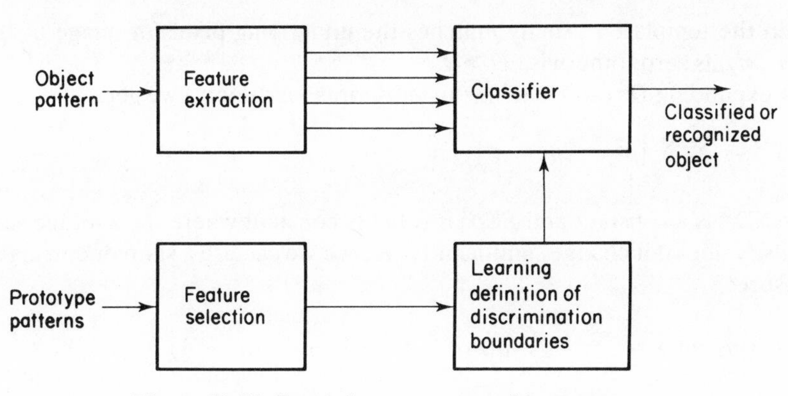

Figure 14.15 General pattern-recognition system

We can summarize this section by reference to Figure 14.15 which shows a general pattern-recognition system. For more information about the uses and theory of pattern recognition the reader is referred to one of the many comprehensive texts such as Kittler *et al.* (1981) and Duda and Hart (1973). Before leaving this topic, however, we must look at one or two specific practical techniques.

14.8.1 Image-template Matching

This is a practical technique which is often used in simple industrial automated inspection systems. As we saw in the last chapter, the basic idea behind template matching is that templates representing expected patterns are computationally compared with test input data. In the image context a correlation measure is then used to assess how well a given template matches the test pattern. The pattern can then be classified on the basis of its degree of similarity to various templates. Normally image templates are smaller than test images and may need to be sequentially shifted over an image until a good match is found. This is illustrated in Figure 14.16, which shows an attempt at matching a simple 2-pixel template to a 4×4 binary test image. The matching procedure consists of a sequence of shifts and array comparisons. The correlation measure used here is simply the arithmetic difference between the template and the underlying pixels.

(More formally we can compute a similarity matrix D whose entries specify the Euclidean geometric distance between template and image pixels in feature space. Referring to array subscripts as in Figure 14.17, we can define the square of the Euclidean distance as

$$D^2(m_1, m_2) = \sum_{n_1=1}^{N_1} \sum_{n_2=1}^{N_2} [p(m_1 + n_1 - 1, m_2 + n_2 + 1) - t(n_1, n_2)]^2$$

When the template t exactly matches the underlying pixels of image p, then $D(m_1,m_2)$ is zero; otherwise $D > 0$.
Now expanding D^2 (and leaving out subscripts for brevity) we get:

$$D^2 = \sum \sum [p^2 - 2pt + t^2]$$

Also $\Sigma\Sigma t^2$ is a constant and $\Sigma\Sigma p^2$ is roughly constant where the average scene intensity does not change significantly. Hence we can use a simpler correlation measure:

$$R(m_1, m_2) = \sum_{n_1=1}^{N_1} \sum_{n_2=1}^{N_2} p(m_1 + n_1 - 1, m_2 + n_2 - 1)\, t(n_1, n_2)$$

which is known as the cross-correlation function. The computation of R is performed by shifting t around on p and at each position multiplying the pixels and summing the results. The maximum value in the R matrix indicates the position and degree of best match to the template—see Figure 14.18 for an example.)

Since it is often found that patterns in test images do not perfectly match prototype templates, some workers in this field have experimented with the use of flexible templates—i.e. the templates are adjusted to see if an improved match can be found.

14.8.3 Syntactic Pattern Recognition

So far we have considered pattern recognition only from the viewpoint of statistically matching input data sets (e.g. images) to prototype patterns or

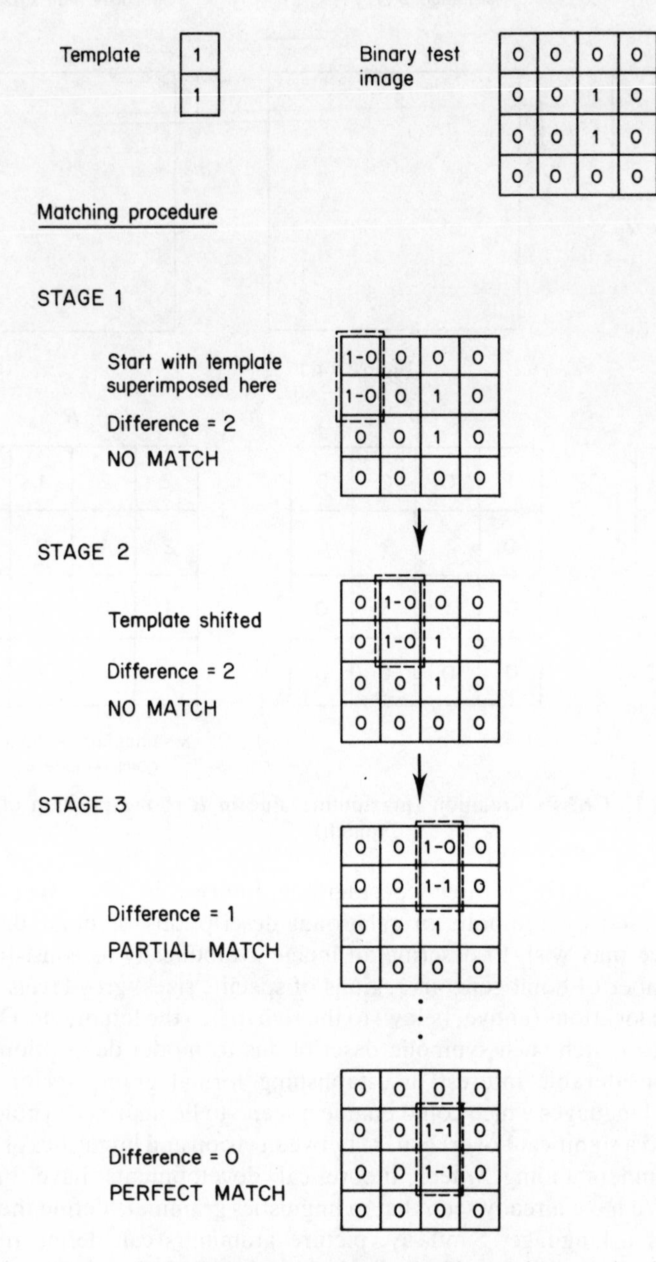

Figure 14.16 Simple template matching using a simple difference correlation measure

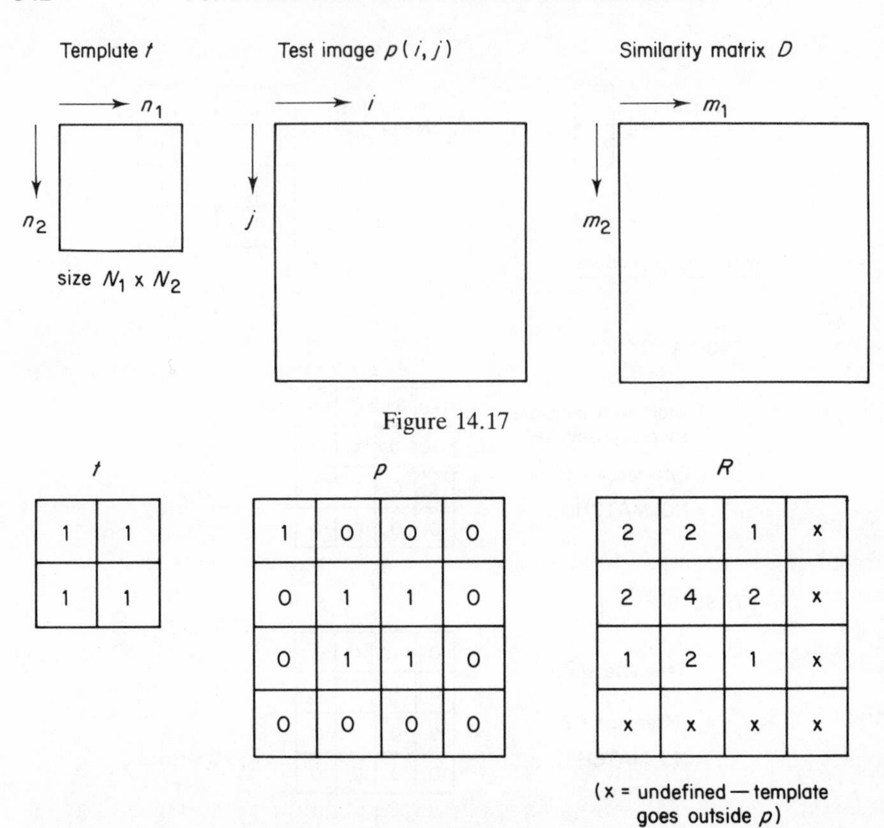

Figure 14.17

Figure 14.18 Cross correlation (maximum value in R shows position of best match)

templates. But there is now considerable interest in high-level pattern matching based on symbolic or relational descriptions of input data. For example, we may wish to describe an image symbolically as consisting of a certain number of homogeneous regions of specific sizes, grey levels, shapes and relative locations (above, below, to the right of, to the left of, etc.) We may then wish to match such symbolic descriptions to model descriptions. Also there is considerable interest in establishing formal grammars or picture description languages which could enable a scene to be analysed syntactically. We thus find a significant overlap here between vision and linguistics or natural language understanding where theoretical developments have much in common. We have already seen that in linguistics grammars define the phrase structure of a language. Similarly, picture grammars can define the basic syntactic structures in scenes built from primitive symbols (see Figure 14.19, for example). Such techniques could be important in machine vision in the future. The problem, however, is to find appropriate symbolic descriptions and

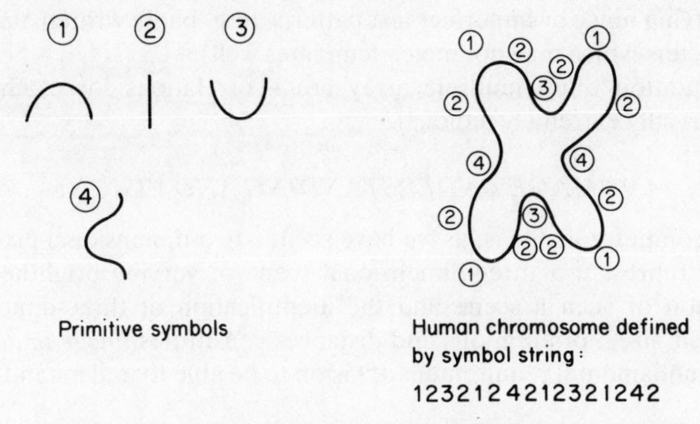

Figure 14.19 Syntactic specification of a human chromosome in terms of image primitives (Adapted from Ledley (1964))

grammars to analyse general image scenes rather than narrowly defined image classes.

Readers interested in taking this topic further are referred to Barrow and Popplestone (1971), Cohen and Feigenbaum (1982), Hodges (1977), and Gonzalez and Wintz (1977).

14.8.4 Applications of Pattern Recognition in IKBS

Before leaving the general topic of pattern recognition it is worth noting that these techniques are directly applicable to diagnostic and consultative expert systems (see Tou 1981 for example). Expert systems such as MYCIN which perform medical diagnoses essentially match given sets of symptoms with disease pattern prototypes built into the system knowledge base. Clearly the diagnosis procedure requires the use of appropriate similarity measures for pattern matching. As noted earlier, many expert systems use a probabilistic basis for inferencing—this is analogous in several respects to statistical pattern recognition used in other contexts.

14.8.5 Problems in Pattern Recognition

In the last few sections we have surveyed the basic principles and techniques of pattern recognition. However, this chapter would not be complete without some mention of the problems which plague pattern recognition in practice and which, for example, prevent successful machine reading of handwritten script at present. The main problems are:

1. difficulty of selecting suitable features and discrimination techniques to perform good classifications;

2. classifying noisy or imperfect test patterns (e.g. badly written alphabetic characters which may not match templates well);
3. computation time (multiple array cross-correlations for example are numerically extremely tedious).

14.9 IMAGE UNDERSTANDING AND VISION

A general computer image is, as we have seen, a two-dimensional pixel array which may represent a three-dimensional scene of varying brightness. The interpretation of such a scene and the identification of three-dimensional objects, their sizes, orientations and distances constitutes *image understanding*. It is a fundamental requirement of vision to be able to understand a scene in this way.

Vision is a high-level problem-solving task which incorporates many ideas from artificial intelligence. It also requires low-level image-enhancement techniques (e.g. edge detection) and pattern-recognition algorithms. Vision is therefore founded on many of the techniques introduced earlier in this chapter; but it must also go very much further.

One of the most important ideas to grasp about machine vision is that it relies fundamentally on *a priori knowledge* about the objects which appear in images. Without such knowledge a computer would be able to do little more than establish a relational description of a scene. Understanding, that is recognizing objects and their relative locations, etc., needs ancillary information. Humans can only 'recognize' objects which they have experienced before.

We can illustrate this with reference to the picture on the cover of the book which shows a painting of the Grand Canal in Venice by Canaletto. Most readers will have been able to identify the scene without having needed to be told. Considering that Venice occupies only a few square miles on a very large planet this is a remarkable feat indeed. Also it is not difficult to recognize a bridge—the Rialto—some classical buildings which appear to have depth, and some gondolas afloat on the canal. Interestingly we can generate a very thorough interpretation of this scene without necessarily ever having seen it in real life—the key to this mental recognition process is the existence of *a priori* knowledge which we can use to make sense of what we see. Without such knowledge our interpretation or comprehension of the scene would be outstandingly poor. Clearly vision requires knowledge or models of objects encountered in scenes. This does in fact prove to be a major stumbling block for artificial machine vision. It has not been found possible to date to provide computers with the models needed to realistically interpret natural world scenes, although steps are being taken in this direction.

14.9.1 Blocks-world Vision

To date many experimental machine vision systems have been developed using artificially trivial scenes, e.g. containing only primitive polyhedral objects: cubes, cylinders, pyramids etc.—so-called 'blocks-world' scenes.

Although there are no definitive image understanding systems in existence at present we can speculate, on the basis of recent research work in this field, that such a system might involve a sequence of computational steps rather like those shown in Figure 14.20.

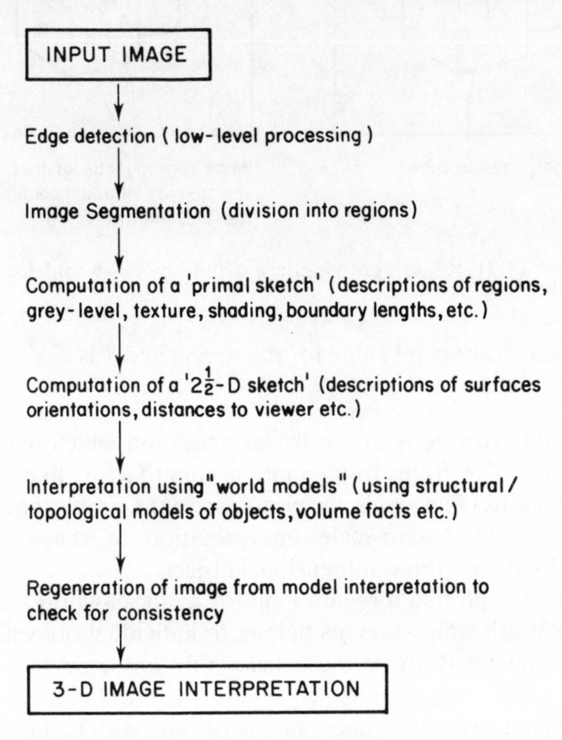

Figure 14.20 A hypothetical image-understanding system

One of the first tasks in any vision system is the computation of an edge map and the segmentation of the image into a number of relatively homogeneous regions by '*region growing*'. Region growing effects a transition from an edge map to a region map (Figure 14.21) and in so doing we must ignore spurious or weak edges which are irrelevant to the interpretation of the scene (e.g. a small crack in an object face). There are many algorithms in existence which perform region growing; many of these are described in Ballard and Brown (1982). Basically they involve sequentially merging pixels together to form regions. For example a pixel $p(x,y)$ may be merged with a region R only on the following basis:

$$p(x,y) \text{ is merged with } R \text{ if and only if } |p(x,y) - \bar{p}(R)| < T$$

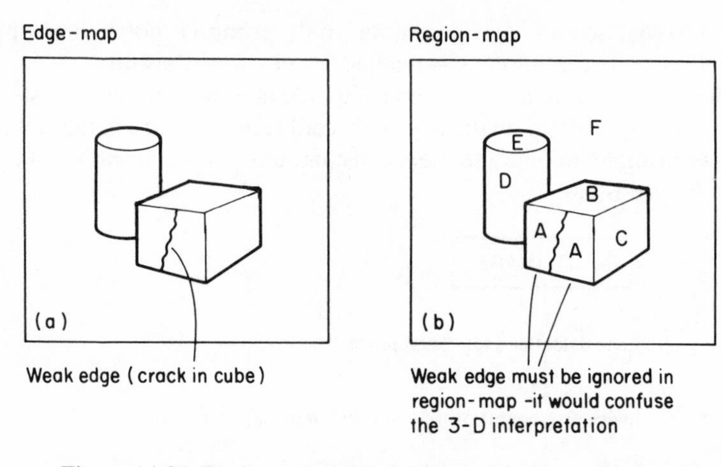

Figure 14.21 Region growing in a simple blocks-world scene

($\bar{p}(R)$ is the average pixel value for the region and T is a threshold value)

In practice region growing is a non-trivial operation which may require far more sophisticated algorithms to take into account factors like region shapes and perimeter lengths. The aim is always to derive the simplest possible region map to assist in the macro-scale interpretation of the scene and the identification of separate three-dimensional objects.

Once we have established a region map for a blocks-world scene it is then necessary to establish which regions belong to individual objects and then to identify those objects. Both of these tasks rely on some form of *a priori* knowledge. For the region map of Figure 14.21(b), for example, it is important to be able to deduce that region A belongs with regions B and C and not with D and E. It is also vital to be able to deduce that A, B, C constitute one object, D and E another and that F makes up the background.

The approach which some workers in this field have adopted is to use topological models for block-world objects and to separate and identify them on the basis of the edge junctions they display. A good example of this is the SEE program devised by Guzman (1968). The SEE program analyses blocks-world scenes in terms of junctions and searches for clues to indicate that two regions belong to the same body. Some examples of Guzman's junction categories are shown in Figure 14.22.

Guzman's program uses heuristics to link regions together. Three typical heuristics are as follows:

1. *Fork:* If three regions meet at a fork, and none is the background, region links are formed as follows:

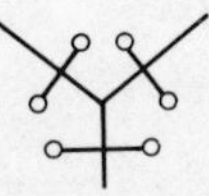

2. *Arrow:* The regions are linked thus:

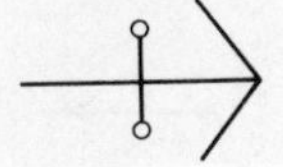

3. *X:* The regions are linked like this:

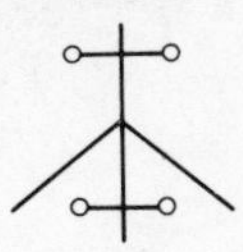

These simple heuristics now enable us to demonstrate how a pair of objects can be separated in a blocks-world scene. Figure 14.23 shows a pair of cubes stacked one on top of the other. There is no way that a computer program could deduce this from the region map alone. However, with the three junction heuristics above, the SEE program can easily separate the two objects by linking *A*, *B* and *C* together and *D* and *E* together. It would then be possible to identify the two objects as cubes if we had prior knowledge about the kinds of edge junctions which cubes display in blocks-world scenes. Clearly such a procedure relies heavily on pattern recognition to identify the edge-junction types. This might be done using template matching, for example.

In this short description we have merely scratched the surface of blocks-world vision and have simply picked out one or two illustrative procedures. We

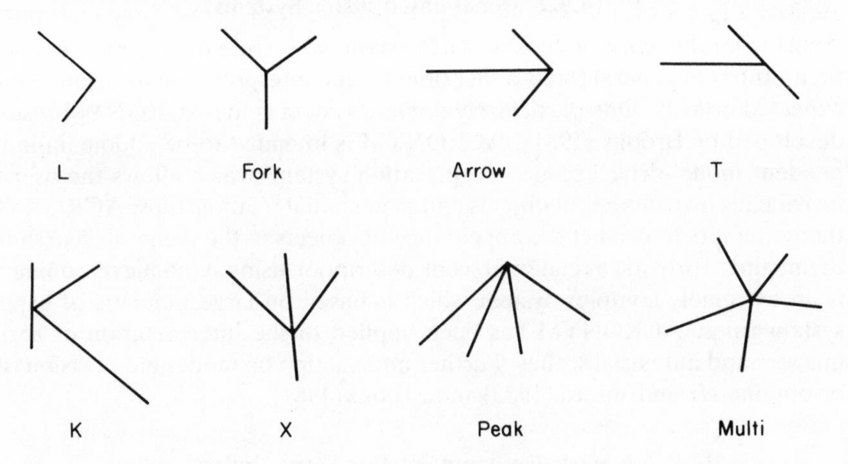

Figure 14.22 Example edge-junction categories for a blocks-world scene (Guzman (1968))

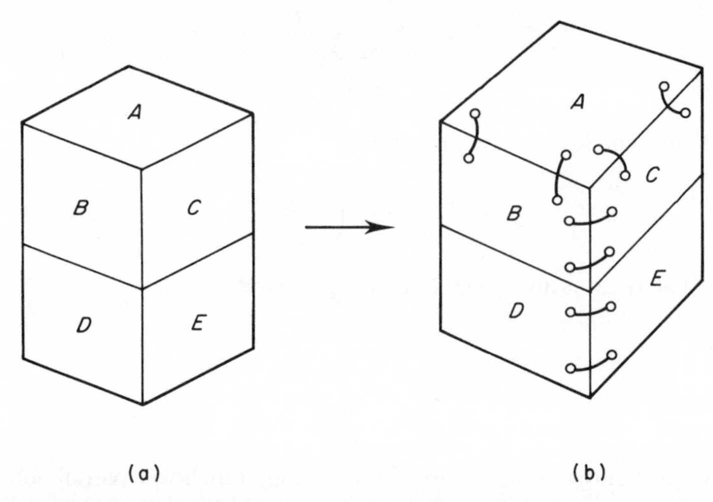

Figure 14.23 (a) Region map; (b) SEE analysis showing region links based on junction heuristics

have omitted any consideration of major problems such as the computation of light flow and the analysis of shadows, etc. In general terms, the whole field is highly experimental and extremely complex, and even some of the simplest scenes require enormous computation time. Also it is not apparent that useful results obtained with blocks-world scenes necessarily take us any closer to methods for interpreting *real*-world scenes. Readers interested in pursuing the history of blocks-world vision are referred to Cohen and Feigenbaum (1982).

14.9.2 Model-based Vision Systems

Apart from the work on blocks-world vision, some researchers have devoted their efforts to general three-dimensional scene interpretation using models of expected objects. One particularly notable system is the ACRONYM system developed by Brooks (1981). ACRONYM is intended to be a 'domain-independent model-driven scene interpretation system' which allows the user to provide his own models of objects and their spatial relationships. ACRONYM then attempts to predict the appearance of objects in the scene, to search for them, and to provide a relational scene description using symbolic reasoning. It is an extremely complex system which is based on large numbers of expert system rules. ACRONYM has been applied to the interpretation of aerial imagery and industrial scenes. Further information on model-based vision can be obtained from Binford (1982) and Brooks (1981).

14.9.3 Knowledge-based Satellite Scene Understanding

Although *a priori* knowledge is essential for three-dimensional scene

Table 14.1 Heuristics applicable to linear feature discrimination in landsat images. (After Peacegood and Wilkinson (1985))

	Road	River	Hedgerow	Railway	Land/sea boundary
Intensity	Variable	Low in infra-red	High infra-red/red ratio in summer	Variable	Low in infra-red on one side of feature
Type	Line/edge	Line	Edge	Line/edge	Edge
Sinuosity	Medium	High	Low	Medium	Medium
Fragmentation	Low	Low	High	Low	Low
Junction frequency	Medium	Variable	High	Low	None
Junction angle	Any	Branch system merging from same direction	90° junctions permissible	Branch junctions < 90°	None

understanding, it can also play an important role in the interpretation of two-dimensional scenes, e.g. from Earth observation satellites. Several satellites (Landsat, SPOT, for example) now provide imagery of the Earth's surface suitable for mapping applications. But with resolutions of 10–30 m there is generally insufficient detail to clearly discriminate between linear features such as roads, railways and rivers. Again prior knowledge has a key role to play in solving this problem. Heuristics based on knowledge about the topologies of land surface features can be extremely useful in scene understanding. Table 14.1 illustrates some of the knowledge which can be used to aid the discrimination process. Note that in this context the knowledge is fuzzy (rivers are *usually* highly sinuous—but not always so). Also the *a priori* information may be context dependent. For example rivers do not terminate on motorways *normally*.

14.10 ROBOTIC VISION

This chapter would not be complete without a brief mention of the requirements of robotic vision. Apart from general three-dimensional scene interpretation which is common to all forms of machine vision, robotics requires in addition a means of fusing multi-sensor data—that is to merge scene interpretations with information received from tactile and other sensors. Also robot vision subsystems are needed to feed back information to control

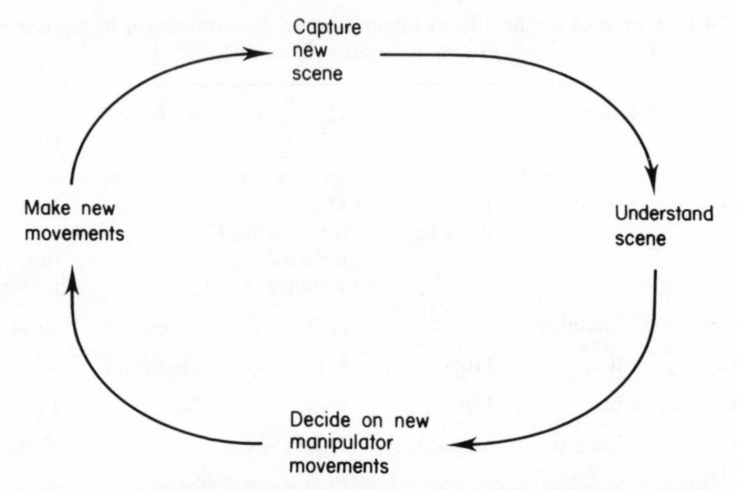

Figure 14.24 Feedback loop in robotic vision
(*Note:* For real-time robot arm control, there should be a cycle time around the loop of < 0.1 s. This is impossible with sophisticated image-understanding algorithms. Most robot vision systems are therefore primitive and normally only use binary images.)

manipulators in real-time (Figure 14.24). Unfortunately the computational demands of such systems are extremely high. Most robot systems in use at the present time merely perform low-level pattern recognition to align machine tools and work-pieces or to spot flaws in finished products. Needless to say, fully integrated three-dimensional robot vision systems are still extremely remote. Machine vision continues to await major breakthroughs in object modelling, symbolic scene description and computer architecture.

References

Abraham, E., Seaton, C. T. and Smith, S. D. (1983): The optical computer, *Scientific American*, February, **248**(2) 63–71.

Ackerman, F. A., Fowler, P. J. and Ebenau, R. G. (1984): Software inspections and the industrial production of software, in Hausen, H.-L. (ed.), *Software Validation*, North Holland, Amsterdam, pp. 13–40.

Addis, T. R. (1983): *Dependency Analysis for Relational Databases*, Technical Report, Man Computer Studies Group, Brunel University, also under the title *DBMS—a Technical Comparison*, in State of the Art Report, Pergamon Infotech Ltd, Maidenhead.

Aho, A. V. and Ullman, J. D. (1972, 1973): *The Theory of Parsing, Translation and Compiling*, Vols I and II, Prentice-Hall, Englewood Cliffs, N.J., 1972 (Vol I) and 1973 (Vol II).

Alexander, I. and Burnett, P. (1983): *Reinventing Man*, Penguin Books, Harmondsworth, Middlesex.

Alvey Committee (1982): *A Programme for Advanced Information Technology*: The Report of the Alvey Committee, Department of Trade and Industry, HMSO, London.

Alvey Directorate (1984): *Alvey Programme Annual Report*, Institute of Electrical Engineers, London.

Anderson, R. B. (1979): *Proving Programs Correct*, John Wiley, Chichester.

Andrews, H. C. and Hunt, B. R. (1977): *Digital Image Restoration*, Prentice-Hall, Englewood Cliffs, N.J.

Atkinson, M. P. *et al.* (1984): The Proteus distributed database system, in *Proceedings of the Third British National Conference on Databases (BNCOD3)*, edited by J. Longstaff, Cambridge University Press, Cambridge, England.

Backus, J. (1978): Can programming be liberated from the Von Neumann style? A functional system and its algebra of programs, *Communications of the ACM*, **21**(8), 613–49.

Baker, F. T. (1972): Chief programmer team management of production programming, *IBM Systems J.* **11**(1).

Ballard, D. H. and Brown, C. M. (1982): *Computer Vision*, Prentice-Hall, Englewood Cliffs, N.J.

Barber, D. C. (1983): The computer and medical images, *Brit. Med. J.*, **287**, 6 August, 413–15.

Barnes, J. G. P. (1984): *Programming in Ada*, Addison-Wesley, Reading, MA.

Barr, A. and Feigenbaum, E. (1982): *Handbook of AI*, Vol 2, Kaufmann, Inc., Los Altos, CA.

Barron, I. M. (1978): The transputer, in Aspinall, D. (ed.), *The Microprocessor and its Application*, Cambridge University Press, pp. 343–57.

Barrow, H. G. and Popplestone, P. J. (1971): Relational descriptions in picture processing, in Meltzer, B. and Mitchie, D. (eds.) *Machine Intelligence 6*, Elsevier, pp. 377–96.

Barwise, J. and Perry, J. (1983): *Situations and Attitudes*, Bradford Books, MIT Press, Cambridge, MA.
Bates, M. (1978): The theory and practice of augmented transition network grammars, in Bolc, L. (ed.) *Natural Language Communication with Computers*, Springer, pp. 191–260.
Bell, T. E., Bixler, D. C. and Dyer, M. E. (1977): An extendable approach to computer-aided software requirements engineering, *IEEE Trans. Software Engineering*, **SE-3**(1), 49–59.
Binford, T. O. (1982): Survey of model based image analysis systems, *Int. J. Robotics Res.*, **1**(1), 18–64.
Bjorner, D. and Jones, C. (1982): *Formal Specifications and Software Development*, Prentice-Hall, Englewood Cliffs, N.J.
Boehm, B. W. (1981): *Software Engineering Economics*, Prentice-Hall, Englewood Cliffs, N.J.
Booch, G. (1983): *Software Engineering with Ada*, Benjamin/Cummings.
Borkin, Sheldon A. (1980): *Data Models: a Semantic Approach for Database Systems*, The MIT press, Cambridge, MA.
Bothon, N. M. (1979): Design structure diagrams: a new standard in flow diagrams, *Computer Bulletin* (British Computer Society), Series 2, No. 19.
Brooks, F. P. (1975): *The Mythical Man-Month*, Addison-Wesley, Reading, MA.
Brooks, R. A (1981): Symbolic reasoning among 3-D objects and 2-D models, *AI Journal*, **16**, 285–348.
Buchanan, B. and Shortliffe, E. (eds.) (1984): *Rule Based Expert Systems: The MYCIN Experiments of the The Stanford Heuristic Programming Project*, Addison-Wesley, Reading, MA.
Burger, R. M., Cavin III, R. K., Holton, W. C. and Sumney, L. W. (1984). The impact of IC's on computer technology, *Computer*, October, 88–95.
Burstall, R. M. and Goguen, J. A. (1981): An informal introduction to specifications using CLEAR, in Boyer, R. S. and Moore, J. S. (eds.), *The Correctness Problem in Computer Science*, Academic Press, pp. 185–213.
Cardenas, A. F. (1985): *Data Base Management Systems*, Allyn and Bacon, Boston.
Chang, C.-L. and Lee, R. C.-T. (1973): *Symbolic Logic and Mechanical Theorem Proving*, Academic Press, New York.
Charniak, E. and McDermott, D. (1985): *Introduction to Artificial Intelligence*, Addison-Wesley, Reading, MA.
Chen, P. P. (1976): The entity–relationship model: towards a unified view of data, *ACM Transactions on Database Systems*, New York, **1**(1), 9–36.
Chen, P. P. (1980) (ed.): *Entity Relationship Approach to Systems Analysis and Design*, North Holland, Amsterdam.
Chen, P. P. (1985): Database design based on entity and relationship, in Yao (1985).
Cheong, V. E. and Hirschheim, R. A. (1983): *Local Area Networks*, John Wiley, Chichester.
Cherry, C. (1957): *On Human Communication*, MIT Press, Cambridge, MA.
Chien, Y. T. (1980): Hierarchical Data Structures for Picture Storage, Retrieval and Classification, in Chaung, S. K. and Fu, K. S. (eds.), *Pictorial Information Systems*, Springer-Verlag, Berlin.
Clarke, K. and McCabe, F. (1984): *Micro-PROLOG*, Prentice-Hall, Englewood Cliffs, N.J.
Clocksin, W. and Mellish, C. (1982): *Programming in PROLOG*, Springer-Verlag, Heidelberg.
Codd, E. F. (1970): A relational model for large shared data bases, *Communications of the ACM*, New York, **13**(6), 377–87.

Codd, E. F. (1972): Further normalization of the data base relational model, in Rustin, R. (ed.), *Data Base Systems*, Prentice-Hall, Englewood Cliffs, N.J., pp. 33–64.

Codd, E. F. (1979): Extending the database relational model to capture more meaning, *ACM Transactions on Database Systems*, New York, **4**(4), 397–434.

Cohen, P. R. and Feigenbaum, E. A. (1982): *The Handbook of Artificial Intelligence*, Vol. 3, Pitman, London.

Cole, R. (1981): *Computer Communications*, Macmillan, London.

Comer, D. (1984): *Operating Systems Design—The XINU Approach*, Prentice-Hall, Englewood Cliffs, N.J.

Computer (1982): Special issue on data-flow systems, **15**(2), February.

Conlon, T. (1985): *Start Problem Solving with PROLOG*, Addison-Wesley, Reading, MA.

Cooke, D. J. and Bez, H. E. (1984): *Computer Mathematics*, Cambridge University Press.

Curran, P. J. (1985): *Principles of Remote Sensing*, Longman, Harlow, Essex.

Dahl, O. J., Dijkstra, E. W. and Hoare, C. A. R. (1972): *Structured Programming*, Academic Press, New York.

Darlington, J., Henderson, P. and Turner, D. A. (1982): *Functional Programming and its Applications*, Cambridge University Press.

Date, C. J. (1981): *An Introduction to Database Systems*, (3rd edn), Addison-Wesley, London.

Date, C. J. (1983): *An Introduction to Database Systems*, Vol II, Addison-Wesley, London.

Davies, D. W., Barber, D. L. A., Price, W. L. and Solomonides, C. M. (1979): *Computer Networks and Their Protocols*, John Wiley, Chichester.

Deen, S. M. (1977): *Fundamentals of Database Systems*, Macmillan, London.

Deen, S. M. (1985): *Principles and Practice of Database Systems*, Macmillan, London.

Deitel, H. M. (1984): *Introduction to Operating Systems*, Addison-Wesley, Reading, MA.

Dijkstra, E. W. (1968): Go To statement considered harmful, *Communications of the ACM*, **11**(3), 147–8.

Downton, A. C. (1984): *Computers and Microprocessors*, Van Nostrand Reinhold, Wokingham, UK.

Duda, R. O. and Hart, P. E. (1973): *Pattern Classification and Scene Analysis*, John Wiley, New York.

Duff, M. J. B. (1980): *Array Processing, Electronics and Power*, November/December, 888–93.

EEC (1984): Council resolutions 84/130/EEC 28 Feb 84 and 85/141/EEC of 11 Feb 1985—see *Official Journal of the European Communities*, L55, **28**(23) Feb. 1985.

Epstein, R. (1977a): *A Tutorial on Ingres*, Memo No ERL—M77-25, Electronics Research Laboratory, College of Engineering, University of California, Berkeley.

Epstein, R. (1977b): *Creating and Maintaining a Database using Ingres*, Memo No ERL—M77-71, Electronics Research Laboratory, College of Engineering, University of California, Berkeley.

Erman, L. D., Hayes-Roth, F., Lesser, V. R. and Reddy, D. R. (1980): The Hearsay II Speech Understanding System: integrating knowledge to resolve uncertainty, *Computing Surveys*, **12**(2).

Escort: Brochure from PA Computers and Telecommunications, Rochester House, 33 Greycoat Street, London SW1P 2QF.

Fagin, R. (1977): Multivalued dependencies and a new normal form for relational database systems, *ACM Trans. on Database Systems*, New York, **2**(3), 201–22.

Feuer, A. R. and Gehani, N. (eds.) (1984): *Comparing and Assessing Programming Languages, Ada, C and Pascal*, Prentice-Hall, Englewood Cliffs, N.J.

Flanders, P. M., Hunt, D. J., Reddaway, S. F. and Parkinson, D. (1977): in Kuck, D. J., Lawrie, D. H. and Sameh, A. H. (eds.), *High Speed Computer and Algorithm Organization*, Academic Press, New York, p. 113.

Fletcher, W. I. (1984): *An Engineering Approach to Digital Design*, Prentice-Hall, Englewood Cliffs, N.J.

Fu, K. S. (ed.) (1980): *Special Computer Architecture for Pattern Processing*, CRC Press, Boca Raton, Florida.

Ghezzi, C. and Jazayeri, M. (1982): *Programming Language Concepts*, John Wiley, Chichester.

Glasgow, J. (1985): *Logic Programming In Nial*, Department of Computing and Info Sc, Queen's University, Canada.

Goguen, J. A., Thatcher, J. W. and Wagner, E. G. (1978): An Initial Algebra Approach to the Specification, Correctness and Implementation of Abstract Data Types, pp. 80–149, in Yeh, R. T. (ed.), *Current Trends in Programming Methodology*, Vol IV, Prentice-Hall.

Goldberg, A. (1984): *Smalltalk-80, The Interactive Programming Environment*, Addison-Wesley, Reading, MA.

Goldberg, A. and Robson, D. (1983): *Smalltalk-80, The Language and its Implementation*, Addison-Wesley, Reading, MA.

Gonzalez, R. C. and Wintz, P. (1977): *Digital Image Processing*, Addison-Wesley, Reading, MA.

Gostick, R. W. (1979): Software and algorithms for the distributed array processors, *ICL Technical Journal*, May, 116–35.

Guzman, A. (1968): Decomposition of a visual scene into three-dimensional bodies, *AFIPS Fall Joint Conferences*, **33**, 291–304.

Habermann, A. N. (1982): System development environments, in Neel, D. (ed.) *Tools and Notations for Program Development*, Cambridge University Press, pp. 273–303.

Harmon, P. and King, D. (1985): *Artificial Intelligence in Business: EXPERT SYSTEMS*, John Wiley, Chichester.

Hayes, J. P. (1978): *Computer Architecture and Organization*, McGraw-Hill, New York.

Hayes-Roth, F., Waterman, D. A. and Lenat, D. B. (1983): *Building Expert Systems*, Addison-Wesley, Reading, MA.

Hockney, R. W. and Jesshope, C. R. (1981): *Parallel Computers: Architecture, Programming and Algorithms*, Adam Hilger, Bristol.

Hodges, W. (1977): *Logic*, Penguin Books, Harmondsworth, Middlesex.

Howe, D. R. (1983): *Data Analysis for Data Base Design*, Arnold, London.

Huang, T. S. (ed.) (1980): *Image Processing Computers*, Springer-Verlag, Berlin.

Hutchison, D. (1983): Ethernet and the Cambridge Ring, *Computer Bulletin*, December, 17–20.

ISO (1982) edited by J. J. van Griethuysen: Concepts and Terminology for the Conceptual Scheme and Information Base, International Organisation for Standardisation, New York, ISO/TC97/SC5/WG3 N 695.

Jackson, M. A. (1975): *Principles of Program Design*, Academic Press, New York.

Jackson, M. A. (1982): *System Development*, Prentice-Hall, Englewood Cliffs, N.J.

Jacob, R. J. K. (1983a): Using formal specifications in the design of a human-computer interface, *Comm ACM*, **26**, April, 259–64.

Jacob, R. J. K. (1983b): Exectable specifications for a human-computer interface, *Proc CHI '83, Human Factors in Computing Systems*, ACM, 28–34.

Jenkins, M. A. (1985): *Q'Nial Reference Manual*, Nial Systems Limited, 20 Hatter Street, Kingston, Canada, also available from Nial UK Contact point, 16 Hurst Lane, East Molesey, Surrey or through the authors.

JIPDEC (1981): *Report on Fifth Generation Computer Systems*, Japan Information Processing Development Centre.

Jones, C. B. (1980): *Software Development: A Rigorous Approach*, Prentice-Hall, Englewood Cliffs, N.J.

Jones, C. B. (1986): *Systematic Software Development Using VDM*, Prentice-Hall, Englewood Cliffs, N.J.

Kelly, M. D. (1971): Edge detection in pictures using planning, in Meltzer, B. and Mitchie, D. (eds.) *Machine Intelligence 6*, Elsevier, New York.

Kernighan, B. W. and Ritchie, D. M. (1978): *The C Programming Language*, Prentice-Hall, Englewood Cliffs, N.J.

King, M. J. and Pardoe, J. P. (1985): *Program Design Using JSP*, Macmillan, London.

King, R. and McLeod, D. (1985): *Semantic Data Models*, In Yao (1985).

Kittler, J. V. (1982): *Pattern Recognition and Image Processing Review*, UK Science and Engineering Research Council, Rutherford Appleton Laboratory.

Kittler, J. V., Fu, K. S. and Pau, L. F. (eds.) (1981): *Pattern Recognition Theory and Applications*, D. Reidel, Dordrecht.

Kowalski, R. (1979): *Logic for Problem Solving*, North Holland, Amsterdam.

Krutz (1980): *Microprocessors and Logic Design*, John Wiley, New York.

Ledley, R. S. (1964): High speed automatic analysis of biomedical pictures, *Science*, **146**, 3461, 216–223.

Lenat, D. (1982): in Davis, R. and Lenat, D., *Knowledge based systems in AI*, McGraw-Hill, New York.

Lerner, E. J. (1984): Data-flow architecture, *IEEE Spectrum*, April, **21**(4), 57–62.

Lien, Y. E. (1985): Relational database design, in Yao (1985).

Liskov, B. H. and Berzins, V. (1979): An appraisal of program specifications, in Wegner, P., (ed.) *Research Directions in Software Technology*, MIT Press, Cambridge Mass, pp. 276–301.

Liskov, B. H. and Zilles, S. (1977): An introduction to formal specifications of data abstractions, in Yeh, R. T. (ed.) *Current Trends in Programming Methodology*, Vol I, Prentice-Hall, Englewood Cliffs, N.J., pp. 1–32.

McCarthy, J. (1967): Towards a mathematical science of computation, pp. 21–28, in *Information Processing, Proc. IFIP Conf 1962*, North Holland, Amsterdam.

McCarthy, J. (1978): History of LISP, *SIGPLAN Notices* **13**, 217–23; quoted in Barr and Feigenbaum (1982), pp. 5 and 7.

McGettrick, A. D. (1980): *The Definition of Programming Languages*, Cambridge University Press.

McGettrick, A. D. (1982): *Program Verification using Ada*, Cambridge University Press.

MacLennan, B. J. (1983): *Principles of Programming Languages*, Holt, Rinehart and Winston, New York.

McLeod, D. (1978): *A Semantic Database Model and Its Associated Structured User Interface*, Technical Report, MIT Laboratory for Computer Science, Cambridge, Massachusetts.

Mano, N. M. (1982): *Computer System Architecture*, Prentice-Hall, Englewood Cliffs, N.J.

Martin, J. (1977): *Computer Database Organisation* (2nd edn), Prentice-Hall, Englewood Cliffs, N.J.

Mead, C. and Conway, L. (eds.) (1980): *Introduction to VLSI Systems*, Addison-Wesley, Reading, Mass.

Meyer-Ebrecht, D. and Wendler, T. (1983): An architectural route through PACS, *Computer*, August 19–28.
Minsky, M. (1979): A framework for representing knowledge, in Winston, P. H. (ed.), *The Psychology of Computer Vision*, McGraw-Hill, New York.
Moto-Oka, T. and Kitsuregawa, M. (1985): *The Fifth Generation Computer*, John Wiley and Sons, Chichester.
Moto-Oka, T. and Stone, H. S. (1984): Fifth-generation computer systems: a Japanese project, *Computer*, **17**(3) March, 6–13.
Naylor, C. (1983): *Build Your Own Expert System*, Sigma Technical Press, Wilmslow.
NCC (1982): *Handbook of Data Communications*, NCC Publications, National Computing Centre, Manchester.
Newell, A. (1984): Foreword to Buchanan and Shortliffe (1984).
Nilsson, N. (1980): *Principles of AI*, Springer Verlag, Berlin.
Norman, D. A. (1983a): Design rules based on analysis of human error, *Communications of the ACM*, **26**, April, 254–58.
Norman, D. A. (1983b): Design principles for human-computer interfaces, *Proc. CHI '83, Human Factors in Computing Systems*, ACM, December 1983, 125–9.
Olle, T. W. (1978): *The CODASYL Approach to Data Base Management Systems*, John Wiley, New York.
O'Shea, T. and Eisenstadt, M. (eds.) (1984): *Artificial Intelligence: Tools, Techniques and Applications*, Harper and Row, New York.
Page-Jones, M. (1980): *The Practical Guide to Structured Systems Design*, Yourdon Press, New York.
Peacegood, G. and Wilkinson, G. G. (1985): A Knowledge-Based System for the Identification of Linear Features in Satellite Imagery, *Proc. Workshop on Image Understanding in Remote Sensing*, University College London, 10 July, Remote Sensing Society/British Pattern Recognition Association.
Peterson, J. L. and Silberschatz, A. (1985): *Operating Systems Concepts* (2nd edn.), Addison-Wesley, Reading, MA.
Pratt, T. W. (1984): *Programming Languages: Design and Implementation*, Prentice-Hall, Englewood Cliffs, N.J.
Pratt, W. K. (1978): *Digital Image Processing*, John Wiley, New York.
Pressman, R. S. (1982): *Software Engineering: A Practitioner's Approach*, McGraw-Hill, New York.
Putnam, L. (1978): A general empirical solution to the macro software sizing and estimating project, *IEEE Transactions on Software Engineering*, **SE-4**(4), 345–61.
Putnam, L. (1980): *Software Cost Estimated and Life Cycle Control*, IEEE Computer Society Press.
Rich, E. (1983): *Artificial Intelligence*, McGraw-Hill, New York.
Richards, M. and Whitby-Strevens, C. (1980): *BCPL—The Language and Its Compiler*, Cambridge University Press.
Rosenfeld, A. and Kak, A. C. (1976): *Digital Image Processing*, Academic Press, New York.
Saib, S. H. (1984): RXVP—today and tomorrow, in Hausen, H. L. (ed.) *Software Validation*, North Holland, Amsterdam, pp. 103–26.
Salton, G. and McGill, M. J. (1983): *Introduction to Modern Information Retrieval*, McGraw-Hill, New York.
Searle, J. (1984): *Minds, Brains and Science*, based on his Reith lectures of 1984, BBC, London.
Shipman, D. W. (1981): The functional data model and data language DAPLEX, *ACM Transactions on Database Systems*, New York, **6**(1).
Shiva, S. G. (1985): *Computer Design and Architecture*, Little, Brown & Co, Boston.

Simons, G. L. (1983): *Towards Fifth Generation Computers*, NCC Publications, Manchester.
Smith, D. C., Irby, C., Kimball, R., Verplank, B. and Harslem, E. (1982): Designing the Star user interface, *Byte*, **1982**, April, 242–82.
Stonebraker, M. (1980): Retrospection on a database system, *ACM Transactions on Database Systems*, New York, **5**(2), June.
Stonebraker, M. (1981): Operating system support for database management, *Communications of the ACM*, New York, **24**(7), July.
Stonebraker, M., Wong, E., Kreps, P. and Held, G. (1976): The design and implementation of Ingres, *ACM Transactions on Database Systems*, New York, **1**(3), September.
Stonham, T. J. (1984): *Digital Logic Techniques*, Van Nostrand Reinhold, Wokingham, U.K.
Stucki, L. G. (1977): New directions in automated tools for improving software quality, in Yeh, R. T. (ed.), *Current Trends in Programming Methodology*, Prentice-Hall, Englewood Cliffs, N.J., pp. 80–111.
Sufrin, B. (1982): Formal specification of a display-orientated text editor, *Science of Computer Programming*, **1**, 157–202.
Tanenbaum, A. S. (1981): *Computer Networks*, Prentice-Hall, Englewood Cliffs, N.J.
Taylor, R. W. and Frank, R. L. (1976): CODASYL data base management systems, *ACM Computing Surveys*, New York, **8**(1).
Teichroew, D. and Hershey, E. A. (1977): PSL/PSA: computer aided techniques for structured documentation and analysis of information processing systems, *IEEE Transactions on Software Engineering*, **SE-3**(1), 41–8.
Teitelbaum, R. and Reps, T. (1981): The Cornell Program Synthesizer: a syntax-directed programming environment, *Communications of the ACM* **24**(9), 563–73.
Tesler, L. (1980): The Smalltalk Environment, *Byte*, **6**, August, 90–147.
Torrance, S. (ed.) (1985): *The Mind and The Machine*, Harper and Row, New York (p. 12 particularly).
Tou, J. T. (1981): Application of pattern recognition to knowledge system design and diagnostic inference, in Kittler, J. V. *et al.* (eds.) *Pattern Recognition Theory and Applications*, D. Reidel, Dordrecht, pp. 413–29.
Treleaven, P. C. and Lima, I. G. (1984): Future computers: logic, data flow, ... , control flow? *Computer*, **1984**, March, 47–58.
Tsichritzis, D. C. and Lochovsky, F. H. (1982): *Data Models*, Prentice-Hall, Englewood Cliffs, N.J.
Turner, D. A. (1982): Functional programming and proofs of program correctness, in Neel, D. (ed.), *Tools and Notions for Program Construction*, Cambridge University Press.
Turner, D. A. (1985): Functional programs as executable specifications, in Hoare, C. A. R. and Sheperdson, J. C. (eds.), *Mathematical Logic and Programming Languages*, Prentice-Hall, Englewood Cliffs, N.J., pp. 29–54.
Vasta, J. (1985): *Understanding Data Base Management Systems*, Wadsworth, Belmont, CA.
Walston, C. E. and Felix, C. P. (1977): A method of programming measurement and estimation, *IBM Systems J.*, **16**(1), 54–73, 1977.
Warnier, J. D. (1974): *Logical Construction of Programs*, Van Nostrand, New York.
Warnier, J. D. (1981): *Logical Construction of Systems*, Van Nostrand, New York.
Weinberg, G. M. (1971): *The Psychology of Computer Programming*, Van Nostrand, New York.
Weizenbaum, J. (1966): ELIZA, *Communications of the ACM*, **9**, January, 36–45.
Weizenbaum, J. (1976): *Computer Power and Human Reason: From Judgement to Calculation*, Penguin Books, Harmondsworth, Middlesex.

Wiest, J. and Levy, F. (1977): *A Management Guide to PERT/CPM* (2nd edn), Prentice-Hall, Englewood Cliffs, N.J.

Williams, J. H. (1982): *Notes on the FP style of functional programming, in Darlington et al.* (1982), pp. 73–101.

Willis, N. and Kerridge, J. (1983): *Introduction to Computer Architecture*, Pitman, London.

Winograd, T. (1983): *Language as a Cognitive Process, Vol 1: Syntax*, Addison-Wesley, Reading, MA.

Winston, P. H. (1984): *Artificial Intelligence*, Addison-Wesley, Reading, MA.

Winston, P. H. and Horn, B. K. P. (1984): *LISP* (2nd edn), Addison-Wesley, Reading, MA.

Winterflood, A. R. (1984): *An Access and Storage Architecture for the Roster System*, Technical Report 84-157, Dept of Computing and Information Science, Queen's University, Kingston, Canada. Also available through the authors.

Wirth, N. (1971a): The programming language Pascal, *Acta Informatica* **1**(1), 35–63.

Wirth, N. (1971b): Program development by stepwise refinement, *Communications of the ACM*, **14**, 221–7.

Woods, W. A. (1970): Transition network grammars for natural language analysis, *Communications of the ACM*, **13**, October, 591–606.

Yao, S. B. (ed.) (1985): *Principles of Database Design*, Vol 1, Prentice-Hall, Englewood Cliffs, N.J.

Yeh, R. T. and Zave, P. (1980): Specifying software requirements, *Proc. IEEE*, **68**(9), 1077–85.

Index